ALSO BY BETTY BOYD CAROLI

First Ladies: From Martha Washington to Michelle Obama

Inside the White House

America's First Ladies

The Roosevelt Women

LADY BIRD
and LYNDON

The Hidden Story of a Marriage
That Made a President

BETTY BOYD CAROLI

SIMON & SCHUSTER
New York London Toronto Sydney New Delhi

Simon & Schuster
1230 Avenue of the Americas
New York, NY 10020

First Simon & Schuster hardcover edition October 2015

SIMON & SCHUSTER and colophon are registered trademarks of Simon & Schuster, Inc.

For information about special discounts for bulk purchases, please contact Simon & Schuster Special Sales at 1-866-506-1949 or business@simonandschuster.com.

The Simon & Schuster Speakers Bureau can bring authors to your live event. For more information or to book an event, contact the Simon & Schuster Speakers Bureau at 1-866-248-3049 or visit our website at www.simonspeakers.com.

Book design by Ellen R. Sasahara

Manufactured in the United States of America

1   3   5   7   9   10   8   6   4   2

Library of Congress Cataloging-in-Publication Data

Caroli, Betty Boyd.
Lady Bird and Lyndon : the hidden story of a marriage that made a president / Betty Boyd Caroli.—First Simon & Schuster hardcover edition.
    pages cm
Includes bibliographical references and index.
1. Johnson, Lady Bird, 1912–2007—Marriage. 2. Johnson, Lyndon B. (Lyndon Baines), 1908–1973—Marriage. 3. Married people—United States—Biography. 4. Presidents' spouses—United States—Biography. 5. Presidents—United States—Biography. I. Title.
    E848.J64C37 2015
    973.923092'2—dc23
[B]   2015011027

ISBN 978-1-4391-9122-4
ISBN 978-1-4391-9124-8 (ebook)

To Livio

CONTENTS

LADY BIRD
and LYNDON

PROLOGUE

A T EXACTLY 4 p.m. on December 9, 1967, Lady Bird Johnson started a slow, dignified descent down the wide stairway from the residential quarters of the White House to the State Floor, where more than six hundred guests were waiting. All of them were dressed for an evening gala, and while some lingered around the foyer at the foot of the stairs, chatting in small groups, others had already taken their places in the huge East Room, where Lady Bird was headed. In the four years of her husband's presidency, she had walked this route dozens of times to greet heads of state and delegations of various sizes from all over the United States. But today was different. And very special. Today her twenty-three-year-old daughter, Lynda, was marrying the military aide she had begun dating that summer.

The press had avidly reported on all the prenuptial festivities leading up to this, the first White House wedding of a president's daughter in more than fifty years, and Lady Bird was determined to deliver an event perfect down to the smallest detail. Since the August morning when she first learned of her daughter's decision to wed Charles "Chuck" Robb, she had devoted more hours than she could count to mulling over white silks for the gown that Geoffrey Beene would design for the bride. She had composed and then revised guest lists and she had considered multiple cake recipes before deciding on the pound cake, flavored with rum and white raisins. She had even taken time to insure that the cameras recording the ceremony would be hidden, their presence indicated only by tiny slits in the white fabric backdrop behind the improvised altar.

Dedicating this much attention to her daughter was uncharacteristic of Lady Bird Johnson, who knew she did not deserve high marks for her mothering. Both her daughters had told her so, sometimes in teary-eyed sorrow or in accusatory tones. In her household, Lyndon always came first, and she had often left Lynda and the younger Luci for weeks at a time so she could appear at his side in political campaigns and cater to his every command. Even when she resolved to stay behind with her daughters, she would change her mind and go to him, unable to resist his plea that he needed her. Rather than offer some excuse for falling short, she admitted to her diary that she had "neglected" her daughters but not "enough for me to get a guilt complex."

On the wintry afternoon of Lynda's wedding, Lady Bird's arrival in the East Room was the signal for the ceremony to begin. As soon as she took her place behind the velvet rope setting off a space around the altar for the wedding party, the groomsmen began filing in, followed by the bridesmaids in their Christmasy red gowns. As the Marine Band struck up "Here Comes the Bride," it was as if a drum roll had suddenly hushed the crowd, and Lady Bird could see all eyes turn toward the door to watch Lynda enter on her daddy's arm. Beautiful as Lynda looked in her "regal" high-necked gown, embroidered with silk flowers and seed pearls, Lady Bird's gaze fastened not on her daughter but on Lyndon. In her account of that day, she described how she watched him "all the way" to the altar, her heart "full of tenderness" for the man whose hair suddenly looked much whiter than before.

The East Room was so packed that everyone had to remain standing, except for a handful of elderly guests who had been provided with benches. How different this glittering crowd was from the motley small gathering that witnessed Lady Bird's wedding thirty-three years earlier in Texas. Surrounding her today were U.S. senators alongside Supreme Court justices and American ambassadors who had journeyed from posts in Europe and Asia to attend. She knew most of the six-hundred-plus by name, while at her own wedding, an impromptu event put together by a friend of Lyndon's, the only familiar face was that of her college roommate.

Although clad for Lynda's wedding in a costly designer outfit, Lady Bird knew there would be odious comparisons made between her and her glamorous predecessor, Jacqueline Kennedy. In the aftermath of JFK's assassination, flustered Americans meeting Lady Bird for the first time occasionally blurted out Mrs. Kennedy's name instead of hers. Even after that stopped and Lady Bird became a household name, she understood she would never match Jackie's "magic," her ability to draw people to her like a "Pied Piper." But the comparisons failed to sting. Lady Bird blithely brushed off derogatory references to her looks and provincial tastes, and when once faced with a portrait emphasizing her prominent nose, she quipped that it "looked just like my nose looks."

When the time came for Chuck and Lynda to repeat their vows, Lady Bird warmed to the way the bridegroom answered in "firm and clear" tones. But it was Lyndon's response to the minister's question, "Who gives this woman in marriage?" that she thought sent a "ripple of emotion" through the crowd. Lyndon had said, "Her mother and I."

It was a remarkable affirmation of a partnership that had caused more than a little comment during their years in public life. Lady Bird knew very well what people were saying, that Lyndon had married a plain Jane for her money after courting more beautiful women. She had registered the descriptions of her as a dish rag, subject to his bellowed orders and demeaning remarks. But it was her reaction to his womanizing that seemed to baffle everyone. Not only did she put up with it and with his talking about it—she was unfailingly polite to every woman with whom he had or was rumored to have had an affair. She invited them to the ranch and complimented them on their looks and accomplishments. Several of them were in the East Room that day. A lot of people were asking each other why.

Lady Bird knew what few others did—that Lyndon trusted her— and only her—with his most important secret—his own frailty. This big strong man, a genius at politics, could be suddenly undone and once undone had trouble getting himself back on track. When faced with a huge problem or disappointment, he would go to bed and pull the covers over his head, and that's when she stepped in, to get him on his feet and moving again. Only she could do that. She had done it time and again, and while she realized that some of his closest staff during these last two years, years she would describe as "pure hell," sensed that something like this was going on, only she knew, and she would never tell. It was their secret.

The fact that he had admitted his problem to her and relied on her to help him deal with it gave her the strength to take the hit. She would rather look weak herself than bring him down. She could blow off what others said about her. Those humiliating descriptions, the comparisons with Jackie, her daughters' complaints about her lack of nurturing— they counted for nothing. She was as sure now, as when she married him, that she was the most important person in Lyndon's life.

In just twenty minutes, the Robb ceremony was finished. As soon as the Marine Band struck up Mendelssohn's special march and the wedding party exited, Bird took Lyndon's arm and moved quickly through the throng of guests and back upstairs for photos. She had not permitted the press pool to witness the taking of vows, but here in the Yellow Oval Room, from which all the furniture had been removed, were dozens of reporters, armed with a "vast array of cameras." After pictures were taken of the wedding party, the bride and groom and their parents went back downstairs to greet every single guest, in a reception line so slowed by all the hugging and kissing that it took two hours to get through it.

By that time the East Room had been converted to a dance hall, and as soon as Peter Duchin's orchestra struck its first notes, everything became such "a swirl" that Bird could not remember who danced with whom first. What she remembered very clearly was how quickly Lyndon had cut in on her, and with one of his broadest smiles quipped how far she had come since that "purple dress" she had worn as a bride thirty-three years earlier. He didn't leave it at that, but, in the very dearest "touches" of the day, he referred three more times to their own wedding ceremony and that "awful purple dress." His jesting words, for her ears only, conjured up so many memories—of the day she married Lyndon and of all that had happened since.

At times like this, when Lady Bird was thinking about marriage in general and her own in particular, her thoughts went to a little metal box she had carried with her through a dozen house moves. It contained the letters she had written to Lyndon and he had written to her, when she was still "Bird" to him and all her friends. Those letters laid out the quid pro quo of their relationship, and that box, now carefully stowed in her sitting room on the second floor of the White House, contained the key to understanding what held this marriage together.

The morning after Lynda's wedding, she took out that box and spent several hours going over the precious letters. Even in the exhilaration of her daughter's big day, an opulent White House wedding, it was her own marriage that Bird wanted to revisit. It had been her husband, not her daughter, who captured and held her gaze in their walk down the aisle, and it had been his teasing remarks about the purple dress that had provided the strongest emotional pull. It would be those letter-reading hours that she would single out as among the very "most satisfying" hours of her time in the White House.

This is the story of that marriage.

———◦◦◦———

BIRD LEARNS TO FLY

A YEAR AFTER her husband died, Lady Bird Johnson sat down for an interview on the *Today* show. With millions of Americans watching, she expected anchorwoman Barbara Walters to ask her about the beautification project she had started as first lady and had continued in the five years since leaving Washington. It was a topic Lady Bird felt comfortable with. She had given countless interviews and speeches on the subject. But Walters quickly veered away from wildflowers and national parks to ask a question that had nothing to do with beautification. It zeroed in on Lady Bird's marriage: "How did you handle your flirt and ladies' man husband?"

After only an instant's hesitation, Lady Bird replied evenly, "Lyndon was a people lover and that certainly did not exclude half the people of the world, women." The unflappable Lady Bird had faced down one of the most renowned interviewers in the world and answered a potentially embarrassing question with honesty and grace.

If Walters had researched Lady Bird's early years, she could have anticipated the sort of response her query would elicit. It was all there, in the first years of Lady Bird's life, how she virtually raised herself in a household where humiliation and adultery were part of the picture. It was also a home where the exercise of raw power was taken for granted, and managing it became vital to survival. Rather than strike back against an attack such as Walters's, Lady Bird relied on the protective carapace she had begun developing as a child—it equipped her to spar, disarm, and vanquish while maintaining what looked like gentle, ladylike composure.

Mrs. Johnson rarely talked about her early years. Perhaps she preferred to forget. More likely, she never knew the whole story—part Gothic novel, part comic opera—of how her aristocratic mother wound up giving birth on a December day in 1912 to her only daughter in a hardscrabble part of Texas that she loathed, among people she wished she had never met.

Lady Bird's father, the big, dynamic Thomas Jefferson Taylor (known as T.J.) was one of those men who had to *feel* he was the most important man in the room. At six foot three, he towered over most people, craved attention, and expected his behavior to be tolerated, no matter how outlandish. The deference he commanded frequently involved money, and he had ingenious methods to keep people owing him. One oft-repeated story had him manipulating an impoverished neighbor back into debt after the man had struggled hard to pay off the last cent owed. The story goes that T. J. Taylor knew the man's weakness for cats and he offered to give him one, but the man, being scrupulously fair, insisted on paying a little something. The two settled on a minuscule amount, but that was enough to put him back on T.J.'s debtor list. While he wheedled to get what he wanted, T.J. also contributed generously to both churches in town, an effective way to keep the entire community in his debt. The local saying was: "T. J. Taylor owns everything."

T.J. so firmly ruled that part of Harrison County, lending at exorbitant fees and collecting on his own timetable, that virtually everyone called him "Mr. Boss." But not his wife, the pampered Minnie, whom he had lured to Texas from more cultured surroundings in Alabama. Miss Minnie called no one "Boss." When the adult Lady Bird offered one of her rare descriptions of her parents, she called theirs a "stressful" union, and those words, though true, did not begin to capture the truth.

Minnie Pattillo and T. J. Taylor grew up in the same Alabama county, but on different planets. Her father, Luther Pattillo (whose Scots ancestors spelled it Patiloch), had begun acquiring land after the Civil War, and by his shrewd (some would say exploitative) management, he had become one of the largest landowners in the state. While most sharecroppers in the region split 50/50 with their landlord whatever the crops brought, Luther Pattillo demanded 60 percent for himself, and because he owned so much land and the general store where many sharecroppers traded, he could get away with it.

Luther and his wife, Sarah, liked to enjoy their wealth by moving around, from one of the homes they owned to another, depending on the social season and the school year. Wherever they lived, they maintained a large library and kept a piano in the drawing room so Minnie and her younger sister Effie could perform for guests. Effie got so proficient she set her sights on attending the Juilliard School in New York City, while Minnie remained the bookworm of the family, content to sit alone reading for hours at a time.

Behind that genteel facade, of piano music and shelves of old books, the Pattillo household reeked of jealousy and malice. Sarah had been a Confederate widow with three young children when Luther married her, and she never let him forget that she came from a background superior to his. While he used his cunning to accumulate wealth, she had been born to it. It would have been appropriate for Luther to treat his stepchildren as his own, but he neglected them in favor of the two boys and two girls—including Minnie—he fathered by Sarah. As a result of his ruthless business practices, he became known as "the meanest man in Autauga County," but his offspring, proud of their self-made father, liked to lord it over their half-siblings and play up to him. Luther called himself a "general merchant," and passed along the label (with the business) to his own son Claude, leaving his stepchildren to fend for themselves.

If Autauga County, Alabama, had been more urbanized, the Pattillos would have looked at T. J. Taylor as coming from the wrong side of the tracks. In rural Alabama, the common phrase for people like the Taylors, who never managed to own much land of their own but had to eke out a living as tenant farmers, was "dirt poor." Polished pianos and store-bought books were foreign to them, and they worried not about the winter social calendar but about winter shoes. Yet Autauga County was small enough that Minnie Pattillo and T. J. Taylor, born within months of each other in 1874, were bound to cross paths. Whether it was the romantic setting of his rescuing her after she had been thrown from a horse, as family lore had it, or some other, less dramatic meeting, the mutual attraction was strong. Standing alongside the much taller T.J., Minnie, with her many freckles and ruddy complexion, made his jet black hair and olive skin appear all the darker.

Who knows what really drew Minnie to the untutored T. J. Taylor? One answer seems obvious. T.J. acted much like Luther Pattillo in his ambition and business practices, and if most women marry their fathers, Minnie was simply following that instinct. Minnie had a rebellious streak, and she may have found T.J.'s rough edges exciting, so at odds with the social snobbery she witnessed at home. Naturally, her parents were dead set against her having anything to do with T.J., and it was all too clear that she could register her defiance to them by sticking with him.

For his part, T.J. set out on the fast track to prove himself worthy. Leaving Autauga with an older brother in late 1898, he managed to pay cash for 116 acres as soon as he crossed the Texas border. Where he got that $500 (about a year's wages for a working man) remains a mystery. He later told his daughter he had sold a saddle, but only a very elaborate saddle would have brought $500. And how would he have acquired such a saddle in the first place? His neighbors decided he must have robbed a train along the way. T.J. soon bought more land, swapping poorer acres for better, and when he opened a shop in Karnack, the sign he put out front, "Dealer in Everything," sounded like a bloated version of his future father-in-law's "general merchant."

In November 1900, when T.J. returned to Alabama for Minnie, the Pattillos still labeled him "white trash." Acquiring a rustic little store in a speck of a Texas town did not catapult him into their class. Even if they made allowances for his lack of education, they weren't likely to forget that his mother had married four times and produced thirteen children, making her something of a joke to their society-minded friends. When Minnie persisted with plans to wed, her family refused to attend, and so the ceremony was a Taylors-only event at the home of T.J.'s older brother.

If Minnie had known where T.J. was taking her, she might have reconsidered. With fewer than one hundred residents, Karnack, Texas, had only recently gotten its own post office. Marshall, the county seat fifteen miles away, had already become one of the wealthiest towns in that part of the state, and it would have suited Minnie better. Its strategic location, on the railroad connecting Dallas and Shreveport, made it a hub for commerce, and prosperous local residents had built imposing large homes along Washington Avenue and opened centers of higher learning, including a Female Institute. But a man on the make, like T.J., needed a less settled spot, with weaker competition. Karnack was his kind of place. He set down his stakes and refused to budge.

The marriage showed cracks from the start. Minnie made clear she detested her new home, and she wanted nothing to do with neighbors she saw as clearly inferior to herself. Most had never seen an opera or traveled outside the county. Her husband offered little consolation. His long workdays, as he continued to accumulate acres, meant she saw little of him. What she might have heard, she would not have liked. His reputation as a "ladies' man" was well deserved, and what's more, he didn't care a whit what people said about him.

Yet Minnie stayed, at least for a while. The son she bore within a year of marriage was named for his father, but by the time the second was born, in August 1904, Minnie wanted a name that had nothing to do with her husband, and she settled on the exotic-sounding "Antonio." Before little Tony could walk, she left Karnack, taking both boys back to Alabama where she farmed them out to relatives, both T.J.'s and hers. To her family, she explained that she had left her husband because he was seeing other women. What had started out as a summer break for Minnie and the boys was going to last a lot longer.

According to court documents T.J. filed in February 1909, Minnie had been gone four years and he wanted a divorce. Whenever he had written her to ask for an explanation, she had pled illness and requested more time to convalesce. But T.J. suspected she was not even with her family but had decamped to more appealing surroundings in the upper Midwest, possibly opera-rich Chicago or Battle Creek, Michigan, where she and all her family liked to go to take cures at the Kellogg Sanitarium.

It's not clear where T.J. was getting his information, but his suspicion was confirmed when he received word from Michigan that Minnie, having left her sons in Alabama, was indeed a patient at the sanitarium. But, as the Kellogg doctors informed him, she had recently undergone surgery and was unable to travel the "two thousand miles" (the actual distance was half of that) to answer T.J.'s charges. She was not too sick, however, to know what she wanted, and through her attorneys, she asked for alimony, payment of her attorneys' fees, and a share of the Texas property considered hers under the state's community property laws. Her counterclaim left out all mention of her two little boys, Tommy and Tony, whose custody T.J. was seeking.

That response raised T.J.'s ire and, through his lawyers, he went after Minnie's father and officials at the Kellogg Sanitarium, demanding to know who was supporting his wife and what ailed her anyway. Luther Pattillo's response has not survived, but Dr. Bertha Moshier, an internist younger than Minnie, signed a statement on October 6, 1909, declaring that Minnie had been under her care in Battle Creek for "5 weeks" (only a tiny bit of the four years she had been gone) and that since she suffered from "nervous prostration" she needed a private nurse day and night. Travel was out of the question for "four or five months at least." Given Minnie's delicate condition, any trip sooner than that carried the risk of "permanent derangement."

Now T.J. sounded baffled: if his wife was indeed suffering from "nervous trouble," would she not be better off in his "quiet country home [than in] a hospital where . . . numerous other people are being treated?"

Minnie continued to dither, even accusing T.J. of taking unfair advantage of her by filing for divorce after he had encouraged her to seek treatment. She had never intended to abandon him permanently, she insisted, but in the meantime she refused to set a date for her return. As for the "valuable . . . real and personal property," accumulated during the marriage, her lawyers noted, she "avers that she has an interest."

During the years Minnie was separated from T.J., she moved back and forth between the sanitarium and the home of one Alabama relative or another. When the census taker came around her parents' house on April 18, 1910, she was there and described herself as a "widow" named "Minnie Pattillo." A different census taker, enumerating Karnack, Texas, a few days later, listed T. J. Taylor as "married" and "head of household." Neither parent claimed the company of Tommy and Tony, now aged nine and six, but a census taker found the boys living with T.J.'s older sister and her family in Alabama.

When T.J. was granted his divorce nearly a year later (on February 6, 1911) Minnie was still in Alabama, but she immediately went into action. It was grossly unfair, she telegraphed her attorneys, that T.J. had won a "judgment by default," without her presence or participation, and she instructed her legal team to obtain a new hearing.

Within weeks, T.J. and Minnie were back together. He dropped his case and she brought the boys to live with him in Karnack. He showed no signs of giving up his womanizing but he did offer Minnie one considerable consolation—a big, showy house, one of the most impressive for miles around. The couple had begun their married life in humble quarters behind the store, but during her absence he had purchased a two-story mansion (with seventeen rooms and six fireplaces) three miles south of Karnack. Built originally by slave labor and always called the Brick House, it had fallen into disrepair, but T.J., who resisted spending money on any personal pleasure, spared no expense in turning the house into one of the most elegant in the county. He put huge white columns out front—giving Minnie something to flaunt if her picky Pattillo kin ever came to visit.

Even without the house, Minnie had her reasons for returning to T.J. She still felt drawn to this big, commanding man, for whom she had once bought barbells and a mat for workouts. More importantly, he provided an escape from the infighting of Luther Pattillo's household in Alabama, where one of his stepdaughters, a widow with four children, had recently returned to live. The always festering resentment between Luther's own offspring and those of his wife Sarah could only grow, now that both parents were failing in health and questions about inheritance became more pressing.

In fact, both parents died within months of Minnie's going back to T.J., and Luther, who managed to survive his wife by only a few weeks, made sure to funnel the bulk of his estate to his own blood, leaving only a pittance to each stepchild. That gave Minnie, now heiress to almost a quarter of her father's holdings, ample reason to put some distance between herself and her disinherited half siblings. Her new wealth wasn't hers to spend immediately—it came in land and revenues to be turned over later, when acres were sold and loans paid back. Even if Minnie had inherited a ready fortune, Southern ladies did not go off to live on their own. Certainly not a woman in her forties with two young sons.

All through the turmoil of the divorce proceedings, the statements of Minnie's attorneys highlight the importance of money. She knew that T.J. had become a wealthy man in her absence, owner of thousands of acres of cotton-growing land. By renting to farmers who paid him back with a share of the crop, and by supplying those same folks with most of the store-bought items they needed, "Mr. Boss" held them in what even his loyal relatives described as a kind of peonage. His continuing good fortune was virtually assured by the fact that his neighbors could not avoid dealing with him—he owned the gins they needed to process their cotton. If Minnie had accepted the terms of the divorce, she would have lost a lot.

On December 22, 1912, little more than a year after Minnie returned to T.J., she gave birth to a baby girl with large brown eyes. Dr. Baldwin, living just over a mile away, arrived in horse and buggy to deliver the newest Taylor, named Claudia, after Minnie's bachelor brother Claude. But very soon, chubby little Claudia Alta Taylor got a nickname that stuck: Lady Bird. The popular version of its origin credits a hired nursemaid, who pronounced her "pretty as a ladybird," but the subject herself admitted that it came from her black playmates— Stuff and Doodlebug—who preferred something more vivid than Claudia. Later, it was "deemed more respectable to assign credit to the nurse" and avoid any mention of interracial socializing.

Nobody suggested that Minnie liked being back in Karnack. She still found it a dreary, lonely place, populated by people who knew nothing about Italian opera or her favorite authors. She had no close friends, and kept clear of her neighbors, who considered her "wacky." She sometimes accompanied T.J. to the store, then walked the three miles back to the Brick House alone. But more often she rode alone in her chauffeured sedan, a veil covering her face. When she went out for a walk, she loped solo through T.J.'s acres, her long skirts swishing through the grass and her reddish blond hair blowing in the wind. Local residents saw her as a dreamer at heart, a woman who yearned for life on a bigger stage than Karnack could offer. It was that deep, overpowering yearning that she passed on to her only daughter.

For her sons, Minnie wanted exposure to a world beyond Texas, and soon after Lady Bird's birth, she dispatched both boys to boarding schools so distant they would find it difficult to come home, even at Christmas holidays. At first enrolled at Riordan, an upstate New York school known for its progressive ways, they were then split up, with Tony transferring to a school in New Mexico. That meant the two brothers, just entering their teens, were deprived of the comfort of each other's companionship, and their little sister saw neither of them. Minnie showed scant interest in making amends for taking the boys away from their father earlier or for leaving them with relatives while she traveled for cures and culture. She reserved her minimal maternal instincts for little Claudia, who remembered her as a gentle figure, who liked to play records of Italian operas on her Victrola and read Norse tales aloud.

Neighbors saw a less benevolent figure, who showed little interest in anyone but herself. On the rare occasion she took a stand on a community matter, T.J. was sure to be found on the opposite side. Her sole foray into politics is a case in point. After Texas granted women the right to vote in primaries in 1918, Minnie began crusading against a popular local candidate, whose relatives were T.J.'s friends. The candidate had been a "slacker" in the war, she argued, and did not deserve public office.

T.J. and Minnie disagreed on just about everything. She still liked to travel, to attend musical events in Shreveport, fifteen miles away in Louisiana, and confer with doctors at the Kellogg Sanitarium. He stayed close to home, going to bed early so he could be up and at work before sunrise. The half of Harrison County that was African American interested him only as subjects for exploitation, but she assembled a few of them in her living room to talk about their religious practices. (She claimed she wanted to write a book on the subject but aggravating T.J. seems a more likely motivation.) He continued to strike back in ways that humiliated her. When a dog sniffed him out at his store one day, T.J. turned to a customer and said, "I've been with a black woman and that dog can smell her on me." What clearer evidence does one need to show that Lady Bird grew up in a home where marital fidelity carried little weight? The black youth named Sugar who came past the store for handouts was widely believed to be T.J.'s son, half brother to his three children borne by Minnie.

What Lady Bird called a "stressful" marriage was actually one from hell, as the adults she called Mother and Daddy fashioned a reunion on the shards of a bitter, multiyear separation. Her brother Tony captured some of the rancor in that household when, as an adult, he talked about T.J. beating both sons. He told his sister that she never knew how bad the boys had it, and perhaps she didn't. But it's far more likely that she began then to learn what later became her strongest defense against what she did not wish to hear or see—she simply shut it out.

The Taylors' marriage ended abruptly in September 1918, when Minnie died, in mysterious circumstances that continue to raise questions nearly a century later. Was it suicide, as some Marshall residents believed? A botched abortion, as others suggested? Or did one historian get it right when he relayed rumors that T.J. had "pushed her down" a flight of stairs?

Claudia, only five years old at the time, remembered little of her mother's death, and since her father permitted no discussion of the subject, she was unlikely to learn more. The sketchy version she relayed as an adult has become the accepted one—that Minnie, forty-four years old and pregnant, was tripped by a dog, causing her to fall down the stairs of her home, and then die from a subsequent infection.

The graphic details haunted one of Minnie's granddaughters, who admitted that during her own pregnancies she stayed on high alert whenever a dog came near.

Other information about Minnie's death raises strong doubts about whether a dog had anything to do with it, and the disappearance of documents that would help resolve those doubts maximizes the suspicion. Minnie's death certificate, on file at the Harrison County Courthouse, gives the cause as "septicemia," commonly called "blood poisoning," but not commonly associated with falls. Although the official date is September 4, multiple family communications place it ten, or even fourteen, days later. Tommy and Tony, aged seventeen and thirteen at the time, could offer little in the way of verification. Still hundreds of miles away, they did not learn of their mother's death for a full year because their father did not tell them.

While it would require an autopsy to pinpoint the exact cause of Minnie Taylor's death, a betting person would put money on a botched abortion. Septicemia frequently resulted—and was often fatal—when women tried to abort using metal objects. Since it was common knowledge around Karnack that she was pregnant, she must have been in an advanced stage. Yet neither her tombstone nor death certificate mentions a fetus or stillborn child. Since she had already sent her sons away and was investigating boarding schools in Washington, D.C., for little Claudia, it is reasonable to suspect she would not welcome a fourth child. She was buried, without a funeral service, within twenty-four hours of her death, highly unusual in that county at the time, and it was another physician, not the trusted neighbor, Dr. Baldwin—who had attended Claudia's delivery—who signed Minnie's death certificate. Issues of the county newspaper, which might fill in details of what happened, are missing for those weeks from the archives at the newspaper office and from an otherwise complete collection at the local college. Most suspicious of all is the completeness with which Minnie was erased from her children's

lives. Not a single photograph of her survives, indicating that whoever possessed pictures taken of her during the forty-four years that
she lived was very angry with her. And T.J. was certainly angry. The
only time Lady Bird saw her father fly into a rage was when the local
minister tried to console him by saying he should view his wife's
passing as "the will of God."

Whatever its cause, Minnie Taylor's death left her daughter, five
months short of celebrating her sixth birthday, even more isolated.
Without those tenuous ties that had once connected her to a remote,
often absent mother, the lonely child became even lonelier. Claudia
would later hear talk about her mother, how she treasured fine leather
bindings on her books and liked to wander alone through the fields.
But the picture emerged only in shadowy outline, like that of a distant
aunt she barely knew.

In the weeks following his wife's death, T.J. took time from management of his business to comfort his daughter. When she admitted
she missed her mother's nighttime stories, he offered to read aloud
to her. It was the first time, she later admitted, that she knew he *could*
read. But this was busy cotton season, and he soon decided to cart her
off to visit her Alabama cousins five hundred miles away. Rather than
engage an adult to accompany her, he hung a sign around her neck and
put her on a train. The sign, which read "Please deliver this child to
Claude Pattillo, Autauga, Alabama," functioned perfectly, and she arrived without mishap. Behind the sign, a smart little five-year-old was
learning the value of self-sufficiency.

After his daughter returned to him, T.J. decided she needed a woman's guidance, and he invited Minnie's younger sister Effie to come
and live with them. It was a little like asking an injured hunt dog to
take care of the pack. Effie Pattillo, who had shown considerable talent as a pianist in her youth, was now in her early forties, a fragile,
wispy woman for whom the phrase "having the vapors" could have
been invented. Smaller and physically weaker than Minnie, Effie had

grown to adulthood pampered like an invalid, and much as she valued appearing the "real lady," she acted more like a spoiled child who
took little responsibility for financial decisions or other life choices.
Shielded by Papa Pattillo's wealth and standing in the community, she
had the luxury of not having to worry about what others thought of
how she dressed or acted, and so she became more and more the eccentric bystander.

Aunt Effie deserves some credit. She widened her niece's view of
the world by taking her along on trips to the Kellogg Sanitarium, and
she tried to foster what Minnie had started, introducing Claudia to
nature's pleasures, teaching her to appreciate a colorful field of wildflowers or the special light of a setting sun. T. J. Taylor's huge land-
holdings provided the space for exploring those joys, but neither he
nor Aunt Effie could provide the reliable companionship of the "piney
pine" woods and "true blue" wildflowers that had sustained Minnie in
a place she hated. Nature was her preferred solace, and it would take
center stage in her daughter's life. As Lady Bird explained later, nature
was "my daily companion. My kingdom, my place, my love." Outdoors, walking across her father's acres, she could shut out ugliness
and forget the envious glances of the neighborhood children who had
far less than she. To transport her to a world of her own, she supplied
her own soundtrack, by humming to herself or whistling.

The country house that T.J. had bought for Minnie was just the
place for their daughter to develop a rock-hard self-sufficiency. With
both brothers away at boarding school and only the children of hired
help for playmates, Claudia Taylor had plenty of time to herself, to
invent games she could play alone, to observe her father's strutting
peacocks, to gaze off into the distance at the verdant hills and lush forests. After T.J. built her a detached two-room playhouse, she isolated
herself within its walls, even sleeping there at night. Sometimes, as if
pulled by a magic cord still connecting mother and daughter, the young
Claudia descended the mansion's front steps and set off to ramble for

hours across T.J.'s fields, just as her troubled mother had done before her. Did she imagine herself following paths her mother had crossed, sitting on rocky outcroppings where her mother had once stopped to rest and observe the exquisite scenery?

As an adult, Lady Bird would always trace her love of the outdoors, its beauty and serenity, back to those solitary years in Karnack's meadows. Driven by her own curiosity and guided by Aunt Effie, she developed an encyclopedic knowledge of wildflowers, so that she became to botany what Theodore Roosevelt was to insect study—she rarely met a species she could not identify. It was an interest she did not pass on to her daughters, and one of them, questioned about her own interest in wildflowers, admitted, "It did not come with the genes."

By the time Claudia was no more than ten or eleven, she had figured out that Aunt Effie was someone to love, but a woman that "passive . . . weak and full of illnesses" did not provide a model to follow. Young Claudia set her "sights on being more like my father, who was one of the most physically strong people I have ever known."

Lady Bird was very much T.J.'s daughter. Not only her dark hair, olive coloring, and oversized nose came from T.J. Taylor, but far more important, the ambition, business savvy, and almost incredible attention to ferreting out every cent in any exchange. She clung to his example in ways her brothers, separated from him at a young age, never did, and she became the risk taker in much bigger ways than they ever did. T.J. clearly loved and nurtured his only daughter, and he raised her, to a large extent, as if she were a son. At least he made no exceptions for the fact that she was a girl. He taught her the rules of success as if he fully expected she would one day run a business herself. Just as importantly, he made her comfortable with the idea of raw power, even if questionably achieved.

Although T.J. was busy as local employer, lending banker, and "dealer in everything," he also served as his daughter's tutor—by example. He never read a book for pleasure, but he was a demon with numbers. Even the tiniest entry on the ledger drew his attention, and his daughter, who would later be described as able to read a balance sheet the way a truck driver reads a map, learned from him. She had her own checking account by the time she reached puberty, and she viewed it as distinctly hers. Informed as an adult that some of her female employees had joint checking accounts with their husbands, she retorted that she "wouldn't share an account with the Angel Gabriel." T.J.'s talk of his own impoverished youth, of his mother being unable to provide "tea cakes" even at her children's birthdays, convinced Claudia that he wanted far more for her. She understood why for him "value-of-a-dollar" was one word.

Unlike most people who knew T.J., his daughter saw only benevolence and kindness in him. She often talked about the time she inquired about a row of large wooden boxes in his store and he had assured her they were packing units. Only later did she learn they were coffins. Most of Karnack's population emphasized his miserly, manipulative ways, but she singled out his rare acts of charitableness, like extending credit to the family of her good friend, Emma Boehringer, whose father had died, leaving his widow with little to support herself and her children. For Lady Bird, T.J. was a gentle, compassionate figure while others were more likely to use the term his father-in-law relished— "the meanest man" around.

Young Lady Bird was too smart not to know how T.J. was making his money. Although some of it was legitimately and fairly earned, much of it came from underhanded tactics and squeezing out his weaker neighbors. At the "company store" he operated, he took advantage of local residents who didn't have the means to go elsewhere, and he gouged them on prices. When local lumber mill workers went to his store with the chits in which they had been paid, he gave them less than face value toward their purchases, but he demanded full credit when he cashed in the chits at the mill. He kept hiring men to fish with nets in the neighboring Caddo Lake even after the state legislature prohibited net fishing. Not until a game warden burned his nets did he stop.

This was the same Caddo Lake where his daughter liked to hang out in summer. As soon as she was old enough, she went with friends to picnic on its banks, under ferny cypress trees, and swim in its murky, green water. In spite of alligator sightings, she was quick to jump in. She took her boyfriends there and had herself photographed vamping in a bathing suit, like a Hollywood pinup as she hugged a tree trunk. She could not have failed to notice that her father was making a very different use of Caddo Lake—for his own profit. Yet he remained her hero.

As Karnack's privileged little rich girl, Lady Bird learned early how to focus on the reality that worked to her benefit and block out the rest. Later in life, she talked about being able to stick her head in the sand, but her associates offered other descriptions of how she managed to ignore unpleasantness. One White House colleague noted she "had resources most people don't have"; she would start whistling and will herself into a place "of birds and sunshine." One acquaintance described her "veil" as a "Southern thing," that came down when she needed to block something out. Her longtime friend Harry Middleton observed, "She put on her mask and let the world go by." Historian Doris Kearns Goodwin called it "psychic leave," and said she witnessed it many times. Lady Bird would be sitting there, in body only, until Lyndon called out, "Bird, are you with me?" Then she would snap back.

The tiny one-room Fern School that Claudia Taylor started attending the year after her mother died offered limited companionship. Enrollment rarely reached ten, and when the number dropped to only two or three, the teacher moved classes to T.J.'s Brick House. After six years at Fern, with its potbellied stove, Claudia enrolled in a considerably larger school in the more upscale Jefferson, ten miles away. Sharing a room with Aunt Effie, she learned to imitate the deep Southern accents of the two retired schoolteachers who ran the boardinghouse, and to roll her eyes, like them, when she wanted to feign ladylike ignorance. With those retired schoolteachers, she had two good examples of how a show of feminine weakness could mask real power.

Cut off from so much in life, young Bird learned to disappear into books. Like her mother, she could spend hours at a time with only printed pages for company. She later singled out "The Emperor's New Clothes" by Hans Christian Andersen as an early favorite. One family acquaintance remembered driving up to the Brick House and seeing the eight-year-old girl on the front porch, a copy of the tome *Ben-Hur* in her little hands.

Although T.J. had little schooling, he wanted the best for his daughter, but he was reluctant to send her away. When it came time for high school, he assigned one of his employees to drive her the fifteen miles to Marshall, the county seat. T.J. put little stock in keeping his vehicles clean, and Minnie's daughter was embarrassed when classmates saw her being delivered each day by a dusty truck that smelled of cowhides. Besides, ferrying her back and forth took a driver's valuable time. So T.J. bought her a car of her own when she was only thirteen, and since Texas did not require a driver's license at the time, she drove herself back and forth. Her privileged status did not go unnoticed. "She had her own car," one jealous classmate remembered, "when my family didn't even have a car."

T.J. had his reasons for granting his daughter her independence. In 1920, two years after Minnie's death, he married his attractive young bookkeeper, Beulah Wisdom, twenty-four years his junior. Local residents knew her as a "looker" who wore the latest flapper fashions, the kind of woman only a rich man could hope to have. Eight-year-old Claudia did not see her new stepmother as a role model, and, when later asked, as an adult, if she found Beulah attractive, she said, "Yes, in a coarse and crude sort of way." The class chasm between the Wisdoms and the Taylors was clear even to a child, and Beulah's young niece remembered that when she was invited to sew doll clothes with Claudia, she carefully saved the scraps to make pants for her own little brother.

When school let out each spring, Claudia and Aunt Effie hustled off to Alabama, putting as much distance as possible between themselves and T.J.'s young wife. Since Aunt Effie had no home of her own, she parked herself with relatives and then pled illness and took to her bed, leaving her niece at the mercy of whoever was willing to take her in. Some of the Pattillo clan clearly welcomed the child and introduced her to watermelon evenings and Sunday picnics; they took her along on sightseeing trips to neighboring states, even as far as Colorado. Always aware that she was the visiting outsider, on probation, she was careful to mind her manners and look grateful as they bounced her from one household to another. One cousin recalled seeing this perfectly groomed little girl, arriving as the lone passenger in the backseat of a large car, her full skirt carefully spread out around her as if she did not mean to be touched.

By the time she was in high school, Claudia Taylor sounded like T.J. on subjects such as finances and international relations. These were written assignments, rather than topics she picked herself, but already, at age fourteen, she appeared opinionated, arguing that the United States should grant independence to the Philippines, not because it was right but because it would give the U.S. a monopoly on all rubber produced there. In another high school essay, on the subject of whether the United States should cancel debts it stood to collect from European nations, she wrote that she favored cancellation, not "because of sympathy" or because it would make other countries "like us better," but because it would help get those nations back on their feet and in a position to buy American products. Sounding like a cagey, mature bookkeeper, she admitted that $26 billion was "a large sum to erase from the 'right side' . . . of the ledger," but she reminded her reader that the U.S. "could make more money" from a strong Europe than from one strapped with debt.

It's no wonder her classmates predicted a bright business future for Claudia Taylor when she graduated from Marshall High at age fifteen. The yearbook compared her to Erie Halliburton, the famed entrepreneur locally revered as the man who started out with only a borrowed wagon and a mule but quickly extended his oil and gas empire around the globe. That judgment was very much on the mark. Late in life she admitted that had she not married Lyndon, she would probably have become a businesswoman.

At high school graduation, she was not yet set on that course but she was determined to strike out on her own. Staying in Karnack meant constant contact with her flashy, unsympathetic stepmother, and accompanying pathetic Aunt Effie to Alabama was equally unappealing. From the daughter of the local Episcopal rector, she learned about St. Mary's College, an Episcopal boarding school for girls in Dallas, and when she told T.J. she wanted to go there, he agreed. (She later said she hoped she granted her own daughters the same independence he gave her.) In Dallas, she would have a big city (population 158,000) and a chance to smooth out the rough edges of the schooling she had received in Marshall (population 14,000). St. Mary's wasn't exactly what her mother had in mind when she investigated boarding schools in Washington, D.C., but it appeared likely to offer similar rewards.

The two years Lady Bird spent at St. Mary's gave her a chance to remake herself. After a religion teacher introduced her to a different version of Christianity than she had heard in the fundamentalist Baptist sermons in Alabama or the Methodist teachings in Karnack she decided to convert to Episcopalianism. An English teacher awakened her to the richness of her native language and encouraged her to write with vivid phrases: "Don't just say 'a man is cruel. Walk him on the stage and have him do a cruel thing. . . . Instead of saying, 'It was stormy,' write, 'Thunder echoed through the valleys and lightning lit up the landscape.'" St. Mary's gave little importance to domestic skills, like cooking and sewing—students at St. Mary's expected to have others do those tasks for them. But it was there that Claudia learned the excitement of live theater. In the world of drama, she could lose herself, and theater became a mainstay pleasure of her adult life. "I loved the theater," she would say: "I fed upon it."

The young Lady Bird was game for adventure. On a trip to Shreveport, she insisted on going up in a tiny airplane, even though the wings looked precariously attached with wire. Her friend hung back, but Lady Bird loved it and called it "the most exciting ride of my young life." Fearless at the wheel of a car, she relished driving herself around. Both her mother and Aunt Effie had owned cars but relied on others to operate them, illustrating a kind of dependence that was not for Miss Claudia Taylor. When Aunt Effie needed her car driven the five hundred miles back to Autauga, Alabama, her sixteen-year-old niece volunteered to do it, accompanied by a friend the same age. Detained by road construction and the need to wire T.J. for more money, the two teens finally arrived more than a day late, in the middle of the night, at the home of a very anxious relative in Alabama.

Before she turned eighteen, Claudia Taylor had formed the traits that would define her adult life. From her father she had learned the value of every cent and the importance of taking risks. From her mother came the equally strong pull to lose herself in nature and drama, in words and dreams of faraway places. The Southern belle demeanor she had absorbed from Aunt Effie and the two ex-schoolteachers in Jefferson, Texas, fooled many people, and when she rolled her eyes and drawled her vowels, she appeared soft and pliable. But her childhood had toughened her, and she had mastered the priceless technique of insulating herself against intrusion and hurt, encasing herself in a protective cocoon that no one could breach. She could rationalize—or ignore—the shortcomings of others, even those adversely affecting her, without sacrificing a whit of her dignity. She had prepared herself to do what her mother never did—leave Karnack for a more exciting life.

2

❖◉◉◉❖

MAMA'S BOY

MOST PEOPLE think of Lyndon Johnson as a commanding, take-charge man, capable of manipulating others and ultra-confident of his own powerful reach. But inside that giant of a human being was an insecure and needy one, always grasping for signs of love and support. He recognized his weaker side as well as anyone else did, and explained how he had first become aware of it when he was only five years old.

By accident, he had hit his pregnant mother in the stomach with a ball, and afraid that he had harmed her and the unborn baby, he started walking to his grandfather's house, half a mile away. His mother had always warned him to stick to the road and not be tempted by the river that ran alongside. But that day, he put her warnings aside and, eager to feel the cool water on his bare feet, he left the dry and dusty road and started skipping along the riverbank. Suddenly he tripped over the exposed root of a dead tree and fell, hitting his head hard.

As he lay there, unable to move, panic set in and he feared night would come and no one would ever find him, that he would die right there, all alone and hurting. It was his punishment, he decided, for exploring this out-of-the-way place he had been told to avoid.

Then his parents miraculously appeared, and his father carefully lifted the injured boy, put him across his shoulder, and carried him all the way home. Lyndon's mother kept murmuring about how worried she had felt, how she had panicked at the thought of never finding him. After his parents bandaged his wounds and tucked him in his own bed, assuring him all the while how much they loved him, Lyndon felt such an overwhelming glow of happiness that he decided he could endure the most extreme pain if it led to an outpouring of attention and affection afterward. That hunger—for approval and adoration—would define the adult Lyndon, and his frustration when it was not fed would fuel his worst behavior.

The power of love was not the only lesson his parents taught him. From his mother, Rebekah Baines Johnson, he learned about the value of refinement, the importance of class differences, and the need to succeed. She made very clear she expected a lot from him. With her degree from Baylor University, she had fancied herself a couple notches above her less schooled neighbors, but that sense of superiority got battered by reality during the first year of her marriage. As she sweated over laundry tubs and toted pails of water from the outdoor pump, those dreams she once had for herself of becoming a famous writer looked entirely beyond reach. "Then I came along," Lyndon later reported, "and suddenly everything was all right again. I could do all the things she never did." The doting attention she lavished on her first-born was returned in kind, and for his first school recitation, he chose the poem, "I'd Rather Be Mama's Boy."

When his mother later put together *A Family Album* for Lyndon, she described his birth on August 27, 1908, in terms usually reserved for another birth, in Bethlehem: "In the rambling old farm house of the young Sam Johnsons, lamps had burned all night. Now the light came in from the east, bringing a deep stillness, a stillness so profound and so pervasive that it seemed as if the earth itself were listening. And then there came a sharp compelling cry—the most awesome, happiest sound known to human ears—the cry of a newborn baby; the first child of Sam Ealy and Rebekah Johnson was 'discovering America.'"

Rebekah uncharacteristically omitted her maiden name from page one of *A Family Album.* Because of the enormous pride she took in her ancestors, she usually found a way to fit "Baines" into any conversation. Her father, Joseph Wilson Baines, had left Louisiana as a child, when his pious, scholarly father was summoned to Texas to edit the state's first Baptist newspaper and then to head the Baptist university, Baylor. With a young British tutor in tow, the family must have caused some amused comment on the rough-and-tumble frontier, but the proud Baineses were not the type to care.

As an adult, Joe Baines started out following in his staid father's footsteps, teaching school and editing a newspaper. But then he ventured into riskier territory, including politics and land speculating. His fragile blond wife, Ruth, who was only fourteen (and his student) when he had proposed marriage, passed on her good looks to their daughter Rebekah but not much more; she rates only a footnote in *A Family Album.* It was Joe Baines who held center stage as the "dominant force" in young Rebekah's life, the "adored parent, reverenced mentor, and most interesting companion."

Just "call me lucky," Rebekah suggested, as she looked back over her youth: lucky to be born in McKinney, Texas, in 1881, just as her father was primed to outdo his devout Baptist parents. When the governor appointed him secretary of state for Texas, Joe moved his family from tiny McKinney to Austin, the state capital. By the time Rebekah started school in 1887, Joe Baines had installed his wife and their three children in an imposing limestone house outside Blanco, where he dealt in land and practiced law. Even without a British tutor, his offspring decided they had a superb education because they had him—Joe Baines taught them to "think and to endure, the principle of mathematics, the beauty of simple things." No wonder Rebekah set her sights high: she would become a journalist, she vowed, and write the great Confederate novel.

But Joe Baines had reached too high. Buying up acres like books, he overextended himself, and when he could not pay his debts, the bank auctioned off his two-thousand-plus acres *and* the family home. The Baineses had to vacate their two-story showplace and move into a much smaller wooden structure in Fredericksburg, slightly further west. Rebekah later glossed over what she called "severe and sudden financial reverses" by claiming that the entire family "adjusted readily and cheerfully to financial change." But that hardly seems an accurate description of how she and her siblings fared in the downsizing. Her brother had to sell his horse and fancy rubber-wheeled buggy, and she went to work. Joe Baines continued to dabble in real estate, and when Rebekah wasn't helping him out, doing secretarial chores, she clerked in a bookstore and submitted articles to regional newspapers, hoping for publication that would bring her a dollar or two. Joe Baines continued to take an interest in politics, and in 1902, at age fifty-six, he won his first election and took a seat in the Texas legislature.

It was a single term, and as Joe's health declined, the downward spiral of his life swirled faster. Bookish and pious, he was a loving and treasured mentor to Rebekah but no match for the competition in the thistly Hill Country. When he died, in 1906, at age sixty, he left a family struggling to support themselves. His wife, once accustomed to live-in servants, started taking in boarders. Rebekah, at twenty-six, had to face facts. She had passed the age when most American women married, and she had not written a page of that novel.

Before Joe Baines died, he had encouraged Rebekah to interview the young legislator elected to the seat Joe had just vacated—Sam Ealy Johnson Jr. The two men had become acquainted during political campaigns, and the older man had taken note of Sam's affability and his ambition. Even without a day in college, Sam had passed a local teachers exam by studying on his own, and he had then taught school for two years. That set him a bit apart from most of the males in his family, who talked rough and showed little interest in education.

The cowboy credentials of the Johnson clan also appealed to Joe Baines, whose own upbringing was light on adventure. Sam Johnson's father and his Uncle Tom had made names for themselves as trail drivers who moved cattle along the Chisholm Trail. It was the golden age for the cattle class, a time when a day's work included sleeping beside a campfire and keeping an eye out for rustlers. Trail drivers dealt with cowhands and ranchers. They rarely crossed paths with book-lined rooms or college presidents, and Baptist abstemiousness of the kind practiced by the Baineses was pretty much a joke with them.

By the time Sam Ealy Johnson was born in 1877, his father (Sam Sr.) and Uncle Tom were recognized across a wide swath of western Texas as major cattle dealers. They had gotten their start before the Civil War, then taken time off to fight before resuming business at their headquarters along the Pedernales River. Between the big slaughter-houses of Abilene and the ranches around Blanco, the Johnson brothers acted as middlemen who bought cattle from locals, maintained a holding pen for keeping herds until they acquired a sufficient number to start the drive north, and then hired hands to help move the animals along the famous trail. The profits could be enormous if all went well. Buying at $3 or $4 a head, they could expect to sell for ten times that at the trail's end. But not all went smoothly during what could be a two-month drive: rivers rose, rustlers stole, cattle took sick or ran off.

Trail driving did not leave a man much time for family life. Tom Johnson never married, and Sam looked for a wife who could take care of herself, run a household, and oversee a family during his long absences. Eliza Bunton, nineteen years old when he married her in 1867, did not disappoint. Besides bearing a large brood of children, she made her way into a book, *Leading Pioneer Women*, for hiding under her kitchen's floorboards an entire day, infant clutched to her chest to stifle his cries, so that invading "Red Warriors" could not find her.

Something of a local heroine by the time Rebekah Baines met her, Eliza Bunton Johnson was known for her good looks and practicality. When times were good and the money plentiful, she gladly accepted from her brother-in-law a splendid silver-mounted carriage and matched span of horses. Then, when times turned bad, she sold them off, using the proceeds to buy a property that later became the Johnson home. A striking, tall woman, with piercing black eyes, and magnolia-white skin, Eliza was often singled out as quintessential Bunton, and the story goes that her grandson, Lyndon, was only a few hours old when one relative looked him over and pronounced him pure Bunton in appearance.

When Rebekah Baines went to interview handsome Sam Ealy Johnson Jr. in 1906, she had a list of questions about what he, as a new state legislator, was going to do for his constituents back in the 89th District. At first she found him cagey, unwilling to provide much in the way of quotable quotes, but she liked his looks. He was, she wrote long after he was dead, a "personable young man, slender and graceful, immaculately groomed, agreeable and affable in manner and with great personal magnetism." For his part, Sam had never been interviewed by a pretty young blonde before, and he was smitten with this one, who could talk as knowingly as he about law making and the problems of the world.

In the months that followed, Sam squired Rebekah to a Confederate reunion and campaign rallies, including one where his hero William Jennings Bryan spoke. He was clearly enchanted with "a girl who really liked politics," and he lost no time proposing marriage. Just eight months after her adored father died, Rebekah accepted. Perhaps she hesitated to spring the news on her still grieving family, but more likely she feared they would not approve her choice. Whatever her reason, she did not tell them until after the fact. Her sister, Josefa, later admitted that the marriage took them all by surprise: "We didn't really know about it at the time." Then she added diplomatically, "We were very much pleased, of course." When Rebekah's own son eloped in similar fashion, she could hardly have objected. He was acting in family tradition.

Sam Johnson settled Rebekah in the same house near Stonewall where he had been living on his own, "batchin it," and occasionally sharing the space with a homeless ranch hand or two. The house lacked any sign of a woman's touch. The overcrowded little rooms, without electricity or indoor plumbing, required hard work if they were to be kept cozy and clean, but Rebekah tried to look on the bright side. Better times surely lay ahead, she kept telling herself, as she "shuddered over the chickens and wrestled with a mammoth iron stove."

The exact size and comfort of the house where Sam and Rebekah started out—and the location of Lyndon's birth—remain in dispute a century later because the family gave such radically different descriptions of it. Although Rebekah liked to emphasize the hardship of living in a small "cabin" in the first years of her marriage, she later tried to give a more upscale image, calling it a "rambling farmhouse." Her claim that she was shocked at its limitations when she first went to live there as a young bride is surely an exaggeration. She had grown up only thirty miles away, and since her father dealt in real estate and was involved in politics, she would have had many opportunities to see houses like this one.

The original structure, a rectangular box with a dividing breezeway, called a "dog run," down the middle, was razed in the 1940s, when Lyndon's political prospects were on the rise, to be replaced by a somewhat larger dwelling, with higher ceilings. It had only four rooms, and the front two did double duty, serving for both sleeping and sitting. Neither the extended shack that some historians describe nor the sprawling homestead occasionally portrayed by Rebekah, Lyndon's birthplace most probably fit somewhere in the murky middle, like so much of the Johnson story. As Lyndon neared the pinnacle in politics, he liked to emphasize his humble beginnings, to the chagrin of his sister Rebekah, who amused her friends by saying: "Lyndon may have been born in a log cabin, but I, sure as hell, wasn't."

Other details of the Johnson story appear just as scrambled, and part of the reason lies with ambitious, class-conscious Rebekah, who kept trying to reconcile the jagged reality of her life with the outsized dreams of her youth. Marriage to Sam Johnson produced plenty of disappointments, but whenever she got the chance, she emphasized his best side and made him (and their life together) sound better than either was. When she recorded details of Lyndon's birth, she wrote that he was delivered by "Dr. John Blunton of Buda." But the evidence makes clear that the good doctor, although summoned, did not arrive at the house in time, and the man who later became the thirty-sixth president of the United States exited his mother's womb attended only by a midwife, not something a proud Baines would like to admit.

Rebekah spent the first five years of her marriage and gave birth to three children in that little house. Her sister and mother pitched in to help during their summer visits, cooking down fruit preserves and canning vegetables for the winter months. When Sam had a bit of extra money, Rebekah hired a neighbor woman to assist with the heavy lifting and endless laundry, but when money ran low and her relatives departed, she had to manage on her own.

Rebekah's rough, red hands attested all her life to that hardship. In 1938, just months after her husband's death, Rebekah was in Washington when Lady Bird gave a small lunch for her and other guests, including Virginia Durr, a white civil rights leader from Alabama. Durr later recalled how she had sat next to this "extremely beautiful woman . . . very aristocratic . . . [with] beautiful bone structure." It was her large, swollen, very red hands that drew Durr's attention, and Rebekah Johnson noticed. As they began eating, she leaned over to Durr and whispered how she had always been "embarrassed and ashamed" of her hands. They had never recovered, she explained, from the hard work of her early married years. But the proud mother of a young man newly elected to the U.S. House of Representatives made clear to Durr that she expected her future to brighten: "Even as a young boy Lyndon used to say to me, 'Oh Mama, when I get big, I'm going to see that you don't have to do any of this hard work so you can have pretty white hands.'"

Rebekah Johnson expected this and more out of her firstborn, and from his earliest years she put every effort into helping him achieve all that she feared she never could. She coddled and pushed the young Lyndon, introducing him to the alphabet before he was toilet-trained and teaching him to read by the time he was four. When he started tagging his older cousins down the road to school, she persuaded the teacher to let him attend classes, although he had not reached the required age. When he acted shy about participating in classroom exercises, she convinced the teacher to let him sit on her lap, a privilege that could not have made him popular with other students.

Even with all the responsibilities of wife and mother, Rebekah clung to the possibility of a career for herself. She still turned out the occasional article for regional newspapers and then enlisted her relatives to help spot any that were published so she could clip them and get paid. Cooking and cleaning bored her, and she liked to sleep late whenever she could, leaving it to her husband to prepare the children's breakfast and herd them off to school. He was the stern one, insisting that the children memorize speeches of William Jennings Bryan, while Rebekah spent her time directing school plays and concentrating on matters of manners and dress.

Appearances meant everything to her, and when Sam brought any of his political cronies home for a meal, she made sure to put a linen cover on the table rather than the practical oilcloth that her neighbors routinely used. In her bedroom, where guests gathered to talk when it was too chilly out in the breezeway, she kept her most prized possession, a writing desk, which helped set her home apart from others in the area. Her emphasis on what she considered the "finer things," such as drama and classical music, fueled her children's conviction that they were superior, destined for a future brighter than that of their Hill Country friends.

Hard-boiled and demanding, this tall, big-boned woman, with her knifelike voice, could cut cold anyone who disagreed with her, even if that person was her own flesh and blood. When Lyndon refused to take violin lessons, which he called "sissy stuff," she did not speak to him for days, even though the two lived in the same house. Her punishing silence hurt all the more because she continued to lavish attention on his siblings. It was a lesson in retribution that Lyndon learned well. Although he did not deal well with cruelty aimed at him, he relished dispensing it, and "freezing out" became a favorite way to deal with those who disappointed or crossed him.

Sam Ealy Johnson Jr. also played a significant part in Lyndon's early years, and one biographer titled his book about the thirty-sixth president: *Sam Johnson's Boy.* As a member of the state legislature from 1905 to 1909, Sam moved easily among the locally important politicos. But by the time of his first son's birth in August 1908, his finances had taken a beating, and Sam left government to concentrate on supporting his growing family.

In spite of the rosy picture Rebekah painted of her husband, his ability to provide spiked and plummeted. Recovering from that first financial downturn soon after his marriage, he made new investments, then went bust again. Years after the fact, D. Jablow Hershman, author of several books on mental disorders, wrote that Sam Ealy Johnson had a "typical manic's career" making repeated changes in occupation and taking foolish gambles that reduced his family to poverty.

Hershman's judgment seems a bit harsh, considering the fact that in the pre-safety-net era, many farmers and small-time investors suffered similar peaks and troughs through no fault of their own. Crops failed; prices fluctuated in ways no one could predict. Like many other Americans in the early 1900s, Sam's dependents had a roller-coaster ride. When times were bad, they cut back or went without. But Hershman was right in that Sam rode the good times to their upper limits. When he felt flush, after making a sizable profit in a real estate deal or a cattle sale, he splurged, moving his family into an upscale house in Johnson City and driving them around in a shiny Model T. Johnson City, named for a Johnson forebear well before Sam and Rebekah arrived, had only a few hundred residents at the time, and the closest railroad was in Fredericksburg, thirty miles to the west. But it felt like a busy metropolis compared to the isolated ranch. Instead of a one-room schoolhouse with a single teacher, Lyndon and his siblings attended the more imposing two-story Johnson City School, with its faculty of five. But when Sam Johnson's luck turned again and his bank account dwindled, it was back to that low-ceilinged house on the Pedernales, where Lyndon and his younger brother slept on the porch.

Between 1918 and 1925, when Lyndon was an impressionable adolescent, his father returned to serve again in the state legislature, providing the boy with an invaluable starter course in politics. Representing his home district in the statehouse was only a part-time job, but when the legislature was in session, Sam had to stay in Austin for days at a time. He often took Lyndon with him so he could sit in on House debates and listen to after-hours discussions in back rooms and public bars. The son watched lobbyists dispense a range of favors, from booze to the company of women, in order to win something for their clients in return. Sam Ealy Johnson had a reputation for being exceptionally honest and hard to corrupt, but it seems unlikely that any legislator survived for long without registering some recognition for his efforts.

Since service in the legislature was compensated at only $5 a day, a little extra help, in the form of payoffs from lobbyists, came in handy. Lawmakers felt justified in accepting assistance, especially if offered in a form other than cash, such as a paid vacation for the lawmaker's family in one of Austin's finer hotels. Sam Johnson's family stayed at the Driskill, and although evidence is lacking for who paid, it is perfectly reasonable to expect that they thought they were entitled to a vacation in Austin, because they sacrificed so much by Sam's being away from home. That kind of recognition—gifting a politician's family for the work he did—was not limited to Texas; nor was it deemed necessarily unethical at the time. When General Motors delivered to the White House a new Cadillac for First Lady (and horse lover) Lou Hoover in 1929, she wrote the car company an enthusiastic "thank you" for adding to her Cadillac stable.

In his trips to Austin, Lyndon picked up a lot from his father, besides the pleasure of staying at the Driskill without leaving a paper trail. Lyndon began to walk and talk just like the older man, so much so that fellow legislator Wright Patman said the resemblance was "laughable." Amiable Sam Johnson prided himself on listening to people (and one of his observations, "When you're talking, you're not learning anything," became a favorite of Lyndon's). But Sam didn't just listen with his ears—he showed his total attention by edging up close to a man, eyeballing him with those piercing black eyes and wrapping a long arm around his shoulders. When Sam Johnson wanted to make a point of his own, he backed it up with a pointed finger, right at his listener's nose. At six foot three, the lanky legislator might have seemed intimidating to shorter men, but his genial manner and obvious concern won them over. To young Lyndon, the message was clear: right-in-your-face pressure had to be modulated with a good dose of friendly concern.

The boy absorbed the legislative gossip that came his father's way, including potentially harmful details about personal improprieties, and he saw how tidbits got stored away for later use. Sam drummed into his son that if you walked into a room and couldn't figure out what every person was thinking, you didn't deserve to be in politics. It was another way of teaching that "every man has his price," and Lyndon learned the lesson well.

During the regular legislative session, which started in January and ran for two months, Sam had to rely on others to operate the ranch. As the eldest of his children, Lyndon became the designated man of the house, charged with helping his mother and seeing that daily chores—feeding chickens and chopping wood—got done. He quickly figured out how to foist tasks on his younger siblings, freeing himself to roam with his buddies. The resentment they later showed him (and the wariness with which they accepted his favors) resulted from bitter experience. After he became president, one of his sisters made headlines with her statement that he was "always bossy."

In his part of Texas, Sam Johnson became known as a populist Democrat, fiercely intent on protecting the underdog. The list of the laws he sponsored included aid for state pensioners and for rural families who needed roads. Small-time investors received his support in a measure called the Blue Sky Law. When the German Americans in Sam's district found themselves demonized as "Huns" during World War I, Sam stood up for and defended them. He earned the goodwill of other constituents by attacking the Ku Klux Klan so fiercely that he received death threats.

Rebekah, in highlighting her husband's accomplishments, overlooked all these and focused on one of his very early legislative victories—the Alamo Purchase Bill, which provided for the state of Texas to buy the historic site in San Antonio and turn over its management to the elite Daughters of the Republic of Texas. Sam was only one of several legislators (and hardly the most significant) who backed the purchase, but it was the measure that Rebekah saw as tying him (and her) to the wealthy tier of old Texas—to the people she thought mattered most.

What Rebekah omitted entirely in telling Sam Johnson's story is striking, although entirely understandable. Her husband drank, and he drank a lot, especially when he was losing money instead of making it. In 1921, when his exaggerated plans to earn a fortune in cotton were ruined by a disastrously bad market, he began a depressing physical decline that lasted until his death sixteen years later. He had taken out huge loans to buy equipment, hire hands, and lease land, and when the price of raw cotton tanked to a fraction of what it had been, he could not begin to pay back all that he owed.

Lyndon would later claim that his father lost $100,000, the equivalent of more than $1 million in 2014 dollars, in that debacle, but it was more likely only about half that. Whatever the exact figure, Sam Johnson never recovered, and it became clear that he would not provide a success story to suit his wife. His political contacts continued to find small jobs for him, on highway projects or streetcar inspecting, but cash was tight. By the time Lyndon entered college in 1927, Sam could not come up with the money for him to enroll, and Lyndon had to borrow from a neighbor. Lyndon's four younger siblings (including three sisters) would all go to college, but on a shoestring of loans and student jobs. At Sam's death in 1937, he left a widow so destitute that Lyndon, a married congressman, was her chief support, and he took out a life insurance policy on himself, naming his mother, not his wife, as beneficiary.

The much diminished Sam Johnson was not the man Lyndon had observed earlier. During his son's most formative years, when tall, rangy Sam was still a respected figure in his community, he stood out as a model. When he started skidding, however, his trips to the local bars growing longer and more destructive, Lyndon was ashamed of him. Enlisting a friend to accompany him one night to the local saloon to entice Sam to come home, Lyndon explained how much his mother, who never permitted a drop of alcohol at her table, suffered at seeing her husband drunk. The son vowed not to disappoint his high-reaching mother as his father had done.

Faced with such opposite parental models when he graduated from high school in 1924, fifteen-year-old Lyndon had not yet figured out how to combine the staid, reverent, class-conscious Baines genes with those of the cussing, imbibing Johnsons. So he did what lots of other young men were doing at the time—he headed west.

California appeared wide open in the 1920s, ready to accommodate dreams of any size. In Hollywood, the embryonic film industry was looking for top talent from New York and Europe, but even a little-schooled farm boy could find employment somewhere—in the burgeoning office buildings, newly opened oil fields, or on truck farms whose owners bragged they were feeding the entire nation. Ben Crider, the older brother of a high school buddy, had already made his way to Los Angeles, and his letters home, outlining the rich opportunities waiting there, were an enticement to others to join him.

Lyndon pooled his meager resources with Ben Crider's younger brother and two others to buy a rattletrap of a car, and then drove off, leaving the Hill Country and a deeply disappointed Rebekah Baines Johnson behind. Although she recognized that her son never developed her interest in books, she still envisioned him going to college and accomplishing more than any man in her family had ever done. When word came back that Lyndon was doing menial jobs, running an elevator and making deliveries, she continued to pray that this was only a temporary deviation from the high road she had in mind for him.

After twenty months, Lyndon returned to Texas, back to the nest and his surest supply of loving attention, which he had already judged as essential to his well-being as oxygen. His father's political connections helped him find a job, driving a truck in road construction, but Lyndon soon angered some of his co-workers by getting out of the hard labor the same way he had offloaded chores on his younger siblings. The road crew's rancor toward him may have set the stage for an exceptionally unpleasant Saturday night brawl when Lyndon evidently got bruised up a bit. A couple days later he surprised and delighted his mother by telling her he was tired of working with his hands. Now he was ready to use his brains. Would she help him get into college?

Rebekah walked to the phone and called Southwest Texas State Teachers College at San Marcos, and before she hung up, she had arranged not only for his admission but also for a job to help pay his expenses. Aware that he lacked some of the entrance requirements, she coached him, and in one bravado performance stayed up to tutor him all night for a math test he barely passed. She had already worked on his public speaking skills, having instructed him and other neighborhood children in what was then called "expression." One of Lyndon's female cousins explained how Aunt Rebekah would drill them on public speaking; she pounced on poor diction or faulty grammar while reminding them to stand tall and gesture and make eye contact with their listeners. Lyndon benefited from his mother's elocution lessons, but his cousin Ava said he never could match his father's eloquence, especially when addressing a large group.

Pious Rebekah, who liked to write across the seal of her letters "Mizpah" from Genesis 31:49, meaning "May the Lord keep Watch between you and me while we are away from the other," made a good choice in sending Lyndon to San Marcos. Southwest Texas State Teachers College, with only seven hundred students, enrolled three females for every male, and Rebekah could expect her lean, six-foot-plus son to make a splash with the farmers' daughters, even if he did have some rough edges. Although University of Texas at Austin was much larger and more prestigious, Johnson City residents favored San Marcos because of its proximity (only forty miles away) and less stringent entry requirements. Rebekah's younger sister had already attended San Marcos, where her mother ran her boardinghouse, so the entire family knew their way around the town.

When he started college classes in February 1927, eighteen-year-old Lyndon was a curious mix. Rebekah's prodding and outsized ambition had produced a cocky young man who thought he could wangle anything from anyone. But his father's depressing downfall remained a stark reminder that failure loomed. Lyndon was haunted by memories of his Grandmother Bunton; the take-charge woman whose name got into history books for outsmarting the men who invaded her household ended up paralyzed by a stroke that left her unable to move or speak. She died when he was only eight, but the image of her shocking incapacity stayed with him for life, a potent warning about the elusiveness of dominance. For a young man who put the highest value on physical strength and maintaining control, the worst nightmare was losing power. At all costs, he did not want to fail like his father and grandmother.

Some of the tools of success were already in the hands of college freshman Lyndon. He had learned to ingratiate himself with older people and pick out those in a position to help him. His boyhood friends noted how he took time to talk with their mothers, complimenting them on their cooking or their appearance; and then their mothers favored him, with an extra piece of pie or a compliment about what a fine example he set for the other boys. At San Marcos, his fellow students called it brownnosing. But to Lyndon, it was a way to improve his chances.

Although his first student job was as janitor, Lyndon soon caught the eye of the college president and became his assistant. With a desk just outside the president's office, he was known as someone who could pull strings: arrange an appointment with President Cecil E. Evans on short notice or reach the right person at the most propitious time.

The small campus provided Lyndon a setting to try out the political skills learned from his father. When he arrived, the "Black Stars," a group of the leading jocks, controlled student activities and the funds that supported them—they decided how money was allotted, which athletic teams got what, and who wrote for the school newspaper. Lyndon quickly organized the opposing "White Stars" to squeeze them out, and by the time he left, the Black Stars had trimmed their expectations and lost their monopoly over dates with the most popular women on campus. Although Lyndon later boasted that he defanged the Black Stars entirely, he actually was more accommodating, beginning to use the looking-for-common-ground approach that would serve him later in Washington.

In campus elections, he became his own polling outfit, counting votes before they were cast. If his candidate was lagging behind, he stayed up all night trying to bend ears and change minds. Using techniques for which he later became famous, he would zero in on the "undecideds" or those who owed him a favor and use every available argument to bring them around. Some classmates complained that he was bossy, self-centered, and employed unfair tactics—like blackmailing the opposition with threats of exposing personal matters that they preferred keeping private. Whether it was an off-the-cuff comment about a candidate's personal failings or a story about a family's closeted skeletons, Lyndon stored tidbits away, to release—or threaten to release—at the opportune time. Using his arsenal of persuasive weapons, he engineered his roommate's election as Senior Class president and his own ascension to editor of the school paper. He perched himself on a three-footed stool of power, supported by the newly formed White Stars, the student newspaper, and a desk near the college president's office.

Not yet old enough to vote in a national election, Lyndon had already figured out a lot about how politics worked. From his mother, he had picked up the importance of charm and refinement as well as the tactics for punishing those on the other side. From his father, he learned how to calculate the odds and increase his own chances in every political deal. The combination was a recipe for achieving real power.

Not every venture succeeded. In a town the size of San Marcos, word of his family's background got around. After Lyndon met and courted Carol Davis, the mayor's daughter, he accompanied the Davis family to the 1928 Democratic nominating convention in Houston. But Carol's parents decided he was still more the product of failed cowhands than of Baines preachers, and on their insistence Carol dropped Lyndon.

A special mentor at San Marcos—Professor Howard M. Greene—encouraged Lyndon's interest in government and politics, and the grateful student would later bring Greene to Washington and introduce him to President John F. Kennedy as "the man who started the fire under me . . . gave me my first course in government and my last." Greene's credentials were not those of the typical academic—he was a maverick, who announced he did not need a Ph.D. because no one had anything to teach him. An eccentric on campus, he fancied plaid shirts and untied ties, and when he lectured, feet on the desk, he kept a spittoon nearby. On a farm outside San Marcos, he raised prized pigs and developed a breed that later made headlines, but the indelible mark he left on many of his students had nothing to do with pigs.

His most famous protégé, Lyndon Johnson, ought to have been walking on air as he surveyed his successes at San Marcos. But the "highs" resulting from on-campus victories were punctuated by periods of despair when he questioned whether he should even be in college. He envied the wealthier students who had fancier clothes than he, and he chafed at the prospect of having to stay three years at San Marcos to earn a degree. After mulling over his prospects, he wrote his old buddy Ben Crider, who had remained in Los Angeles, and inquired about the current job market. Once again, Rebekah stepped in. She wrote her own letter to Crider, begging him to help her keep Lyndon in school. Crider didn't mention Mrs. Johnson's letter when he replied to Lyndon's, but he enclosed a loan of $80, and Lyndon remained in college.

Lyndon often mused that he felt short-changed, with a degree from a state teachers college rather than an elite Eastern university. Although his parents argued it was the man, not the alma mater, that determined success, he never could make himself believe it. Yet San Marcos served him well. It gave him the confidence to stand out and test his power. His cousin Ava recalled that he could convince the women students to do just about anything he wanted, to support his White Stars or any changes he advocated in his newspaper columns. When his co-workers and critics later labeled Lyndon's manipulative ways "the treatment," they often added that it was at San Marcos that he refined the basics of how "the treatment" worked.

Southwest Texas State Teachers College also provided a flexible academic calendar so students could withdraw temporarily to earn money. When his own funds ran low, Lyndon took off the academic year 1928–1929 and taught school in Cotulla, a tiny town 130 miles south of San Marcos, halfway to the Mexican border, in a school that enrolled mostly Mexican Americans. As the only male on the faculty of four, he automatically became principal, although he had just turned twenty and had never taught a day in his life.

That one year at Cotulla probably did more to shape Lyndon than all his classes at San Marcos. He developed a genuine sympathy for the underdog. Coming from a family that had struggled at times, he now encountered students from homes where they never had enough to eat. Although his salary was only $125 a month, he started taking from it to buy pencils and school supplies for those who didn't have them, and he set up a sports field and supervised after-school games.

The Cotulla students loved him, and he garnered their lifelong regard for staying after the closing bell to help them. Some of them followed him doggedly after he left their town, asking him for jobs as soon as they were old enough to work in his office. A busload of alumni later traveled miles to watch him, as president of the United States, sign a new law that would inject much needed funds into schools like theirs. He had touched their lives in ways they would never forget, and they had touched his. He would repeatedly cite them for making him understand how poverty crippled people, and how lack of opportunity set the stage for a lifetime of failure.

Back at San Marcos at the end of his teaching year, Lyndon finished up his bachelor's degree. But he faced a miserable market at graduation in August 1930, when nearly one in ten of the nation's workers did not have a job. His Uncle George, head of the history department in one of Houston's biggest high schools, tried to make a place for him there, but failed, leaving Lyndon to accept the best offer he received—from a sleepy little town south of San Antonio, Pearsall. With a population of only a couple hundred, it was not the sort of place a restless go-getter like Lyndon Baines Johnson wanted to tarry.

In just one month, he was out of there, geared for something bigger. He was twenty-two years old, with a college degree that even he knew was second-rate. But he had a healthy respect for the opinions of strong women, like his mother, and she had made very clear she thought he could outdo everyone, including her adored father and her disappointing husband. He still had to find a remedy for his bottomless pit of self-doubt, and he had to find someone to supply the inexhaustible, unwavering support that he absolutely required. But if he could manage that, who knew how high he could climb?

3

GETTING OUT OF KARNACK, WITH THE RIGHT MAN

O N A bright Sunday morning in 1930, seventeen-year-old Claudia Taylor, now "Bird" to her friends, was back in Karnack at the Brick House. It was April, spring vacation time at St. Mary's College in Dallas, and she was spending a few days with her father. Since that meant having as little as possible to do with her stepmother, she set off on one of her favorite walks, looking for any magnolia trees that were already flowering.

Bird had a lot more on her mind than magnolias that day. Her time at St. Mary's would end in a month, and she still had no firm plans for what to do next. Her well-heeled classmates, who had traveled far more than she and enjoyed the kind of adventures she suspected her mother had yearned for but never found in Karnack, had widened her eyes, and she liked to think she was making some progress toward a life as exciting as theirs. With a virtually unlimited checking account and a little black Studebaker her father had given her, she liked to treat her classmate Emma Boehringer, whose widowed mother could provide her children with few luxuries, to trips to Shreveport where the two young women would eat in a fancy restaurant and then see whatever was playing at the Strand, a theater so ornate they imagined it must have been imported from Europe. One weekend, Bird gathered up a couple of Karnack friends and struck out for New Orleans, 350 miles away. Discussing that trip much later in her life, she could not remember if they had a chaperone, but brushed off the question with: "Well, let's hope we did."

But her permanent address was still "Karnack, Texas," a town so small people laughed at the pretension implied in naming it after a monumental temple complex in Egypt and then changing the spelling from Karnak. If the two years away from home had clarified anything for Bird—it was just how wide a chasm separated Karnack from the woman she wanted to become.

As much as she adored her father, she already knew that she could not live his life, or anything remotely like it, talking only about weather and crops. She had long ago dismissed Aunt Effie as a role model. Without a life of her own, Effie had had to attach herself to one or another kin, like a clingy, injured dog, just to survive. Neither of Bird's two humdrum brothers presented an example worth following. Tommy was becoming paunchy like his father, and both brothers were running modest businesses. No, there had to be something beyond what any of them were doing, perhaps that place her mother was looking for on those trips to Chicago, or the one she seemed to dream about while riding around Karnack in a chauffeured car, a veil covering her face.

The popular magazines that Bird read offered examples of women who had made careers for themselves and utterly altered their lives— journalists like Bess Furman, who covered Washington for the Associated Press, and Amelia Earhart, who gained headlines as the first woman to fly across the Atlantic. Even if Bird could not imagine matching their feats, she felt confident she could do something similar, on a smaller scale. But she wanted more than a career—she wanted to marry and have children. So she had to find the right man, one who took her breath away and was going places, but one who would also let her deploy her ambition. How could she manage all that?

It was on that Sunday morning walk that Bird came face-to-face with the answer. Eugenia "Gene" Boehringer, Emma's older sister, was also visiting her hometown, and like Bird, had gone out exploring the countryside. Although only six years older than Bird, her confident bearing and take-charge manner made her seem at least a generation wiser and more experienced. As Gene started updating Bird on all that had happened since the two last met, it became clear that Gene was living exactly the life that Bird had dreamed of.

Gene had made the brave decision to leave Karnack and go to college in Austin, the state capital, three hundred miles away. It wasn't easy. Knowing her mother could not possibly pay her way, Gene, the oldest of six children, got a job and worked while also studying at the University of Texas. After she graduated, she didn't take the easy route, retreating back to Harrison County where she knew people and could live near her mother. She remained in Austin.

But the eye-popping part of Gene's story was the job she now held—as a secretary at the Railroad Commission. In spite of its bland-sounding name, the Railroad Commission regulated far more than trains—it controlled the gas and oil industry as well as the pipelines that delivered those vital commodities all across the immense Lone Star State. Working there, as a secretary, Gene met the most important businessmen and leading lawmakers, and she regaled a wide-eyed Bird with stories of how she regularly chatted up big-time investors about deals they were making, and how she ferreted out details of pending legislation from the legislators themselves. Here was a flesh-and-blood example of those career women Bird had read about, but unlike them, Gene had grown up just down the road from Bird, and she, too, planned to find a husband and combine marriage with a career.

Before the two women parted that spring day, Bird had accepted an invitation to come visit Austin. Rather than drive or take the train, she flew, something few of her friends would risk in 1930. The three-hundred-mile flight got bumpy and made her sick, but as soon as she landed, any reservations about why she had come to Austin vanished. She fell in love with the city at first sight.

Bluebonnets, in bloom from March to May, swathed the hillsides in lush color. Around the state capitol, its dome an imitation of the Capitol in Washington, D.C., stood a mixture of buildings that looked nothing like Harrison County. The Driskill Hotel, a few blocks south of the capitol, dwarfed anything Bird had seen in Shreveport, and its huge chandeliered lobby and uniformed doormen suggested an opulent world she had explored only in books. A fifteen-minute walk northeast of the capitol took her to the University of Texas campus, which spread across several blocks, its vine-covered fraternity houses flanking rambling Victorian buildings where classes met. To the west lay a motley collection of homes, some close to the ground but others three stories high, surrounded by well-tended lawns. Beyond them, across the Colorado River, stretched an unsettled hilly expanse, with leafy trees, flowery patches, and trails for hiking and horseback riding. It was a world away from Karnack and Bird immediately decided this was a "magic place" for her.

The following September, she drove down to Dallas in her little black Studebaker, hoping that the experience would be all that Gene had made it out to be. Though she was one of only a few students who did not have to worry about money (this was less than a year after the stock market crash of 1929) she did not rent an apartment for herself but shared a room in a very modest house at 301 West 21st Street. The owners, Mr. and Mrs. Felix Matthews, provided breakfast for their half dozen paying guests but sent them for other meals to cheap eateries in the neighborhood. Bird, who had grown up with hired cooks preparing food just the way she liked it, now ate from set menus in greasy spoons. The biggest impression she left on her housemates was how disciplined she was. She stuck to healthful dishes and ate lots of vegetables, as she had been taught to do on her excursions to the Kellogg Sanitarium with Aunt Effie. Bird's housemates, thrilled to be liberated from parental supervision, liked to indulge in rich desserts with whipped cream.

The highlight on weekends was a visit to Gene Boehringer's quarters at the Austin Women's Club. Bird counted on Gene to introduce her to the most promising of the state capital's young set, especially handsome bachelors who had already made names for themselves. Dawson Duncan, a reporter, was one of her first blind dates, and he struck her as exactly what "a romantic newspaperman" should look like. When he dropped her, after a single date, she took it stoically, realizing how naive and unworldly she must have seemed to him. But she did not forget him, and decades later when their paths crossed again she would be the one in a position to ignore him.

In Austin, Bird was a little T.J., sleuthing out opportunities at UT and sizing up her options. She wasn't going to rob a train, but she would look for a ladylike equivalent to get her where she wanted to go. That meant taking the right courses and meeting the right man.

Only about one third of the 5,400 students lived in fraternities and sororities, but Bird quickly decided she wanted to be part of that third. They were the big names on campus, the men and women who got their photos in the school paper; they captained the athletic teams and ran the student government. But in a rare show of parental will, T.J., probably influenced by stories of fraternities' hazing rites, vetoed his daughter's plans to join a sorority, and she remained at the Matthewses' rooming house her entire time at UT.

Still, there was no stopping T.J.'s little Bird from tasting all that life had to offer, including double dates with her roommate, Cecille Harrison, on two-hundred-mile trips across the Mexican border, where they partied until dawn. Spring was a particularly exciting time.

Bird remembered falling in love every April, when she and Cecille went with their current boyfriends to Dillingham's Pasture, just north of Austin, for what they called "Navajo parties." The "Navajo" came from the blankets they spread out on the grass, with an alarm clock alongside, so they would be sure to be back in their room before the Matthewses' 11 p.m. curfew.

Bird may have fallen in love every spring, but any man she dated more than once had to have something special. From student body president Chilton O'Brien to politically motivated Victor McCrea and personable premed Jack Mayfield, they were all very ambitious. While still students, they managed to distinguish themselves as go-getters, a cut above their less achieving classmates. Gene Boehringer's brother, on the other hand, got dropped immediately when Bird decided he would "never amount to anything."

While sizing up young marriage material, Bird also wanted to see what older, more experienced men could teach her. When Gene introduced her to well-heeled business types and retired lawmen, some of them old enough to be her father, she accepted their invitations for afternoon horseback rides in the hills and late night suppers. Why would a UT coed do that, except to find something that was missing on campus? The older men could pay for Prohibition-outlawed cocktails, and Bird discovered her very favorite was a Tom Collins, with extra lime. She left no evidence that she became sexually involved with any of these older men, but she admitted to a curiosity about what they knew. At the home of a retired Texas Ranger, she took to reading his large collection of fully illustrated, sexually graphic books, until he stopped her, saying, "That one's not for you."

In UT classrooms, Bird played it safe. With a major in history, she knew she would have trouble finding a job. So she also took the education classes required of teachers, and to maximize her chance of employment she signed up for typing and shorthand. But she didn't stop there. Although slated to pick up a bachelor's degree in May 1933, she stayed another year to take more journalism classes. She had already written a few columns for the university's *Daily Texan,* and now, rather than becoming a teacher or secretary, she envisioned herself as a reporter somewhere beyond the forty-eight states, maybe Alaska or Hawaii.

Not much escaped Bird at UT, and later descriptions of her as shy and timid just don't fit. Active enough in college sports to be elected to the board of the Women's Athletic Association, she appeared in the group's yearbook photo in a fetchingly low-cut black dress, looking more like a debutante than a team player. Politically engaged, she liked to fill a free afternoon by walking over to the capitol and listening to debates; intrigued by new places, she booked herself a trip east as a graduation present.

Many of her classmates settled for destinations close to home after picking up their degrees in June 1934. But not Bird. She had listened so many times to her Karnack neighbor Dorris Powell extol the fascinations of New York City that she knew she had to see it, and her roommate, Cecille, agreed to go with her. Leaving the port of Galveston, they stopped briefly in Miami, and then sailed up the Atlantic Coast to Manhattan, where they intended to get a firsthand look at the Broadway lights and see some plays before going to Washington for a tour of the national landmarks.

New York City was a huge disappointment. Dorris Powell had touted its raised rail tracks and multiethnic throngs as gritty and exotic. But Bird, who got a lot more excited about a field of bluebonnets than about jam-packed streets, failed to see the appeal of a city with nearly seven million people. She liked the Broadway shows she saw with Cecille and made sure to reconnect with some of those Texas "oil men" who were also in New York and took her to the "Casino de Paree" nightclub. But the thrill that Dorris promised just wasn't there.

Washington, on the other hand, with its wide streets and imposing monuments, intrigued her. She dragged her roommate along with her to the Supreme Court building, where they sat in the justices' chairs, and then to 1600 Pennsylvania Avenue, where they peered through the iron fence at the White House. Cecille soon had enough of what she considered dry civics lessons and went back to New York. That left Bird on her own, and she immediately looked up an old boyfriend, Victor McCrea. He introduced her to his sister and other young Texans, who had also taken summer jobs in the capital, keeping her so busy she forgot all about the telephone number Gene Boehringer had given her, with instructions to call a young man named Lyndon Johnson.

Back in Texas, Bird had to decide what to do with herself now. At twenty-one, she had two bachelor degrees from the University of Texas, one in liberal arts, with a major in history, and the other in journalism. But she had no prospects for a job. It was the gloomiest trough of the Great Depression, when one out of four Americans did not have work, and even with shorthand and typing skills she was unlikely to get hired. T.J. was still making money, and he could have afforded to cover the costs of her staying in Austin. But remaining in the capital without a paycheck was hard to justify, and most of Bird's friends, including Cecille, were going back home to live with their parents.

In Bird's case, the home scene had drastically changed. After fourteen years of marriage to his second wife, Beulah, T.J. had sent her packing and sued for divorce on the grounds that she was enjoying male companionship that did not include him. Although he had shown utter disregard for monogamy himself, and even his daughter recognized that he kept women on the side, or as she cryptically put it, "lady friends" who had no place in "his domestic life," he was not about to permit his wife the same freedom. It was a painful ego buster for "Mr. Boss" to find himself cuckolded, and one neighbor expressed surprise that he did not kill Beulah.

The daughter who still worshipped T.J. as "the gentlest of men" decided she would come to his aid, while her two older brothers looked the other way. Tommy and Tony had collected their portions of their mother's estate as soon as they were old enough, but they had little to do with their father. They still called him "Mr. Boss," because that's what he insisted they call him, but like their deceased mother, they saw the title as nothing more than a hollow honorific. Bird and her father had so little contact with Tommy, who lived only a few miles from the Brick House, that she admitted it was easy to "forget we've got him."

Bird's return to Karnack was definitely a marking of time, until the right job and/or the right man showed up. It wasn't what she wanted but she would make the best of what she had, and in the process do something for her father. After fourteen years under Beulah's management, the Brick House was showing signs of neglect. Her very modest origins had not prepared her to manage a large showplace residence: the handmade bricks were crumbling and flaking away, and the once meticulously tended garden, where young Lady Bird spent hours in solitary contemplation, was now so wildly overgrown she had to stoop to distinguish vines from weeds.

A project to renovate and spruce up the property fit nicely with Bird's work ethic—the idea that one always had to have a project or a goal. She certainly wasn't feeding any nesting instinct because she had no intention of living there for long. Her father wasn't asking her to do it—he spent all his time at work and showed little interest in what his house or garden looked like. And he never read books. So why would he care about the bookcases Bird intended to have built? Were they just to serve as showcases for the precious leather-bound volumes that Minnie Pattillo had brought with her from Alabama? Bird may very well have been thinking ahead—to the day when she would bring a prospective husband to meet T.J. and want the Brick House to show at its best.

Like a graduate student in home economics, the methodical Bird started drawing up a list of proposed repairs to the house. For professional advice, she turned first to architects in Shreveport, and then when they lacked the sophistication she sought, she went to a bigger name, architect Hugo Kuehne, in Austin. It was on a trip to confer with him, on September 5, 1934, that she dropped in at the Railroad Commission office to catch up with Gene Boehringer. Someone else happened to come by for a visit at the same time, giving Gene the chance to make in person the introduction she had tried to engineer from a distance, when she had given Bird that Washington phone number three months earlier.

In the years Bird had been distancing herself from Karnack, first in Dallas and then in Austin, Lyndon Baines Johnson had made much bigger strides away from Johnson City. Following his few weeks teaching in Pearsall, he moved to Houston, where a job teaching civics and coaching debate had just opened up at the school where his Uncle George taught. Lyndon immediately turned loose his immense energy on his work and flabbergasted his colleagues by the amount of extra time he spent, in evenings and on weekends, drilling the debaters and escorting them to tournaments. It all paid off. His team won so many trophies they became local heroes, rivaling the football players.

Even with all the glory and recognition his debaters earned him, Lyndon was restless, eager to move on. Ignited by the legislative forays with his father and then by his San Marcos professor's passion for government, he wanted to get into politics, and even before graduating he had begun moving in that direction. Pat Neff, a former governor who currently headed the very important Railroad Commission, was running for reelection in 1930, and since he had once given Sam Johnson a job, Sam was eager to do what he could to help in the campaign. He suggested Lyndon get involved, too, and at the next Neff rally Lyndon was there, prepared like one of his debaters. When the candidate failed to appear, Lyndon stepped forward, and in what one observer described as a ten-minute "stem-winding, arm-swinging speech" from the tailgate of a vehicle, he delivered a glowing endorsement of Neff in terms so enthusiastic and persuasive that few of those present ever forgot it.

Welly Hopkins, a candidate for the state legislature, was in the crowd that day, and he was so struck with Lyndon's performance that he invited him to work in his own campaign. A year later it was Hopkins who passed the young man's name to newly elected Congressman Richard Kleberg, who immediately invited Lyndon for an interview at his gargantuan ranch near Corpus Christi. On the way, Lyndon stopped in Floresville to meet Sam Fore, publisher of the local newspaper and a respected figure throughout the state. Not yet twenty-four years old, Lyndon made such a favorable impression that Fore invited him to stay the night. After Lyndon drove away the next morning, Fore told his wife: "That's one of the most brilliant men I've ever met. I wouldn't be surprised to see him President of the United States some day."

Congressman Kleberg quickly hired Lyndon, and only eighteen months after graduating from college he was in Washington, running the congressman's office. Lyndon's father and grandfather had never gone further than the state legislature, and he jumped at the prospect of beginning his political career in a place they never managed to find employment, in the nation's capital.

It was a rocky start. Arriving as a scared twenty-three-year-old, with absolutely no experience in a congressman's office, Lyndon faced a mountain of requests from his employer's constituents. Since Kleberg preferred the playboy's life to that of a diligent lawmaker, he was often absent, leaving Lyndon and his co-worker, Estelle Harbin, to act for him. Whether it was a veteran's question about a pension or a farmer's problem securing a loan, Lyndon knew neither the answer nor where to go to find one. Estelle Harbin admitted that the two of them appeared so utterly clueless—they had trouble finding their way through the corridors to the right office—that the boss's wife referred to them as "children."

But Lyndon Johnson learned fast. He befriended elderly, lonely secretaries who carried many of those answers in their heads. With a charming young newcomer who complimented them, even on their last year's dresses, they were ready to share what they knew. In order to pick brains, Lyndon hung out at the cafeterias favored by his co-workers. One colleague noted he liked to arrive before everyone else and gobble his food so he could concentrate on the conversation while the others ate. Estelle Harbin observed he could "charm" a woman right out of her chair, and he soon learned to identify the source that would lead him to the right office or agency.

Success begat confidence, and when things went well for him, Lyndon showed a cocky buoyancy. On bad days, he could be grumpy and self-pitying, and one of the young men he had coached in debate, who had followed him to Washington and taken a job in Kleberg's office, complained that he was not easy to work for. But it was the triumphs that his fans emphasized. William S. White, the Texas journalist who wrote for the Associated Press in Washington, singled him out from the hundred or so new congressional employees as having exceptional potential. Sam Fore, the newspaperman Lyndon met in Floresville, Texas, backed up that observation, praising Lyndon as the only employee in Congress who made a name for himself outside his circle of co-workers because "he had something." The congressional employees had organized themselves into a "Little Congress" in 1919, and now they elected Lyndon Johnson to be their speaker. As accolades rolled in, Estelle Harbin observed that he "didn't know what he wanted to be, but he wanted to be *somebody.*"

That was the up-and-coming Lyndon Johnson who met the curious and ambitious Bird Taylor on a September Wednesday in 1934. Each already knew something about the other, and they had heard it from a person they trusted—Gene Boehringer. It did not take either one very long to see what the other had. Bird's two college degrees, especially the one in journalism, would impress Lyndon's mother, to say nothing of the fact that she combined a rock-solid personality with an upscale background, including two years at the elite St. Mary's. Lyndon was less than four years her senior, but his time in the nation's capital had catapulted him way out ahead of the young men Bird had been dating at UT. She didn't have to ask herself if this was the sort of man who would take her away from Karnack.

Gene had already lined up a dinner date for Lyndon that night with one of her other friends, but he quickly zeroed in on Bird and invited her to breakfast the next morning. After regaling everyone in the Railroad Commission office with Washington tidbits, he had her full attention, and she was flummoxed by the strong current of attraction she felt for him. She had always prided herself on being able to compartmentalize her feelings about people and keep a rein on her emotions. But not this time. Unlike the commendable, but entirely predictable, young men she knew, this big bundle of energy who called himself Lyndon Baines Johnson did not fit into any of her people-sorting categories. He dazzled her in a way she had never experienced, and set her feelings churning.

While he "came on strong . . . very direct and dynamic," she hesitated to accept his invitation to breakfast. She already had an early morning appointment with architect Kuehne, and she prided herself on keeping her word. Yet she was intrigued by Lyndon's talk about big-name legislators and his life in Washington, and she wanted to hear more. She felt herself being propelled toward him, like "the moth in the flame."

The following morning, Bird still had not decided what to do. As she walked to the architect's office, she could have avoided passing the window of the Driskill coffee shop, but she didn't, and just inside was Lyndon, ready to flag her down. Before she knew it, she had sat down beside him. A few minutes later she had a word with the architect, then climbed into Lyndon's shiny coupé for a drive around Austin.

For the entire day she listened as he bombarded her with details of his life, mixing braggadocio and charm, persuasion and mild warnings. He told her how hard he had struggled to get through school and then help his younger siblings earn their diplomas; he laid out the particulars of his current employment, how much he earned and what the job entailed. Although he cautioned that she was seeing only his "best side," he asked her to marry him. Bird felt inexplicably drawn to this macho, lanky man who talked the earthy talk of a "real" Texan. But marry him? Who would agree to that on such short acquaintance?

The next day, when he drove her to meet his family in San Marcos, she had a chance to see the seamier side of his life. His father, Sam Johnson, was only fifty-six years old, but he had the face of defeat, a painful summary of disappointments. Rebekah Johnson still struggled to project a genteel image, but Bird saw right through her camouflage into a pile of discarded hopes. The woman who had once envisioned herself becoming a famous writer was now fifty-three years old, and she had not published a paragraph in years. She could still assume a superior stance when meeting someone for the first time, and Bird sized her up immediately as "very much a gentlewoman" who found herself up against "a lot of work." The only dreams left to her were those she had pinned on her offspring—that at least one of them would find the success that had eluded her.

Bird picked up immediately the wariness in the family's welcome, and she understood why Rebekah would naturally feel suspicious about any woman likely to take away her favorite son. Even Lyndon's sister Josefa watched Bird with such mistrust that Bird wanted to pat both mother and daughter on the shoulder and assure them she had no intention of marrying their precious Lyndon.

After registering the poverty in his parents' home, Bird was dazzled by where Lyndon took her next. Following a night in a Corpus Christi hotel, where they had separate rooms, he drove her to meet his boss, Congressman Kleberg, at the famous King Ranch. Even by Texas standards, the King Ranch, which Kleberg's family owned, was mammoth. The largest privately held tract of land in the United States, it could fit the entire state of Rhode Island within its borders. Twice.

Congressman Kleberg and his wife lived in a showy style, unlike anything Bird had ever seen, more Hollywood than Karnack. They favored buttery smooth leather upholstery in their vehicles and jewels that spilled over the settings in their rings. Nearly everything they owned was emblazoned with the two horns that formed the King Ranch brand.

Bird was so excited by all that was happening to her, she could hardly wait to tell Cecille, and she persuaded Lyndon to stop in San Antonio and meet her former roommate. Cecille liked Lyndon and found "an eagerness about his face that you didn't see on other people," but it was the branded leather upholstery of his boss-provided car that stuck most vividly in her memory.

As Bird introduced Lyndon to more of her friends and she met some of his, he showed the same Henry Higgins side that female employees in Kleberg's office had observed. He was always telling them to pay more attention to their appearance—comb their hair, touch up faded lipstick, straighten their stocking seams—and now he started in with Bird. He ordered her to avoid "mule" colors, stick to straight skirts, and wear high heels to make her look taller than her five foot four. Associates who witnessed his testy bossing thought it rude, far outside the norm for a courting man, even one determined to show off his girlfriend at her very best. But Bird tossed off the humiliation of being criticized in front of others and took his advice as part of the initiation into his exhilarating world. After all, he was introducing her to people she found "rather overpowering," like the legendary Alice Gertrudis King Kleberg, who looked to Bird like an "aging duchess."

By Monday, September 10, only five days after meeting Lyndon, Bird was ready to introduce him to T.J., and she invited him to stay at the Brick House on his way back to Washington. The two oversized males, both six foot three, one stick thin with shiny black hair and the other paunchy and turning gray, took each other's measure immediately. They would never spend much time together or become close allies, but each recognized something of himself in the other—a driving determination to get ahead.

Lyndon went out of his way to make a good impression, and when Malcolm Baldwell, the congressional aide who was traveling with him, showed up in pajamas at breakfast, Lyndon ordered him back to his room to get fully dressed. This was the family of the woman Lyndon meant to marry and he wanted no disrespect shown them. T.J. signaled his approval immediately. "You've brought home a lot of boys," he told Bird. "This one looks like a man."

The next morning, Lyndon repeated his invitation that Bird come away with him to Washington, but she knew she could not. Although so much about him seemed right—and he had offered to take her out of Karnack—she had known him only five days, a ridiculously short time to make a decision for a lifetime. So he drove off without her, and she would not see him again for seven long weeks.

4

———◆◎◎◆———

MORE THAN
"ELECTRIC GOING"

S EPARATED BY more than a thousand miles during the fall of 1934,
Bird Taylor and Lyndon Baines Johnson communicated mostly
by words on paper. They had a few phone calls, but it was via letter that
both spelled out their thoughts and dreams and fears. Those dozens
of letters, laying out the terms of what would become a four-decade
relationship, became treasured possessions of Bird's, and she would
take them out at milestone times, such as Lyndon's 1965 inauguration
or a birthday of his, and read them over. That made her feel "so rich,"
she said.

Daughter Lynda's wedding day in 1967 provided another trigger
for reliving a time when the young Lyndon was "very close." He had
bolted the wedding reception, only an hour after it started, taking
daughter Luci and her baby son with him to Texas. That left Bird to
toss rice at the beaming bridal couple and see the last guest off. It was
nearly midnight when she went to bed.

The next morning, after a big pot of coffee and a look at the day's newspapers, she retrieved a small green metal box from her office/sitting room. Inside were the two precious packets. The first, tied with a red ribbon, contained the forty letters, postcards, and telegrams that Lyndon sent her during their brief courtship, and the second had the forty-five letters she had mailed to him. Now, only hours after watching her daughter become a bride, she needed to revisit those few weeks in 1934, the weeks leading up to her own marriage. With all her current worries that Lyndon was falling apart, wrecked by doubt and disappointment about his Vietnam policies and Great Society programs, she needed to concentrate on another time, when both of them were young and the future lay wide open, in wait.

The fact that Lyndon had fled his own daughter's wedding reception to go back to Texas indicated how disillusioned he had become with himself. Bird never could predict how much benefit he would gain from a few days of downtime, inspecting his cattle and fences without a single antiwar sign in sight. But she knew from the sag in his shoulders he badly needed a break. In the meanwhile, she wanted to go through the letters he had written at a time when he seemed primed to confront any challenge and she wanted nothing more than to go with him.

Once she started reading, she became so fully engrossed in the words and the memories ignited that she did not get up from her chair until three in the afternoon, when she had a commitment she could not ignore. But after fulfilling that obligation and catching a few hours sleep, she found herself wide awake and eager to get back to the letters. It was 4 a.m. and she was hungry. After finding herself some cookies and milk, she crawled back into bed, this time with the other packet, those she had written to Lyndon. Slipping back in time, she read every letter, "the excitement of Lyndon mounting" with each one. When she had finished the last one and closed the metal box, it was 6 a.m. and she decided it had been "one of the strangest, most off-key" days she could remember.

Those letters, most of them not available to researchers until Valentine's Day in 2013 and not used by a Johnson biographer until now, contain the key to their marriage: what he saw that she could do for him, and what she saw that he could do for her. They are romantic and raw and brimming with lust. But they also reveal the implicit deal the pair struck with each other: that Lyndon would fulfill her ambition of being matched with a man as charismatic and as comfortable with power as her father while taking her away from him, and that Bird would provide Lyndon with a ferocious devotion equal to his mother's and the emotional ballast he needed to achieve his ambition.

As daughter of T.J., the richest man around, Bird had grown up around power and the will it takes to acquire it. She loved her father's take-charge attitude and his penchant for staying stage center, the focus of all attention. Lyndon matched T.J. in all these traits, and while he would remove Bird from T.J. country, he would retain T.J.'s spirit and his approach to life.

Bird's value to Lyndon was equally obvious, in what both of them wrote. He made his weaknesses abundantly clear: he was often sick, and he lived on a seesaw, with his moods shifting wildly from top-of-the-world, when he thought he could do anything, to very low, when he registered only doom and failure. She could be his stabilizer. She had the toughness for both of them, the resilience to be his medicine— to encourage him to put one foot in front of the other and keep going, when all he wanted to do was quit.

Over the years, when outsiders saw Lyndon as a domineering, abusive husband, Bird knew the truth because it was right there, in the letters of 1934. She was essential to him; he needed her. His outbursts and humiliating words were the best evidence that he recognized, deep down, his reliance on her. Like anyone so dependent, he would resent her for it.

Biographers of LBJ who suggest he married Lady Bird for her money miss a major point: money—even a bigger amount than she had—would have counted for little if the woman who came with it was unwilling to take huge risks, like betting a large part of her inheritance on a candidate who looked like a loser, as she did in 1937. Money could also not provide what Lyndon needed most: someone who would engage fully in his career and keep bucking him up instead of compounding his fundamental insecurity by pointing out his failures. History shows that most American presidents before 1968 married up, but not all of them found a wife equal to Bird Taylor, with the steely resolve to help her man get what even he sometimes feared was out of reach.

There were other advantages to having Bird as a partner, starting with her natural grace. For a go-getter with rough edges like Lyndon, social charm and some pedigree could be at least as valuable as net worth. Besides the two college degrees—very unusual for a woman at the time—she had impeccable manners and appeared at ease wherever she went. Lyndon had watched her manage his family's frosty reception and then converse smoothly with a congressman whose wealth made T. J. Taylor look like a pauper. The few days Lyndon spent with Bird in early September 1934 revealed some of her winning qualities, and the letters they exchanged between September 11 and mid-November underlined them all.

When Lyndon sat down to write Bird that first letter, only a few hours after he left her, he was in a Memphis hotel room at the end of the initial leg of his drive back to Washington. He told her how "hard" it was to leave her that morning and "how satisfying and gratifying it was to be with you in your home." Although he left out any reference to her appearance or to the sexual charge between them, he had obviously placed her on a pedestal. He confessed that he "beamed with pride" at seeing how graciously she presided as "the lady of [her father's] house." Lyndon's only regret, and it was a big one, was that she had not come away with him.

Such a long letter in his own hand was something of a stretch for

Lyndon. In Kleberg's office, he dictated letters and let someone else type them up. But his heightened emotions that evening must have staved off writer's cramp because he ran on for five pages, telling Bird that she was "my first love in years." Then, to underscore his meaning, he added, "I love you."

He fully counted on her to match his enthusiasm and have a letter waiting for him when he reached Washington on Thursday evening. But cautious Bird was holding off. She still couldn't quite believe the last week had really happened, and she was taking things slowly, trying to make sense of her feelings. It took four days for his letter to get to Karnack, but it would take even longer for him to receive a written word from her.

This is how Bird came to see how vulnerable Lyndon could be, and how quickly he lashed out when faced with that sense of vulnerability. When he still had not heard from her on Saturday morning, his temper flared, and he sent another letter, verging on the nasty, accusing her of "indifference" and lack of "sentiments of affection" or "expressions of love." He felt "terribly blue," and blamed her. Sounding like a self-pitying bully, he wrote: "I'm lonesome. I'm disappointed, but what of it. Do you care?"

Lyndon wired her and then followed up with a letter, saying he would phone her on Sunday to find out "definitely just how and where you stand." In what sounds like an ultimatum, he underscored how much he resembled her father—an untiring deal maker who never took no for an answer. This young man wanted her commitment, and he wasn't going to wait for her letter to tell him she would marry him.

Excited at the prospect of hearing Lyndon's voice again, Bird wired him a number to call. Since the Brick House had no telephone, she had to talk with him from a neighbor's home, and too wound up to wait she arrived at the appointed place half an hour ahead of the time set. Afterward, she gloated a bit about how the call had aroused her friends' curiosity and envy, and she wrote Lyndon: "Nobody in Marshall knows you can talk that far over the phone—especially just for fun and not business."

Her very first letter to him (written before the phone conversation but reaching him after they had talked) was on the cool side. This was a woman who knew part of her appeal to Lyndon was her self-reliance. Rather than admitting to any "electric going," as she had after their first meeting, she sounded like Miss Competence as she listed the "simple things" she had been doing since he left, like overseeing repairs on bookcases and on a white wooden fence around her father's garden. Only a tiny hint of the romantic crept in when she mentioned the "lovely moon" they had admired together on the night before he left. She signed off, "love, Bird," no match at all for his head-over-heels declaration.

Although Lyndon was busy in Washington, juggling his day job with law school classes at night, he made time to write passionate letters, but with ample evidence of his fragility. Here was a man who could never be satisfied with what he had but was never sure he deserved what he got. Baring his insecurities, he confessed he felt like a defeated candidate, so "blue and depressed" that he came home from the office one day at 3:30 in the afternoon and went to bed. He questioned his "own perseverance, will power and self-control" and regretted his "moodiness," the fact of "always feeling blue" when he didn't hear from her. He admitted to having a restless nature, and being "never sure, never contented—always doubtful" about much of life. But of one thing he was sure—how he felt about her: "Again I repeat—I love you—only you. Want to always love—only you."

His letters were very specific about what he expected from her: limitless, nurturing support regardless of whatever he said or did. He wanted a woman "who loved me, would pet me, and be as affectionate as I am," someone "to nurse me," and "help me to climb." Why wouldn't she show those feelings in her letters to him? He prodded her to keep writing and "Mix some 'I love you' in the lines and not between them."

During those weeks they were apart, his mood swings reflected what he heard from Bird. He relied on her letters to recharge him; when none arrived, his spirits sank and he protested. If the morning mail yielded nothing from Karnack, he did not wait for the afternoon delivery but fired off an angry letter accusing Bird of neglecting him. When she wrote that "right this minute I'd rather see you than anybody in the world," he called it the "best letter you have written . . . gave me new life—a real inspiration and a determination to make you the most happy and contented little woman in all the world." He kept her letters lined up in his room, "one by one," so he could take them down and reread them when feeling low. Her most recent letter had raised his spirits, giving him "new hope, new interest, new plans . . . just thrilled . . . to death."

Her constraint annoyed him, and he kept urging her to loosen up and reveal the depth of her emotion. He knew some people found any demonstration of "real . . . inward feelings 'silly,'" but he assured her that he did not. He had bared his deepest longings and admitted to faults; now he wanted evidence that she meant to rescue him with her love. How could she continue to hold back? After he had already told her how "depressed" he was?

Throughout their correspondence he repeatedly confessed to having a temperamental personality that caused him to jump too quickly, act hastily, and become far "too sentimental." Here was a man who stopped to help hurt dogs and welled up in sad movies, while Bird could walk right past injured animals and rarely shed a tear over anything. No one had to tell her who was the more grounded partner in this relationship, and that if she married him, it would be up to her to keep him on track.

In her letters, she began playing the cheerleading role that she would continue to hone throughout their long marriage, rousing him time and again out of his gloom. After he wrote on October 14, "For weeks I've only half heartedly done anything," she ordered him to "Stop it, dear! (That's a command!)" She reminded him that it was his enthu-siasm and "que vive" [*sic*] that had attracted her to him in the first place. Always the optimist, she saw better times ahead: "In the next few months or one year we shall find the way out of our difficulties . . . [and in the meantime] I shall not let you forget me."

Because his letters did not always arrive in sequence, Bird scram-bled to decipher what lay behind his rapid mood changes. He began one letter, "I'm very unhappy tonight. All week I've felt this way." But buoyed by a subsequent upbeat letter from her, he turned jolly. Then his mood plummeted again, and shortly after begging her to marry him immediately, he warned that she might have to wait "four or five years." Puzzled by the erratic shifts and turns, Bird inquired what caused them. What *was* he thinking?

In a sunny reply, Lyndon urged his "dear Bird" to forget all about the despair expressed in his previous letter because "this morning I'm ambitious, proud, energetic and very madly in love with you. . . . Plans, ideas, hopes. I'm bubbling over with them." He regretted he had been "cruel" and let her know "how despondent" he had "felt last week."

That high did not last either, and he sounded really dejected in a subsequent letter. Glum about his prospects in Washington, he was again considering a return to Texas. That would mean delaying mar-riage, because "No, honey, I haven't over estimated what my Bird should have."

Bird understood that it wasn't just in temperament that she was the hardier of the two. She rarely fell ill, but Lyndon was often in bed with one malady or another, and he sounded very sorry for him-self at those times. In September 1934, he had to miss work and law school classes because of influenza, and he wrote her that he feared a recurrence of the pneumonia he had suffered two years earlier, when he could not work for six weeks. In a poignant signal of how much he needed a strong, nurturing maternal figure to nurse him back to health, he wrote her that he felt like a "sick little man," who missed his "real friends" and "yearned" to be with them, like a child, "wanting to get to its mother."

While he rattled on like a schoolboy, bouncing back and forth between loving her to death and scolding her for not caring enough about him, she remained unruffled. She had already concluded that if she lashed out at him, "something awful might happen to us," and she would not allow that, no matter what unflattering names he called her. When days went by without a letter from him, she felt "forsaken," but refused to retaliate by not writing or by answering in a pout. No, that was "one thing I won't do," she assured him, thus providing a clue to what others, who later witnessed his nastiness and infidelities, could never understand. She had promised him in one of her earliest letters that nothing would ever come between them, because: "I simply will not let it." And both of them knew she was a woman who kept her promises.

When his letters dropped off slightly, she was disappointed but understood that his frailty would brook no punishment. Not from her. She promised to mete none out: "I think its [*sic*] plain silly (besides presumptious [*sic*]) to fuss at someone you love." She was only twenty-one when she wrote that letter but it contained the basis of their grand bargain—that no matter how he treated her, she could take it because she was the stronger of the two.

Lyndon made very clear he was seeing other women at the same time he was begging Bird to marry him. One of them, named Helen, whom he referred to as "my little radio writer," was the daughter of a judge in New York. Lyndon wrote Bird that he had gone drinking and dancing with Helen, then talked with her into the morning hours. Bird made no mention of the "little radio writer" when she replied to his letter in 1934, but she later explained that she had known it was not a platonic relationship. Rather than object, she was grateful that the sophisticated New Yorker had "sharpened [Lyndon] up."

If Lyndon had been using Helen to ignite a bit of jealousy back in Karnack and move Bird to the altar more quickly, it did not work. She kept giving her reasons for holding off. They did not know each other well enough—she needed more time. Without a trace of coyness or deceit, she spelled out how she felt: "I love you [but] I don't know how everlastingly I love you,—so I can't answer you yet." When he kept nagging, she replied, "Darling, don't you see that I'm just trying to be perfectly sane and level-headed? I want to do what is best for both of us." Like a mother tending a cantankerous child, she stayed steady, letting his tantrums play out without losing her temper or sense of who was in charge. She worried in one letter that her "poor lamb" was overworking and asked him, "Whenever do you play?"

Her letters gradually picked up in passion, with less about her renovation project and more about the "hundred kisses" she was sending him. Some days she wrote more than once, and in one letter she enclosed a newspaper clipping of a poem about love: "Why you are all my laughter and my light—why it is sheer delight to love you so." But the last words in the letter were hers, with ratcheted up affection: "Goodnight, dearest love. Did you know you are my dearest love?"

Bird was entirely open about what she liked in Lyndon. Much more than a persistent suitor whose attentions she relished, he was part of that big "Outside World" she had been looking for, with its exciting "gay life beyond the 'provinces.'" She shrank from the possibility that this life might elude her, and she admitted to feeling depressed by the prospect. Although normally cheerful and optimistic, she wrote him on September 27 that she did not feel "very happy, nor content" that evening and she thought it was because of her "wanderlust." She pictured herself, not in dreary Karnack, but in "all sorts of queer, faraway places where Things are Happening!" She wanted to be "dining in some gay attractive place, with someone I enjoyed." Maybe that someone was Lyndon: "Wouldn't I adore being with you!"

In idle moments, she leafed through magazines, searching for photos of glamorous settings, and she felt "so cosmopolitan" when she recognized the Dodge Hotel in Washington, where she knew Lyndon was staying, and the Casino de Paree in New York, where she had gone nightclubbing with Cecille and those suave businessmen. In provincial Texas, she felt isolated, cut off from lively discussions, like those she had savored in Austin with her friends—the "richest, raciest conversations about the Russian playwrights and the value of money, and the relative merits of Viennese music and Spanish music, and college love, and life with a capital L." In Karnack, all she heard was talk "about what we're going to plant when it rains, and recipes for Mayhaw jelly."

When she kept refusing to set a date for marrying him, his tone grew harsher: "I don't want to wait. I want you now—when I need you most. . . . If you are still sure you want to wait I'll make my letters less affectionate and consequently less embarrassing." Rather than viewing his message as a threat, she saw it as more evidence of his weakness, and she sent a sunny reply. The packages of sweets and books arriving from Washington made her feel "Better than [on] a birthday—most as nice as Christmas!" When he supplied her with a book of recipes contributed by congressional wives, she tried her hand at baking a lemon pie and wrote him a description of the result. For someone who had zero experience in a kitchen, she decided she had produced a "creditable" dessert.

About a month after he had returned to Washington, Bird went to Dallas for the weekend to cheer for the Texas Longhorns in their annual football game against the Oklahoma Sooners. Since her classmate at St. Mary's, Emily Crow, was living in Dallas with her family, Bird stayed with them, and Lyndon tracked her down with a person-to-person phone call. However did he find her, Bird marveled, when "there are so many Crows in the Dallas telephone book!" That she already knew the answer was clear in her next line: "But then you are a young man who generally gets what he goes after, aren't you?" She had found her own T.J.

That weekend gave Bird a chance to catch up with old friends, including Gene Boehringer, who took the ninety-mile-per-hour Zephyr train from Austin. But Bird's most definitive meeting was with her old boyfriend, Victor McCrea. The ambitious UT alumnus, who had dated her in college and squired her around the nation's capital in June, had returned to Texas to work at a Fort Worth law firm, "so of course," Bird explained in her next letter to Lyndon, "he came over [to Dallas] to see me, Sunday afternoon." After driving around town and drinking Tom Collinses at the Shamrock bar, they went to the Adolphus Hotel for dinner, where she mustered the courage to tell him about her new love. Victor had been her most serious suitor, and she thought it important that he hear from her that she intended to marry "one Lyndon Baines Johnson" within the year.

Victor was so upset by her news that he couldn't eat a bite, and Bird, seeing his distress, left her plate untouched. What disappointed Lyndon in Bird's account of that meeting was the mention of a date—she kept pushing marriage way out into the future. He still hoped for a wedding at Thanksgiving, when he would be back in Texas, but she remained adamant that she wouldn't consider a time "so terribly close!"

Although Bird kept writing that she wasn't going to let him get away, she had objections to a quick marriage. Would it not be wise, she wrote him, to wait a year so she could "go traveling around a few months,—when I like being so free and foot-loose"? She recognized she had competition (Lyndon was dancing with more than one "Helen" in Washington) and the possibility of losing him "frightens me," she wrote him. "I can't imagine being quite without you." But she would not be rushed on a matter as important as marriage. That "wouldn't be fair to either of us—or safe." As if he needed any reminder that she was not the impetuous type, she added that something prevented her "from caring deeply about people or things suddenly. . . . They have to grow on me."

His obsession with keeping secrets bothered her, and she begged him to tell her more about the "New York [job] offer and whatever was troubling you in South Texas." After he confessed that he had written her long letters and then torn them up without mailing them, she suggested he reconsider and clue her in on why he was thinking about moving back to Texas. On October 22, she wrote, "Lyndon, please tell me as soon as you can what the deal is. . . . I am afraid its [*sic*] politics. Oh, I know I haven't any business—not any 'proprietary interest'—but I would hate for you to go into politics."

Rather than spell things out, he continued to stonewall, writing that he had no intention of telling her more because he feared the "outcome." That was another of his traits that she would have to learn to accept—this was a man who took enormous pleasure in keeping secrets and then springing a surprise when it was least expected.

Separated by twelve hundred miles, the two arranged to exchange photos, but Lyndon was quicker to get himself to a professional photographer than Bird was. She encouraged him to proceed quickly so she could show her friends how handsome he was, but she hung back from going herself, admitting, "I've an awful inferiority complex about having my picture made." In an unusually physical sign-off, she wished he was with her "this minute because I feel silly and gay and I want to ruffle up your hair and kiss you and say silly things!"

From the photographer's proofs he sent, she immediately picked out her favorite. Her father preferred the more formal shot of Lyndon in a suit jacket, but she chose the casual pose in "shirt sleeves with your arms on the desk." She very much disliked arrogance in a person, "And you do look very arrogant there!" she wrote Lyndon. But the more she considered his pose, the more she warmed to the "proud, sure look out of your eyes." It was an early example of the Midas touch she learned to apply to Lyndon's less admirable traits—she simply converted them into something she liked.

His extravagance upset thrifty Bird, and after he spent an extra few cents on "special delivery," she ordered him to "save that dime" on letters "cause one gets them at the post office just the same." Much as she thrilled to hear a telephone operator say "Washington calling Bird

Taylor," she was shocked at what person-to-person calls cost, and she chided him on his "dreadful" spending habits.

In all those letters Bird wrote to Lyndon she never mentioned Aunt Effie until October 29, when she unveiled a plan to come east for two weeks. She had decided she wanted to see Lyndon, and she could justify a trip to Washington by combining it with a dutiful visit to Aunt Effie in Georgia. Unbeknownst to her, Lyndon had already decided to set out for Texas without telling her. Driving night and day, he made the three-day trip in two and arrived in Karnack on Halloween to deliver his marriage proposal in person. He pressed her: "If you don't love me enough now, you never will." But Bird, who still considered herself a "slow, considered sort of person . . . not given to quick conclusions or much rash behavior," refused to say "yes." Finally, she agreed to go with him to Austin and pick out an engagement ring, but she returned alone to Karnack by bus on November 7, still uncertain what to do.

Nearly everyone she knew was urging her to wait. Even T.J. was wavering, in spite of what he liked about Lyndon: his looks, prospects for a bright future, his apparently genuine love for Bird. This courtship was entirely too accelerated for T.J., and he joined other relatives and friends who cautioned Bird that two months wasn't long enough to know the man you would take as a partner for life. If Lyndon *really* loved her, he would wait. Even matchmaker Gene Boehringer decided this courtship was much too rushed. Bird understood they all spoke out of concern for her, but her head ached with their dire warnings. She pled with Lyndon not to "hate" her for listening to them and to give her some leeway.

Still hoping a trip east would clarify things, Bird left Lyndon to take care of his boss's business in Corpus Christi while she visited her Alabama cousins and Aunt Effie. She knew he was still counting on a wedding at Thanksgiving, which came on November 29, and he had already sketched out an itinerary for a honeymoon in Mexico. But she wanted to hear what others thought about this faster-than-whirlwind romance before she made up her mind.

The physical separation did not mean the two lovers forgot about each other, even for a minute. He had flowers waiting when she arrived at her cousin's in Montgomery, and Bird wrote immediately to say that the distance between them had made her "want" him even more and see their situation "in a clearer perspective." She went on and on about how she thought him "a superior person, as a lover and as a man," and she had already convinced her cousin Elaine that he was a "wonderful person." Another line from that letter indicates she was prepared to serve as his chief marketer for life: "I could sell you to your worst enemy, if you ever had one!"

After visiting her cousins, Bird moved on to secure the blessing of Aunt Effie, who was residing in Atlanta, 160 miles east of Montgomery. When Bird arrived there on Tuesday, November 13, she planned to stay several days since she knew it would "break" Aunt Effie's heart if she rushed off. But she was counting on making it back to Texas and Lyndon by the following Saturday.

That much anticipated visit quickly turned into a disaster. Frail Aunt Effie, whom Bird had not seen in a year, could barely manage a few steps, and when the subject of marrying Lyndon came up, Aunt Effie let loose with a string of reasons why Bird should not go ahead (she was too young; she would be missing out on a career of her own; she didn't even know this young man yet; if he loved her he would wait). Rather than argue, Bird became so upset, exhausted "both mentally and physically," that she fled. Before nightfall, she was on a train west, planning to stop briefly at her Alabama cousins before going on to Karnack.

All she could think about was getting back to Lyndon: "I want to rush on home and meet you somewhere and I want you to put your arms around me and kiss me and let's us laugh! I'm so damned tired of being serious (please pardon me one 'damn' will you?)" Her evening prayer was that the two of them could have fun and "be gay."

Lyndon was waiting for her in Karnack, and now his plan to marry immediately made more sense. Alongside Aunt Effie's warnings, which still rang in her ears, Bird could hear her father's pronouncements about how the best bargains were made in a hurry. She had not yet unpacked her suitcase on the morning of Saturday, November 17, but without promising Lyndon anything she added two of her best dresses, including a new lavender one, and climbed into his black coupé. She could always get out in Austin, she told herself, but that was not how she was leaning. When Lyndon stopped briefly in Marshall to have a blood test, she used the time to buy herself a "beautiful negligee."

With stops only to make phone calls, buy gas, and eat, they completed the 320-mile drive to San Antonio by early evening. During his three years in Congressman Kleberg's employ, Lyndon had rendered many favors to people in the 14th District, and now he meant to collect on them. He phoned Postmaster Dan Quill, whose sister he had found a job for in Washington, and in his peremptory style ordered Quill to make all the preparations for a wedding that evening. He didn't ask Quill if he could; he didn't give details about what he wanted. He just said, "Fix everything" and hung up the phone, leaving Quill to solve them on his own.

Quill disobeyed several laws and ignored strong traditions that day as he put aside his own plans for the weekend and tried to satisfy Lyndon's request. Texas required a marriage license, not easy for out-of-towners to manage on short notice and virtually impossible on a Saturday; St. Mark's Episcopal Church had its own rules against uniting couples not fully instructed in church teachings on the subject of matrimony. When the Reverend Arthur K. McKinstry, a much loved liberal rector, refused to perform the ceremony until he had talked with the couple, Quill reminded him of the favorable postage rates Lyndon had procured for St. Mark's weekly newsletter, and McKinstry decided that in this case he would make an exception.

By the time Lyndon and Bird checked in at the Plaza Hotel about six that evening, Quill had secured the license and lined up a priest but ignored other conventions typically associated with a marriage ceremony. When Bird inquired about a ring, bachelor Quill rushed across the street to Sears, Roebuck to buy one, and clueless about sizes he brought back several for her to try. When she selected the $2.50 one, he made it his wedding gift to the couple. Getting either family there in time was out of the question, but Bird couldn't envision herself taking this huge step without at least one friendly face by her side, and she phoned Cecille Harrison, who lived nearby, to join her. When Cecille arrived at the Plaza, she found a jittery Bird, talking a "mile a minute" about whether she should marry Lyndon or "jump out the window."

After Cecille helped her into the lavender dress, the two of them walked to St. Mark's where a motley group waited, talking so loudly that the Reverend McKinstry had to shush them. Dan Quill had not found it easy to put together a jolly wedding party on a few hours' notice, and he was not happy to have skipped a much anticipated hunting trip with Vice President John Nance Garner so he could witness the nuptials himself. Those he had rounded up for the evening included attorney Henry Hirshberg, accompanied by his wife and his brother-in-law. Hirshberg's law partner and his wife were also there, but Bird had never met any of them. Except for Malcolm Baldwell, one of Lyndon's co-workers whom she had met briefly, they were all strangers to the bride.

As Bird Taylor and Lyndon Johnson approached the altar to take their vows, Henry Hirshberg ended up next to the groom, and he signed the registry as "witness" alongside Cecille Harrison. After the very brief ceremony, the guests agreed that some kind of celebratory dinner was in order, but Quill had done as much as he intended to do for Lyndon Johnson that day and he took off, leaving the others to manage as best they could.

The Hirshbergs, who were well-established residents of San Antonio, took charge and prevailed on the St. Anthony Hotel to find rooftop space and a music ensemble appropriate for the occasion. Providing alcohol for the celebratory toast was more difficult. Although the Twenty-first Amendment had technically ended Prohibition a year earlier, Texas still had a dry law on the books, and the hotel was obeying it. Attorney Hirshberg had to send his brother-in-law to his own special stash to get "four or five bottles of sparkling burgundy." Then Hirshberg used his connections with the hotel management to make sure "the stuff was properly dispensed despite the law." Bird's wedding was a ragtag, impromptu affair, arranged by people she didn't know and toasted with illegal booze. At the reception, talk focused on politics and the health status of a newly elected congressman rather than on prospects for the newlyweds.

The next morning, the bride and groom phoned friends and family to relay the news. To Gene Boehringer, Bird used enthusiastic, earthy terms: "Lyndon and I committed matrimony last night." Back in Karnack, T.J. received instructions to have wedding announcements printed up, and with the help of neighbor Dorris Powell, he proceeded. The marriage certificate, with incorrect details supplied by Dan Quill, had listed the bride as "Bird Taylor," but in the announcement T.J. managed to tack on one of the names he and Minnie had given their daughter at birth. Christened Claudia Alta Taylor, she was "Claudia Bird," when her father officially announced her marriage "to Mr. Lyndon Johnson on Saturday, the 17th of November, San Antonio, Texas."

The day after the ceremony the newlyweds set off on a honeymoon to Mexico, with no set date for returning. They would stay "as long as our money lasted." Ecstatic Bird was so caught up in the excitement, she did not register all the details of the trip: the drive to Saltillo, about 250 miles south of the border; the train to Monterrey; the flight to Mexico City to tour a pyramid excavation; the little boat they took through the floating gardens of Xochimilco. But she was fully aware that Lyndon was buying her "loads of flowers" and that the two of them looked exultant. In the photos of that trip, their broad grins and sparkling eyes betrayed such an erotic charge between them that Bird suggested the negatives should be destroyed.

The trip lasted ten days, time enough for both bride and groom to realize that his enthusiasm for picturesque and scenic places did not match hers. Her hope that they could have fun and be "gay" came up against his workaholic, impatient bid to get back home. His friends could not believe he stuck it out as long as he did. They had predicted he would be back in four days, but Bird had managed to keep him occupied more than double that time.

Reentry to Texas brought Bird a list of assignments. After seeing a gynecologist (for reasons she kept to herself), she went to work on becoming Lyndon's political partner. In the courtship letters, she had made very clear her strong interest in contemporary issues and expressed some decided opinions. So Lyndon had ample notice that she was a woman who thought for herself. Even on matters that she knew his colleagues disagreed with her, she was blunt, writing him that she abhorred "protective tariffs" but did not consider socialism "essentially a malignant system." When he told her that his good friend Welly Hopkins was critical of "ultra liberal" New Deal laws, she replied that she liked them and she had no objection at all to what Hopkins was calling the "increasing paternalism of our government." People who insisted on a strict interpretation of the Constitution were wrong, she argued, because "I think it can be bent to suit new needs." Offering to debate any of these subjects, she taunted Lyndon to join her: "Do you like to argue about economics and religions and . . .social systems, et cetera ad infinitum??? I do!"

Having gone on record about so many issues of the day, Bird was primed to take part in a political alliance, and Lyndon had an assignment ready as soon as the honeymoon ended. He wanted her to memorize the names of all the county seats in Kleberg's congressional district and the most important bosses, or "jefes," in each. Now when she accompanied Lyndon to political meetings, she could greet people as individuals and talk with them about what Lyndon could do to help them. If he was going to be the "best secretary that a congressman ever had," they both knew she had an important role to play.

By late December, when Bird turned twenty-two, she was packing for Washington, where she would have to run a household for the very first time. She had met Lyndon less than four months earlier and had spent only a fraction of that time with him. But that was sufficient to delineate the terms for a long, mutually beneficial partnership. She had married a power-seeking man like her father who would take her away from boring talk of planting crops and making jelly. That journey would incorporate Bird into her husband's career and make her part of his ambitious climb. Lyndon had found the mate essential to his success. She was his mood stabilizer, a gracious people pleaser, and incredibly strong shield of steel.

5

BECOMING A PRICELESS POLITICAL PARTNER

ONE STORY Lady Bird Johnson liked to tell about her husband concerned a meeting he had soon after becoming congressman for Texas's 10th District. His mentor, the corporation attorney Alvin Wirtz, had arranged for him to talk with the top executive of a power company to work out a deal beneficial to his constituents. The two men talked and talked but the congressman got nowhere, and in a huff Lyndon stood up, told the businessman to "go to hell," and stomped out.

A few hours later, when Lyndon returned to Wirtz for advice on how to proceed, Wirtz told him that he was very disappointed. It had taken months to get the businessman to meet and now Lyndon's outburst had undone all that hard work. "Just remember," Wirtz counseled, "you can tell a man to go to hell, but you can't make him go."

This was a punch line whose wisdom Lady Bird knew only too well. Lyndon was forever losing his temper, lambasting aides, telling off associates, and offending the very people he needed on his side. He could flatter and charm, yes. No one could do that better, and she marveled at how often he remembered an employee's birthday or inquired about an ailing family member. But he could also let loose with biting ridicule and nasty insults. He brought his loyal, hardworking secretary, Mary Rather, to tears by telling her in front of her co-workers that she had made an "ass" of herself by drinking too many martinis. Walter Jenkins and John Connally, early hires to Lyndon's congressional staff, endured more tongue-lashings than they dared count, and Connally's wife, Nellie, who worked as secretary in the same office, learned to duck when Lyndon threw a phone book at her.

All of them found some satisfaction in knowing their boss's mood could improve in a flash and then he would be passing out gifts (Mary Rather received an expensive handbag). But it was Lady Bird who provided the best consolation. She treated Rather like a sister, inviting her along on driving trips and including her at parties. The same solicitous attention went to the Connallys and to the Jenkinses, along with repeated admonitions to disregard whatever Lyndon said in the heat of the moment. He hadn't meant a word of it, Bird insisted. It was all part of that promise she had made before their marriage to sell him to his "worst enemy." As "fixer" of the liaisons he broke and mediator in the messes he made, she aimed to be right there, ever ready to help his political climb.

It wasn't just to others that she needed to "sell" Lyndon. When he was in one of his down moods, sick and pessimistic about accomplishing anything, she would remind him that things were sure to turn around. Sherman Birdwell, who managed Lyndon's Washington office for three years, noted how his boss's moods shifted rapidly. He could be the most exciting leader, laying out ambitious plans with such infectious enthusiasm that Birdwell worked eighteen-hour days to put those plans into action. But then Lyndon would take to his bed, refusing to budge, "next to death's door." That's when Birdwell needed Bird.

To the amazement of his associates, Lyndon sometimes directed his derogatory comments and brusque demands at his wife. Martha James, whose husband worked with Lyndon, remembered being in the Johnson home chatting with Bird in perfectly normal tones when Lyndon starting yelling at them to stop: "Cut out the damn noise. I'm playing dominoes. I can't think." Mrs. James, not accustomed to being yelled at, was so upset she insisted her husband take her home immediately. But Lady Bird treated the reprimand like a puff of harmless hot air—she seemed not to have heard it. She was taking the advice she gave others—to toss off those angry words as meaningless.

Call it what you wish—fixer, enabler, smoother-of-feelings—it was the role Lady Bird played in the career of a political genius who had trouble managing his own moods and his relations with others. She got started early, almost as soon as she arrived in Washington in late December 1934, and she combined that responsibility with a crash course in household management.

Here was a woman who had grown up with servants who did everything for her. She had approached the oven, when she baked that lemon pie from the congressional wives cookbook, like a student entering a science lab, moving slowly, step by step, through the printed instructions. In Washington, as the wife of a congressional assistant, she would have to do much more than bake a lemon pie now and then. She would have to oversee cleaning, take care of laundry, and shop for and prepare meals, not only for herself and Lyndon, but for all those they invited to their home.

Lyndon liked to tease her that she got off to a rocky start in Washington. The two of them had driven up from Texas (the first of what would become dozens of such trips for Bird) and arrived on December 31, 1934, in time for a big party at the Alexandria home of newspaperman William S. White. Bird hadn't the slightest idea how to get there—her acquaintance with Washington was limited to those few days she had spent there the previous June—but she knew a bit about reporters and how they partied. This was a crowd with a reputation for heavy drinking and they didn't go for the sweet, citrusy Tom Collinses that she liked. They drank whiskey and they drank it straight.

On a festive occasion like New Year's Eve, the reporters had an added incentive to keep their own glasses (and Bird's) full, and in the excitement of the evening she lost count of how much she had drunk. When she got sick, Lyndon blamed the host for serving bad booze, but White thought the problem was Bird's. Like a lot of country girls, she didn't know how to hold her liquor.

White's assumption was an early example of how people underrated Mrs. Johnson. She never missed an opportunity to learn and, in this case, she made sure it was the last time she over-imbibed. She also set to work becoming the perfect political partner, and in this she had a mentor in Terrell Maverick, wife of Texas congressman Maury Maverick. Although only a dozen years Bird's senior, Mrs. Maverick was a city woman, from San Antonio, and self-appointed guide to those younger and newer than herself to Washington. She gathered up a group of young wives, including Bird, and took them on a tour of the Capitol, followed by lunch in the VIP dining room. There she delivered her lecture on how to survive in the city. She told the neophyte wives that each had to get deeply involved in her husband's work, learn the names of his colleagues, read up on the issues he was voting on, understand his responsibility to the voters who put him there. Otherwise, the women risked ending up like so many Washington wives before them, drifting apart from their husbands and getting divorced.

That advice fit neatly with Bird's own ideas, and she set to work immediately, showing the same adaptability she had shown earlier on her summer stays with relatives in Alabama and at the Matthewses' rooming house in Austin. No matter how drastically her circumstances changed, she never complained. She simply sized up the scene and fit in, dealing with what she had rather than wishing for something else.

If she had been as well-heeled as Lyndon's biographers would later describe her, she might have hired a maid and found a large, elegant place like the seventeen-room house where she grew up. But T.J. was not about to subsidize his married daughter, and she didn't expect that. She knew she could count on him and Aunt Effie to help out in a real pinch. Maybe they would pitch in on something extra, like a car, but for day-to-day expenses she meant to manage on what her husband earned.

The apartment the Johnsons found in Northwest Washington, at 1910 Kalorama Road, was pathetically small. It had only two rooms and a tiny kitchen, which meant that when Aunt Effie came to visit (and claimed the bedroom) Bird and Lyndon had to sleep on the living room couch.

None of that mattered for long because Bird had to pack up and move out a few months later. She had gone for a summer visit to her father in Karnack when Lyndon phoned to tell her that he had been chosen to head the Texas division of the National Youth Administration, a new federal program to retrain young people and place them in jobs. For Bird, the most thrilling aspect about the job was its location: they would be living in Austin, a place she still thought of as "sheer heaven."

Those next eighteen months turned out to be one of the very best times in Bird's marriage, as she found new ways of following Mrs. Maverick's advice. Lyndon, at twenty-seven, was the youngest of all NYA directors, and he needed a large staff to develop NYA programs for his gigantic state. He started hiring even before receiving final clearance for his own job. Although a couple of his underlings were already familiar to Bird because they had worked with Lyndon in Washington, most were new, and she immediately started treating them all like family.

Whether at the "romantic and charming" house she rented first at 2808 San Pedro Street, or at the "dull little place" at 4 Happy Hollow

Lane, where the Johnsons moved next, the door was always open. Bird was still doing most of her own housework and trying to learn to cook, but she welcomed her husband's co-workers and contacts at any hour of the day with a coffeepot perking and a home-baked cake ready for cutting. If an unexpected visitor needed a full meal, she prepared it, and she attempted to please the finickiest eater. Lyndon's second in command, Jesse Kellam, maintained that his mother, although an excellent cook, was no match for Lady Bird, who did something special to spinach so that even he liked it.

All this entertaining cost money, and Lyndon's starting NYA salary was only slightly more than he had made as a congressman's assistant. Even after he got a raise, to $5,000 on August 1, 1936 (equivalent to about $83,000 in 2014 dollars), she had to scrutinize every purchase. He lopped off a good chunk for personal incidentals, like cigarettes and car expenses, and continued to send money to his parents and younger siblings. From what was left, she bought a $25 savings bond every month and stretched the rest to cover groceries, utilities, and everything else.

Staff tended to congregate at her place on weekends and these gatherings set the stage for her own environmental and highway beautification work decades later. One evening when NYA aides were sitting in her living room, mulling over ideas for new ways to put young people to work, they began talking about a recent highway tragedy. A Mexican family had stopped at the side of the road to rest, when their car was struck from behind, killing them all. If a space had been provided for resting, at a safe distance from the traffic, the tragedy could have been avoided. Someone suggested using NYA workers to build those rest stops, and that conversation stayed with Bird, triggering a lifelong interest in roadside parks. She was still handing out prizes for superior park projects fifty years later.

Staff members were not the only guests at Bird's table. Lyndon was always bringing home extra mouths to feed, without so much as a warning telephone call to her. It could be someone he had just met, or a group of people he wanted to impress or influence. To stay within her budget she shopped for liquor by the case and ferreted out the butcher's cheapest cuts. Objecting to the extra guests was not an option. Bird knew the value of a gracious hostess, and she was not going to miss a chance to win points for Lyndon.

While others used force of nature terms—"hurricane," "tornado," "volcano"—to describe how Lyndon operated, Bird saw him as a machine, in full throttle much of the time. Although his high-energy mode remained a mystery to her, she fully recognized his zeal in moving toward a definite, worthwhile goal. He didn't have to explain to her why he worked such long hours and was incredibly demanding of those he hired to help him. At the central office he rented in downtown Austin, he kept badgering his staff to come up with programs suitable for Texas, and he arranged with building management to keep the electricity on until midnight so everyone could work late and still have an elevator running to take them down.

In spite of her close involvement with her husband's aides and work, Lady Bird didn't know everything that was going through his mind because he didn't tell her. He still had that fixation with secrecy that she had observed in the courtship letters. So when one of his aides alerted her in mid-1936 that Lyndon would soon leave the NYA job to run for office himself, it came as such a shock that she nearly drove the car off the road.

Lyndon's chance came just a few months later, when popular James Buchanan, representative of Texas's 10th District, died suddenly on February 22, 1937. This was the district where Lyndon grew up, and many of his best friends still lived there. But his prospects did not look good. Eight other men, older and more experienced, had also filed to run, and Lyndon's strength was in the western, sparsely populated Hill

Country rather than in the city of Austin, which had the bulk of the 10th District's votes.

Lyndon did have one advantage, and Alvin Wirtz, one of the district's savvy politicos, spotted it. During those three years working for Congressman Kleberg, Lyndon had learned a lot about how things worked in Washington. He knew the people who got money funneled to the states. For attorney Wirtz—always called Senator Wirtz because of his service in the state senate—that Washington experience could be extremely valuable. Wirtz was currently heading a project that required heavy federal funding, and he threw his support to Lyndon and engaged one of the best campaign managers in the state, Claude C. Wild Sr., to take charge.

Now that Bird had a chance to participate in her husband's first campaign, she provided much more than fresh shirts and a hot meal at the end of a long day. Lyndon needed cash, and Bird's inheritance from her mother remained untapped. The first installment of $7,000 was not due for another six months, but Bird thought T.J. would advance that payment if she asked him.

First, however, she wanted to do some checking of her own about the soundness of this investment. Even to advance the career of a husband she adored, she was not about to risk her money without checking out the odds. So she went to Senator Wirtz, the man she called our "adviser . . . our brain trust," and asked him two questions: Did Lyndon have any chance at all? And how much would a campaign cost? Wirtz replied in the affirmative and set the price at $10,000.

That was twice what her husband made in a year, a sum likely to dismay many a wife, but Bird never flinched. She phoned her father immediately, and when he tried to bargain her down to $5,000, she remained firm, showing she could stand on her own, even against tough T.J. "We have to have ten," she insisted, and he transferred the money to Lyndon's bank within hours.

The candidate's wife soon clashed with the campaign manager over

tactics. Wild had convinced Lyndon that he had to come on stronger, go on the offensive, and attack the other candidates. He could
never win with just a meek presentation of his own record; he needed
to go negative. When Bird heard Lyndon delivering what sounded to
her like mudslinging, labeling one of the other candidates a lobbyist,
another guilty of unsavory connections, she didn't just sit back and
watch. She went to Wild to complain that she had put up money for
this race and she deserved a say in how it was run. She didn't like the
tone Lyndon was taking, and she wanted him to stop the name-calling.

Wild immediately gave her a choice: "Mrs. Johnson, you're going
to have to make up your mind whether you want your husband to be
a Congressman or a gentleman." Put that way, the decision was easy,
and she raised no more objections. But to remind herself of the important part she had in that campaign, she carried the bank withdrawal slip
in her purse until it became ragged and faint.

Like so many other people, Wild underestimated how well those
wheels in Bird's head turned. He acknowledged that she tried to get
her husband to eat better, something healthier than the canned sar-
dines and cured sausage he picked up along the way, and she answered
the phone and drove voters to the polls on election day. But she was,
Wild naively concluded, "quite young . . . a delightful person at that
time" but without any interest in politics.

That was what she looked like to outsiders, but she was fooling Wild
the way she would fool others for the rest of her life. She had quickly
recognized that Wild "did not want women in politics. No, Sir," and
she wasn't going to annoy him by making herself too visible. Already,
at twenty-four, she had learned rule number one for a successful politician's spouse: give your advice privately if it might antagonize when
delivered in public.

The total amount spent on that race ballooned far beyond her
$10,000, and although campaign rules did not yet require precise fil-
ings, one insider speculated that Lyndon's six-week campaign cost be-

tween $75,000 and $100,000, making it one of the most expensive in the nation for a House seat at the time. Beyond Bird's inheritance, Lyndon drew on her father and her brother, Tony Taylor, and on his own kin, including bachelor Uncle George, who put up his life savings. But family contributions made up only a fraction of what came from Senator Wirtz's wealthy clients.

The race for victory on April 10 was a fast-paced, winner-take-all contest, with no provision for a runoff between the top two, and Lyndon used every ounce of his powerhouse energy to follow the strategy his team worked out. Ray Lee, the pipe-smoking journalist who quit his teaching job at the University of Texas to help in the campaign, explained that Lyndon campaigned the old-fashioned way, going after one vote at a time. Targeting undecided voters, he moved doggedly down unpaved country roads, shaking hands with one farm couple after another. He never missed a rally, regardless of weather, and he kept attention focused on himself. As one local newspaper reported, Lyndon Johnson "spoke first, last and the loudest."

The exhausting schedule exacted a price, and Lyndon lost pounds, as well as his voice. He complained of stomach pains, even vomited from time to time, but he kept going and refused to see a doctor. Then, just two days before the election, his condition worsened. While greeting a line of voters, including Mr. and Mrs. Matthews, who owned the rooming house where Bird stayed as a UT student, he collapsed and was taken to the hospital. Doctors diagnosed acute appendicitis and ordered immediate surgery. While Lyndon worried that voters might suspect his illness was just a ruse to win their sympathy, he had no choice—not when doctors told him he had an appendix ready to burst.

Election the following Saturday produced a huge victory. Lyndon was still recuperating from his surgery on Thursday when news came that he had won big, with nearly three thousand votes more than his closest rival. Suddenly it seemed everyone he ever knew wanted to congratulate him, and as a parade of well-wishers streamed by his hospital bed, the doctors insisted Bird stop them. She just laughed and pointed out that he was encouraging the flow of enthusiastic fans. Far be it from her to quash his celebration or hold him back.

By the time President Franklin Roosevelt completed his spring fishing trip off the Texas coast, Bird had Lyndon in good enough shape to greet him personally and get photographed at his side. A few weeks at the Brick House had put some of those lost pounds back on Lyndon's slim frame, and he wanted to underscore his campaign pledge to back whatever the president proposed. The 10th District had given FDR four out of every five presidential votes cast in 1936, and for the district's brand-new congressman, a picture at his side would mean a lot. FDR took an immediate liking to Lyndon, in spite of his rather brash questions about the Roosevelt family and how much fish the president caught. FDR instructed one of his cabinet members to help the young congressman "with anything you can."

Bird stayed behind to organize things when Lyndon took the train to Washington in early May to start his service in the House of Representatives. This would be her fourth move in three years, and she needed some time to decide what to take with her. After packing bed linens and housewares into her car, she started driving east, accompanied by the wife of one of Lyndon's aides. With only a slight detour, she could spend some time with Aunt Effie, who never failed to tell her how much she enjoyed those visits.

As soon as she arrived in Washington, Bird immediately set out to be her husband's number one aide, without appearing on his payroll or putting a foot in his office. Most congressmen's wives who accompanied their husbands to Washington stuck to social events and planned their days around hairdressers and wardrobes, but not Bird. In the few months she spent in Washington in 1935, she had begun guiding visiting Texans around, showing them the chief monuments, and she observed how grateful they were. Now, as a congressman's wife, she became a one-woman welcome wagon for any 10th District Texans visiting the capital. She obtained tickets for them to hear House debates, ferried them from one landmark to another in her own car, and invited some of them back to her apartment for a meal.

Now that she had a bigger apartment than the one in 1935, she found entertaining easier. It was furnished, which meant she was still using someone else's chairs and tables, but it had two bedrooms so that Aunt Effie could stay for weeks at a time. Even when she was there in the guest room, Lyndon's brother or one of his staffers could sleep on the living room sofa or put up an extra cot. It was a hectic household, with a constantly shifting list of residents, and Bird could never be sure who or how many would turn up at breakfast. "Friends of friends" moved in and out in such antic succession that she felt like she was living in a Marx Brothers movie. After one overnight guest left, she and Lyndon conferred, then concluded that neither of them had any idea who that last guest was.

That the unflappable Lady Bird adapted so easily and without complaint to what another wife might call excessive intrusions was a big part of her social genius. It was certainly a considerable advantage for a congressman, especially since she managed to make a favorable impression on nearly everyone she met. Lyndon was a mastermind at picking out the most important people in any room or situation and then currying their favor, but he didn't always succeed in winning them over. Bird did. While his brash, public courting of VIPs could strike associates as blatant self-promotion, her wide smiles and frequent invitations signaled caring and genuine concern. Virtually everyone liked her, and most people liked her a lot.

Sam Rayburn is a case in point. Lyndon had known the Texas congressman since childhood, and now with Rayburn newly elected to be house majority leader, Lyndon flattered him shamelessly. When Lyndon planted a kiss on Rayburn's shiny bald pate, the recipient accepted it as his due, in the manner of a Mafia godfather collecting respect, but other colleagues thought the gesture ridiculously inappropriate.

Bird used softer, subtler tactics to win favor with people who counted. As soon as she realized that bachelor Rayburn was a lonely man after his workday ended, she started inviting him to Friday suppers and Sunday lunches that she cooked herself. Other Washington wives found it awkward to include a solitary male at their dinner tables. But Bird treated him like a favorite uncle. She made a big fuss over his birthday each January and inquired frequently about his health and well-being. By 1940, when he became the powerful speaker of the House of Representatives, she had become one of his top favorites. He sometimes clashed with Lyndon, on both substance and style, but his fondness for Bird never wavered. He stood up for her when Lyndon criticized her cooking and decided she was the best woman he ever knew.

More evidence of her social skills showed up in her conversation. The woman who once warned Lyndon that she loved to debate hot topics, like whether New Deal laws were socialist, now calibrated carefully what she said. She wasn't about to argue or take sides if that offended anyone. Although she had once relished discussions involving differences, about politics and theater and life, she now recognized that confrontation rarely won friends, and she advised other newcomers to Washington to just "ask questions" if they wanted to make a good impression. That deference won her many admirers, including some who actively disliked her outspoken husband, and he, realizing that fact, started taking her along to dinners when no other wives were present.

Behind Bird's genial smile and easy chatter was the same spunky woman with her own opinions, and she found a way to make those known to her husband, who could be hardheaded about advice offered. She called her method "infiltration," and explained how it worked. She would listen thoughtfully to his long monologues about some problem he was facing, and then, in the softest tones, without a hint of challenge in her voice, she would tell him what she thought. It

could be a tentative suggestion, such as "You might also consider . . ."
Or a gentle query: "Do you mean perhaps . . . ?" Then she would
sometimes hear him recycle her position as his a few days later, giving ample proof that he had, indeed, "listened to me." Although she
probably never read ancient Chinese philosophy, she was very much
attuned to one of its teachings—that leading by pretending to follow is
how real power is wielded.

Lyndon's first big challenge as a congressman gave Lady Bird more
chances to polish her political wife skills. Senator Wirtz had backed
Lyndon in the 1937 election because of what he could do for Texas's
10th District—specifically for Wirtz's current project, the Lower Colorado River Authority. The Texas legislature had set up the LCRA
in 1934 to control the Colorado River's destructive force by building dams at crucial junctures, and it was to be paid for out of federal
money. By 1937, huge cost overruns had consumed the LCRA's entire
allocation, and the dams remained unfinished. It was up to Congressman Johnson to get money flowing again. That meant convincing officials to grant exceptions to the rules and persuading his colleagues
that the 10th District's claim was more worthy than others.

Lyndon came through, with considerable help from Bird. Of
course it was not a smooth or easy victory—not when competition for
funds was so fierce—and Bird reported that he had "nights of elation"
mixed with "nights of discouragement." It was up to her to keep him
on course, using the same kind of cheery advice that she had used in
the courtship letters.

She also put her own special brand of persuasion to work on a key
figure. John Carmody, head of the Rural Electrification Administration, had the responsibility of deciding which parts of the 10th District
qualified for federal help in getting electric power lines. REA policy
did not allow subsidizing very sparsely populated regions—the cost

was too high—and without those subsidies, parts of Lyndon's district would not get access to electricity even after the necessary dams had been built to supply the power. If Carmody did not make an exception, residents on those isolated ranches and farms would be pumping water by hand and reading at night by lanterns just like their grandfathers had done.

Carmody was known as hard-nosed, a stickler for rules, but that didn't deter Lyndon from trying to change his mind. He sent him a gargantuan, forty-pound turkey, so big it was rumored to have been cross-bred with a beef. And Carmody, sniffing a hint of bribery, sent it back. Bird proceeded more gingerly, with her usual mix of dinner invitations, broad smiles, and solicitous words about his family, and Carmody changed course, permitting electric lines into the Hill Country. It was a life-changing event for farm families who could now push a button to pump water or light the dark, and Bird knew they would not forget the congressman behind that transformation.

Although it is impossible to calculate precisely Bird's worth to her husband's career, the evidence is overwhelming that she, unlike him, found common ground with everyone, from the acerbic curmudgeon to the sweetest, smiling face. The wives of Herman and George Brown, who started bankrolling Lyndon after they landed contracts to build the LCRA dams, both became her friends although they had wildly different personalities. Margaret Brown, Herman's outspoken, combative wife, did not make friends easily, and although her husband found her scrappy ways refreshing, others tried to avoid her. But not Bird, who praised her as "very stimulating, intellectual and independent . . . [the kind of person who ignites] firecrackers . . . [of the] intellect." The less outspoken Alice Brown, wife of Herman's younger brother, George, was more attuned to Bird's subdued style, and the two women vacationed together in the summer of 1940 at the Prude Ranch, a working ranch that hosted paying guests, where the Brown children camped out and rode horseback.

Who knows how their wives' friendship with Bird figured in the Brown brothers' decision to support Lyndon? They had ignored him in the 1937 race, but once his value to them was clear, they flooded him with favors, making his subsequent campaigns much easier. In 1939, Herman Brown wrote to reassure him: "Remember that I am *for* you, right or wrong. . . . If you want it, I am for it 100%." The Browns began by sending Lyndon a new car, but their gratitude soon ballooned to include offers to use their private planes and vacation properties, and, most important, virtually unlimited campaign dollars. As Bird put it, Lyndon got a "free ride" in his next three congressional elections.

Bird had helped Lyndon deliver so many favors to folks back in the 10th District, she knew his supporters were loyal. They weren't going to hold a single vote against him. When he backed an increase in the minimum wage—an extremely unpopular stand in the eyes of business owners and farmers—she found nothing strange in the fact that he was reelected while other House members, including Terrell Maverick's husband, who took the same position, lost their next election. Letters to his office confirmed his popularity. One man, who had been trying unsuccessfully for five years to get a response from the Veterans Administration, was stunned by Congressman Johnson's efficiency: "I never saw anything like it. Why, I'd vote for that fellow for president."

With her husband so busy, Bird carried the bulk of family responsibility, both his and hers. The Taylors were getting along fine. T.J. had married again, this time to a blonde who was younger than Bird; both Tommy and Tony were thriving. It was Lyndon's side that required Bird's help. His oldest sister, Rebekah, and youngest sister, Lucia, could take care of themselves, but the other two siblings provided enough trouble for all four. Brother Sam Houston had difficulty keeping a job, and he was often drunk, making his long stays with Lyndon and Bird strained and unpleasant. The middle sister, Josefa, had the same problems as Sam Houston, in even greater severity.

To add to her difficulties, the normally healthy Bird found 1939 one of the "few times in my life when I was not physically very up to par." She lost weight, getting down to 113 pounds, and after five years of marriage she had not yet become pregnant. On the advice of a friend, she consulted a Baltimore physician who performed a medical procedure to increase her chances of conceiving, and, determined to get as much as possible out of the short hospitalization, Bird had her appendix removed at the same time.

To some who watched her in the 1930s, Lady Bird Johnson looked like a mousy servant performing housekeeping tasks—laying out her husband's clothes each morning, filling his cigarette case, and polishing his shoes, all without a murmur of complaint. But Lyndon needed far more to stay afloat, and Bird knew what the deal was. From the wide-eyed newcomer who drank too much at the New Year's Eve party, she had transformed herself into the valuable partner of an up-and-coming congressman. Flexible about so many things—where she lived, how many guests she had to feed, Lyndon's mood changes and secrecy about his plans—she seemed to get along with everyone. And she was one of the few people who could offer him "good judgment" without raising his ire. Her mentor, Terrell Maverick, might well have been proud—Bird had become a model political wife.

6

---⊷◉◉◉⊶---

NETWORK BUILDER

O N CHRISTMAS night in 1968, longtime Washingtonians Jim and Elizabeth "Libby" Rowe invited a few of their closest friends to a holiday dinner. Among the fifteen or so regulars at this annual event were Assistant Secretary of State William Bundy, his wife and their three children, and journalist Bill White and his wife, June. About 6:30, as the adults sipped cocktails and the young set entertained themselves in an adjoining room, ten-year-old Michael Bundy spotted some unusual activity in the hedges outside. The doorbell rang, and when the Rowes' son went to answer it, he found the president of the United States standing there, and the first lady, with a big smile on her face, behind him.

The Johnsons had not been invited, but here they were, and none of the adults showed much surprise. They were accustomed to Lyndon's impromptu appearances. He and Bird had appeared at the Whites' door a few weeks earlier, bringing their own dinner, and since the Whites had already eaten, there was nothing to do but seat the Johnsons at the dining room table and watch them consume their chili. June White decided Lyndon got a kick out of popping surprises. Bird, who knew better than most wives how unexpected guests can upend things, admitted she did not try to temper his spontaneity because he was "so enthusiastic and sweet."

On this Christmas night, the Rowes immediately welcomed the Johnsons inside. As Secret Service agents took up strategic posts around the house and Lady Bird settled into a chair, the president launched into a recitation of his accomplishments. He did not stop until he left an hour later.

It was vintage Johnson: Lyndon gleefully surprising the hosts by crashing their party and then monopolizing the conversation; Lady Bird compensating for his social ineptness by thanking the Rowes for what she kept calling an "open house." Young Michael Bundy noted how raptly the adults listened as the president went on and on about how much he had done for them and for the nation.

Everyone present knew that his upbeat assessment of his record did not coincide with what most Americans were thinking. With less than a month left before Richard Nixon moved into the White House, LBJ was besieged by critics of his Vietnam policies and nothing he could do would change that. As if trying to prove his worth to himself and his audience, he kept going back to the legislation of which he was proudest—in education and medical insurance and civil rights.

At ten, Michael Bundy thought it odd for a grown-up to brag like that, but the adults were not at all surprised. They had known Lyndon a long time, and they had known Bird. They knew he would have not gotten where he was without her, always there in the background, smiling and smoothing the way. When Bird got a chance to pass on advice to her daughter, Lynda, who had married an aspiring politician and asked her mother how best to help him, the answer came back that she should learn to walk behind him and keep saying, "Thank you."

It is easy to misinterpret such a role as unacceptably docile, laughably passive. But it was anything but. If Bird hadn't covered up her husband's gaffes, smoothed out the feathers he ruffled, and helped build a powerful network of supporters and friends, how would he ever have reached the success that he did? She knew how essential her social skills were to his success, and so did he. Toward the end of his life, when a friend reminded him that the best thing he ever did was marry Bird, he confirmed that not a day passed that he did not think of that.

Of course the network building she started right after her marriage was not just for Lyndon—she had her own reasons for wanting to rub shoulders with the movers and shakers of Washington. She had let Lyndon know in the courtship letters of the deep yearning she had to be where "Things are Happening," and in a position to meet the people who made those things happen, people who knew all about life "beyond the provinces" and talked about "life with a capital L." Bird never wanted to be the insignificant wife who sat on the sidelines; she wanted a central role in the action, and getting acquainted with the star players in Washington was the way to do that.

Libby and Jim Rowe were not the first Washingtonians she got to know, but they were among those who lasted longest. Both had taken their first jobs in Washington in the mid-1930s and then stayed. Libby grew up in a conservative Republican D.C. household but after four years at Bryn Mawr she returned as a convinced liberal and worked at the United Mine Workers headquarters, where she wrote speeches and helped elect labor-friendly legislators in 1936. Jim Rowe moved to the capital to clerk for Supreme Court Justice Oliver Wendell Holmes, then took a position at the Securities and Exchange Commission. In 1937, shortly after he and Libby married, he became an assistant to FDR's son Jimmy, putting him very close to the center of Washington's power hub. Libby Rowe had to quit her job because of a United Mine Workers rule against employing married women, but she continued to move in labor circles and spearhead community projects.

As first lady, Mrs. Johnson would look to Libby Rowe for help in beautifying Washington and President Johnson would count on Jim

Rowe for counsel. The relationship between the two couples, overlapping social and work lives for nearly four decades, hit a very rough spot in 1960, when Jim Rowe grew so disgusted with Lyndon's boorish behavior, especially his heavy drinking, that he quit speaking to him. But Jim reentered the Johnson fold in November 1963, and Libby became a stalwart leader in Bird's environmental work.

Southerners predominated on Bird's early list of allies, including many Alabamans who spoke with the same accent as hers. With them, she didn't have to worry that they would ridicule her for saying LIE-BERRY (instead of LIE-BRARY) and CANE-T (instead of CAN-T.) She could relax and enjoy herself, knowing they would serve the foods she preferred, like grits and cornbread.

Alabaman Virginia Durr, nine years Bird's senior, figured in the younger woman's initiation to Washington. Durr would later explain in a book about herself that she had realized at an early age that a young Southern woman of means, like herself, had only two choices, either act the perfect lady or "go crazy." Determined to do neither, she looked for a way out, and at age twenty-three married another ambitious Alabaman, Clifford Durr, who had already distinguished himself by winning a Rhodes Scholarship. With Virginia's help (and she was in a position to help since her sister was married to U.S. senator Hugo Black) Cliff Durr obtained a job in Washington in 1933 with the newly formed Reconstruction Finance Corporation, and Virginia Durr immediately began creating her own niche in the capital as a civil rights activist.

Transplanted couples like the Durrs and the Johnsons drifted easily into friendship, and Bird remembered how she absolutely "loved . . . trips out to [the Durrs'] rambling, old country house." She met other powerful people there, like Virginia's brother-in-law, Hugo Black, who left the Senate in 1937 to join the U.S. Supreme Court. He was still on the Court in 1948, when Lyndon needed a highly placed jurist to keep his name on the ballot in Texas; he turned to Black, who delivered.

Just as she had looked to those older "oil men" back in Austin to enlighten her, Bird enlisted friends somewhat senior to her in Washington. The Durrs, although only slightly older, stepped quickly into a mentoring role. After originally misjudging diminutive Bird as lacking both maturity and confidence, Cliff Durr changed his mind, and, impressed by her intelligence and journalism background, he eventually encouraged her to buy her first radio station. Virginia Durr was equally struck by Lyndon's dedication and intensity. Although he talked full speed and waved his arms like an impetuous, out-of-control youth, she recognized that his resolution to abolish poverty was genuine. As he rose in politics, she would call on him for support in securing voting rights for African Americans, and he would come to her defense when she was vilified as a communist in the 1950s.

A good friend of the Durrs, Aubrey Williams, was soon a guest at Bird's table, where he could make her mouth drop with accounts of his storybook life. He had begun working at an age when most boys start school and then used his wages to put himself through high school and college. He went to France to earn a doctorate, and after returning to the United States was spotted by federal officials as an unusually competent and innovative social worker. By the time he was forty-five, he headed one of the largest, most effective programs of the New Deal— the National Youth Administration—and was the person to whom all forty-eight state directors, including Lyndon Johnson, reported.

Williams had traveled in places that Bird had only dreamed about, and the talk at his home never bored her. No matter how the conversation started, it always got back to politics, she noted, with a "social-economic bent." The mood stayed upbeat and passionate, as everyone jumped in with ideas about how to obliterate city slums and get the economy moving again. Reform and improvement were not just vague dreams, they were goals deemed within reach, and Bird decided these "were the people who were going to do it." At their get-togethers at the Durr home on Seminary Hill or at one of the Johnsons' rentals, "You didn't bother much about the food," Bird remembered, "but the mental stimulation was first class."

At her table sat people with wildly different views—the ultraliberal Durrs, who fought their whole lives to extend rights for blacks and farmworkers, alongside racists like Alvin Wirtz, a father figure to Lyndon when he first entered Congress. When the Durrs were fighting hard to eliminate the poll tax, Wirtz was vigorously defending its retention. At one Johnson dinner, when the subject came up, Wirtz complained in the Durrs' presence that without the poll tax more blacks would vote and that would be like giving the right to animals: "I like mules but you don't bring them into the parlor." Of course, Cliff Durr explained, that was typical of the thinking of many Southerners at the time, and Wirtz was more progressive on other issues, such as the need to extend electrification to rural areas. But on matters of race, the Wirtzes and the Durrs were at opposite poles, and Bird managed to incorporate them all into her circle.

Her friendship with Alvin Wirtz's wife, Kitty, had started during the NYA stint in Austin, and it continued when both couples were living in Washington. Whatever their views on race, the Wirtzes were important people in Texas's 10th District, and their daughter, Ida May, became a central figure in Bird's life after she married a physician, James Cain, in 1938. It was Dr. Cain who furnished Bird with valued medical advice, right up through the White House years. He was the person she called, having him paged out of a theater, when Lyndon had his heart attack in 1955, and he was one of the two doctors she summoned to tell her what was wrong with her seriously depressed husband a decade later.

Many of the ambitious achievers that Bird latched on to in the 1930s came from religious groups alien to WASP East Texas, and she was struck by the breadth of their accomplishments and the depth of their interests. Abe Fortas, son of a Jewish cabinetmaker in Tennessee, had become an excellent amateur violinist by the time he enrolled at Yale Law School, and he kept playing for his friends after taking an important job at the Securities and Exchange Commission in Washington when he was only twenty-five.

His wife was even more remarkable. Fortas spotted Carolyn Agger, another fervent New Dealer, only months after both arrived in Washington, and the two married in 1935. A New Yorker and graduate of Barnard College, Carol, as her friends called her, had also earned a master's in economics from that hotbed of New Deal ideas at the time, the University of Wisconsin, academic home to Professor Edwin E. Witte, known as the "Father of Social Security."

Outstanding as Agger's credentials were, her new husband encouraged her to add to them, and the couple moved to New Haven, so she could earn, in 1938, the same Yale law degree that he held. By the time Bird met her, Carol Fortas had three first-rate degrees from top-notch schools, providing her with special distinction even among super achieving Washingtonians. But it was the Fortases' multifaceted lifestyle, mixing high-culture chamber music, tax talk, and a colorful circle of acquaintances, that intrigued Bird. The diminutive, cigar-smoking Mrs. Fortas, in her purple designer outfits, stood out in any crowd, and after she and her husband settled in Georgetown, their home became a favorite gathering spot for liberal thinkers and aficionados of classical music.

Carol had her run-ins, some of them fierce, with Lyndon Johnson. But she refused to let those disagreements color her relationship with his wife. Open-minded Bird reciprocated the high regard, and although she, herself, would never have paraded in extravagant colors or smoked a cigar, she found something captivating about a woman who did. Nearly three decades after their first meeting, Bird was still relying on Mrs. Fortas for help in her campaign to beautify Washington, and she mused in admiration: "Carol, with her cigar . . . sentimental, and pragmatic, and tough, and soft-hearted. . . . Such a queer combination of a person."

Georgetown, where the Fortases and others of their circle took up residence in the 1930s, was a rather shabby section of Washington, only a few minutes' drive from the Johnsons' apartment. Many of the Georgetown houses were run-down, and in a bold statement of deprivation by choice, the occupants did not bother to fix up or prettify them. They had weightier matters on their minds. Bird found the home of Arthur and Wicky Goldschmidt particularly inviting, with its "narrow little staircases" and "aura of age," and she relished trips to their part of Georgetown, before it "really became fashionable."

To say Georgetown had not yet become fashionable was an understatement. Once a city of its own, it had technically been part of the District of Columbia since the 1890s, but the factories lining its waterfront and the decrepit houses along Rock Creek Park made it undesirable. The massive influx of New Dealers, searching for inexpensive rentals, changed that. The little row houses were only a few minutes' commute to government offices, and newcomers gravitated to Georgetown, beginning a transformation that would turn that section of Washington into one of the most expensive and fashionable addresses in the nation's capital—home to a glitzy list of senators, judges, and writers.

As a congressman's wife, Bird understood that the minute the House speaker's gavel came down, ending the legislative session, she had to have everything ready to get back to Texas. With a new election every two years, it was important to keep close contact with voters in the 10th District, and she couldn't afford to dally. "Dark didn't catch us," she explained, one extra night away from those precious "Constituents" (which she spelled with a capital C). Since thrifty Bird objected to paying for a place she wasn't occupying, she either sublet her current Washington apartment or gave it up entirely, which meant she had to find a new place when she came back. She also thought it extravagant to have more than one set of housewares, and so she packed up the sheets, towels, and tableware and transported them back and forth, along with clothing. Lyndon, who refused to fritter away three days on an automobile trip, took the train or flew, leaving the driving and transfer of their belongings to his wife. One of his secretaries or a staffer would sometimes go along to spell her at the wheel, but Bird frequently had to negotiate the 1,500-mile route on her own, or with just Aunt Effie or another elderly, nondriving relative for company.

Back in Texas, Bird encountered friends and constituents who had little in common with her liberal circle on the Potomac. The 10th District was full of voters who thought more like the Wirtzes than the Durrs and they were openly disdainful of Virginia Durr's thinking about women's independence and Aubrey Williams's projects to help the disadvantaged. Fiercely self-reliant ranchers in the Hill Country saw no reason to guarantee factory workers a minimum wage, and independent-minded Austinites had little use for the plethora of New Deal rules and regulations radiating out of Washington. Although the Lone Star State was still overwhelmingly Democratic, a conservative faction was growing, led by FDR's disgruntled vice president, John Nance Garner. Lyndon, who had won in 1937 after billing himself as closely aligned with FDR, had to find a way to appeal to those who felt less warmly toward the president. A wife who made no enemies could be an enormous asset.

Bird became adept at tailoring her talk to the recipient. When conversing with conservative voters in the 10th District, who wanted to keep things the way they had always been, she left out any reference to positions advocated by the Fortases and the Durrs on subjects like states' rights and the Constitution. Some of her closest friends (like Gene Boehringer, now the married Mrs. Lasseter) and beloved family (such as T. J. Taylor) were unabashedly part of the conservative faction of Democrats, and Bird listened to them all, without clarifying how she or her husband might feel differently about big government and civil rights.

People who wrote what others read were plum targets for Bird's solicitous attention. Lyndon's good friend Bill White, the newsman who hosted the New Year's Eve party where she got woozy, was an early favorite. Like her, White had grown up in small-town Texas and become interested in journalism while still a student at the University of Texas. Unlike her, he had found a job at *The Austin Statesman* and quickly won promotion to Washington. When Bird first met him, much of his distinguished career still lay ahead, but she remained his ally as he piled one accomplishment on top of another, compiling the kind of record she might have envisioned for herself: writing for *The New York Times* by 1945; having a syndicated column running in 175 newspapers nationwide by 1955; winning a Pulitzer Prize for his book on Senator Robert A. Taft.

These high-powered people—smart, strong-minded, ambitious men and women—were far from homogenous, and they clashed on many issues, sometimes so strongly that they had nothing to do with each other for years. But the warm camaraderie born in the 1930s persisted for decades, with careers intersecting time and time again before diverging and separating, then crisscrossing again. Names like Fortas, Durr, Rowe, and White all appeared in Johnson date books in the late 1930s, and they would still be there in the 1960s, on White House invitation lists and potential appointments to the Supreme Court. Their homes were the places Lyndon felt free to drop in on, unannounced.

Of all the personal allies who figured in the early Johnson story, no name ranks higher than that of Charles Marsh. The six-foot-three newspaper tycoon was an imposing figure, his big nose and arrogant demeanor giving him the look of a Roman potentate. Marsh had started out poor, working his way through college, but the vast wealth he acquired by the time Lyndon arrived in Washington gave him enormous clout. While still in his twenties, he began buying newspapers and bank stock as easily as some men buy suits. He guaranteed loans for oilman Sid Richardson, and when Richardson struck it rich, so did Marsh. Although his home base was Austin (and he kept a wife there), he considered himself a national figure and built a rambling Virginia estate, Longlea, near Washington, to accommodate that conceit.

Longlea also accommodated a woman who was not his wife—Alice Glass. A statuesque blonde with a remarkable head of hair, she had the aura of a Hollywood star, but Bird knew her real story, how she had left small-town Texas and reinvented herself as a sophisticated, worldly intellectual. Just a year older than Bird, Alice Glass had hopped from one college to another, dropping out of Texas Christian in favor of the more cosmopolitan Columbia in New York City, and then returning to her home state. She was only twenty, working as a secretary in Austin, when she met Charles Marsh, owner of the city's two leading newspapers.

Marsh installed Alice as his live-in companion and travel mate. On the couple's European trips she proved a quick study, rapidly enlarging her knowledge of wine, fashion, and foreign affairs. Longlea, with its stone facade and baronial drawing rooms, offered a perfect setting for Alice to flaunt her elegance and impress her guests. Young Lady Bird Johnson found Longlea a virtual seminar in style. Alongside Alice, in her silky evening gowns, the congressman's wife felt woefully unsophisticated, but she resolved to learn. It was at Longlea that she absorbed her first lessons in how wealthy globe-trotters lived. Until then, she admitted, "I was happily provincial."

Through Marsh, Bird met international artists, like the gifted young conductor Erich Leinsdorf. In late 1937, at age twenty-five, Leinsdorf had left his native Vienna for performances at the Metropolitan Opera in New York. His visa permitted only a six-months stay, but after the Nazi Anschluss in March 1938, he feared returning to Austria where Jews like himself were no longer safe. He applied to American officials for a visa extension, but with only days left on the old one he had not yet received a response. So he turned to Charles Marsh and Alice Glass (whom he had met the previous summer in Salzburg as "Mr. and Mrs. Marsh") to help, and they enlisted the most can-do congressman they knew.

Neophyte legislator Lyndon Johnson did not have the "foggiest notion," according to Leinsdorf, how to get a visa extended, but he wanted to please the mogul Marsh, and he went to work "with the kind of energy which I think we all [later saw] in action." Lyndon first obtained an extension on Leinsdorf's old visa, giving him time to get himself to Cuba, where there was an abundance of visas—enough "to feed the pigs." From Cuba, Leinsdorf reentered the United States on a permanent resident visa.

The heterogeneity of their Washington friends (Jews, Irish Catholics, and Protestants, from all parts of the nation) suggests the Johnsons chose their associates with less regard for religion, ethnicity, or Southern roots than for brains and power. As Bird put it, she was on the lookout for "fascinating characters of the New Deal."

Secretary of the Interior Harold L. Ickes and his young wife, Jane, easily qualified. As the cabinet member overseeing much of the New Deal's big spending, he was a key player but his admittedly difficult personality (he titled his memoir *Autobiography of a Curmudgeon*) could be off-putting. Bird turned to his amiable young wife to cement a friendship between the two couples. Only twenty-five when she married the sixty-four-year-old secretary in 1938 (after his first wife died in an automobile accident), Jane Ickes soon was running the Maryland farm the couple acquired, and she prided herself on serving suckling pigs raised on her own land. She remained a Johnson friend long after her husband died and the pigs and the farm were sold. Three decades later, Bird looked back over the 1930s, and claimed Jane Ickes as "remarkably durable."

Already in the 1930s, Bird's list of fascinating characters included a sprinkling of oddballs who flouted mainstream values. One of them was William O. Douglas. He had survived an impoverished childhood on the West Coast to earn a law degree at Columbia University and become a prized professor at Yale. Brilliant but endlessly restless, he attracted the notice of President Roosevelt, and after working for the Securities and Exchange Commission he was appointed one of its commissioners in 1936. Three years later, when Justice Louis Brandeis retired from the Supreme Court, FDR nominated the forty-year-old Douglas for the job. He served thirty-six years, longer than any other justice up to that time, and formed a camaraderie with fellow justice Hugo Black, the Johnsons' longtime friend. In 1975, *Time* magazine singled out Douglas as the Supreme Court's "most undeviating liberal voice" up to the time of "his retirement last week."

His libertarian views applied to his private life as well. He produced the first divorce in Supreme Court history in 1953 when he left the mother of his two children and wed a woman eighteen years his junior. Then he divorced two more times, marrying a younger woman each time. (The last two were twenty-three and twenty-two, respectively.)

Although this parade of wives struck some Americans as scandalous for a member of the nation's highest tribunal, nonjudgmental Bird accepted Douglas's behavior as just part of who he was. Others might snub him socially and refuse to have anything to do with his young wives but she cheerfully saw them all, right through the White House years. She attended a weekly Spanish language class at the home of one, chatted with another whenever they met at the beauty salon both frequented, and invited the third to dinner. After meeting the justice's latest mate in 1964, Bird described her as an emaciated adolescent: "there's only 86 pounds of her—very young, and sweet, and trusting and nice." But Douglas's permanent place on Bird's list of cherished friends was never in question: "I guess sometime I'll give up trying to understand people—but I'll always love Bill and hope for the best for him."

As a newcomer to Washington in the 1930s, Bird might have shied away from the prospect of talking with men whose pictures appeared on the covers of national magazines. But she wasn't fazed a bit. She entertained Thomas "Tommy the Cork" Corcoran and Ben Cohen, who were touted as the "Gold Dust Twins" in the September 13, 1938, issue of *Time*. The fast-talking Corcoran and the shy, retiring Cohen hardly qualified as twins, except for the fact that both had come to Washington at the invitation of their former Harvard Law professor Felix Frankfurter and they had collaborated in the drafting of milestone New Deal legislation, including the Fair Labor Standards Act of 1938. Leon Henderson, the financial wizard who annoyed a lot of people by vehemently disagreeing with them, was another welcome guest at Bird's table.

Some of those enchanting characters of New Deal Washington were women, and Bird had to face the fact that her husband was paying more than platonic and intellectual attention to several of them. It seemed he could not keep his hands off them, and from his very first campaign in 1937 gossip circulated about how he spent his nights. He showed little sign of caring what people thought and, in 1939, shocked his aide Walter Jenkins by saying he paid close attention to constituents' opinions on all matters but two—the car he drove and the women he slept with.

Although Lyndon had told Bird he was seeing other women while courting her in 1934, the subject of marital infidelity had not figured in their letters, and Bird apparently had not included it in their unwritten agreement on what she would tolerate from her husband. He later told his good friend Richard Russell, senator from Georgia, that she had threatened to divorce him in the 1930s. But she was more than familiar with extramarital relationships, having watched her adored father preen in his reputation as a ladies' man. His example, among others, convinced her that many men had women who came and went, while their complaisant wives remained steadfast, the permanent centers in their families' lives. And so Bird amended her side of the Great Bargain, adding yet another to the long list of Lyndon's imperfections and transgressions that she would not permit to wreck their partnership. Pulling down the famous veil, she would choose not to notice his attentions to other women, and keep reminding herself that he loved her best.

Much of Lyndon's flirtation occurred right under Bird's nose—in his office or his home—with the women who worked for him. He liked to employ couples—because long hours were more easily incorporated into family routine if both husband and wife served the same boss. The wives could be convinced to accept meager pay and sometimes even work for free. Billie Bullion, the wife of the Johnsons' tax attorney, John Bullion, refused to sign on, and she later told her son that Lyndon's Lothario reputation was one of the reasons. (Lack of pay was another.) It was disgraceful for Lyndon to humiliate his wife, Mrs. Bullion argued, and to flaunt so openly his disregard for his marriage vows.

Others closed an eye, or covered for Lyndon's sexual adventures, at his request. John Connally remembered a tongue-lashing from his boss for not doing so. As Connally told it, Lyndon arranged a rendezvous with Alice Glass in New York City but failed to enlighten Connally. When Charles Marsh, with whom Glass still lived, phoned Connally to inquire about Lyndon's whereabouts, Connally told him, unaware that the newspaperman might put that information together with what he knew about Alice and come to a conclusion disastrous for Lyndon.

Evidence for what historians later described as a serious, decade-long romance between Lyndon Johnson and Alice Glass is not very convincing. The two no doubt enjoyed an intimate tryst from time to time, like the one reported by John Connally. Glass had a reputation for being in the adventure business and Lyndon's weakness in the face of temptation was legendary. But theirs was hardly a relationship that threatened Bird's marriage. Lyndon was not about to leave his wife to marry Alice, and the wife understood that. It was unthinkable for an ambitious young congressman to risk a rupture with one of his most important backers, a man so powerful he could have ended Lyndon's political career right then. Lyndon invariably deferred to Marsh, made himself available whenever summoned, and hustled to do him favors. As Marsh's secretary recalled, "I saw a young man [Lyndon] who wanted to be on good terms with an older man [Marsh] . . . absolutely *determined* to be on good terms with him." If Connally, Lyndon's right-hand man, had not registered that something was going on between Lyndon and Alice, how serious could it have been?

Even if Lyndon had dared to steal Marsh's woman, Alice was hardly the stable, centered helpmate an ambitious politico needed. According to "The Alice Glass Story," which Dorothy Lane, a graduate student at the University of Texas, wrote for Professor Lewis L. Gould, it was a tangled life, and Alice had "invented" a husband named Manners so she could present herself as the respected "Mrs. Manners," whose spouse was temporarily absent, while she continued to travel with Marsh. After Charles Marsh divorced his first wife in 1942, he married Alice, but she left him to wed a civil rights activist, then a professional pianist, and two more men of uncertain occupation. That makes a total of six, if the enigmatic Manners is included. After her last husband died in 1974, Alice went back to Texas, where she had started out, and lived with her sister in Marlin. Such a record raises the question: Would anyone know the name of Lyndon Johnson today if he had divorced Lady Bird to marry Alice Glass?

What is absolutely clear is that Bird regarded Marsh's Longlea as one of her very favorite retreats. She bought a tract of land nearby, although she never built there, and when listing the few places where she liked to go to relax and put her feet up, even in the most frantic times, she singled out Longlea for its "velvet warmth." Charles Marsh and Alice Glass continued to dot the Johnson record for the rest of their lives. President and First Lady Johnson made a final visit to Charles Marsh not long before his death in 1964, and Alice Glass was an overnight guest at the Johnson White House and then sent Lyndon a valuable sculpture just before he died.

In the spring of 1941, it was to their wide circle of friends that the Johnsons turned for advice on what to do next. After only four years in the House, Lyndon was restless to move up, and he saw his chance when U.S. senator Morris Sheppard died of a brain hemorrhage on April 9. Although only two years past the minimum age (thirty) required of senators, Lyndon felt confident his work for the 10th District had won him a following all across the huge state, enough votes to win him a seat in that very select club of ninety-four men and one woman who made up the U.S. Senate at the time. Marsh and other friends agreed that his chances looked good, and they enthusiastically backed him. Tom Clark, an attorney in the U.S. attorney general's office, was so involved in the race that his son Ramsey (who later served as LBJ's attorney general) remembered that the whole family tuned in on shortwave radio while on a vacation in Alaska to see how their candidate was doing.

After an upbeat start, Lyndon's prospects plummeted when a man far more popular than he entered the picture. Texas governor Wilbert Lee "Pappy" O'Daniel, who had said he was not a candidate, suddenly changed his mind and entered the contest. Although born in Ohio and raised in Kansas, O'Daniel had become a legend in his adopted Texas, where he operated a profitable flour business and hosted a midday radio show.

Faced with an opponent as beloved as Santa Claus, Lyndon did what was becoming his usual—he overworked and fell apart. He spoke so loud and so often that his throat turned raw, and he became so debilitated he was hospitalized. As his time in bed grew to nearly two weeks Bird recognized that his problem was more than physical—he was badly depressed. His campaign manager, John Connally, rounded up substitutes for the speaking appearances but that could not continue indefinitely, not without giving some explanation for the candidate's absences. When Connally decided to prepare an innocuous press release, to allay voters' suspicions, Lyndon was furious. He countermanded Connally, ordered him out of his sight, and promised never to speak to him again.

It was Bird who saved the day. Going against everything Lyndon had said, she cajoled Connally, saying her husband's tirade meant nothing and that Connally's continued work in the campaign meant everything. She kept the campaign manager on the job and her husband in the race.

By primary voting day, the field had narrowed to just the two—Johnson and O'Daniel—and Lyndon's spirits lifted. Staffs of both men kept careful watch on the numbers as the tallies dribbled in over several days. At first O'Daniel was winning; then a new box of votes put Lyndon ahead. The Johnson camp holed up in an Austin hotel, and when news accounts indicated victory for their man, congratulatory telegrams poured in. On bad days, everyone just waited. In the end, O'Daniel claimed the seat, and Lyndon's staff admitted they had erred: by permitting preliminary unofficial results to be turned in early, they had allowed the opponent to calculate just how many votes he needed to "find" in order to take the lead. When Lyndon's staff suggested challenging the result, he demurred, knowing any investigation could reveal shortcomings in his own operation as well.

One innovation marked that contest. For the first time a "Women's Division" formed to help Lyndon. Bird played a small public part, preferring to let her outgoing friend Marietta Brooks, who had been a schoolteacher and relished speaking to large crowds, take charge. Bird gamely attended ladies' lunches and tea parties, but her sweating hands left no doubt about how little she enjoyed such appearances. If any of the Johnson women were going to make Lyndon's case to voters, it had to be his mother and his middle sister, Josefa, who felt comfortable singing Lyndon's praises in public. Bird preferred to follow the example of Eleanor Roosevelt, who thought it unseemly for a wife to campaign for her husband—until 1940, when his audacious run for a third term drew even Eleanor into the race. Southerners, in particular, objected to wives campaigning, and Bird resolved to heed the advice of one senator's wife who explained what worked for her: "I just go along with Mr. George and sit on the platform to show them I don't have a cleft foot."

That did not mean Bird sat out the campaign. In this, Lyndon's fourth contest in as many years, she went on the road with him, sounding very unlike the young woman who wrote him in 1934 that she dreaded the prospect of his becoming a politician. Now she was toting the little movie camera that he had given her and, in what would later be called "opposition research," she made notes of what his opponent said. In the soundtrack she subsequently added, she delivered commentary on how "Pappy O'Daniel . . . flashed like a comet across the Texas landscape" and how her nine-year-old niece passed out campaign literature. She played down her own role ("All I did those days was wait and see") and she poked fun at her very limited wardrobe. After her movie camera, in the hands of someone else, caught her day after day in the same nondescript suit, she laughingly noted that she finally managed to show up in "a different blouse."

Lyndon lost that election—the only one he ever lost—but one lesson from it was clear. Lady Bird could override a husband's command, even a husband as unassailable as hers, and she would not hesitate to intervene when she judged the circumstances called for it.

The other lesson was equally significant. She had learned how exciting and invigorating a campaign can be. In those few weeks she immersed herself so completely in the purpose that marks a vibrant political contest that she called it a highlight of her life. She felt like she was "living among people who were working at the very top of their capacity." Thrilled by the "rich wine of youth . . . running in our veins very strongly," she decided that even though it ended in defeat, she wouldn't have missed it for anything, not even for "a million dollars."

Lyndon was clearly dejected with the result. As she watched him, in a rumpled seersucker suit, amble out to the plane that would take him back to Washington, she knew it was time for some high-spirited cheerleading. The morale-boosting letter she wrote him emphasized the fact that they had all done their best. "It was all right we lost. I'll always remember the campaign of 1941 as just about my favorite campaign."

A few weeks later, she had another reason to give a Pollyanna slant to the outcome. In July 1941, when the House of Representatives considered extending the military draft, opinion was so divided that the measure passed by a single vote. Pearl Harbor would soon startle Americans out of their complacency and spin the country into full military buildup. If Lyndon had not been there to cast the vote that kept the draft in place, the mobilization would have been far more difficult. Bird decided this was a good case of her husband being "in the right place at the right time."

As Lady Bird was making her way in Washington in the early years of Lyndon's political ascendancy, only a few people took time to size her up carefully. Jonathan Daniels, a North Carolina newspaperman, was one who did. He wrote in his diary soon after joining FDR's staff in Washington in 1941: "Lyndon Johnson's wife is the sharp-eyed type who looks at every piece of furniture in the house, knows its period and design—though sometimes she is wrong. She is confident that her husband is going places and in her head she is furnishing the mansions of his future."

Even the astute Daniels had no way of knowing the kind of mansions Bird had in mind or the number of fascinating characters she would incorporate into her network along the way.

7

CEO AND FINANCE MANAGER

O N A Sunday afternoon in 1951, attorney Leonard Marks went to the home of a client in Northwest Washington. He didn't usually do house calls and almost never on Sunday. But this case was special. The wife of Lyndon Johnson, elected to the U.S. Senate in 1948, had been Marks's client for about five years, long enough for him to know that she liked to talk business in the comfort of her own home. If the day was warm, she would have drinks served on the porch or in the backyard, and since this was Sunday, the senator would be there, too. Lady Bird would get the conversation started with warm and chatty questions about Marks's health and that of his family, making this sound to an outsider more like a social occasion than what it was—a highly charged business session with fortune-changing implications.

With pleasantries out of the way, Mrs. Johnson would move on to the subject of the day, and to the list of questions she had prepared for Marks. The time had come for her to decide whether or not to make a huge investment, and she had summoned Marks to give her some background information. She had bought her first radio station in 1943, then added others, and she was making money. But now it looked like those boxy radios in people's homes might be supplanted by little screens with pictures in black and white, and the Federal Communications Commission would soon start taking applications from those who wanted to operate the stations that delivered television via those screens. If Lady Bird Johnson intended to get in on this new venture, she had to decide now.

Although invented decades earlier, TV had not yet caught on, and too few Americans owned sets to interest advertisers. Outlay—to equip a TV station, hire staff, and provide content—would be huge, compared to radio, and Lady Bird Johnson's right-hand man in Texas, Jesse Kellam, was advising her to hold back. Her husband was warning her about betting on a loser. But she wanted to hear from Marks. She wouldn't be asking him for a yes or a no. She made her own decisions. What she needed from Marks was his perspective on the costs and the risks, his predictions for making money.

It would have been hard to find a better placed expert on the subject than Leonard Marks. As a former member of the Federal Communications Commission, the agency that set rules and issued operating permits, he had been involved in broadcasting long enough to know more on the subject than even Lyndon Johnson, who sat on the Senate committee to which the FCC reported. Marks had left the federal agency to join a law firm that specialized in communications, and he was personally acquainted with leaders in the business and with their critics. No one could be sure, of course, how profitable television would turn out to be but Marks was bullish. He fully expected Americans would soon be getting the bulk of their news from TV and they would rely on those little screens in their own homes for entertainment, even educational programs that would rival what schools could teach.

Marks had scheduled only a two-hour meeting that Sunday, but as he laid out the pros and cons and the relative advantages of VHF [very high frequency] as opposed to UHF [ultra high frequency] the afternoon meeting stretched into evening. As the Johnsons mulled over what Marks said, Lyndon remained wary, unsure if this investment was sound. But Lady Bird was gung ho to go ahead with VHF. "It may take everything we have but it is a gamble that I want to make," she told Marks. All Lyndon could say was, "Well, it's your money." This was T.J.'s daughter, and she wasn't going to let a risk-averse husband hold her back.

That confidence, nurtured in her youth, had registered remarkable gains in the decade preceding that important meeting with Marks in 1951. In fact, it could be said that she had used those years, beginning with the U.S. entry into World War II, to turn herself into a confident CEO. She had never taken a course in business management but in the early stage of the war she had on-the-job training, which she valued more than years in a classroom.

Lady Bird Johnson was not in Washington on Sunday, December 7, 1941, when she heard on the radio the shocking announcement about the Japanese attack on Pearl Harbor. She was in tiny village in Alabama, carefully checking financial records at a relative's home. Her mother's bachelor brother, Claude Pattillo, had died a few weeks earlier, but Bird missed the funeral because of a medical problem. Painfully aware of how much Lyndon wanted a son, she had checked herself into a hospital for a gynecological procedure to increase her chances of becoming pregnant, and only after her doctor approved travel did she make her way south. She knew her Uncle Claude owned a huge chunk of Autauga County's valuable pine forests, and that she, as his niece and namesake, would inherit part of it. She could have waited to hear from one of her Alabama relatives or an attorney how much she was getting, but that was not how she operated. She went to Billings to examine the papers herself.

That year had already been a turbulent one for the Johnsons. Besides her medical problem, Lyndon had racked up a trio of losses—the Senate race and time out for two hospitalizations. Talk of the United States becoming involved in a war already under way in Europe had made the year even grimmer, and Congressman Johnson's summer vote to extend the draft reflected his pessimism. Now, with the U.S. under attack, the time for debate had ended. The nation was at war. By the time Bird returned to Washington, Lyndon had already signed up for active Navy duty, fulfilling a promise made months earlier, that if any young men were drafted he would be right beside them, ready to fight.

Lyndon hadn't bothered to say who would run his congressional office while he was gone and take care of all the requests coming in from his 10th District constituents. Like other House members, he had employed female secretaries, but the office manager and top aides were male. Now, with so many men signing up for service, new hires were in short supply, and over the Christmas holidays, which Bird and Lyndon spent with his mother (always "Mrs. Johnson" to Bird) in Austin, the decision was made. Lady Bird would run the office, and she would start her administrative duties immediately by accompanying her husband to California, his first military assignment. Her notes from that trip show how very diligent and precise she could be—she kept a record of every expenditure down to the last penny, including a tiny tip to a porter and 75 cents "for medicine."

By January 20, 1942, after watching tearful wives and mothers say poignant good-byes to servicemen who were shipping out, Lady Bird was on a train back to Washington. Lyndon would stay stateside for now, checking on production and manpower problems for the undersecretary of the navy. It was a natural assignment for a member of the House Committee on Naval Affairs, but it would keep him out of Washington, flying around the country, leaving her to manage not only household finances but also office spending. With his pay reduced to that of a Navy man, she decided to economize by giving up her rented apartment and moving in with Nellie Connally, whose husband was on active duty.

Every day was packed, starting with classes in typing and shorthand to improve her speed. By a little past noon, she was grunting in an exercise class, hoping to shed some of the "deplorable" pounds she had put on. As long as he had known her, Lyndon kept a sharp eye on her figure, and when she added to the 113 pounds she registered in 1939, he started nagging her to take them off. While he was away, he wanted her to update him on her waist and hip measurements in every letter she sent him.

By three or four in the afternoon, all her classes finished, she headed to his office where three or four secretaries were responding to the mail that came in every day. As the person in charge, Lady Bird went over each response, checking wording and spelling, before signing, "Mrs. Lyndon Johnson." Her husband had insisted she be very clear about her volunteer status and include in every letter, "I am working without pay in the office." But Bird thought something less "awful bald and ugly" could make the point just as clearly, and she came up with a subtle, slightly longer alternative: "I'm contributing my time while Lyndon is away on active duty, doing what I can to help out in the office."

The pile of correspondence sometimes kept her busy until 10:30 at night, and by the end of February she decided to drop out of business school and quit the exercise class so she could devote full time to the "substance [of my life], the real thing," which was, of course, Lyndon's office. A few weeks later, she wrote an old friend in Marshall that she had a "full time job now. . . . I get down to the office about eight-thirty, stay until seven, frequently come back at night to finish up."

A clever executive allocates her time wisely and spends as little of it as possible doing what others can do for her, and Lady Bird Johnson knew that. In April, she moved out of Nellie Connally's apartment and back to a place of her own at Woodley Park Towers, where she hired a maid to clean and prepare her meals. It was her thirteenth move in seven years, but it freed her from domestic chores and gave her more time at the office. Then the African American maid, Otha Ree, quit. With the war opening up so many new opportunities for women, Ree could finally put her college degree to use. Rather than settling for domestic service, which was the only job she could find earlier, she started teaching school back in her hometown in Texas.

Bird was as careful about hiring a replacement for Ree as she was about new hires at the office. She favored Texans in both cases and insisted on recommendations from a trustworthy source. For domestic staff, she liked to get referrals from professors at Wiley College, the small African American college in her hometown, and that meant she would have to wait until August, when she planned to drive her current car, a Buick convertible, back to Texas. In Marshall she learned from Wiley College President Matthew Dogan that student Zephyr Black was looking for work. After verifying that Black's aunt had once worked for T.J., Bird set up an interview with the young niece, and it took only twenty minutes for the two women to come to an agreement. Then the young African American rode with the congressman's wife in the Buick to Washington, beginning a relationship that would last twenty-seven years.

By the time Zephyr started cooking for the Johnsons in the fall of 1942, Lyndon had shed his Navy uniform and returned full time to his congressional office. During his seven months of active duty, he had been out of the country only about six weeks when he was deployed to the South Pacific. But he was not in Washington, where his office had to deal with major decisions. Since he was up for reelection that year, good publicity was essential, and Lady Bird had to keep newspapers supplied with updates on what Congressman Johnson's office was doing for constituents. Lyndon suggested that she write a personal note to as many voters as possible—the specific number he had in mind was 1,500—and he chided her that all she had to do to reach that goal was write twenty-five letters every day of the week for two months.

That was in addition to the responses she had to get out to the dozens of letters that came in every day, some asking for significant help. Requests could be as easy to fulfill as supplying information on a son in the service, or as difficult as obtaining a lucrative government contract for a slaughterhouse, getting a new highway rerouted, or arranging for an ammonia plant to be moved. The hardships of the Great Depression and the exigencies of war had caused Americans to turn to their legislators for help, and the head of the Austin post office noted that people expected a lot. He had asked for help himself and admitted: "I get right ashamed of the many requests we send in."

Secretaries Mary Rather and Nellie Connally put in long hours, too, but they lacked entrée to the offices where some of the biggest decisions were hammered out. They knew a congressman's wife could obtain appointments that underlings could not, and that meant Bird had to approach complete strangers and ask for favors. Her coworkers reported she would sit staring at the phone for a while before mustering the nerve to dial the number. On one occasion, although she counted Jane Ickes, the wife of the secretary of interior, among her friends and went to the Ickes home for dinners, she dreaded the prospect of appealing directly to the grumpy secretary to satisfy a constituent's request. But she knew it was her job. So she did it. And she must have done it well. By the time she returned to her desk, the message was waiting for her: Secretary Ickes had granted her request. What better boost to her confidence could she want? The next time it would be easier.

Like Lyndon in his first years with Congressman Kleberg, Bird rec-ognized that doing business in Washington often meant going to the secretaries and assistants, who worked in the background, their roles discounted as insignificant. In wartime Washington, female networks were even more important than usual because so many men were off fighting, leaving women to make decisions and disseminate the crucial information that a congressman's office needed. As Bird explained in one letter, "We rely on a net-work of friends throughout the various departments [to help solve] the multitudinous problems with which our constituents present us."

Even if it meant staying late, after a long day at the desk, and spend-ing extra money on dinners out, Bird knew the value of her female network and she was constantly adding to it. Lyndon, fully aware of her frugal side, was thrilled to see her political skills at work, and he encouraged her to spend whatever she had to for the lunches and out-ings involved.

One young female reporter who stopped by Congressman John-son's office in early 1942 was eight years younger than Bird, but the two women had so much in common they immediately became friends. Both came from small-town Texas and had graduated from UT where they wrote for the school paper. Although Elizabeth "Liz" Sutherland was far more exuberant and outgoing (she was the first woman elected vice president of UT's student body) and could easily overshadow the more reserved Bird, the two became solid, loyal allies for life. The married Liz Carpenter would later become Bird's right-hand aide in the White House.

Although Bird's classes at UT had provided the basics of journal-ism, the congressional office job gave her the chance to develop the skills of a superb press secretary. That meant learning how newspapers operated in the real world. Nobody had to tell her the importance of releasing frequent bulletins to every editor in the 10th District. But if she wanted to be fair and not appear to favor one paper over another, she had to keep up with staff changes on every paper so she could reach the right person in a hurry. Once, when she sent an important news item to a single reporter, who happened to be absent that day, his editor blamed Bird for costing him a huge scoop. She replied that she was "mortified and embarrassed" and she would never repeat the gaffe because she well understood the pain of taking "a licking" from a rival.

To maximize her husband's popularity with voters, she organized an effective PR campaign in his absence. She instructed county officials in the 10th District to send her lists of all births and deaths so she could write personal notes of congratulation or condolence. She prodded her friends and relatives to make suggestions, and she appealed to Buck Hood at Austin's major newspaper: "I wish you'll drop me a line whenever you think of anything, big or trivial, that Lyndon's office ought to be doing, whenever you run across any news we ought to know, whenever you have any advice or ideas that will help to do the job."

Unlike her husband, Bird insisted on authenticity in her press releases and correspondence. He liked to put a grandiose slant on his naval service, describing it as a "mission for the President." One staffer picked up the phrase and used it in a letter to a constituent, explaining that Congressman Johnson was not in his office but "serving his country where the President considers he is most needed." Bird, in checking that letter, circled the phrase about the president and penned in the margin that she didn't like it and "besides [it's] untrue." Indeed, Lyndon's enlistment had been more his idea than that of his commander-in-chief, and when FDR requested all congressmen to return to their legislative jobs, he did, as did most of the others.

In her husband's absence, Bird continued his efforts to funnel federal money to Texas. Even before Pearl Harbor, Congress had allocated $10 billion for defense contracts, and Lyndon immediately started pushing for locating a military base in his district. Austin's mayor and other city leaders also pressed the case but the competition was fierce in early 1942, and the final decision was looking "a little bit too close."

With people back in Austin eager to get a plum military installation there, Bird went to a key figure, assistant secretary of war for air Robert Lovett, and reiterated the advantages of the 10th District. When she left she wasn't sure of the outcome but the press secretary side of her asked for another favor. Before the decision was announced, she wanted Lovett to give her advance notice so she could issue the press release and make sure her husband received credit for his efforts. It is impossible to know what weight she carried in the final decision, but in September 1942 a military base, later renamed Bergstrom Air Force Base, opened on three thousand leased acres in Lyndon's district, and the congressman's name figured prominently in the announcement.

Lady Bird Johnson's role in funneling more money to Texas, to a defense plant hundreds of miles away from Lyndon's district, is even more intriguing. The federal government, in its rapid conversion to a war economy, had to open up factories all across the nation to produce whatever its servicemen needed to fight—ammunition and guns, uniforms, fighter planes. While some factories could retool—to make tanks instead of cars—others had to start from scratch, and countless towns wanted the privilege of starting them. Among the winners was tiny Karnack, Texas, where Lady Bird's father still lived. Not all of the land for Longhorn Ordnance Works came out of T. J. Taylor's considerable holdings, but a lot of it did. By mid-1942, he and his then wife, Ruth, were busy buying land from their neighbors and selling it to the government, sometimes for nearly twice what others received for the same acreage. In the month of August alone, T.J. and Ruth Taylor recorded $70,000 in land sales, equivalent to more than $1 million in 2014 dollars.

There was nothing illegal about the land deals—T.J. had been buying and selling bits of Harrison County for more than forty years. But the rapidity of his acquisitions in 1942, followed by quick resale at inflated prices, does raise the question of whether he had inside information about the location of the new ordnance factory. Since Lady

Bird and Lyndon had signed away any claim to her father's immediate profits, there is no paper trail connecting them to his windfall. But the question remains: Was Bird using her Washington network to gather information that substantially increased her father's net worth?

As the summer of 1942 ended, it must have felt a lot like Christmas in T.J.'s big Brick House. Bird had come back for a visit and her two brothers had their own reasons for celebrating. Tony showed up with a new bride, Matianna, and Tommy, who still lived in Texas, had become the proud father of a baby girl. With Longhorn Ordnance set to open, the local economy looked good.

During the half year that Bird managed Lyndon's congressional office, she performed so flawlessly that some of his constituents didn't even know he was gone, and others suggested she could win a House seat on her own if she chose to run. Jake Pickle, who handled the Texas office until he, too, went off to fight, praised the "bang-up job" she was doing. He proposed organizing some extra publicity for her: "I feel we could and should get some good stories and features about her work. It would go over big." But Lyndon, always a little squeamish when anyone but himself was getting credit, did not push for flattering articles about Bird, and none appeared. As soon as he got out of uniform, in July 1942, he ended her work in his office. This behavior followed a pattern that would be repeated again and again in their marriage: he pushed and prodded her to excel, taunting her that anyone with two degrees from the University of Texas should certainly be able to manage the project he had in mind. But when she delivered— making a useful contact or solving a thorny problem—he could turn petulant, not liking to be upstaged.

The woman who exited Lyndon's office in the summer of 1942 was fully aware and justly proud of what she had accomplished in those few months. They had provided her the equivalent of a graduate degree in business management, and she had learned more about how government worked, she wrote, than in all those years at the University of Texas. She had gained confidence in her financial skills and boasted that she could "hold down a job" and make a living for herself if she had to.

Armed with this elevated self-assurance, Bird initiated some important changes in her life, starting with buying a house. Fed up with those rented apartments she had been using since her marriage, she wanted a place of her own. Nothing fancy or even as grand as her family home in Karnack, but a house she could come back to after every sojourn in Texas. While Lyndon was away on active duty, she had used some of her precious, rationed gasoline to drive other wives around Washington in search of a "dream house" to buy, and she had stored up real estate tips. Now that he was back, she had more time for house hunting, and she found a place that seemed just right. Aunt Effie, in one of her generous moments, had offered to supplement Bird's own savings to meet the down payment, and all Bird had to do was convince Lyndon that this was the right move. He had always objected to owning a home in Washington because he thought it sent a cocky message to constituents, making the congressman look overly confident of reelection.

Bird was too astute politically not to understand that reluctance, but she was so excited about her most recent property find that she broke into her husband's meeting with John Connally to describe the modest house, with a perfect floor plan and a charming garden, on a quiet, dead-end street. When she finished, Lyndon ignored her completely, as if she had not spoken. He wouldn't even look at her. That made her so furious that she unleashed a torrent of uncharacteristic anger: "I want that house. I have no place of my own, no children. All I have to look forward to is the next election." It was extraordinary for this normally self-controlled woman to explode like that, and, according to Connally, Lyndon was nonplussed. He turned to Connally to ask what he should do. When Connally advised, "Buy the damned house," Lyndon finally gave his okay.

The Johnsons moved to 4921 30th Place in Northwest Washington in early 1943, and to Bird's amusement Lyndon soon became even more enthusiastic about the house than she. He started purchasing outsized furniture for it, and she heard him pontificating to incoming congressmen about the importance of owning a home in the capital. He did insist on showing his populist side by listing his residential phone number in the city directory, where it remained until he became vice president. Anyone with access to a phone could dial a number and reach Lyndon Johnson—or more likely his wife.

Bird turned the house into an income-producing investment. Before she drove back to Texas at the end of each congressional session, she made sure she had rented the house out, fully furnished, for the time she would be gone. Other legislators' wives might object to strangers using their cutlery and sleeping in their beds, but not Bird. As for why she never had a problem with her temporary tenants, she explained: "I'm not much of a housekeeper, and I always went over inventory with the renters very carefully before I left." And the subletting continued long after she had become a wealthy woman.

At the very same time Lady Bird Johnson was negotiating for her dream house, she was initiating another, far more significant investment—in a radio station. She and Lyndon had talked of owning a newspaper as a way to supplement his income, but they decided they couldn't afford one. So they turned to broadcasting. In late 1942, they found KTBC, an Austin radio station with a low price tag to match its poor prospects. In four years of operation, it had never produced a profit, and according to its most recent balance sheet it had spent about 25 percent more than the paltry $26,795 it took in the previous year.

Although bad management might appear the likeliest explanation for such pitiful performance, the station's owners were neither naive nor poorly connected. One of them, Robert B. Anderson, was about the same age as Bird, but he had already, at age thirty-two, served as Texas's assistant attorney general and then its tax commissioner. (He would go on to hold three different positions in President Dwight Eisenhower's cabinet, including secretary of the treasury, before ending up a convicted criminal for bank fraud.) His success in the radio business had been stymied by the refusal of the FCC to grant his station more broadcasting power. Limited to a tiny 250 watt band to be shared with Texas A&M University, KTBC could air programs for only a few hours a day, not enough to attract sufficient advertising revenue.

After hearing that KTBC was up for sale (more than one person later took credit for steering the Johnsons to Anderson), Bird (signing herself Claudia T. Johnson) made an offer. Hardly a backroom deal since all such purchases require approval from the FCC, her application put her personal worth at $64,332, equivalent to nearly a million dollars in 2014. As management experience, she listed her time running Lyndon's congressional office. None of this would have come as news to Clifford Durr, a commissioner on the FCC. Bird had already approached him as a friend and asked for his advice on the deal, and not until he assured her that KTBC looked promising did she proceed with the acquisition.

What happened next shows the enormous error of seeing Lady Bird Johnson as a woman unacquainted with the business world. She left Lyndon in Washington in the spring of 1943 and moved to Austin, where she worked full-time to put her radio station on its feet. With a confidence to match T.J.'s, she examined the balance sheets, evaluated staff, and assessed the programs transmitted. She even pitched in on cleaning. Donning a blue housedress that she designated especially for this task, and toting a mop and bucket, she started washing windows. Grime weighed down staff morale, she explained, and spic-and-span windows and hallways would lift employees' spirits and her profits.

Unlike KTBC's previous owners, the congressman's wife received almost immediate FCC approval to expand and thus make more money. Chaired by Texan James Lawrence Fly, the commission quickly granted KTBC a much larger broadcast band all its own, allowing it to remain on the air twenty-four hours and offer advertisers a more enticing market. With a higher audience potential, it needed additional programming, and since a fledgling station could not assemble all the content needed, it had to look elsewhere.

Networks to supply programming to radio stations had been slowly taking shape over the preceding fifteen years, but only a handful had achieved national visibility. Edward R. Murrow's throaty tones had helped raise the profile of CBS, causing NBC and the smaller networks to scramble for turf. The Johnsons approached NBC first but that network had already aligned with a San Antonio station that did not want competition for the territory between it and Austin. So the next stop was CBS.

As the Johnsons began amassing what would become a huge fortune in broadcasting, both husband and wife played crucial, but very different parts, illustrating the synergy in their partnership. Neither could have made a success of the station without the other. Although she had the money to buy the station and she kept a careful eye on daily operations, he was the one, with his reputation as a can-do congressman, who could make the alliances to put a station on the national map. Donning his Stetson, he went to the New York office of CBS chairman William Paley, who had no idea why a congressman from Texas's 10th District would show up without an appointment. But Paley took time from a busy schedule to see him. Like most people who met the young Lyndon Johnson, Paley was struck by his energy and ambition. The CBS chair quickly grasped the fact that KTBC was far more important than the investment of a Texas housewife, and he arranged for its affiliation with his network.

Lyndon intervened at other key times. In early 1946, when it appeared Austin was slated to receive a second station license, giving KTBC competition for listeners and advertiser dollars, a group of ten Texans applied. All veterans, just back from war service, they took the call letters KVET, and Congressman Johnson, who insisted he had no objection to competition but wanted the "responsible" kind, put in a good word for them. Why wouldn't he? KVET's owners came right off his old buddies list, and they included Jake Pickle and John Connally, who had worked for him since before the war, as well as others he had known even longer. KVET owners indicated they would focus on sports, a subject Bird's KTBC rarely touched.

Until the vets got their station up and running, Lyndon suggested some of them work at KTBC, and they did. Jesse Kellam, his friend from San Marcos days, stayed on, managing the Johnson station for decades; Sherman Birdwell, whose connection to Lyndon's family went back three generations, sold advertising time. He found it easy— even people who disliked Lyndon bought because KTBC had a virtual monopoly on Austin's airwaves. Since radio advertising was relatively new, Lyndon kept coming up with strategies to attract new clients. He suggested the station's salesmen line up people to go into stores and announce they were there because of what they heard on KTBC.

Charges later surfaced that the Johnsons' staff applied much more direct pressure on clients, such as requiring them to purchase advertising time in return for political favors or perform personal service as part of the deal. But the proof of these claims failed to materialize.

Broadcasting was in takeoff mode in 1943, a little like California before the 1849 Gold Rush, with very visible risks and rules not yet written. Following the right hunch could mean a big payout, but in the meantime expenses added up as new equipment was purchased and staff salaries climbed. Carol Fortas, the attorney friend of the Johnsons, insisted anyone who went into broadcasting in the 1940s with a little money and a bit of luck stood a good chance of striking gold. But the Johnsons had more than luck. They had personal friends on the FCC and the access and credibility that Lyndon's elective office provided. Their advantages soared after Lyndon was seated on the Senate Commerce Committee, with its mandate to oversee the nation's broadcasting. A word from him could have enormous effect on other stations. But in the early 1940s, the Johnson fortune was not yet made, and when KTBC reported its first tiny profit ($18 in August 1943) Bird used the entire amount to pay a dental bill.

As the station's profits began to climb, Bird marked a huge milestone in her personal life. After nearly ten years of marriage, she had finally become pregnant. It was a snowy Sunday morning, March 19, 1944, when delivery seemed imminent, and Lyndon should have been available to drive her to the hospital. But he already had a reputation for liking to talk on the phone and even in a personally charged time like that he was reluctant to hang up the receiver. When Bird went out to the car and got in it, he remained in the house, and she had tapped her foot a while before he finally got into the car and drove her to the hospital. He didn't stick around to see how the delivery went. In his usual not-wanting-to-be-alone mode, he gathered up a few male friends and drove around Washington, stopping frequently to phone the hospital for an update. When word came that delivery had proceeded smoothly, he took the "whole crowd," his wife remembered, to the hospital for a viewing of the baby. It was vintage Lyndon, seeking companionship at what others might think the most private of family times.

The new parents had been so sure they were getting a son they had discussed only boys' names, and now the appearance of a healthy baby girl required a turn in thinking. It was Grandmother Rebekah Johnson who came up with "Lynda Bird." Not every newborn in Washington that year received the kind of welcome that the firstborn of a Texas congressman did. President Roosevelt sent her a book about his dog, Fala. Speaker of the House Sam Rayburn, who had become a frequent guest at the Johnsons' home by the time Lynda Bird was born, immediately took a liking to the scrappy child.

Bird parented in the same CEO style that she used at the radio station, at Lyndon's office, or in running her busy household. She directed and delegated, hiring the best help she could find and then keeping an eye on results. Lynda walked and had her own tricycle by the time she was one, and Bird recorded her antics in home movies. In the filmed footage of birthday parties and play group gatherings that followed, Lyndon rarely figures, and in one of his short appearances, he looks oddly out of place as he squats beside little Lynda Bird on the lawn and she keeps staring at him, as if seeing him for the first time.

The inconveniences of caring for a youngster stretched the patience of both parents and put serious pressure on the marriage. The already overextended congressman and his wife had little time or energy left to tend to a child, and friends and staffers later described some tense, unpleasant scenes during Lynda's early years. Bird's expertise at book-keeping and business management did not extend to caring for fidgety infants, and when she failed to keep Lynda quiet, Lyndon complained. Billie Bullion remembered going to the house on 30th Place with her husband and a few other couples for "drinks, sandwiches and talk." The wives all pitched in to help Bird with the food while "Lyndon pretty much monopolized the talk." But infant Lynda soon put an end to it all. As Mrs. Bullion recalled: "Colicky babies . . . can cry and cry, until they start howling." Even with all the doors shut, the sound of the bawling baby reverberated throughout the house. The other wives offered their own solutions for how to calm her, but nothing worked. She kept crying, stopping only to catch her breath before resuming at even higher volume until she drowned out Lyndon. That made him so mad, he yelled, "Dammit, Bird, do something to shut that kid up." That sent guests heading for the door, leaving Bird with a sick baby and a furious husband. "How she handled that I don't know," Billie Bullion later told her son.

Bird's management skills translated more easily into property renovation and management, and in the last two years of the war she began upgrading the house on 30th Place. No larger than the average American home, it had a living room, dining room, and kitchen on the first floor, and three bedrooms and a small office for Bird on the second. She converted the basement into housing for domestic staff and turned over the unfinished attic to servicemen who needed a place to sleep for a night or two. Following the lead of her friendly next-door neighbor, who raised his own vegetables and a patch of corn, Bird tried growing tomatoes. But she paid much more attention to the flowers that bloomed in succession: in early spring, she counted on forsythia and hydrangeas, followed by peonies, her very favorite, in May. She planted morning glories outside the dining room window and roses that climbed up the sides of the screened porch.

With a house that size, Bird could accommodate Aunt Effie more easily. Now in her early sixties, with her demure, outdated outfits, featuring lace at the neck and long, swishy skirts, she injected a hint of another world into her niece's chaotic household. Myopic and slow-moving, Aunt Effie gave the impression of a misplaced Dresden doll, as oblivious to the political talk around her as if it were in a foreign tongue. While the rest of the household worried about the excessive alcohol consumption of Lyndon's brother, Sam Houston, who also stayed from time to time at 30th Place, Aunt Effie blithely continued mixing drinks for him.

On April 12, 1945, after hearing a radio announcement, Aunt Effie rushed into her niece's tiny home office to share the news that President Roosevelt had died. At first, Bird discounted the report, thinking it just another example of the older woman's confused state. But when confirming broadcasts followed, Bird came to the shocking realization that it was accurate. She had accompanied Lyndon to FDR's fourth inauguration three months earlier but had taken the president's ashen complexion as a sign of overwork, not drastic deterioration. Unprepared for his death, she was stunned, as was much of the nation, who had to face the prospect of a new leader in wartime.

FDR was the only president some Americans had ever known. His jaunty attitude throughout the darkest days of the Great Depression and the traumatic attack on Pearl Harbor had made him a hero in many homes. At the Johnsons' home, he was much more. Lyndon, who described him as "like a Daddy to me," reacted to the death as if it were that of a close family member. He went to bed, and he stayed there. When Bird suggested they go to Union Station and view the cortege bringing the body back to the capital, Lyndon accused her of callousness and not caring. "This is not a circus, you know," he reminded her sarcastically, thus shaming her into staying home, a decision she later regretted.

A few months later, the war ended, and as car horns blasted victory sounds around Washington, thirty-two-year-old Lady Bird Johnson had reasons for joining the merriment. She had made enormous strides since Pearl Harbor. Although she had never collected a salary, she had developed the confidence of an eager entrepreneur and was already the sole owner of a radio station. She no longer had to make do with a shabby, rented apartments—she had her own two-story, brick, colonial house, where she supervised the cook and other domestic help as efficiently as she managed child care for her toddler daughter.

But along with celebrating the war's end, Mrs. Johnson had some concerns. She had just left the hospital after multiple blood transfusions needed when a tubal pregnancy ended, and she worried she would never be able to deliver that son her husband desired so much. On the public front, she could see Lyndon's visibility increasing, both in Washington and back in Texas, but if he continued in politics she needed to nurture her broadcasting business into something far more profitable in order to provide the level of financial security she wanted for her family. She had not yet encountered communications wizard Leonard Marks or learned anything about television's potential for making money.

8

CRUCIAL CAMPAIGNER AND MARKETER

W HEN BIRD blithely promised Lyndon in a before-marriage letter that she could sell him to his "worst enemy" if he "ever had one," she had no idea what lay ahead. Or how that vow would be put to the test. By 1946, her husband, a congressman since 1937, was in a nasty political campaign, facing his first real challenge for reelection to the House of Representatives. To make matters worse, she herself had become an issue, her business record under scrutiny for evidence of impropriety. Congressional wives were used to snide, private re-marks about how they dressed or spoke, but Lady Bird Johnson was facing questions about how she made her money, and how she spent it, and voters wanted answers before they marked their ballots.

Lyndon always ran scared in elections. Even when he was way out ahead, he kept focused on the possible misstep or unexpected event that could derail him. In 1946, those anxieties had some foundation because his political base was falling apart. With the turmoil of the war and its aftermath, Texas Democrats had split into two factions, and

Lyndon, as one of the "Loyal" Democrats, was going to have to defend himself in the primary election against the "Regular" Democrats, who were fed up with what they saw as excessive federal intervention in their lives, in matters such as price controls, rationing, and labor laws.

The Johnsons had a hint of coming trouble in 1944, when Lyndon's strongest opponent in the Democratic primary, Buck Taylor, attacked him on both political and ethical grounds. Taylor, one of the Regulars, put Lyndon on the defensive by pressing him to explain why he had backed all those big federal programs. It was Buck Taylor's second charge, however, that stung deepest. He pointed out that the Johnsons had become very wealthy and he challenged them to show how they came into that money, since it was far more than a congressman's salary could have produced.

Buck Taylor was a bit of a windbag, without the personal credibility to make his charges stick, and Lyndon beat him. But a stronger opponent appeared in 1946 to raise the same nettlesome questions. Hardy Hollers, a forty-five-year-old attorney and decorated war veteran, ridiculed Congressman Johnson as an "errand boy for war-rich contractors" and implicated Bird, claiming that her KTBC had received favorable treatment from the FCC because of her husband's intervention. Hollers even brought T. J. Taylor into the debate, asking voters how a seventy-year-old man like Lady Bird's father could have started a construction business and immediately made so much money.

The then popular singer Gene Autry agreed to help Lyndon out by opening up political rallies with "Back in the Saddle Again," but it was going to take more than a sentimental cowboy song to win this race. Bird went into action. First, she turned to her able, "not a bit timorous" friend Marietta Brooks, who would "just as soon talk to a bunch of men" as at a ladies' lunch. Through family connections and her successful architect husband, Brooks knew her way around the 10th District and had access to people who mattered. She immediately turned to a network already in place, the Federation of Women's

Clubs, to line up volunteers in every county. Women who had already committed to Lyndon's renomination were encouraged to speak to their undecided friends and to send out campaign literature to people they didn't know.

Like most political campaigns at the time, this one expected a lot of women volunteers. They had to cover all their own expenses, such as gasoline and meals while on the road, while the men working directly with Lyndon were given a sizable expense account to pay for their whiskey, steaks, and hotel suites. Although husbands and sons could be recruited to tack up campaign posters on remote country roads, the women themselves had the task of going to local merchants and asking for space to put up Lyndon's posters in the storefront windows. The women would be a lot more effective, Bird suggested, if they were bill-paying customers and went with a smile.

When the female brigade proved insufficient to deal with Hollers's charges, both Johnsons knew they had to do more. Lyndon scheduled a big public rally at Austin's Wooldridge Park on July 6. He publicized the event in county newspapers, with ads that questioned his opponent's integrity ("Thou Shalt Not Bear False Witness") and promised complete honesty in his own campaign ("Statesmanship Not Slander"). To all who came to the park (or listened in on radio station KTBC) Lyndon pledged to "Read the Record . . . Call the Roll! . . . Empty the Garbage Can."

As hundreds gathered in Wooldridge Park that Saturday evening, they saw Lyndon, all alone on the platform except for his mother and his wife, both dressed in righteous white. With arms swinging and voice ringing, he reminded the audience that Texas Regulars had started attacking him in the previous election. Now they were continuing to smear him "with slanderous yellow sheets . . . every foul rumor these evil minds could concoct." They even "dragged into the mire the name of my sweet wife."

The sweet wife came prepared with ammunition to shoot back. For days, she had gathered up documents to substantiate what she had made herself believe—that neither she nor Lyndon had profited unfairly from his office. She collected papers on KTBC, the 30th Place house in Washington, and the duplex the Johnsons had recently bought in Austin for what Hollers was calling a suspiciously low price. She went through her files for letters from Aunt Effie and Uncle Claude; she located canceled checks and statements of what her father had given her. While Lyndon talked to the crowd, he kept gesturing to the pile of documents she had put together, and invited anyone dubious of Johnson integrity to come up and check the written records.

Bird admitted she was disappointed when, after all her hard work, not a single person stepped up for even a glance. The lack of interest may well have resulted from doubts that the full record was there—Lyndon was already known for not leaving much documentation behind. But the campaign, even though it resulted in an overwhelming victory (Lyndon's 42,672 to Hollers's 17,628), left Bird with a bad taste, "kind of a slur, a dark mark on our life that existed . . . for all the rest of time."

Having prevailed in the primary, the Johnsons could skip the general election and that was fortunate because Lyndon was a physical wreck. As Bird described the situation: "His body finally reached the point of exhaustion and the physical bill came in." It was at times like this that Bird's help and encouragement were most crucial.

Although his aides publicly described this latest confinement as due to a recurring respiratory infection, they admitted privately that he suffered from "nervous exhaustion." Walter Jenkins, Lyndon's chief aide, went further, calling it "bad." Lyndon acknowledged it was "six weeks or two months of not being worth much." This was one of those times he had predicted back in 1934 when he warned her he would need a woman to nurse him and help him to climb.

Even at his most robust, Lyndon required considerable caretaking. Like a potentate with a throng of lackeys, he counted on someone always at the ready, to fetch his glasses, find him the right newspaper, take notes. On the road he depended on a secretary or female reporter to deal with personal needs—keep tabs on his supply of fresh shirts and whatever medicine he was taking. Margaret Mayer, who covered the 1946 campaign for the *Austin-American*, complained she had to provide "semi-valet" service. In addition to writing favorable articles about him, she carried his throat lozenges and hand cream. At each stop, he waited for her to hand over the right Stetson. In the car, he liked to wear the clean one, but when he got out to face a crowd, he wanted the worn, greasy one.

Whenever Bird was within earshot, she was the one expected to respond to his every cry for help: to reach someone on the phone, untangle a botched appointment, talk with a crotchety associate, help choose between thorny alternatives. Although relieved when others filled in for her, she registered no complaints about his dependence on her, and when he once yelled out, "Bird, where are you?" she reminded him sweetly, "Right behind you, dear. Where I've always been."

Her contemporaries continued to be appalled by what they saw as her complaisance, and they questioned why she did not strike back at what sounded like excessive, even abusive demands. But she understood how important it was to keep him on an even keel. She strongly objected to descriptions of her as being treated unfairly and once told her daughter that Lyndon was "my lover, my friend, my identity." She understood that she not only contributed to his success but found her own power through him. The need for a woman to assert an identity of her own, separate and apart from her husband's, belonged to a later generation—not hers.

By January 1947, Lyndon was fit and ready to begin his sixth term in the House of Representatives, his first under Republican control. Annoyed at price controls and shortages of items they wanted to buy,

unhappy voters had, in the November election, turned out the party
that had controlled Congress as long as he had been in Washington.
Bird's good friend Sam Rayburn would no longer be holding the gavel
when the House came to order—that honor would go to a Republican,
as would every chairmanship of the House committees.

Fortunately for Bird, the wives remained solidly nonpartisan at
their regular Congressional Club meetings. She had become a stalwart member as soon as she was eligible and relished the lectures,
discussions of contemporary topics, and how-to-do-it presenta-
tions. Whether it was actress Gloria Swanson sharing tips on how
to look younger or an ambassador talking about some exotic foreign
destination, Bird was there. When the Congressional Club offered
a course in interior decorating, she signed up and never missed a
session. But it was the possibility of making friendships across the
political aisle that proved most valuable of all. While chatting with
the wives of congressmen from states far removed from Texas, she
made sure to leave the kind of favorable impression that would serve
Lyndon.

It could have been at one of these meetings that Bird came up
against a test of her own. At the wives' club, it was no secret that Bird's
husband was being seen around Washington with the beautiful new
congresswoman from California—Helen Gahagan Douglas. No one
would make a direct reference to the relationship in Bird's presence,
of course. That was just not done. But the tight friendship between
the two members of Congress was common talk in Washington because they made such a public showing of it during House debates
and in after-hours socializing. Extramarital relationships were commonplace in the capital but conducted in private, with intense effort
to keep them hidden from colleagues, reporters, and spouses. Lyndon and Helen were breaking those rules—flouting them, by walking
hand in hand and driving around the capital together, even in the
early morning hours.

What could Bird do? If she showed any jealousy or expressed hurt to the other wives, some of them would no doubt have sided with her. But that meant they were taking her part against Lyndon, and as his "marketer" she was not in the business of making enemies for him. Any verification from her of an intimate relationship between her husband and Douglas would fuel the rumors, while keeping mum might possibly weaken those rumors by calling into question their validity. So Bird's prior decision, to treat Lyndon's womanizing as invisible, continued as her operating mode. Faced with irrefutable evidence of its existence, she would laugh it off or indicate it mattered not at all to her. Lyndon took his cue from her, and when Sam Rayburn warned him about the consequences of his behavior, he countered that Bird knew all about his women and didn't care.

Helen Gahagan Douglas was formidable competition for Lyndon's affection. Only nine women served in the 79th Congress (1945–1947), but Douglas, a curvaceous blonde from Hollywood, would have attracted attention in any gathering. In the overwhelmingly male House of Representatives, she stood out like a birthday cake on a salad bar.

But Douglas was far more than a beautiful face on a beautiful body: she had the kind of life that awed Bird. At age forty-four, Douglas had already conquered several worlds: the Broadway stage, where she rated star billing before she was twenty; European opera houses, where she sang prima donna roles; and in glamour magazines, where she was pictured alongside her handsome husband, Melvyn Douglas, reputedly the highest paid actor in the world and leading man to legendary divas Joan Crawford and Greta Garbo.

That stage-and-screen gloss obscured a more serious, conscientious side of the Douglas partnership. Helen's operatic tours in Austria in the 1930s exposed her to blatant anti-Semitism, and both she and her Jewish husband worried about the threat Nazi Germany posed to the entire world. In their cross-country drives, necessitated by their bicoastal careers, the Douglases resolved to do something about the stark poverty they witnessed—the barefoot children in Appalachia and dispossessed families in makeshift caravans moving west. While other Hollywood celebrities ridiculed the "Oakies" as good-for-nothings and showed little interest in Europe's problems, the Douglases enthusiastically pitched in to help both poor Americans as well as targeted Europeans. Melvyn joined the Anti-Nazi League, and Helen changed her voter registration from Republican to Democrat and served on the board of the National Youth Administration. The couple's public service brought them to the attention of Eleanor Roosevelt, who invited them to stay overnight at the White House.

By 1940, Helen, whose stage talent did not transfer easily to film, decided to devote more of her energy to politics, and she agreed to head the Women's Division of California's Democratic Party. Her success in that organization led directly to an invitation to run for the House of Representatives in 1944, and without consulting her husband, who was thousands of miles away serving with the Army, she accepted the nomination and won the seat. President Roosevelt sent a sly congratulatory note, predicting she would be more than "just a beautiful cloak model," an apparent slap at Connecticut Republican Clare Boothe Luce, the socialite author and wife of influential media mogul Henry Luce, who was beginning her second term in the House.

A celebrity like Helen Gahagan Douglas held enormous appeal for Lyndon Johnson: being publicly linked with her could burnish his Lothario reputation and feed his ego. Within days of Douglas's arrival in the capital in January 1945, he was in her office, eager to mentor her in how things worked on Capitol Hill. Although eight years her junior, he had already served four terms in the House, and he knew the committee chairmen by first name. Democratic leader Rayburn treated him like a son. Who could guide a neophyte, especially a gorgeous one, more expertly than he through the intricacies of the House of Representatives?

When others attacked her for her leftist views, Lyndon rushed to defend her publicly. After ultraconservative Mississippi representative John Rankin took on a group of liberal, freshman representatives that Douglas belonged to and labled them "Communists," she got to her feet and, in a voice perfected on Broadway stages, demanded to know "if the gentleman from Mississippi is addressing me." Rankin ignored her completely, as if she had not spoken, and kept on warning about the threat of communism. That sent Lyndon to Speaker Rayburn with a request to make Rankin apologize. The speaker could not be ignored, and when he pressed Rankin to answer if it was indeed Douglas whom Rankin meant, the unconvincing answer came back that he was *not* addressing the "gentlewoman from California." Lyndon had made his point, however, that the new congresswoman was under his protection.

Rather than snub Douglas at social events, Bird treated her like a firm ally, and it was to Douglas's house in Chevy Chase that she went with Lyndon to commiserate with other grieving friends when President Roosevelt died. Rather than turn people off, because of its clutter and chaos, Douglas's understaffed household seemed to attract first-rate conversationalists, and talk centered not on the weather and social arrangements but on solutions to economic problems and changes on the international front, exactly the kind of talk that Bird called "first rate."

But it was Lyndon's trips to Helen's house *without* his wife that set Washington talking. Creekmore Fath, an Austin lawyer who later became an outspoken Johnson critic, resided in the capital at the time, and he reported that Helen and Lyndon virtually "lived together. . . . It was an open scandal in Washington because Lyndon would park his car in front of [Helen's] house, night after night after night and then would get up in the morning and drive off at 6:30." Another Texas native, Mary Louise Glass, who was Alice Glass's sister, observed that

Helen and Lyndon drove together to the Capitol in the morning, and after parking in a conspicuous place they walked hand in hand to their respective offices.

Creekmore Fath exaggerated when he described the Lyndon-Helen relationship as cohabitation. The congressman had a packed schedule, with many obligations that could not possibly include the congresswoman, including a month-long European trip in 1945, and in 1946 that tough election as well as three lengthy hospitalizations. As for Helen's real interest in Lyndon, shrewd Bird might have suspected what one Douglas biographer later concluded: Douglas had a knack from her early acting days of playing up to powerful men who could advance her career.

Lyndon was certainly the right man for that, and he could always use an extra woman of Douglas's beauty to bolster his morale. Bird had learned long ago that she could not call him on his weaknesses—he could not handle that. She was not about to change course now. Convinced that her continued nurturing was essential to his career and that he knew that as well as she, she would incorporate his other women into her life and try to learn from them. It was not an entirely new form of accommodation. Lyndon had been up-front with Bird about his fondness for the "little radio writer" in 1934, and Bird had accepted her as useful in smoothing out his rough edges.

Lady Bird Johnson's vow to help market her husband became critical in 1948, when Lyndon, at age forty, decided to make a second try for a seat in the U.S. Senate. Although one of the most chronicled Senate races in American history, Bird's significant role in it is rarely mentioned. She did far more than wifely catering: she kept him in the race, and she did it more than once that year.

To gain entrée to the Senate, Lyndon had to campaign all across the huge Lone Star State rather than just a single congressional district. For this much bigger field, he opted to use a helicopter to reach sparsely populated rural areas. The chopper, with "Lyndon Johnson—US Senator" painted in big letters on the side, was a novelty at the time, and since many Texans doubted its efficacy and deemed it too newfangled and noisy, it was dubbed the "Johnson City Windmill."

Lyndon liked the helicopter, however. Moving faster than a car, it would swoop down on short notice, delivering the candidate to a town square or farm field if even half a dozen adults had been spotted as a potential audience. A slim and cocky-looking Lyndon would bound out, ready to shake hands and deliver a rousing campaign talk. Bird worried the helicopter was unsafe and she refused to ride in it, but Lyndon blew off the risks. He liked the attention it brought him, and he relished the excitement it delivered to voters who had never before come within shouting distance of a candidate for the U.S. Senate.

Helicopters were expensive, though, and cash flow became a problem during the first round of the 1948 primary. Campaign worker Joe Phipps told of one tense moment in early July when the race was tight, and the candidate and his wife were locked in an intense discussion about where they were going to find the funds to continue. They could not even pay the hotel and restaurant bills for their crew and get them on the road that morning.

While Bird kept suggesting ways to come up with more money, Lyndon wanted to give up and quit. When she recommended calling Sid Richardson, who had by now become an affluent Fort Worth investor, Lyndon scoffed at the idea, reminding her that Richardson had already come out for his opponent, Coke Stevenson. But that was "before you entered the race," Bird chided her husband, and anyway, "It doesn't make any difference who Sid says publicly he's for. . . . He's our friend. He will always be our friend." When stubborn Lyndon couldn't bring himself to make the call, she volunteered: "And if you're too stiff-necked to call him, I certainly am not. Do you want me to call?" According to Joe Phipps, who witnessed the whole exchange, Lyndon uttered not a word but his "slow, lean nodding up and down movement" registered consent. As Phipps left the room, Bird was dialing the phone, and half an hour later the money was there to pay the bill for the overnight stay and get the staff moving.

The candidate performed tirelessly, starting each day early and finishing late, and he expected his employees to work equally hard. Secretaries found the schedule so grueling they rotated, one week on the road and one week back at headquarters. Under the stress of this arduous campaign, Lyndon suffered a recurrence of an old problem: kidney stones. He tried to keep going, arguing that he would eventually pass this stone, as he had passed the others, but the pain became excruciating. Racked with intermittent fever and chills, he sweated through more than his usual number of shirts each day. Shivering at night in his rail berth, he prevailed on newly hired aide Warren Woodward to crawl in beside him and share some of his body heat. For Lyndon, undergoing surgery to remove the kidney stone was out of the question—it would take him off his feet for weeks, unthinkable in a tight race.

Finally, when the pain became intolerable, Lyndon agreed to check into a Dallas hospital—but only temporarily and in absolute secrecy. With her hands virtually tied, Bird reached out to an old friend—the celebrity aviator Jacqueline Cochran, who happened to be in Dallas at the time for an event honoring Stuart Symington, secretary of the newly created air force.

Cochran first met Lyndon in 1937 when she was looking for federal funding for a pet cause of hers, research on the effects of unpressurized cabins in airplanes. She had already carried out some experiments on her own, assessing the effect of high altitudes on chickens and other farm animals. When her money ran low, she approached the Texas congressman with ties to San Antonio's Randolph Field Medical School, one of the few places in the nation doing research on the subject. She found Lyndon Johnson "terribly interested," and she became a regular at his Washington home, where she went for Sunday brunch and helped Lady Bird change diapers.

By 1948, Cochran was the one in a position to do favors for Lyndon. Her 1936 marriage to Floyd Odlum, head of RKO and one of the richest men in America, provided her with many luxuries, including her own airplane, which she updated at whim and used to flit between both coasts. As a result of her altitude research, she had ties to medical personnel at the most prestigious institutions. Although a lifelong registered Republican, she maintained tight ties with Democrats.

Using a back entrance to the Dallas hospital, as instructed, Cochran took one look at Lyndon and was shocked. Having trained as a nurse, she could size up a patient quickly, and this one looked bad. He lacked color and appeared so listless and dejected that she feared he might die if not treated quickly. When he refused to even consider surgery, she proposed an alternative treatment that she had heard about from her contacts at the Mayo Clinic—a new technique that crushed the kidney stones, then extracted the fragments, without surgery. Lyndon was game.

Cochran quickly converted her plane into a mini-clinic, stocked with painkillers and cots, which she had made up with fresh sheets for Lyndon and the exhausted Bird and aide Warren Woodward. With just one young flight assistant beside her, Cochran took off, headed to Rochester, Minnesota. When Lyndon's pain got so bad he cried for help, she relinquished the controls long enough to administer a narcotic injection. When he sweated through his pajamas, she removed them and wrapped him in sheets and blankets.

On landing in Rochester, Cochran watched medics wheel Lyndon into the clinic, and then she left. She was famous enough that her presence in Rochester might be reported in the papers, leading to speculation about Lyndon's health. He had made very clear he wanted to avoid that. Physicians quickly went to work on him, using the non-invasive technique that required little time for convalescence. A week later Lyndon was back in Texas, ready to resume campaigning.

After all this trauma, the results of the first primary round on July 24 were hard to accept. Lyndon came in second, forcing him into a runoff scheduled for five weeks later. Front-runner Coke Stevenson's lead (he took 40 percent) was bound to grow now that the race had narrowed to just two men and supporters of the eliminated candidates were climbing on the Stevenson bandwagon.

Lyndon went into one of his very worst funks. The prospect of facing more of those long, exhausting days was too much. After all he had put into this fight, another month seemed an impossible stretch, and he wanted to quit. "He was depressed . . . exhausted, depleted. So was I," Lady Bird told an interviewer. Then she corrected herself, explaining she was "exhausted and depleted" but definitely *not* "depressed." That was Lyndon.

Although she, too, had been disappointed with the initial round of the primary, she took it as a challenge to do better in the runoff. While Lyndon prepared his staff to give up, she offered to give her all into keeping his chances alive: "I said I would rather fight and fight and put in everything we could and get all the more money and all the more hours and lose by 50,000 than lose by 71,000. If we could reduce it to 40,000, let's strive for that, and maybe we could bring it down to 25,000 and just possibly, barely, we might win." She had done it again, stepped in at a crucial time to keep the campaign alive.

In preparation for the runoff on August 28, the Johnson camp shifted strategy. Instead of flying helicopters over remote farm fields, they concentrated their efforts on densely populated urban centers. Women organized rallies to attract the female vote, and Bird started accepting invitations to speak at gatherings and on the radio.

Even a serious car accident could not keep her from a scheduled appearance. On the very last day of the campaign, Marietta Brooks was driving her to Seguin for a reception hosted by friends, when on a wet, slippery patch of road Brooks lost control of the car. It flipped, rolled over, and ended up wedged in a ditch, nose in the air. Bird couldn't even get the car door open, and Brooks was too seriously injured to move. Squeezing through a window, Bird made her way to the road and tried to flag down a passing car. The sight of a disheveled woman waving at them caused the first two drivers to speed up, but the next car, with an elderly gentleman at the wheel, stopped. Bird never knew his name, but he helped extricate Brooks, and while he was driving the two women to a doctor, Bird kept regretting that both of them had not voted absentee. The doctor hospitalized Brooks but released Bird, who immediately proceeded to the reception where she was scheduled to greet voters. She had another dress in her overnight bag to replace the torn, dirty one she was wearing, but she had to borrow stockings from her hostess.

After she finished that event, Bird continued another forty miles to San Antonio, where a big rally had been scheduled to celebrate both her husband's birthday and election eve. She didn't say a word to Lyndon about the accident, and he was too busy playing to the crowd to notice her cuts and bruises, severe enough to discolor her legs for months and leave a hard bump on her right thigh.

Unaware of her close call, he issued her an assignment for the following day, which was election Saturday. He wanted her to join his three sisters and mother in a phone blitz of Austin. In a last-minute move to get out the vote, the Johnson women tore the city's phone directory into five segments, and each took responsibility for calling every name on her sheaf of pages.

The first reported tallies justified Bird's optimism about the election. Lyndon looked like a winner. Then Coke Stevenson pulled ahead. For four long days the Johnson camp waited in an Austin hotel, watching the numbers shift and change. Bird likened the tension to that on "a violin string," but she refused to give up the fight. The final count in the primary, showing Lyndon with a paltry eighty-seven votes more than Stevenson, provided a nickname that stuck: "Landslide Lyndon." Charges immediately surfaced that Lyndon's side had tampered with ballot boxes, an embarrassing development after all those campaign spots highlighting Lyndon's honesty and authenticity, touting him as the "Straight Shooter" candidate who could "look you in the eye."

Bird remembered the 1948 election as a turning point in Texas politics. The division between the Regular branch of the Democratic Party and the Loyal segment had widened, and some of the Johnsons' old support had moved away. Even the woman who brought Lyndon and Bird together, Gene Boehringer Lasseter, was deserting them and siding with less liberal Democrats. Losses were part of politics—and the shrewd campaigner in Bird knew that one has to accept some.

The long campaign in 1948 and the anxious wait for results left Bird feeling like she had "climbed to the mountain." It was nearly Christmas before she was ready to celebrate. Back at the house on 30th Place, where nurse Patsy White looked after four-year-old Lynda and toddler Luci (born July 2, 1947), Bird prepared to entertain family and aides over the holidays. Exhausted staffers Mary Rather and Warren Woodward joined with Walter Jenkins and his family to make merry over the political victory and watch Lyndon pass out presents. John Connally, although tired from overseeing the campaign, drove up from Texas with Nellie and their children, arriving on Christmas Eve. It was a jolly end to an exhausting year.

As Bird prepared to join the Senate Wives' Club in 1949, she could look back over a dozen full years as a Washington wife. Once a neophyte, she now considered herself a seasoned player, with two healthy daughters, a flourishing radio station, and a husband eager to make his mark in the U.S. Senate. No one could say she hadn't made good on that vow—to sell him to his worst enemy, who sometimes seemed to be Lyndon himself.

9

"A WONDERFUL, WONDERFUL WIFE"

I N THE Johnson White House, reporter Sarah McClendon was about the last person the president wanted to see. A small woman with a very big voice, she had been covering the capital for a string of small-town newspapers since the 1940s, and he knew her questions could be brazen, her penchant for revealing secrets absolutely infuriating. But in earlier times, McClendon enjoyed a more congenial relationship with the Johnsons. She and Bird came from the same part of East Texas, and in Washington they got together frequently with other transplanted Southerners for after-hours partying and weekend fun. McClendon's daughter, Sally, and Lynda Bird Johnson were classmates at Mrs. Gladstone Williams's charm school.

During that amiable phase, McClendon would go to Lyndon's Washington office for news she could use in an article, and in 1952 she got a story that surprised her. It would have surprised others, too, if she had dared print it at the time. The senator, who had a reputation for paying much more attention to other women than to his wife, had just received a telegram from Lady Bird, who was in Texas, recovering from another miscarriage. Lyndon was so exuberant over the contents of the telegram that he read it aloud to McClendon. His wife had written that she had felt so discouraged after this latest loss that she had considered "dropping out altogether" and not returning to Washington. But then she had changed her mind. She was going to stick with Lyndon and "plan her life along with his, to work beside him in politics or anything that might come up."

It was not Bird's dejection that surprised McClendon. That would be expected in a time of bereavement. Nor was it her resolution—Bird was not a quitter. But Lyndon's reaction to the telegram was as bright as a big neon light proclaiming his feelings for his wife. His face "lit up with love and joy," showing the tough reporter a side of him that she thought few people ever witnessed or understood. The man often depicted as cruel and insensitive to his wife was actually head over heels in love with her. He needed her, and he knew it, and her promise to come back to Washington and continue their partnership was such welcome news he could not keep it to himself.

In fact, Lady Bird Johnson had become what he would later call "a wonderful, wonderful wife," an invaluable asset who served as sounding board, financial manager, network builder, and resolver of family problems. Only she could talk him out of his depressed funks and keep him moving. That was clear by the time he entered the Senate in 1949, and it would be underscored again and again as he kept climbing, first to a leadership position in the Senate and then higher.

Lyndon hadn't been in his Senate seat a week when he and Lady Bird had to decide how to handle a very tricky problem. Southern Democrats were caucusing on how to kill a proposed civil rights bill, and the filibuster was at the top of their list of tools to use. By relying on an old Senate rule that allowed unlimited debate, a minority could talk a bill they despised right into oblivion. *The Dallas Morning News*, where Dawson Duncan, Bird's one-time date at UT, still worked, was watching the state's brand-new senator very closely, and when he didn't show up at the Southern Democrats' meeting, the *News* reported his absence. Puzzled readers understandably questioned why anyone would skip a caucus, especially one on this important topic. Did Senator Johnson have something to hide about how he stood on civil rights?

Lyndon had already unveiled his thinking on the subject to his aide, Horace Busby, telling him that he and Lady Bird had been talking over the matter "for the last several nights . . . And we both feel very strongly that we did not come to the Senate to engage in filibusters, and I don't expect to be part of a filibuster this year." Of course, Lyndon couldn't admit that publicly. Not when so many of his Texas voters were counting on the filibuster to save them from a change they abhorred. When reporters tried to track him down, he used every trick he knew to avoid them, darting in and out of doorways and then taking refuge in the dining room reserved for "Members Only."

But he couldn't keep running, and Dawson Duncan's paper reported that the senator and his wife *both* changed their minds. Rather than play the maverick (and endanger his reelection) Lyndon would go along with his Southern colleagues on the filibuster. Georgia senator Richard Russell, a staunch opponent of the proposed civil rights bill, offered to mentor him, as Speaker Sam Rayburn had in the House of Representatives, and both Johnsons were more than willing. Bird began inviting Russell to her home, where he was such a frequent guest that the Johnson daughters started calling him "Uncle Dickie." The patrician bachelor could be a bit reserved and aloof, not a relaxed, casual guest like Speaker Rayburn. But that did not deter Bird from finding out how Russell liked his black-eyed peas and turnip greens and then serving them whenever he came over.

Bird was in the visitors' gallery, along with secretary Mary Rather, when Lyndon gave his "maiden" speech to the Senate on March 9. She listened as he attacked President Harry Truman's new civil rights initiative and *defended* the filibuster as a legitimate tool to use against its passage. Lyndon pointed out that President Truman faced no limits on how long he spoke, and neither should senators. Using a bit of cowboy talk, he concluded: "No mount is free once the bit is in his mouth."

Fully aware that her husband had to straddle a barbed ideological fence to survive in Texas politics, Lady Bird turned on her warmest smile and gracious hospitality to keep him from getting bloodied. While he won over colleagues with genial cloakroom talk, leading to his election as his party's whip in 1951 at the phenomenally young age of forty-two, she showered everyone with generous invitations and unfailing charm. Criticism was a language she never mastered; confrontation was not in her vocabulary. A wife like Eleanor Roosevelt, who expressed strong views of her own, would have made Lyndon's balancing act more difficult. A less supportive wife, or one with a greater commitment to self and children, would not have had the time and energy to host as many dinners and teas as Bird did. If she had refused to pick up and move twice a year, between Texas and Washington, she would not have been able to chat up powerful figures in the capital and then stand at Lyndon's side when he spoke to voters back home.

Mrs. Johnson had always maintained an open house for staff and friends, and now, as a senator's wife, she operated a virtual hospitality center for a wide range of guests, including the capital's most powerful leaders and their spouses. The house on 30th Place was not large, but she could accommodate a dozen or so Senate wives for lunch, and she knew how hard it was for senators to be harsh on each other if their wives were sharing a chicken salad a few blocks away.

Single men and men whose wives remained back in their home state were often at a loss for something to do on weekends, and they knew that the Johnsons' door was always open. Even those who appeared without warning at mealtime were warmly welcomed. Bird would just tell the cook to add some filler to the main course.

Bill Moyers, who joined Senator Johnson's staff in 1954, described how Bird's generosity worked. When she invited him for Sunday brunch, Moyers, a Texas Baptist, had no idea what she was talking about, and knowing she was Episcopalian, he decided brunch might be something that Episcopalians did on Sunday. He arrived about eleven in the morning of the appointed day and found three of the most influential men in Washington sitting in the dining room, reading the morning papers—Speaker of the House Sam Rayburn; Senate icon Richard Russell; and FBI director J. Edgar Hoover, who lived across the street.

Each of those men played an important part in Lyndon's success and two of them would continue to figure in his viability in the White House. (Rayburn died in November 1961.) What other Washington wife could have attracted such a distinguished lineup to her table?

Women who knew Bird best maintained she always stayed a bit detached in her relationships. She never became so fully involved in an effort or so committed to an individual that she could not disassociate herself, in order to reposition herself into more neutral territory. Marjorie "Marny" Clifford, wife of the prominent attorney Clark Clifford, observed that Bird remembered "everything," but she kept things separate, using "pigeonholes in her mind that open when she wants them to." She had the gift of making the person with her at any given minute feel her full attention—an ego enhancer for even the loftiest of senators. When Lyndon inquired how she managed to capture the attention of the most important person in the room and then keep it for much of the evening, she replied: "I don't know. I just asked him, 'Tell me all about yourself.'"

Lyndon's Senate colleagues included some very wealthy men, like Robert Kerr, of the famed Kansas oil family, and Clinton Anderson, who had made a fortune in insurance in New Mexico. Both Kerr and Anderson entertained with flair in their home states, staging grandiose parties in houses that easily accommodated dozens. If Lyndon planned to stay in their league, he needed a showier residence in his home state than the unremarkable duplex on Austin's Dillman Street, and he immediately focused on an area he knew well—the Hill Country where he had grown up.

One place in particular appealed—the 240-acre ranch that had been in his family for decades. Just down the road from the little house where he was born, it had most recently belonged to his Aunt Frank and her husband, who liked to host summer picnics and holiday get-togethers. Lyndon treasured such special memories of the house, it was one of the first places he took Bird, and in 1951 he bought what would quickly become known as the LBJ Ranch.

The house had deteriorated considerably under Aunt Frank's ownership. After her husband died and her son went his own way, she lacked the energy to oversee repairs and updating. With its sagging beams and dangling eaves, the structure looked to Bird like a haunted house out of Charles Addams. Rather than try to rehabilitate it, she thought it wiser to follow the advice of her friend Neva West, who suggested demolishing it. It was the house's superb setting that made the new owners reconsider. Perched high enough to provide a good view of both the winding Pedernales River down below and the setting sun behind the undulating hills to the back, it stood on the perfect spot for a house. Why not salvage at least the foundation and some of the walls? Bird set to work to turn the ruins into what she called her "heart's home."

In order to make the house livable as quickly as possible, Bird spent several weeks in early 1952 in the Austin area. Making innumerable drives between her mother-in-law's house on Harris Boulevard, where she slept, and the ranch seventy miles west, Bird acted as contractor and purchasing agent. For advice, she relied on old friends, including architect Max Brooks. Before his sudden death in October 1951, Senator Wirtz had walked the land with her to advise on where to block the river's flow with small dams; neighbor A. W. Moursund contributed his ideas on converting the neglected fields and slumping buildings into a working ranch.

This was not the first time Bird had left Lyndon in Washington for an extended period, but this separation was different from the one in 1943 when she got KTBC up and running. Now the couple had two daughters, aged eight and five, and Lyndon found himself in the rare role of parent-in-charge.

Lynda, the older, had developed a special *simpatia* with her grandmother Rebekah Johnson, whom she called "Madda," but neither girl had had much chance to form a tight bond with either parent. Lyndon worked late hours, and both he and Bird were often separated from the girls for days or weeks at a time. Marie Fehmer, one of Lyndon's secretaries, observed that they grew up "almost orphans in a sense." Fehmer concluded that her boss never understood his daughters and "they don't understand him."

That disconnect was already obvious in a letter he wrote to Bird, describing a Sunday in May 1952 when she was busy at the ranch. Thinking to please his daughters, he took them to an amusement park. But the outing quickly soured for all three. The bossy older Lynda insisted on supervising her little sister and choosing rides for both of them. That riled Luci. To smooth things over, their father joined them in a ride on fast-moving, colliding cars, which he called "whip outfits," but he found it scary and unpleasant. Although he was only forty-three, he was "completely worn out" and decided the girls "should be my grandchildren instead of my children." Grateful when a light rain started, he welcomed an excuse to cut the excursion short.

He fared even worse when he got the girls home. They continued to wrangle, and when Luci, who had a cold, refused to sleep with Lynda, Lynda "got her feelings hurt at her sister's lack of affection and insisted on sleeping with me. That meant I did not sleep any." Then "Luci woke up and insisted that she did not want to sleep alone and that she had a sore throat." Finally, the girls wound up in their own beds, leaving him free to watch the 7 a.m. morning news. In framing what is probably the most extensive written account he ever gave of his relationship with his daughters during their early years, Lyndon relied on a typist. So the words may not be all his. But he left no doubt that he was "counting the days" until Bird returned to take charge. If parenting was not Bird's forte, it was even less Lyndon's.

After the girls passed the age of needing a baby nurse, Bird expanded the list of caregivers whom she could count on to take over while she tended to her investments and catered to Lyndon. Besides the domestic staff, she used her husband's secretaries and other office aides, and Willie Day Taylor (no relation to Bird) became a favorite. She had left the University of Texas just before graduation in 1948 to join the Johnson election team, and the job became her life. Unmarried, with a pronounced limp and a very limited social life, she worked a full day in the office as press aide and then stayed after five to take care of Lynda and Luci. While Bird attended Senate wives' gatherings and went off with Lyndon to receptions with other power couples, it was Willie Day Taylor who oversaw play dates and became such a beloved nurturer that Luci begged to spend weekends at her home.

In other ways, Bird looked for the cheapest solutions regarding her daughters. She had Lynda's hair cut in an easy-to-keep Dutch boy bob, which suited neither her face nor contemporary style, and she negotiated with a beauty shop in Austin to cut and style her hair and that of her daughters in return for airtime on KTBC. Later in life, when she looked over photos of the girls as youngsters, she admitted, "I hadn't been as good a mother as I should. They were too fat, and also I had not paid enough attention to their clothes. But, one divides the hours of one's life as best we can."

When Lynda was ready to start first grade in September 1950, her parents decided to split her school year the same way they divided their time, half in Washington and half in Austin. Since it looked like the legislative talks would continue late that summer, Bird returned to Texas ahead of Lyndon and enrolled their six-year-old in Miss Hubrick's school just down the street from the Dillman Street duplex. Four months later, when Congress convened in January, Bird withdrew Lynda and took her back to Washington and entered her in school there. It was an unsatisfactory arrangement, and Bird could see that change upset her daughter. But she stuck to the plan because it suited her and Lyndon's work schedules.

In September 1952, when the family was finally installed at the LBJ Ranch, Lynda started attending the Johnson City school, only a few miles away. But in January, she had to say good-bye to her newly made friends and start all over with a different teacher in Washington. Anyone could see it was a rough adaptation for an elementary school child. Bird realized her older daughter lacked playmates and was getting pudgy by the time she turned eight.

At age ten, Lynda developed a mysterious medical problem that attracted some long overdue parental attention—at least from her mother. That year—1954—was particularly stressful in the Johnson household. Bird miscarried again in April, and while the Senate grappled with how to treat Senator Joseph McCarthy for raising sullying charges against a list of persons he accused of communist leanings, Bird took off with Mary Rather for a restorative cruise in the Caribbean. That summer, when Lynda started going into baffling "spasmodic, uncontrollable movements, jerkings" that doctors in Austin could not explain, her mother took her to Scott & White, a medical center in College Station, Texas. During the three-hour drives from the ranch for each consultation, Lynda finally had her mother to herself, and the two learned to sing along together.

When doctors prescribed home rest, Lynda didn't have to go to school anywhere for the months of September and October, giving her an unprecedented amount of time with her mother. In November, when doctors pronounced Lynda well enough to resume school half-time, she enrolled in St. Andrews, a small Episcopal School near the ranch, where she received "special care and attention." By Christmas, she was "quite all right again." Although Bird worried about the illness (and thought the spasms affected Lynda's handwriting into adulthood), Lyndon showed little concern. Bird judged him "impatient" with their daughter, as if she fell ill to spite him, and years later was still "mad" that Lyndon "wasn't as understanding as I think he ought to have been."

Anyone doing an efficiency study of the Johnson household would have rated Lady Bird a top-notch manager. At the house on 30th Place she nosed out the best bargains on cleaning supplies, insisted on multiple estimates for repairs, and kept upgrading the property. The house had a constantly shifting cast of characters, with visiting relatives, not-yet-settled staff, and Texans passing through Washington, but they all had to fit around husband, wife, and two little girls. Lyndon remained the kingpin, his needs and wishes paramount at all times, beginning with breakfast served in bed. Bird explained to an aide that she lit on that solution after having trouble getting him to the table while his eggs were still warm.

To keep all three households running smoothly, Lady Bird supervised a constantly shifting staff of cooks, cleaners, repair people, yard workers, and caterers in each place. She had her mainstays, such as Zephyr Wright, née Black, who moved with the Johnsons back and forth between Washington and Texas, and Helen and Gene Williams, who joined the household in 1952 and became durable, valued employees. Amiable Helen got along with everyone, even "more or less" with the sometimes snappish Zephyr. Helen could size up Lyndon's swiftly shifting moods as well as anyone. She patiently taught little Luci to bake cookies, and she helped out with child care when needed. Gene Williams did gardening, heavy household chores, and whatever else needed doing. Since he wore the same size shoe as Lyndon, he broke in his boss's new purchases so the busy senator never had to worry about suffering from blistered heels or bruised toes. Gene Williams did balk at one assignment: When Lyndon asked him to take the family dog on his next driving trip to Texas, he refused, explaining, "It's hard enough for me [an African American] to find a place to sleep [on these cross-country trips]. Can you imagine what it would be like if I had a dog?"

Besides everything else she did to help Lyndon win elections and stay as popular as possible with his colleagues, Bird was the one who had to look after Lyndon's two exceedingly needy siblings. Two of his sisters—the youngest, Lucia, and the oldest, Rebekah—remained settled in apparently happy lives. Rebekah's husband, Oscar, went to work for KTBC after finishing law school, and her son Philip (born 1948) struck Bird as incredibly neat, his clothes remaining as spanking clean as when he first put them on.

But the other two, brother Sam Houston and middle sister Josefa, continued to supply the headaches. Sam Houston couldn't keep a job. A tall, good-looking charmer who fancied himself more talented than Lyndon, he was still drinking too much and that excess consumption, along with extravagant spending, wiped out any advantages accruing from either looks or brains. His marriage to Albertine Summers in 1940 ended in divorce after the birth of two children, and his dissipation continued. In 1948, his relationship with one of his brother's secretaries produced a child, Rodney, who was promptly adopted by Josefa and her husband. In spite of Lyndon's finding Sam Houston job after job, he continued to decline—in health and reliability. In the bad periods, Bird found herself checking him in and out of hospitals more often than she could count. Lyndon admitted he was inclined to give up on his brother, but Bird clung to the hope she could save him.

Josefa, the sister Bird found most congenial, was even more exasperating. Tall and attractive, Josefa achieved a reputation in college for "looseness" and "wildness" and drinking too much. Her promiscuous pairings were not youthful indiscretions that abated with the years—they continued into adulthood. As Lyndon's career soared, he had to turn to staff and supporters to help bail her out of multiple scrapes.

Like Lyndon, Josefa had periods of very high productivity, during which she campaigned effectively for him and recruited other women to do the same. Then she dropped into listless downs or flaunted her licentious behavior. One reporter who observed her at various political conventions claimed, "If there was a man to be picked up, Josefa picked him up." By the time Josefa turned forty, Bird described her as "bedeviled with drink and too much medication." Hard as Bird worked to rescue her, putting her up at 30th Place for months at a time and ferrying her to doctors' appointments, nothing worked. Josefa remained "in very bad shape."

As if Bird did not have enough family drama on Lyndon's side, she had to contend with the troubles of her own relatives. Her father, now in his seventies, had lost the swagger of his younger years and the ability to drive a sharp bargain. With a dubious business partner he ran up huge debts in 1949 and then could not repay them. Bird and Lyndon enlisted help to bail T.J. out, but it was a sad comedown for the once proud man who liked being called "Mr. Boss." He eventually found some forgotten bank stock of his own to offset his debts, but he could no longer brag about either his business know-how or his physical fitness. Signs of arteriosclerosis, which complicated his circulation and made his last years miserable, were already showing up.

Bird's strained relationship with her stepmother, Ruth, had worsened. Worried about the possibility that T.J.'s heirs might face difficulties when he died, leaving lots of land but little cash to pay the inheritance taxes, the Johnsons engaged a lawyer friend to help him set up an irrevocable trust to shield the estate from taxes. T.J. was amenable and signed the document while his wife was away, a move that infuriated her when she came back. She insisted on invalidating the arrangement. Even after receiving a careful explanation of the meaning of "irrevocable," she remained adamant, and the attorney was reduced to taking the blame, saying he had not fully spelled out the consequences to T.J. After the irrevocable will was nullified, T.J. was free to make a new will, which he did, without involving Lady Bird, who surmised correctly that it favored his young wife over his three children.

The bright spot in all this financial gloom was Bird's broadcasting business. It was doing well, producing the income essential to keeping her family comfortable. Under the careful management of Jesse Kellam after 1946, KTBC had turned in steady profits, and by 1952 Bird submitted papers to the FCC showing that her original investment of $17,500 was now worth nearly half a million dollars. KTBC had returned a healthy profit the previous year of $57,983, equivalent to almost half a million in 2014 dollars. Bigger fortune lay ahead. Bird's decision to invest in TV and bet on VHF rather than UHF would turn out to be propitious.

Embarrassing questions would continue to arise about how much she had been favored by the FCC. It looked very suspicious that the FCC had granted only one VHF license to Austin (population 160,000) and granted it to her, giving her a monopoly. Much smaller cities were assigned more stations. Johnson critics noted that channel 7, owned by the senator's wife (whose business name was always Claudia T. Johnson), could charge high rates for TV advertising because it lacked competition.

The timing also looked suspicious. From more than seven hundred applications that the FCC received from across the nation, after its four-year freeze, it singled out only eighteen for immediate approval, and one of the eighteen came from the wife of a man who sat on the Senate's Commerce Committee, to whom the FCC reported. Leonard Marks, the communications lawyer who had encouraged Bird to invest in television in the first place, insisted that her application had been carefully scrutinized by many investigators over many years, and not one bit of evidence surfaced to show any improper interference. But of course not all interference gets recorded on paper.

An account of the Johnsons' intricate maneuvering in the media world of the 1940s and 1950s would make a book of its own, but the short version is that fortune came quickly. When managers of KWTX in nearby Waco objected that Bird's proposal to increase broadcast strength would cut into their turf, she bought a small UHF station in Waco. She then negotiated with KWTX to sign over to her 29 percent of its stock in return for the right to use her network affiliation. The value of that stock grew exponentially so that by 1964 it was worth an estimated $600,000. Her investment in the Weslaco broadcasting station in the Rio Grande Valley also showed a remarkably large and quick gain— something over a hundred percent in just a couple of years. When two cable companies competed for Austin's market, the corporation Bird controlled voted to team up with the eventual winner.

Through it all, T. J. Taylor's daughter kept careful watch over operations. In her small office on the second floor at 30th Place, she signed every check, except for payroll, and monitored the staff's detailed reports that came to her every week. She wanted to see how the station's earnings on any single day compared to those of two years earlier. In the margins she made her suggestions, including how to word sales pitches to potential advertisers. She demanded a full accounting of all purchases and procedures, including what to offer new hires and how much was spent on toilet paper. Station employees understood that they couldn't bluff when dealing with her. If she asked them a question, they had better know the answer, and it had to make sense. A *Wall Street Journal* reporter concluded that she "deserved credit for effective attention to both grand strategy and minutiae of business right up to the time her husband became President."

Those profits were essential to the Johnsons' lifestyle and to their sense of security. His salary of $12,500 was not nearly enough to staff and run three households (Washington, Austin, and the ranch). His leadership position earned him a bit extra, and he had additional allotments for staff and travel, but he needed more than he earned to keep upgrading his cattle herds, to say nothing of the expensive boats and cars he liked acquiring. Bird had absorbed her father's intense fear of being left poor, as his own mother had been, and she knew how important a thriving business could be to Lyndon's continued political climb.

The Texas papers left no doubt that Lyndon Johnson was headed for a bright future and he had a wife who would help. In 1949, the *News* had headlined one of its articles, "Young-Man-Going-Places," and explained how Lyndon managed that by keeping everyone happy. If he had to go against the president, he gave advance notice, to ward off possible anger or disappointment. He had delivered so many favors to constituents that when he voted for measures they did not want (public housing, slum clearance, and aid to education) he knew voters would stick with him. The *News* concluded that the state's young senator had figured out how to make a name for himself. He maintained strong ties with the leaders that counted while he "ate, slept and dreamed strategy that would lead to influence."

The senator's wife kept up a busy schedule to supplement his list of contacts, and she got noticed. As a congressman's spouse, she had rated barely a mention at national charity benefits and political fund-raisers, but now she got a seat at the head table. Earlier she had contented herself with a cup of tea at receptions; now she was asked to pour, giving her a new level of prominence and allowing her to talk with almost everyone in attendance. She never missed a chance to make a friend for Lyndon.

In the blitz of publicity that he received, she was credited—not so much for her social skills and campaign role as for her business savvy. When respected reporter Paul F. Healy wrote a May 1951 article for the popular *Saturday Evening Post*, he titled it, "The Frantic Gentleman from Texas," and described how a lovable Lyndon, though clearly not an intellectual, used his "dogged Texas charm" to win the favor of his colleagues. According to Healy, Senator Johnson had his quirks— a tendency to talk too much on the phone, an incredible ignorance about Hollywood (he didn't even know who Lana Turner was), and so little interest in sports that he talked politics at football games. But his staff adored him. Though overworked and underpaid, they remained among the most loyal and enthusiastic employees on Capitol Hill because of their admiration for their boss.

Healy made Lady Bird sound like Superwoman, essential to Lyndon's success and a power in her own right. Healy called her the "staple pivot," the woman who made sure her man did not "burn out or break down." On her own she had compiled an enviable record as a "clever business woman who owns and runs by remote control a profitable radio station in Austin and looks out for her 3000 acres of cotton and timber land in Alabama." Besides keeping her husband's fountain pens filled, his wardrobe laid out, and the table set for any number of guests he decided to bring home for dinner, she continued to welcome his constituents who visited Washington. Even in heavy snowstorms, she drove them around to see the sights.

By the end of 1954, Bird could read in *U.S. News & World Report* that her husband was on its list of "History Makers," alongside such international powerhouses as Ho Chi Minh, Nehru, and Mao Zedong. Just weeks earlier, another article had hinted that he had presidential potential in the next election: "Knowland and Johnson in '56?"

A lot of Washingtonians didn't like Lyndon Johnson, and many bristled at his blatant egotism and self-promotion. Katie Louchheim, leader of the Democratic Women's Division, listed the multiple ways he annoyed people: "antagonizing the press. . . . Giving them little admonishing lectures before and after hearings. And having a news ticker in his office." Everything pointed to outsized aspirations: "his eyes turned up PA Ave. His ambition . . . so overpowering, it insults you." By early 1955, Louchheim complained that a seat alongside him at dinner meant listening to one topic the whole evening—Lyndon. After regaling her with a litany of his "operations and ailments" during the soup and fish courses, he moved on to brag about what *he* would do for his fellow senators. She was inclined to agree with him on the latter point ("no one will do it better") but she found his braggadocio hard to take.

Louchheim found nothing offputting about Lady Bird. After a critical survey of all the women present one particular evening, catty Louchheim described Hubert Humphrey's wife, Muriel, as presentable in a dress she had made herself, but the prize "for poise and peculiar beauty" went to Mrs. Johnson. Although lacking "a single good feature," she possessed the "charm and a leisurely paced intelligent, lacquered veneer that takes on greatness." In her "black tulle [dress] 'with little touches of pink'" she remained unfailingly courteous while her needy husband was "rapidly becoming her 'charge,' her ridiculously impossible charge." Together, the two showed a remarkable fit: the tightly reined wife alongside a husband "wound up from here to eternity."

Husband and wife could divide the territory, with her showing up at social events while he took care of work. In a "Washington Scene" piece in the *New Orleans Times-Picayune* on May 26, 1953, columnist George Dixon described Lady Bird as enjoying what Lyndon dismissed as "gallivanting," while he worked himself to a "frazzle." When Bird chided him that another senator, eighty-five-year-old Theodore Francis Green of Rhode Island, had been at the party she just left, a party Lyndon refused to attend because of Senate work, he was annoyed. "Migawd," he replied. "I stayed on the Hill all night working to get [Green's] bill through."

On the morning of July 2, 1955, Bird had to choose how to spend the day. Daughter Luci turned eight that day, and she wanted a party; Lyndon, frazzled by the stress of Senate leadership (he had been elected

Democratic majority leader in January), had other plans. With his ego swollen by recent national attention, he thought he deserved some time to himself, without rambunctious eight-year-olds anywhere around. Just a week earlier, *Newsweek* headlined him as the "Texan Who Is Jolting Washington"; earlier that year, *The New York Times* had named him one of the few "Who Will Run Congress." But in spite of all the kudos, he had had a tough year, and the long days, heavy smoking, and poor eating habits showed in his lined face. He clearly needed respite from a punishing schedule, but that morning his wife chose their daughter, a decision she would reverse by nightfall.

While Bird tended to her daughter that Saturday, Lyndon confronted inquisitive journalists, who pressed him with questions until he lost his temper and gave one of the reporters a tongue-lashing. Then, discouraged by how things were going, Lyndon wolfed down an unhealthy lunch of baked beans and frankfurters and directed his driver to take him to Middleburg, Virginia. He could always count on finding refuge at Huntland, the farm retreat owned by his long-time backer, George Brown. Although Brown's official residence was still in Texas, he and his wife often entertained at Huntland, and the Johnsons had an open invitation to join them. With old cronies like the Browns, Lyndon could forget D.C. troubles and irritating reporters. He could say whatever he wanted without worrying that it would show up in the next morning's paper. The fact that Bird stayed behind meant that Lyndon would feel freer to drink more, without worrying about her keeping tabs on his intake.

By late afternoon when he reached Huntland, he had an upset stomach but attributed it to the heavy lunch. His friends thought otherwise. Senator Clinton Anderson, another guest, recognized the symptoms of a heart attack because he had recently suffered the same himself. The Browns summoned a local doctor, who advised rushing Lyndon to a hospital. Within the hour, he was on a stretcher, headed to Bethesda Medical Center. The pain was excruciating but, when told that stopping to administer medication would cost precious time, he instructed the driver to "keep going."

Through the hour-long trip, Lyndon kept up a conversation with Frank Oltorf, the Brown employee who sat beside him in the back of a hearse that doubled as ambulance. The two men had known each other for more than a decade, and they tried to get through the stressful ride by reminiscing about a woman they both knew—Alice Glass— although Oltorf would refuse to divulge what either of them said. Lyndon clearly understood the gravity of his condition when he queried the physician, who was riding in the front seat beside the driver: "Doctor, let me ask you something. Will I ever be able to smoke again if this is a heart attack?" When the doctor replied that he would not, Lyndon sighed and said, "I'd rather have my pecker cut off."

Then Lyndon turned talk back to end-of-life matters. He told Oltorf about the will he had made, a copy of which he had left in the bottom drawer of his desk at the radio station. To thwart any misunderstanding of his intentions, Lyndon spelled out the will's provisions: "I just want to tell you what I want. I want Lady Bird to have everything I have. . . . She's been a wonderful, wonderful wife, and she's done so much for me. She just deserves everything that I have."

IO

STRUGGLING WITH
BALANCE AND MOMENTUM

THE PHONE CALL Lady Bird Johnson made one Sunday morning in 1959 could not have been easy. She was in Texas with Lyndon and realized that there was no way she could keep her promise to her daughters to be back in Washington with them by that evening. Lyndon needed her, and he always came first. Yet the telephone call was distressing. As she kept trying to explain that something had come up to detain her, Luci threw a tantrum. She became very emotional, "got frantic . . . screamed and yelled" that she wanted her mother back by nightfall. Finally Lynda took the phone and said, "Don't worry, Mamma. We'll take care of her. You stay. I understand that you have to stay. You come as soon as you can, and we'll look after Luci."

That call, showing the difficulties of balancing family and work, took place when the Johnson daughters were in their early teens. But they had lost their mother's primary attention years earlier. In fairness to her, it should be noted that the children of other political couples complained of being similarly shuffled aside by career-conscious parents. Sally MacDonald, daughter of journalist Sarah McClendon and part of the same informal group of "Texas kids" as Luci and Lynda, explained how peripheral she and the others felt to their parents' busy lives. The "kids" were taught to smile for photographers and look for their "toe marks" in picture lineups, but otherwise remain invisible. MacDonald decided political couples "didn't know or care" what happened to family. They preferred to "step over the kids, throw people out." She remembered Lyndon as particularly insensitive to his daughters' feelings—he referred to Lynda as the brainy one and Luci as the beauty.

Although Lady Bird did better than her husband at showing her affection, it was a struggle to give attention to family while also overseeing a thriving business and adding momentum to a flourishing political career. Whenever she phoned, to catch up on what her daughters were doing, she always ended the conversation with, "Remember you are loved." Sally MacDonald, who witnessed many of these exchanges, found the sign-off "hokey" at the time, but as an adult, with a daughter of her own, she admitted she became "teary" just thinking about how hard the busy senator's wife, pulled in many directions, kept trying to remain connected to the girls she obviously loved. Sally did not note, but it is all too clear: the message was delivered in the passive voice, rather than the more direct "I love you."

Never the recipient of much mothering herself, Bird remained detached, out of touch with what young girls needed and what their contemporaries were wearing and doing. She took Lynda to a pediatrician until age twelve, when the daughter rebelled. With height and heft to appear older than her years, she had been mistaken by the receptionist as the mother of nine-year-old Luci. Splitting the academic year, half in Washington and half in Texas, made it hard for the girls to keep friends and maintain academic continuity. But their mother kept them in that pattern until 1958, when school officials intervened and insisted the girls stick with the same school through the academic year.

The choice was Washington, which meant that, except for vacations, they lived at 30th Place, even when their parents were back in Texas for long stretches and could speak only by phone. Luci likened her treatment to neglect and described her youth as deprived. She accused Bird of not being "a real mother. A real mother stays home." The more sanguine Lynda blamed the situation, more than the individuals, and she often reminded her mother that Washington was made for legislators and their spouses but it was no place for children.

It wasn't that Bird didn't love her daughters—she simply put other responsibilities ahead of them. That was the life she had chosen. She was not the only first lady to make that choice. Theodore Roosevelt's wife, Edith, usually described by historians as a model for all presidents' wives, admitted privately that she would "not have hesitated to chop all my children into pieces for their father." In the twenty-nine years that Edith survived Theodore, she remained so cruelly judgmental and neglectful of her children and their offspring that one of her great-granddaughters described her as "mean as a snake." Bird, who had a little longer than Edith to mend family ties, did much better. She traveled in her widowed years with her daughters and showered their children and grandchildren with enormous affection. At her funeral, the outpouring of warmth and fondness for "Nini," as the younger set dubbed her, showed no hint of the disappointment registered earlier by Luci and Lynda.

Lady Bird's decision to elevate her husband's needs over those of her children became abundantly clear in 1955, when he was hospitalized for a month after his heart attack. Except for two brief breaks, she remained within hearing distance around-the-clock so that her feet could "hit the floor" whenever he called for her. That meant that Lynda, aged eleven, and Luci, eight, were left to the care of Willie Day Taylor and other hired help, and they were, as George Reedy, their father's aide, pointed out, further "deprived of [Bird's] presence and her motherhood."

Of course Lady Bird was concerned, as any wife would be, to receive a phone call July 2 telling her that her husband was being rushed to the Naval Medical Center in Bethesda with what appeared to be a heart attack. The center was less than ten miles from 30th Place, and in the light traffic of the holiday weekend she drove herself quickly to the hospital and arrived before Lyndon. From the waiting room, she could not see his big frame being lifted out on a stretcher but when he was carried into the cardiac unit on the seventeenth floor, the sight of his pallid, sunken face shocked her. In twenty-one years of marriage, she had seen him hospitalized again and again for respiratory infections and kidney stones, but never, even with the excruciating pain of a ready-to-burst appendix, had he looked this bad. His attempt at humor did nothing to quell her fears. He had just been measured for two new suits, and now he told her to "go ahead with the blue" since he could use that "no matter what happens."

Aides Walter Jenkins and George Reedy, who had also been summoned to Bethesda that sultry Saturday evening, knew Bird well enough to expect full control, total calm. The woman who rarely cried (and was mortified when Lyndon began weeping during a scene of the movie *The Grapes of Wrath*) stayed stoic. Her face a mirror of composure, she kept reassuring Lyndon, "Honey, everything will be all right." She watched, without a word, as he smoked what he promised would be his last cigarette, and turned "gray as pavement, motionless as stone, and cold to touch." Then Dr. J. Willis Hurst, the young cardiologist on duty that Independence Day weekend, explained that in cases like this, of myocardial infarction, the survival rate was only fifty-fifty; the first few hours would be critical.

Before Lyndon went into shock and was wheeled away, he rattled off instructions—how to find his will and where to get a second opinion on the competence of Dr. Hurst. But his most emphatic order concerned Bird: "stay here. I'd rather fight this with you beside me." He could have saved his breath on that one.

Since Lyndon's election to Senate majority leader in January, Bird had struggled to get him in better health. He had put on noticeable weight, and none of her subtle advice to eat less had the least restraining effect. He had already been hospitalized once that year, for kidney stone surgery, and was going frequently to doctors with complaints of sore throat and fatigue. He looked stressed, but she knew it was useless to encourage him to slow down—too much depended on making his mark as the most effective Senate leader in history. Much as she wanted him to take things easier, she could not forget that it had been his tremendous ambition that had attracted her to him in the first place.

For the entire four weeks he stayed at the medical center, she watched over him like a mother in a neonatal ward, and as his chances of survival improved, his hospital suite became a virtual office, with her in charge. With typewriter-topped desks filling much of the space and his aides coming and going, the white-capped nurses looked oddly out of place. This setup was against all the rules, and Dr. Hurst knew that. Complete rest was the prescribed medicine for cardiac patients. But in this case, he had decided he had a patient who didn't heal without the spur of work; only the push of a bustling office would pull him through.

Even with that concession, Lyndon's recuperation did not proceed smoothly. Always a worrier, he kept voicing reservations about how his replacement as majority leader was doing. Even more, he worried that he himself was losing precious ground. The 1956 presidential election was little more than a year away, and newspapers across the nation had taken his name off the list of potential candidates. After an AP story ran under the headline "Heart Attack Drops Johnson from White House Hopefuls," Lyndon became really depressed. His brother insisted that he had found him in tears, mumbling, "I'll never get a chance to be President now."

Lady Bird could see how distraught he had become, and she called in a physician she trusted even more than Dr. Hurst—Dr. James Cain, the Mayo Clinic internist who had married Senator Wirtz's daughter Ida May and become close to the Johnsons. Cain's diagnosis was alarming. Although he emphasized that heart attack patients typically become depressed, he had rarely seen a depression as deep as Lyndon's.

Cain's dire pronouncements were underscored by reports of aides and secretarial staff who had to deal with Lyndon's despondency every day. Much as they tried to make allowances, mindful of the disappointment he would understandably feel at being sidelined at age forty-seven, possibly for life, they found his mood swings exasperating. George Reedy struggled to wring decisions out of him and then to navigate through conflicting orders and unreasonable demands. Secretary Mary Rather remembered the convalescence as a "quiet, long, lonesome, sad" time. Booth Mooney, a Johnson staffer since 1953, reported that his boss started having nightmares about his incapacity. In the worst episodes, he panicked at the prospect of becoming as immobilized as his paralyzed Grandmother Bunton or as dispossessed and impotent as President Woodrow Wilson after his 1919 stroke.

Lady Bird had two decades of dealing with Lyndon's mood slumps, and she started looking for what would bring him out now. As the person who knew him best, she zeroed in on the thousands of well-wishing letters and cards that poured in, mostly from Texas but some from as far away as India. Knowing how her man cherished words of loving support, she started reading the messages to him, even when he lacked the energy to lift his head from the pillow. She pasted the most poignant, handwritten messages in fat scrapbooks so he could keep them at his side and pat them for reassurance, even in the dark of night. In addition to the letters, he received an array of gifts, and she kept reminding him of them: enough flowers to open a shop, along with piles of books, crates of soft drinks, and half a dozen watermelons. Staff followed Bird's lead and clipped upbeat editorials from formerly unfriendly newspapers to add to the cheerleading pile.

For a man who fed on adulation, it was a virtual feast. Lyndon became obsessive about those letters, picking them up and tracing the writing on the page as if to confirm the existence of each word. Then he decided every one of them deserved an individual response. Completely disregarding the fact that his staff was already overworked and worn out, he ordered them to answer every single letter. Bird would handle the personal ones, writing by hand to people she and her husband knew, but staff had to type up all the others. Laboring long hours, aides accomplished a seemingly impossible task, and thousands of letters went out.

Even with all that encouragement, Lyndon had times when he despaired of ever resuming his old life. Walter Jenkins reported that he would be fine for a few days, outlining big plans for the future. Then, suddenly, for no observable reason, he would lapse into a dejected silence and lose interest in everything around him. One minute he was barking orders like a general and the next he became morose; he wanted no one near him.

When doctors pronounced the patient well enough to travel, he flew in a private plane to Texas to observe his August 27 birthday and continue his convalescence at the ranch. This began the Johnsons' fourth year in that house, and what looked like the home of a relatively prosperous rancher was quickly converted to a rehab center. Bird installed everything required for the patient's comfort and recovery—a special bed, a huge TV, multiple sunlamps, and an array of exercise equipment. To accommodate his staffers George Reedy, Jim Rowe, and others, she put up card tables in the living room so three secretaries could work simultaneously. She installed extra phone lines to maintain communication with the rest of the world, and made hospitality arrangements for the parade of important visitors she expected to pass through.

Among the many guests who came to talk with the newly skinny, tanned Lyndon were political leaders from all over the state, along with national celebrities, including Arthur Godfrey and Adlai Stevenson. Old friends like Sam Rayburn and Les and Liz Carpenter stopped by to cheer the patient up. The Carpenters may have regretted their visit. After Lyndon provided Les with one of his hunting guns that "kicked back," he left with a bandaged right eye.

The Johnsons used those months of recuperation to make further improvements around the ranch. They installed an irrigation system to get them through dry stretches. To increase space for visitors, they built a new guesthouse, so appealing to Hubert and Muriel Humphrey, who stopped by on their way home from an Arizona vacation, that they took a set of the architect's drawings back to Minnesota. The swimming pool in the Johnsons' yard, with a white board fence around it, still had no landscaping, but it remained a favorite gathering place because temperatures stayed warm enough to swim well into December.

The fall of 1955 had its high points. During one of Lyndon's good patches, the whole family went to California, where the girls, on one of only a handful of vacations they ever took with their father, had the "time of their life" at Disneyland. Bird's home movies of those months show a placid, happy family, quite at odds with the sad reality described by staff. Lyndon pats the family dog and examines his prize Herefords. He swims across the pool, wearing dark glasses like a movie star, while a slim, smiling Bird floats faceup, savoring the blue sky overhead. Plump Lynda teases her younger sister with water splashes, and the two girls pose with "Daddy" at one end of the pool. This last footage is especially notable, since secretary Mary Rather reported the girls spent very little time with their parents that fall.

Everything revolved around Lyndon and how he could resume his leadership of the Senate. During her visit to the ranch, Katie Louchheim noted that he wore monogrammed socks and reclined imperially in a chair, spewing out big plans, while Bird "perched on the bed" and listened. To Louchheim, the patient sounded like an enthusiastic athletic coach, putting together a team. He quizzed her for names of women he could appoint to important jobs and talked excitedly about all he was going to do when he returned to Washington.

These meetings with Louchheim and others were all part of a careful strategy by Lyndon's PR team to make him look productive and upbeat. George Reedy and Horace Busby planted stories that made him sound like a changed, contented, and grateful man. Once reputed to relish driving fast around the ranch, he now claimed to enjoy nature walks; the father who had never paid much attention to his daughters bragged about getting acquainted with them; the man who famously eschewed reading books now expressed a liking for biography and Plato. An article written by Busby but published under Lyndon's name, claimed the heart attack had actually been a plus: "My Heart Attack Taught Me How to Live."

Many of the articles about Lyndon credited Lady Bird as his chief caretaker. *The Dallas Morning News* praised "her devotion and intelligence and diligence," measuring every calorie that Lyndon consumed and greeting every guest who dropped in. She enlisted the help of longtime secretary Juanita Roberts, who had acquired nutrition training during a previous job, to help her keep Lyndon on a high-protein diet of only 1,500 calories a day. Joining him in that regime, Bird lost ten pounds herself, and like a proud teacher showing off her prize student, she told the *Morning News*, "I've never seen anybody go after something the way Lyndon has this new way of living."

What she did not tell the papers was another, much less happy story: Lyndon Johnson was a cranky, incredibly difficult patient and, cut out of much control over anything, he made life miserable for everyone around him. He shouted at Juanita Roberts that he never wanted to hear the word "protein" again. After he lambasted Bird for telling him what he could and could not eat, she started making up lists, like restaurant menus, so he could place his orders himself. Dealing with the fallout from his other temperamental outbursts was not so easy. When he chastised office staff, she could ease the sting of his ugly words by reminding them that they were dealing with a sick man; when he tore into salesmen at the broadcasting company for not making more money, she could gently cut him off, with, "Now I think that's enough of that, Lyndon." But she was finding this recuperation very difficult and she admitted to a friend that when it was all over, she just wanted to "cry for about two hours."

By mid-October, the recuperation was going better. Lyndon had regained enough strength and confidence to accept an invitation to speak to an audience of one thousand in Whitney, Texas. It was a rousing performance. As he outlined his vision for America, he touched on a whole range of subjects, from education and housing to civil rights and full employment. Echoing an energetic young FDR, he made Adlai Stevenson, the current Democratic favorite, sound old-fashioned, and that speech was later singled out as a major milestone in elevating Lyndon to national prominence. Boosted by his showing in Whitney, he started giving more speeches, and Bird was right there beside him, slipping him little reminders or tugging his jacket tails when she thought he had talked long enough.

By January 1956, Lyndon Johnson was back in the Senate, but his associates found him more cantankerous than ever. Katie Louchheim questioned some of his committee appointments, and, after a discussion with Texas newspaperman Bill White, she decided that the effects of a coronary on an ambitious man could be disastrous. Lyndon had "gone sour," in her opinion, and become "sick mentally as well as physically . . . impossible . . . [and his arrogance] worse than ever."

Rather than cultivating members of the press, Lyndon seemed bent on provoking them. After keeping reporters waiting more than an hour, he antagonized them further by saying he had to leave for another appointment. White, who had been a Johnson friend since the early 1930s, continued to defend him but admitted "he's somewhat unbalanced because of his bottomless ambition and the frustration his heart attack imposes upon him. Can't stand any criticism . . . [or any]

thwarting." Louchheim agreed that Lyndon needed a lot of attention; it was up to Bird to keep him happy.

By May 1956, media outside Texas were reporting that Senator Johnson had made a surprisingly strong comeback. The Cleveland *Plain Dealer* retracted its earlier, pessimistic conclusion that his career was over and now included him in the "two or three most powerful men in the Democratic Party . . . [with] a strong, perhaps decisive voice at the [upcoming presidential nominating] convention." While his place as front-runner was still in question, Lyndon was his usual undecided self. He would not go after the nomination, he insisted, but "if it comes [my] way. . . ."

Bird strongly opposed a presidential run at that point—it was too soon after his heart attack. When she accompanied him to the Democratic nominating convention in August 1956, the first national convention she had ever attended, *The Dallas Morning News* ran a headline: "Lady Bird Likes Job in Senate." After describing her as "a slim, pretty brunette with sparkling brown eyes" who serves as her husband's sounding board, the *News* quoted her: "I think being a Senator from Texas is a wonderful job for which Lyndon is well suited, and he loves it. I like it where he is."

The same Dallas paper indicated Lyndon had problems beyond his health if he ran for national office. Simply put, he was considered too conservative for Northern liberals and too liberal for Southerners who saw him as too pro-labor and too pro-blacks. To capture the Democratic nomination, Lyndon would have to appeal to voters with widely different views on labor laws, taxes, and the role of the federal government in their lives.

After Adlai Stevenson lost to Republican incumbent Dwight Eisenhower in November, Senator Johnson began tweaking his credentials on civil rights, one of the most divisive issues in the nation. He had already edged away from the anti–civil rights stance he had taken in House votes on the poll tax and lynching and in his strident speech to the Senate in March 1949. In 1954, when one hundred of his fellow legislators (nineteen senators and eighty-one congressmen) defied the Supreme Court's *Brown v. Board of Education* decision by signing what was known as the Southern Manifesto, vowing never to obey it, Lyndon Johnson was one of only three Southerners who refused to join them. But he was still on very friendly terms with some of the most outspoken opponents of equal rights for blacks, including Senator Richard Russell, and Bird was still serving Russell his favorite meals whenever he dropped by.

When Eisenhower's attorney general, Herbert Brownell, outlined a new civil rights act in 1957, Lyndon saw his chance to gain some points with liberal voters without antagonizing Senator Russell and like-minded Southerners. Lyndon's assistant, Jim Rowe, had warned him he had to move quickly. Either he jumped on the civil rights bandwagon now or he was doomed to be stranded, a sectional leader without any hope of ever reaching the White House. This was the kind of challenge that brought out the political genius of LBJ, and he zeroed in on the one segment of the civil rights act that held potential for compromise—the section that segregationists would never accept and liberals might be persuaded to give up. Without that section, giving the federal government expanded power to prosecute discrimination, the Senate might pass the civil rights act, and Senate leader Johnson would collect credit from both sides—from the South for warding off the worst and from the North for backing the section of the act that extended voting rights to blacks.

To have round-the-clock access to his Senate colleagues while the bill was being hashed out, Senator Johnson set up a cot in his office. Bird provided him with fresh shirts, some hot meals cooked by Zephyr Wright, and the latest family news. Probably more important to the eventual outcome, she remained equally charming to the wives of senators opposed to Lyndon's compromise and to those who supported him. She hadn't been meeting with other Senate wives for nearly a decade just to roll bandages. She knew most of the women by first name, had entertained many of them at 30th Place, and knew the value of her solicitous inquiries about their health and that of their families.

Enacted on September 9, the 1957 Civil Rights Act did not accomplish all that its initiators wanted, but it was the first civil rights act passed in nearly one hundred years, and Senator Johnson deserved some of the credit. As did his wife, who later saw this victory as part of "a chain."

People who had previously written LBJ off for national office now began taking another look, and Lady Bird figured in the assessments. The *New Orleans Times-Picayune* on December 8, 1957, ran a headline, "Wife of Senate Majority Leader Highly Efficient." The article extolled her ability to adapt to her husband's frenetic schedule and its constant changes. With the cooperation of her "fabulous" cook, she sometimes stretched a meal prepared for four to feed twelve. After all was set for a big dinner, he might cancel entirely, to go elsewhere or work late. "Only a wife with the patience of Job" would manage to say, as Lady Bird did, "Oh well, we'll eat it tomorrow night." In addition to the usual portrayal of her as a "slender, pretty brunette" and good household manager, she was now being praised as "smart . . . one of the most astute business women in Texas, chairman of the board of the Texas Broadcasting company which owns three television and radio stations." It would be difficult to find any spouse in American political history up to that time with credentials to match those of Senator Johnson's wife in 1957. The article noted that besides managing her households, she "runs up to New York to confer with the big networks and national advertisers and keeps a weather eye out for a way to expand."

Like Dolley Madison, Lady Bird Johnson refused to admit the existence of enemies, and like Mrs. Madison, she confused some Washingtonians with her equanimity. Katie Louchheim mused in her diary about whether the "poised and sure" Bird knew more than she was letting on. When she gushed with admiration for her dinner partners, many of whom detested Lyndon, was she being "as arch as I think her," or did she really not know what those dinner partners thought of her husband?

Only rarely did Bird lower her guard among friendly faces, and once Louchheim overheard her complaining about how hard it was to please everybody: "If only people knew . . ." But mostly, Bird kept the smile pasted on and the flattery flowing—to make up for her husband's brashness and gaffes. She had long ago learned to conceal her true feelings so that only she had the key to them, and even the shrewd, inquisitive Louchheim couldn't get access.

Although both her husband's political prospects and her own broadcasting business were thriving in the late 1950s, Mrs. Johnson singled out those years as a low point in her life. Or, as she put it, not "personally my most joyous [years]." Her biggest problems were indeed personal—with family, both her husband's and hers, and matters of the heart.

In 1959 she hit a nadir when she realized she was going to lose a brother without ever having taken the time to get to know him. Tommy, the elder of her two brothers, had received a diagnosis of pancreatic cancer, and when Bird phoned her friend Dr. Cain for clarification of what that meant, she learned that it was almost always fatal. Nearly a dozen years older than she, Tommy had been away at boarding school during much of her youth, and after she married Lyndon and became so focused on his career, she had seen very little of her brother. Now his death sentence came as a painful reminder of how she had sacrificed blood relatives for the man she married, and it must have caused some soul-searching. Alone at the ranch at the time, she felt a sorrow deeper than any she could ever remember, and the woman who rarely cried let herself explode in grief. She confessed that she "cried and cried and cried. And I really don't know," she remarked twenty-five years later, after Lyndon's death, "whether I have ever cried since."

More than Tommy's death pushed the late 1950s into one of the worst periods of Bird's life, as she faced a litany of disappointments. She was in her late forties, and after the 1954 miscarriage, she had little hope left of ever bearing Lyndon a son. The ongoing friction between her daughters and herself was bound to grow as they matured and asserted their independence, and her combative relationship with her stepmother was affecting Bird's access to T.J.

But her top worry might well have been something else. For the first time in nearly a quarter century of marriage, she had to consider the possibility that her husband might leave her for another woman. She had plenty of evidence of his philandering—he made no secret of it—and of his other-than-employer relationship with his young secretaries. But now he was singling out one particular secretary as a favorite. Hired in 1954, Mary Margaret Wiley had gradually taken center stage in his Washington office, where she sat at a desk right alongside his, privy to every discussion he had. Her ubiquitous presence was noted in the press, and one newspaper described her as his "cute-as-a-button secretary" who went everywhere with Senator Johnson and recorded his speeches on her "little machine."

Bird treated this secretary as she treated all the women who caught Lyndon's eye—she incorporated them into the family routine and included them in social events. But this particular secretary's omnipresence and her apparent delight in her boss's generous attention fueled speculation that his interest in her might be more than short term. Wiley seemed highly tuned to her boss's moods and preferences and able to accommodate them as smoothly as Bird did. And this secretary was young enough to be his daughter, easily of an age to bear him a son.

To add to Bird's concern, Lyndon seemed changed. His recovery from the heart attack had not been accompanied by renewed satisfaction with his job and his life. He appeared disgruntled with politics and talked longingly about having a more relaxed workday, maybe in a low-key business of his own, like selling insurance. It seemed unthinkable that a man in his early fifties, with a flourishing national reputation, would do what he had often threatened—quit politics and start a new life. But some of his closest associates thought he meant it this time. The heart attack had caused a reassessment of goals, and the Senate had begun to bore him. His wife wasn't the only one who saw signs that Lyndon might make a drastic change in his life. One of his top aides later confessed to biographer Herbert Parmet that he thought Lyndon would "divorce" his wife and marry the secretary.

How does any wife treat a threat like that? By either opting out and letting someone else decide what happens or taking charge and doing everything she can to steer toward the outcome she wants.

Bird did the latter, by trying to increase her political visibility and thus her value to Lyndon, and she started by signing up for a course in public speaking. She had been giving short campaign talks since the mid-1940s, but addressing an audience on any subject but her husband's candidacy required an entirely different kind of preparation and Bird decided to take classes with Hester Provensen, who had an excellent reputation in the capital for tutoring inexperienced orators, both male and female. Provensen operated pretty much like a college professor—she required her students to avoid manuscripts and give short extemporaneous speeches, with only a few notes in front of them, and then critique each other. For Bird, who much preferred turning out a newspaper article, this was a big challenge, and she had to outline carefully what she wanted to say and then rehearse again and again before she attained the natural, convincing delivery that Provensen required.

When reporters came for an interview about Lyndon's presidential prospects and how she figured in his future, Bird made sure she had something substantial to say. The job of first lady, she told the Portland *Oregonian,* included a lot more than just lying "by the pool." It was not her style to be snide, and there is no reason to think that she was making a gratuitous comparison between herself and the others that *Newsweek* would later include in an article, "Will One of These Five Be First Lady?" But any discerning reader could see that none of the others—Muriel Humphrey, Jacqueline Kennedy, Pat Nixon, and Evelyn Symington—could begin to match Lady Bird's record, not in Washington experience or supportive networks or business accomplishments. All five were current or former Senate wives (and Pat Nixon's husband was completing a second term as vice president) but only Lady Bird was dubbed by *Newsweek* a "Human Dynamo." As the 1960 Democratic nominating convention grew near, the "Human Dynamo" was being pulled in multiple directions, as she tried to maintain balance in her personal life and help keep up the momentum in Lyndon's climb. Although there was much talk about how he coveted the nomination, he had refused to formally declare himself a candidate until a week before the convention opened. In the meantime, Senator John F. Kennedy had captured enough primaries to make him a front-runner.

Bird, who accompanied Lyndon to the convention in Los Angeles, still loved the man she had fallen hard for in 1934, the man who embodied her ambition and dreams. Although he could dumbfound her with some of his actions and words, she could not envision life without him. But the future looked uncertain. He seemed fully recovered from his 1955 heart attack, but who could tell how upcoming stresses might affect him? If he somehow managed to get his party's nod, would he not face even longer hours and tougher decisions in an exhausting campaign? In the unlikely event he triumphed in November and won the Oval Office, she would be up against more daunting challenges than she could yet imagine. If, on the other hand, one of his competitors became president, Lyndon could count on keeping his Senate seat. But would he want it? Would he want her?

II

———◆◉◉◉◆———

OUTSHINING HER
HUSBAND

O N FRIDAY, November 4, 1960, only hours before Americans
were scheduled to select their next president, polls showed
John Kennedy and Richard Nixon locked in a dead heat, with Texas's
twenty-four electoral votes still in doubt. Lady Bird knew that Dallas,
where Lyndon was scheduled to speak at noon at the Adolphus Hotel,
was hostile territory: "Never . . . a strong hold for us. . . . Very conservative town." But even she was shocked by what happened that day.
As she made her way alongside her husband to the hotel entrance, a
boisterous crowd surrounded them, shouting obscenities and blocking
their way.

Mrs. Johnson recognized some of the women, whom she knew as
well-to-do, courteous Republicans. Now they looked more like a street
mob, jostling her and shouting in her face. Unaccustomed to physical assault, she kept nodding and trying to smile, as Lyndon wrapped
his arms around her and started a slow, trancelike walk that made her
feel like "Marie Antoinette in the tumbrel." The Johnsons could have

covered the distance to the ballroom, where an audience awaited them, in a few minutes, but they inched along, multiplying the time of the walk by four.

The protesters turned rowdier and more menacing when photographers started snapping their pictures and TV cameras shot footage for the evening news. One sign labeled the senator "Judas," and shouters demeaned his wife as the "Yellow Thorn of Texas." Police offered the Johnsons protection, but Lyndon declined, and he later explained why: "If the time had come when I couldn't walk unaided through the lobby of a Dallas hotel with my lady, I wanted to know it."

Those few minutes provided a turning point for Bird and for the campaign. After she was safely in the Adolphus ballroom and found a window from which to observe the fracas outside, she observed sadly to herself, "Things will never be the same." Many of her fellow Americans agreed. After seeing the confrontation played out in vivid images in newspapers and on TV screens, they registered their dismay that Texas Republicans had behaved so badly.

Georgia senator Richard Russell, Lyndon's onetime mentor but more recently his adversary because of differences on civil rights, had retained his fondness for Bird. That she should suffer such abuse outraged him, and he volunteered to campaign for the Democratic ticket he had formerly scorned. The courtly bachelor vowed to concentrate on parts of the nation where his accent still carried some weight. Other Southerners mirrored his chagrin at how their reputation for chivalry had been besmirched, and historians have concluded the result was an upswing in favor of the Democrats. Bird's calm response to an explosive situation had helped create a sympathy factor for the Johnsons, siphoning votes away from the Republican ticket and aiding JFK's bid for the presidency.

Ironically, by helping Kennedy win, the Johnsons would be saddling Lyndon with a job that neither he nor Bird wanted him to have—the vice presidency. Texan John Nance Garner, who served unhappily as

FDR's VP from 1933 to 1941, is remembered mostly for declaring it "not worth a bucket of warm spit" (although he used a less polite word than "spit"). Presidential candidates had a record of using that slot on the ticket to get rid of loudmouths or to send them into obscurity, and neither of the Johnsons wanted such an indignity for Lyndon.

Lady Bird initially urged her husband to turn down JFK's invitation to join the ticket when he phoned the Johnsons' convention suite the day after his own nomination. Like most of her husband's supporters, she found humiliating the prospect that Lyndon would take the subordinate position to a man younger and less able than himself. With twenty-three years of experience in Congress, nine of them as a Senate leader, Lyndon saw himself as infinitely better suited for the Oval Office than "sonny boy," as he referred to JFK, who could claim less than half that time, none of it in a leadership position. It wasn't that the Johnsons disliked the young Kennedy—they just thought him green, impatient to wait his turn, and backed by a wealthy, overly pushy father.

But the Democratic nominee was facing a tough battle that year, and Lyndon's team realized a Texan running mate could give JFK an enormous boost. A Roman Catholic had never claimed the White House, and if Kennedy was going to be the first, he had to increase his appeal among voters who were suspicious of—even fiercely opposed to—a pope-friendly family living in the White House. Lyndon's Texas roots and accent could help offset the Eastern/Catholic taint to the top of the ticket, and if he declined to run, and the ticket lost, who would collect the blame?

Besides that consideration, the Johnsons had other incentives for deciding to join Senator Kennedy on the Democratic ticket. Even with his big negatives of youth and inexperience, he was a far more palatable occupant of the Oval Office than the likely Republican nominee, Richard Nixon. For Bird personally, the motive was partly selfish. She judged the VP job less stressful than managing an unruly Senate, and since his heart attack she had given a lot of thought to keeping him healthy. She loved him, and that scare in 1955 had clarified how quickly she could lose him.

After several hectic hours of discussion with Bird and Democratic colleagues, Lyndon agreed to join the Democratic ticket, and on July 29 he and Bird went to the Kennedy compound on Cape Cod to work out the details of the upcoming campaign. The Johnsons and the Kennedys were hardly strangers. The men had worked together in the Senate, and Lady Bird had included Jackie in one of the lunches she gave for Senate wives at 30th Place. But the Cape Cod get-together had little of the camaraderie of old-time friends. It was more like a forced meeting of wary business associates, who had resolved to be on best behavior and show only the utmost respect for each other. The Kennedys, who had no guest suite, cleared all clothing and family photos out of their own bedroom, and gave it to the Johnsons.

The stay lasted less than twenty-four hours, but it produced enough fallout to fill a book. Johnson aides, who had to be billeted at a local hotel, picked up what they deemed clear evidence for what would become a tangled, long story about how little regard the Kennedy camp had for the Johnsons. Although JFK treated his running mate with dignity and respect, his aides heard a different assessment when he warned them that Lyndon was a "very insecure, sensitive man with a huge ego" and they were to "literally kiss his ass from one end of Washington to the other."

Some of the snide comments attributed to Kennedy loyalists may have been exaggerated—or even invented—for humorous effect, but that did not keep them from turning up in conversations at Georgetown dinner parties and in the pages of tabloids. Among the nastiest (and oft repeated) was the one that dubbed the Johnsons "Uncle Cornpone" and his "little Pork Chop," which seemed especially cruel to five-foot-four Bird, who struggled to keep her weight down and knew how ruthlessly Easterners ridiculed her Southern accent.

If Bird registered any signs of disrespect on that visit, she never showed it. She could not have been more cordial. When Jackie admitted she was confused about what she could do to help in this campaign when she was "pregnant and helpless," the older, more experienced Mrs. Johnson immediately offered advice that Jackie took: "Why don't you call reporters in and show them the lovely sketches you have done of sailboats. . . . You can do that." It was unprecedented counsel: the spouse of a vice presidential nominee telling the wife of the top of the ticket how to behave. In stepping in to help the floundering Jackie, Bird was offering a preview of what lay ahead.

In the next three years, as LBJ struggled in JFK's shadow, Lady Bird emerged as a strong and active political spouse, complementing a ticket and then an administration as none of her predecessors had ever done. In the very last interview of her life, when asked what years she enjoyed the most, she picked the VP years, citing the chance to travel and meet important people. But, she admitted, those were very bleak years for Lyndon.

On the Cape Cod visit, Mrs. Kennedy got a chance to observe how Lady Bird worked. While the husbands conferred in one corner of the house, the wives chatted nearby, and Bird kept her little spiral notebook open at all times. Whenever she heard a name or a number from the men's side, she jotted it down without missing a beat of her own conversation with Jackie and her sister, Lee Radziwill. Although Jackie later disdained Bird's attentiveness to Lyndon as resembling that of a servile "hunting dog," she recognized the cool competence that accompanied it. Lady Bird looked "so calm," Jackie marveled. "I was very impressed."

That judgment would be underlined time and again in the weeks following the Cape Cod meeting. This was Lady Bird's tenth campaign as Lyndon's partner and she had ratcheted up her visibility in each one. This time, as Jackie's pregnancy sidelined her, Bird carried the load for both of them. Considering the fact that she still harbored misgivings about JFK's qualifications, it is remarkable that she expended so much energy on getting him elected. If the comments from the Kennedy camp about her were as unkind as later reported (on her accent, her subservience, her appearance) why didn't she withdraw to the ranch and sit this election out? After all, spouses of vice presidential candidates were not yet expected to exert much effort in campaigns.

But Lady Bird worked as if her very life depended on winning. Even while her father lay near death in Karnack, she stayed at Lyndon's side on a whistle-stop train trip through the South. His leadership in passing the 1957 Civil Rights Act had made him a pariah in those parts, and now she wanted to help mitigate that anger and keep disaffected voters in the Democratic fold. While Lyndon launched a practical appeal, saying that a vote for Kennedy was a vote for a stronger, more prosperous South, Lady Bird knew that it was the personal connection that moved people. She talked about her memories of Sunday picnics and watermelon evenings with her Alabama cousins, and how she felt most at home in that part of the nation. To Southerners, Lyndon's accent marked him as a Westerner, but Bird was one of them.

Then Mrs. Johnson did something far more daring—she went out campaigning without Lyndon, either on her own or with one of the Kennedy women. Jack's mother, Rose, had already enlisted to help her son win primaries, and she soon found herself in "great demand as a speaker." She had started giving talks about her travels while still in her forties, and now, at seventy, had become a confident speaker. She boasted that she could "carry a women's audience myself," while her daughters were "apt to be with [Jack]."

In the general election, when Rose Kennedy teamed up with Lady Bird to woo voters in fourteen states, the two women had some differences on how to proceed. Efficiency-minded Rose disliked losing precious time by engaging in small talk with the masses, and she liked to deliver her remarks as soon as she arrived, shake a few hands, and move on. Let them drink their coffee on their own time, she reasoned.

Bird had been doing these events for a long time, and she had her rules. Every single person there, even if the total ran into hundreds, was to be greeted individually, hand shaken, and a few words, including names, exchanged. Even the content of two women's speeches differed: Rose kept replaying the same stories about how she had raised an achieving, handsome brood; Lady Bird tailored each speech to the audience, with references to some local hero or historic site. Rather than talk about her children, she extolled Lyndon's ability to produce results.

Although Rose mildly praised Bird for working hard and handling volunteer campaign workers well, she never doubted for a minute that she was the more effective speaker. But the fact is the two women did not communicate in the same language. Alongside the septuagenarian beauty, Lady Bird resorted to a Texas colloquialism to describe where she found herself—in "tall cotton." Southerners used the phrase to describe feeling good about themselves, as if in the midst of an excellent crop ready to yield big profits. But haughty Rose Kennedy mistakenly interpreted it as meaning "not quite up to me."

Other Kennedy females, including Rose's daughter Eunice Shriver and daughter-in-law Ethel Kennedy (Robert's wife), agreed to appear with Lady Bird in areas where opposition to a Catholic candidate remained high. With the help of Liz Carpenter, Bird planned large receptions and teas across the country, with special emphasis on her home state, where Carpenter vowed to show Texans that Roman Catholics possessed no "horns or tails." Not yet reconciled to the sacrifices of gritty, on-the-road campaigning, Ethel Kennedy and Eunice Shriver objected to sharing hotel quarters, and Carpenter had to provide two suites of equal size and luxury so that neither woman felt slighted. Like Rose Kennedy, Ethel and Eunice attracted large crowds, with their designer clothes and movie star magnetism, but they drew the line at some parts of vote courting. When Liz Carpenter provided them with perky little campaign hats, they refused to wear them and "practically sat on them."

Even in a campaign as tense as this one, Bird had to peel off a couple times to check on her father in East Texas. He had already undergone amputation of one leg, and the once powerfully built "Mr. Boss" had shrunk to a feeble invalid. On October 22, he died. Lyndon's daily diary is blank for October 23, but the next day, a Monday, he was back on the campaign trail, headed to Los Angeles. Bird, whose relationship with her stepmother, Ruth, had remained sour after the episode with the irrevocable trust, soon learned that her father's will left the bulk of his estate to his wife and only a pittance to Bird. The two children of her deceased brother, Tommy, inherited portions of T.J's Texas land, as did her brother Tony and some of her cousins.

It was a painful slap from the grave, to be virtually dismissed from her adored father's affections, and it underscored how a woman who had virtually no enemies had made a powerful one this time—her stepmother. But Bird could not take off from electioneering to pursue her case against the will. That would come later and take a long time. Eight years elapsed before the executor dealt with all the challenges to the document, including those of Mrs. Johnson, who hated to see her father's estate "eaten up and eroded" in a way that reminded her of one of those dark plots in the plays of Tennessee Williams or the books of William Faulkner. In the final distribution of T.J.'s estate, she received only an insignificant building in Mauldin, Missouri, that yielded a mere $1,500 a year in rent.

In any tight race, Lyndon's mercurial moods became more pronounced, and the 1960 contest looked very close. When he didn't have Bird with him, he became morose and often spent the better part of the day in bed. In the log his secretaries kept, they sometimes cited a worn-out voice as reason for his inactivity, but more often they gave no reason at all. At the ranch, he stayed in bed until nearly noon, then went for a swim and took a nap before dinner. In Washington, with less than three weeks to go, he loafed two whole days away.

Of course he wanted to win, and he campaigned vigorously on some days. But a victory this time was going to be tinged with regret—the VP desk had not been a goal of his. That ambivalence might explain why he vented his frustrations so freely on subordinates. He complained about whatever disappointed him: puny crowds, an inadequate supply of fresh shirts, malfunctioning microphones. He quarreled with his schedulers—for giving him too much free time or too little. Aide Jim Rowe got so tired of his tirades he accused Lyndon of acting like a "Mogul emperor" and wondered to himself why someone on the staff didn't kill him.

Bird responded to Lyndon's verbal attacks as she had done in the past—she pulled down her protective veil and acted like she didn't hear them. When the commercial flight she was on arrived late, he "bawled her out" in front of others, using terms too foul for his aide George Reedy to repeat: "The whole thing was so revolting that it's the sort of thing you wanted to forget."

Lady Bird encouraged staff to treat Lyndon's outbursts the same way she did. After he lambasted aides, calling them "a bunch of god-damn, son-of-a-bitching bastards" who couldn't do anything right, she would come in afterward to assure them that he hadn't meant a word of it. Reedy, whom Lyndon ridiculed unmercifully for his corpulent behind and hammertoed walk, admitted that some of the staff became so upset with Lyndon's outrageous behavior they quit. But Reedy stayed, along with most of the others, because they did not want to desert their co-workers in the middle of a tight campaign and disappoint Bird. On his best days Lyndon excited aides with his vision and energy, and he enticed them to their highest productivity by setting an example. But on the down days, he repulsed, rather than attracted, and that was when he needed Bird, to talk him out of his funk and cauterize the hurt he caused.

———————

The 1960 presidential election was one of the closest in American history, and victory went to Kennedy by a tiny margin, less than one tenth of 1 percent in the popular vote. The electoral college produced a clearer winner, with the Democrats claiming 303 votes to Nixon's 219 (Senator Harry Byrd of Virginia got 15). A big chunk of the 303 votes came from the South, where Bird had campaigned alone or with Lyndon. Her home state, which had seemed very iffy, provided its 24, and the Carolinas another 22. If the combined (24 plus 22) 46 electoral votes had gone to the Republicans, Richard Nixon would have been taking the inaugural oath on January 20 instead of JFK. Mrs. Johnson's energetic campaigning did not go unnoticed. Robert Kennedy observed: "Lady Bird carried Texas." Although she cannot be credited directly for attracting a precise number of votes to the Democratic ticket, she certainly helped—in ways that no vice presidential candidate's spouse had ever done before.

As Bird began preparing to take up the job often dubbed "second lady," she had nearly three decades of watching how her five predecessors had done, and she did not want to duplicate their mistakes. The very private Bess Truman had only a few months in the role, but during that time she had lived in a small apartment, rarely entertained, and was such a nonentity in the capital that she could do her own shopping without being recognized. Both Mrs. Truman's predecessor, Ilo Wallace, and her successor, Jane Barkley, had longer tenures but limited themselves to social roles, hostessing dinners and teas. VP Garner's wife, Mariette "Ettie" Rheiner Garner, left a slightly larger mark because, as her husband's secretary, she was acquainted with many of his colleagues and knew who his enemies were. But Bird was used to *having* a secretary, not *being* one. Pat Nixon had received very favorable publicity for her bravery in South America, where she faced demonstrators who attacked the car she and her husband were riding in. But in Washington, she lived the low-profile life of an ordinary housewife. With only part-time domestic help and a tiny family budget, she had to do most of her housework herself, and she told reporters she still pressed her husband's pants.

With financial reserves dwarfing those of her immediate predecessors, Bird resolved to make more of a mark. Vice presidents did not yet have the perk of government housing, and their wives were expected to do what they could to entertain, either in their very modest homes or in local restaurants. An event like that rarely made much of a splash on the society pages, and Bird was looking for a house suitable for the family of a man who was going to make more of his job than a "bucket of warm spit." She found it at 4040 52nd Street, in Northwest Washington, a house that had previously belonged to the legendary hostess ("with the mostest") Perle Mesta. With a dining room large enough to seat thirty and landscaped grounds to accommodate al fresco receptions for more than one hundred, it seemed perfect. Lyndon objected that the property's French name, "Les Ormes," would cost him votes, but that was easily remedied by switching to the English equivalent, "The Elms." The buying price ($200,000 in 1960, equivalent to about $1.5 million in 2014 dollars) came out of the Johnson pockets, but it seemed an investment worth making.

In preparation for the move, Bird sold off some of her less stylish furnishings and purchased Mesta's French dining room chairs. To fit the casual entertaining style that she and her family preferred, she added a $15,000 swimming pool. But remodeling took time, and after the house on 30th Place sold, the Johnsons lived temporarily in a suite at the Shoreham Park Hotel. Not until late August did The Elms become fully habitable. While other wives might have been intimidated by the prospect of tampering with anything the illustrious Mesta had touched, Bird was not. She added some Lone Star touches throughout the house to remind her "where I came from."

Mrs. Johnson now got the chance to put her speech training with Mrs. Provensen to use. With two small children (Caroline, born 1957, and John Jr., born 1960) Jacqueline Kennedy wanted to keep her public appearances to a minimum, especially the routine, humdrum ones, like greeting obscure dignitaries and accepting awards and citations. So she asked Lady Bird to substitute for her. Sometimes the appeal came at the very last minute, causing Johnson aides to suspect that the first lady's staff had deliberately dallied in order to put Mrs. Johnson on the spot, but she gamely accepted every summons and refused to blame Jackie for the timing. Since Jackie also liked to escape on long vacations of her own, to Europe or India, Bird became her number one pinch hitter.

It wasn't just in Washington that Mrs. Johnson wanted to attract favorable attention for her VP husband. She entertained countless guests at the ranch, including foreign leaders, whose different religions and ethnic preferences could prove challenging to any hostess. When the chancellor of West Germany, Konrad Adenauer, a strict Catholic, arrived in heavily Protestant Texas on an April Sunday in 1961, he found a special Mass ready for him at nearby Stonewall's tiny St. Francis Xavier church. Four hundred guests gathered at the ranch afterward to dine with the chancellor and his daughter in tents, carpeted with Oriental rugs to resemble a "rich Turk's harem." Catering to those who did not eat pork was especially hard—Texans like barbecues and barbecues mean pork. When Pakistani field marshal Mohammed Ayub Khan and his Muslim entourage visited the ranch, Lady Bird had to make sure that waiters received strict instructions to code the trays and pass only the chicken and beef to the Pakistanis. Any mix-up could have had serious consequences because these events received heavy press coverage, not just in the United States but abroad.

Regardless of the number and status of those who landed on the newly built airstrip behind the ranch house, journalists commented on how remarkably unflustered Lady Bird remained. In June 1962, when the Women's National Press Club in Washington produced a skit demonstrating the hectic pace at the Johnson ranch, it was titled

"Life in a Goldfish Bowl." A few nights later, Lady Bird demonstrated the truth in the skit (and how that truth applied equally to both her homes) by welcoming twenty-six members of Congress, the press, and the cabinet to The Elms. She knew enough about each guest to tailor her comments and queries to fit the individual. Her mentor, Terrell Maverick, who had advised her back in 1937 to get involved in her husband's job, had no idea how that counsel would be taken to heart.

Now that Mrs. Johnson was in demand as a speaker, she spent hours deploying what she had learned. Starting with an outline, she would revise through multiple drafts and then practice from notes until she had the smooth transitions and fluid, conversational delivery she wanted. One of Lyndon's aides judged the result "awfully good. You could always depend upon Lady Bird to say exactly the right thing." Now that she found herself frequently facing cameras, she paid more attention to her wardrobe and heeded Lyndon's advice to visit the hair salon often. A friend suggested she could save time by having the hair stylist come to her home, but that struck her as excessively extravagant, and she kept trooping to Georgetown for a shampoo and a set. Very seldom did she allow herself time off for fun, and an aide's report that she once spent an hour trying to learn how to dance the new craze, the twist, stands out as a rarity.

As a Senate wife, she had been one of dozens; now she had a national podium, not nearly as high-powered as Jackie's but one she was determined to use. Behind the gracious hostess and polished public speaker was a very disciplined woman who kept herself to a tight, tough schedule. Booth Mooney, one of Lyndon's aides at the time, observed: "If ever a woman transformed herself—deliberately, knowingly, painstakingly—it was she. A modest, introspective girl gradually became a figure of steel cloaked in velvet. Both metal and fabric were genuine."

Lyndon was another story. The vice presidential years were the worst of his life, a fact that obviously affected his marriage. One associate described him as: "thoroughly, visibly and persistently miserable." While his wife was obviously relishing her new celebrity status, he sank into a long torpor, despondent at his loss of power and prickly about his subservient status. He initially tried to retain a measure of his Senate leadership, but his colleagues balked, reminding him that the Constitution provided for a division of powers between the executive and legislative branches. It was their way of telling him that he should stay where he now belonged.

Unfortunately for Lyndon, a VP has very few official duties, and if the president does not pull him into the power circle, he can feel superfluous, like an insignificant bystander. The once powerful Senate leader now looked more like Bert Parks at a Miss America contest. This was a job that had him posing with Miss Muffin at the National Retail Bakers Association, then with the Cherry Blossom Queen and the Azalea Queen. At least the Azalea event put him in the same picture frame as his daughter Lynda, who wore the Azalea crown that year.

While Lyndon vegetated, Lady Bird started hiring some very competent staff to help her. She knew that busy wives of top leaders, like Eleanor Roosevelt, had typically engaged close friends or relatives to assist in handling mail and managing social events, and she understood the value of trustworthy staff. But she wanted more—expertise and experience, the same traits she looked for when hiring at her radio station. She had brought her longtime friend, newspaperwoman Liz Carpenter, onto the family team during the 1960 campaign, when she invited her to be part of "the great adventure of our lives." At first Carpenter demurred. She hated flying and knew working for a vice presidential candidate would include a lot of time in the air. It was Carpenter's son, Scott, who convinced her to accept, saying, "You'll be flying with Lady Bird, and birds never crash." All through the campaign and after the victorious election, Carpenter drew her salary from

Lyndon's payroll, but she took her assignment as aiding the boss's wife as much as the boss, in planning public appearances, shaping speeches, and encouraging favorable press.

The other key assistant to Lady Bird came on board a little more gradually. Mrs. Johnson had known young Bess Clements since the time her father served with Lyndon in the U.S. Senate. After Bess eloped with Tyler Abell, stepson of the influential columnist Drew Pearson, it was the Johnsons who hosted the couple's wedding reception. By 1960, Bess Abell found herself bored with domestic duties and, tired of talking to her cats, she volunteered to assist Mrs. Johnson with her mail and entertaining. Besides her sunny personality, Bess brought a good deal of Washington savvy to the job. As the daughter of a senator and daughter-in-law of a syndicated columnist, she had access to most of official Washington and she knew how the capital operated. She and Carpenter would become Mrs. Johnson's top staff in the White House, and they would remain until she left Washington in 1969.

The one big assignment President Kennedy gave his VP—foreign travel—was undertaken with mixed appreciation in the Johnson household. Lyndon objected that these missions were manufactured busywork, created to keep him out of the power loop, or worse, designed to make him look bad. But Bird loved seeing exotic new places. Up to that time, she had rarely moved beyond U.S. borders, and when given the chance to accompany the vice president on an Africa-Europe tour, beginning April 1, 1961, she eagerly accepted. On landing in Senegal, she marveled it was like being "dumped right down in the middle of what seemed like pages of the *National Geographic.*"

Lyndon could not have been more obvious about his wish to be somewhere else. He tangled with local officials, and when an ambassador strongly advised against visiting a local village, he went anyway. To show his populist side and soak up the adulation of crowds who had never before gotten close to a major world leader, he moved through throngs with little Secret Service protection. He shook hands with everyone who reached out, including lepers with mangled hands, their fingers missing because of the disease.

Bird took on her usual role—damage controller—and tried to camouflage or limit Lyndon's misbehavior. After the vice president's party reached Paris and checked into the George V hotel, Lyndon went shopping with Bird and secretary Mary Margaret Wiley. But that evening, at a late dinner at Maxim's, he was in no mood to play the dignified diplomat. He drank too much and engaged in sexy bantering and suggestive physical exchanges that exceeded what even hedonistic Parisians were likely to condone. According to aide Horace Busby, Mrs. Johnson, who was seated at the far end of the table, kept silent watch on her husband—until a diplomat's wife, with Lyndon's full cooperation, climbed on his lap. Then Bird moved quickly, ordering Busby to call a car and escort her to it, leaving her husband little choice but to follow her out.

On another official trip a few weeks later, taking him through the Far East and then to Greece, the VP acted like a spoiled potentate, traveling with a huge entourage that included President Kennedy's sister and brother-in-law, Jean and Stephen Smith, and a posse of reporters that required a separate plane. He insisted on bringing cases of his favorite scotch, his own oversized bed, and his super shower heads, powerful enough to produce water blasts even in places where water was scarce. He loudly criticized an American diplomat in front of others, and implied in his speeches to impoverished locals that they could raise their living standards by following the example of Texans.

While he treated each of these foreign trips as a hardship, Bird acted like she had won the lottery. That she, a woman from Karnack, Texas, was actually exploring places along the South China Sea dazzled her. This was more than she had dared dream of when writing those 1934 letters to Lyndon about how much she wanted to see the world. On a swim in the Gulf of Thailand (which she knew as the Gulf of Siam) she took secretary Ashton Gonella, a Louisiana native, with her, and as the two women paddled alongside their Secret Service agents, Bird jubilantly reminded Ashton, "We've come a long way."

Lady Bird's natural curiosity kept pushing her to explore, even when her exhausted staff pled time out to recuperate. Soon after arriving in Beirut in August 1962, she phoned Bess Abell to announce that she wanted a car and guide to take her to Baalbek, fifty miles north of Beirut, to see an archaeological site dating back to the Romans. Abell tried to deter her, saying that after a very long flight aboard Air Force Two, she needed some sleep. But Abell got nowhere. Mrs. Johnson was firm: "We may never pass this way again, and I really want to see Baalbek." Abell reluctantly made the arrangements and then went along. As they wound their way up the mountain roads, she watched her employer jot down notes in her omnipresent notebook, using Gregg shorthand to describe the people, the open-air markets, and the groves of olive trees they saw along the route.

It must have rankled Lyndon to see his wife thrive in her side of the vice presidency while he floundered in his. He had always pushed her to do more, gibing her about how her advanced education had prepared her to do just about anything. But then, when she produced, as in his congressional office or some other assignment, he seemed reluctant to concede much credit. Her excelling should have reflected well on him, but he treated it as his failing, as if the two of them were in some sort of zero sum game, where any gain on one side had to be reflected in an equivalent loss on the other.

Since Lyndon's only official assignment as VP was to chair infrequent meetings of the National Aeronautics and Space Council and the Equal Employment Opportunity Commission, he had a lot of time on his hands. But he wasn't using it for physical fitness. Katie Louchheim, who had known him a long time, described him as "waggish" and "fat." Lyndon's aide Harry McPherson reported after a swim at

The Elms that the vice president "looked absolutely gross. His belly was enormous and his face looked bad, flushed, maybe he had been drinking a good deal. . . . . His life was not causing him to come together physically, morally, intellectually, in any way."

Obviously unhappy, cut off from what he did best—managing a legislature and converting visions into concrete laws that improved people's lives—he took out his frustrations on those closest to him. That left Bird to clean up his messes and escape whenever she could. When on one trip to Asia, Lyndon ordered aide Horace Busby out of his plane immediately, and Busby objected "But we're over the ocean," the VP shouted back, "I don't give a fucking damn." It took Bird's calm intervention to restore peace between the two. In Istanbul, when her husband was especially downcast and nasty, Bird took Liz Carpenter for a sail on the Bosporus and encouraged George Reedy to fulfill a lifelong dream by exploring the Hagia Sophia on his own.

The trip that included Turkey was a lemon from the start. Setting out on the afternoon of August 22, 1962, the vice president and his party made a brief stop in the Azores, where it was past midnight local time. Even at that late hour, a welcoming party of local dignitaries had gathered to fete the American officials, but, according to George Reedy, Lyndon was too drunk to get off the plane. A smiling, perfectly coiffed Bird greeted the crowd in his stead. Subsequent stops saw the vice president "deeply fatigued," in spite of the fact that large crowds lined the roads to cheer him on.

Back home at The Elms, Lady Bird had no better luck dealing with Lyndon's foul moods. She encouraged him to exercise, but he was an erratic complier, enthusiastic for two consecutive days about using the Senate gym, then refusing to go near it for weeks. He preferred nightly rubdowns from his always-on-call masseur. He indulged in junk food, then tried to undo the damage by limiting himself to Metrecal (a popular diet drink). At dinner parties, alcohol flowed freely and he drank enough to gain back the pounds he had taken off with the Metrecal lunches.

Some of the energy Lyndon could no longer expend as Senate leader now went to Bird's broadcasting business. The fledgling little radio station that she bought with her own money in 1943 had grown under her careful watch to a media empire comprising radio and television stations, and Lyndon wanted a bigger role in running them. Although Bird still appeared at meetings of KTBC employees, Lyndon met more often with them solo, and it was he who conferred with outsiders, including executives of a large media conglomerate, Ling-Temco-Vought, about mergers and affiliations in February 1963. After the Johnsons began spending more time at the ranch following his heart attack, they needed an Austin residence less and gradually started relying on an apartment they kept at the broadcasting headquarters for entertaining and overnight stays. So Bird may have been more on the premises and involved in business decisions than the written record indicates. But Lyndon's official diary shows a definite spike in his involvement in the business during his VP years.

By the summer of 1963, Bird was watching her husband's frustrations grow as he dealt with old medical problems and confronted new political challenges. For one ailment or another, he was consulting White House doctors and dentists more than once a week. Even more troubling were headlines alleging that Bobby Baker, the Senate secretary, had acted improperly in the Johnsons' behalf, soliciting a stereo set for them as a kickback on a life insurance policy they had bought. Any scandal involving Baker, dubbed "Little Lyndon" because of his close relationship with LBJ, was bound to besmirch his mentor, and this was the very worst time to weather stories about nefarious dealings. Rumors were already circulating that JFK felt confident he could drop Lyndon from the ticket in 1964, and reports of an unsavory association with Baker would provide reason for following through. The entire vice presidency had been trying for LBJ, but mid-1963 marked the nadir. With more than a year to go, Bird had reason to wonder how it would end.

In November, she spent the first weeks preparing the ranch for a visit from the Kennedys. Jack had been there, but this was a first for Jackie. Lady Bird installed the special bed that JFK required for his bad back, and she laid in a supply of Jackie's favorite brand of cigarettes and plenty of good champagne. Just before noon on Thursday, November 21, she left the ranch with Lyndon to go to San Antonio and welcome the Kennedys to Texas. By Friday, they would all be in Dallas.

12

PRESIDENTIAL PARTNERING

ON NOVEMBER 22, 1963, as word spread of what had happened in Dallas, Americans tried to make sense out of disconnected images on their TV screens and shocking reports from their radios. All across the nation, people who had admired the magnetic, future-oriented President Kennedy struggled with the realization that he had been inexplicably taken from them by an assassin's bullet, and many looked to like-minded friends for consolation in their grief.

One such get-together occurred that evening in Montgomery, Alabama, twenty miles south of Prattville, where some of Bird's relatives still lived. Liberal Democrats were in short supply in that region, but a small group of them gathered at the home of Cliff and Virginia Durr, the civil rights activists whose friendship with the Johnsons reached back to the 1930s. When the conversation turned to what lay ahead, Cliff Durr said, "We just wish Bird could be President." Rollin Shaw, a longtime friend of the Durrs' daughter, was present that night and she remembered, "Everyone chuckled a bit, realizing that the jest contained much truth."

At least they could take comfort in knowing she would be right there beside Lyndon, taking a full partner role, offering both support and judgment, as she had been doing since she married him. He counted on that, and on the plane back from Dallas he turned the phone over to her to help him convey condolences to Rose Kennedy, mother of the slain president.

Within days, Mrs. Johnson started speaking out on subjects that mattered. She was not going to be another Bess Truman or Mamie Eisenhower, who thought a first lady should keep her mouth shut. After Lyndon delivered a rousing call to arms, with his State of the Union message on January 8, declaring "unconditional war" on poverty, Bird met with reporters to tell them what she thought of the speech. With its emphasis on education, retraining, and health, it pretty well summed up, she noted, "Lyndon's living and working for the last thirty years." She even quoted the line she liked best: "You must be strong enough to win a war and wise enough to prevent one."

Lyndon's war on poverty was going to be her war, too. Before he gave that speech, she had already begun preparing for a trip of her own to coal mining areas in Pennsylvania where unemployment was high. She knew, of course, that Eleanor Roosevelt had made similar forays to the poorest parts of Appalachia, and had explained them as part of being the "eyes and ears" for her husband. In fact, Mrs. Roosevelt played down her authority in general and insisted she "never tried to influence [her husband] on anything he ever did." To suggest otherwise was "embarrassing." Lady Bird Johnson was not about to offer a similar disclaimer. Quite the contrary. In planning her own trips to poverty-stricken areas, she called in experts to tell her how she could help Lyndon's efforts. When she returned to Washington on January 11, after visiting dilapidated schools and shaking hands with out-of-work miners, she exuberantly described the day as one of her very best yet as first lady.

Both Mrs. Johnson and her ingenious press secretary, Liz Carpenter, began immediately shaping an image of a first lady fully involved in the presidency. Veteran newswoman Marie Smith had already started a highly laudatory biography, *The President's Lady,* due out late in 1964, and Elizabeth Janeway was slated to publish a flattering article in the April issue of *Ladies' Home Journal* entitled "The First Lady, A Professional at Getting Things." But when *Look* magazine, with a circulation of more than seven million, approached Mrs. Johnson in early 1964 with the proposal for an article on "Wifemanship at the White House," she turned to a writer she admired, the wife of aviation hero Charles Lindbergh.

Anne Morrow Lindbergh and Lady Bird Johnson had taken an immediate liking to each other when they met briefly at the Kennedy White House, and Lady Bird was impressed by two of Lindbergh's books, *Gift from the Sea* and *Dearly Beloved*, although she found them so different she could hardly believe they came "out of the same mind." Who better to write about the role of spouse to a famous man than the woman who had married the most famous man in the world and then won celebrity status for herself by publishing bestsellers? Lindbergh's *Gift from the Sea* (1955) was particularly relevant to Bird's situation because it recounted how a busy wife and mother of five found precious time for herself on an isolated island.

At first Lindbergh did not know how to respond to Mrs. Johnson's invitation. She wasn't sure she wanted to write for *Look*, and the topic of first ladies was not in her repertory. But after talking with Lady Bird, she agreed, and the lengthy piece, "As I See Our First Lady," appeared in the May 19, 1964, issue. It was an eye-opener, spelling out how Mrs. Johnson meant to expand the limits in the job. A first lady could no longer just sit demurely beside her husband in public and quietly run his household.

Providing a tranquil home life for a busy chief executive was, of course, part of the job, and Lady Bird promised to make sure Lyndon had a "balm" from the pressures of his office. But she meant to do much more, according to Lindbergh. Besides monitoring her husband's speeches and actions, she would point out his shortcomings, and let him know her thinking on important issues. When Lindbergh observed that she sounded like one of those American women who want to "dominate" their men, Bird "tartly" corrected her: "American women have been partners since pioneer days. . . . It was not a question of one dominating the other side."

It was a remarkable statement, so unlike Eleanor Roosevelt's description of her own marriage. Nearly twenty years had passed since Mrs. Roosevelt left the White House, and many American women were currently reading Betty Friedan's best-seller, *The Feminine Mystique,* and talking about a new wave of feminism. But Bird didn't regard herself as a feminist, not then nor later. She was fashioning her own hybrid model for marriage, growing out of both Southern and Western roots, and it combined traditional nurturing of others with achievement on one's own. Like the pioneer women she admired, she considered marriage a team of equals; like the Southern women she loved, she would not challenge her husband in public, but in private would let him know what she thought.

In that 1964 article, when Lady Bird Johnson revealed the kind of marriage she had, Lindbergh agreed with her, describing the Johnson partnership as an admirable one in which each respected and relied on the other. Unfortunately, most reporters did not pick up on what Lindbergh wrote, and they continued to treat Mrs. Johnson as the subservient underling to an overpowering, domineering husband rather than an equal who acted as his aide and in-house critic.

Although Mrs. Johnson started off her interview with Lindbergh by saying she felt, as first lady, "as if I'm on stage for a part I never rehearsed," both she and the author knew that was an exaggeration.

No woman had ever come better equipped for that role. Her thirty years of Washington apprenticeship could serve as a guidebook to anyone aspiring to the job. Since arriving in 1934, as the bride of a congressman's young assistant, she had scrutinized the capital so carefully she could have written a tourist guidebook, with the opening and closing hours of all the major monuments, and a rundown on all the important leaders in her own *Who's Who*.

From the network she had in place, she could count on lots of help. Libby Rowe, Marny Clifford, and Carol Fortas, whose husbands provided counsel to Lyndon, stood ready to advise Bird on everything from wardrobe selection to cleaning up the capital city. Nearly a quarter century of hearty interaction with members of the Congressional Club and the Senate Wives' Club circle had provided a roster of friends, who volunteered to come to The Elms and help answer the hundreds of condolence messages pouring in. Eventually, four rooms in the Executive Office Building were set aside for dealing with approximately five thousand letters that arrived each week, while eight telephone operators, "busy as cats on a hot stove," fielded calls. Bird oversaw it all. She was used to delegating tasks—she had been doing it all her life—and her decades-long foray into broadcasting had bolstered her confidence as a manager.

Any move from one home to another produces stress, but the move Mrs. Johnson had to oversee involved the most famous house in America, and millions were watching to see how she managed it. Mrs. Kennedy could not be expected to vacate the premises overnight. She had to find a place to go, transfer Caroline's school out of the third floor of the White House, and deal with the myriad of decisions that sudden widowhood produces. When someone suggested Bird should hurry things along, she directed her press secretary to relay this response: "I wish to heaven I could serve Mrs. Kennedy's happiness. I can at least serve her convenience."

That cordiality took on added significance when contrasted with

Lyndon's impatience. He sought, but did not get, possession of the Oval Office for a meeting on Saturday morning, November 23, before Evelyn Lincoln, JFK's distraught secretary, had a chance to clear the desk. When the residence was ready for the Johnsons on December 7, he insisted on moving in immediately, although Lady Bird pled for waiting a day, so as not to begin their time there on the anniversary of Pearl Harbor. Lyndon prevailed, and the move occurred on a date that seared in Bird's memory like "salt in your eye." As she adjusted to management of the 134-room executive mansion, she continued emptying out The Elms, and preparing to sell it. Only she could make the necessary decisions about which of the furniture, rugs, and house-wares should go to Texas, which to storage, and which got sold or junked.

The upright piano was easy—Sheldon Cohen bought it for his young children. His association with the Johnsons started within hours of the Kennedy assassination, after they phoned Abe Fortas, their long-time friend and trusted adviser, to ask for advice. They were still on Air Force One, returning to Washington, when they went to work on the question of how to manage their personal wealth, especially their broadcasting stations. In the relative obscurity of the vice presidency, both Johnsons remained in constant communication with their business manager, Jesse Kellam, and they freely offered him their views on programming, sales, and staffing. But now that Lyndon was president, with the responsibility of appointing members of the FCC, such inter-vention was clearly inappropriate, if not illegal.

Abe Fortas immediately turned to Sheldon Cohen, a thirty-eight-year-old lawyer in his firm, who went to work on the matter before Air Force One touched down that evening. Cohen's first response was that the Johnsons should sell the stations, but when Fortas assured him that they would never agree to do that, Cohen had to find another solution. For six days, he devoted every waking moment to unrav-eling the labyrinth of financial holdings that comprised the Johnson wealth at that time. Although he slept at home, he barely saw his wife and children. On Sunday, November 24, while most of Washington prepared for the slain Kennedy's funeral on Monday and Abe Fortas held his weekly string quartet rehearsal at his home, Cohen plodded through mounds of financial papers in an adjacent room of the Fortases' house in Georgetown. He was so oblivious to what was happening outside that room that when told that Jack Ruby had killed Lee Harvey Oswald, he had to ask, "Who is Oswald? Who is Ruby?"

What Cohen gleaned from his investigation (and what diligent reporters would reveal a few months later) was that the Johnsons had massive holdings, including banks, land, and businesses. By far the biggest single component was the Texas Broadcasting Company, held in the name of Claudia T. Johnson. Her husband owned not a single share. But Cohen determined that a spouse's name on a deed provided no protection against charges of conflict of interest: he had to treat her property as belonging equally to Lyndon and he had to find a way to separate both Johnsons from decisions about their investments.

Cohen looked for some precedent. He had heard talk of JFK setting up a "blind trust" when he became president, but that turned out to be false. Cohen had already drawn up "blind trusts" for ambassadors who, faced with assignments in countries where they held significant investments, protected themselves from charges of conflict of interest by turning over control of everything they owned to another person or entity, such as a bank. Why not something similar for a president?

The snag was the Johnsons, especially Lady Bird, who showed a more dogged devotion to the dollar than did Lyndon. She had worked long and hard for that nest egg and neither she nor Lyndon wanted to relinquish control. Both talked about the uncertainty of politics and the possibility that voters would turn them out at the next election. They had daughters to educate, and a comfortable retirement to safeguard for themselves. Even if reelected, they needed the income to support a constantly rising living standard. Lyndon kept adding ranchlands and upgrading his cattle, and after building a landing strip behind the ranch house, he had started buying airplanes. Only if all their investments could be safely put under the control of loyal, old friends would the Johnsons agree to step aside.

The two men who emerged as the best candidates for trusteeship were superbly qualified: John Bullion had been preparing their taxes since 1940, and rancher/attorney A. W. Moursund was their longtime neighbor. It was his family who lent Lyndon money to go to college. With two such reliable trustees lined up, Lyndon and Claudia T. Johnson were willing to proceed, and on November 28, Cohen had the papers ready for them to sign.

Although technically the first "blind trust" in American presidential history, it was hardly "blind." Both Johnsons continued to communicate freely with the two trustees. Moursund had his own direct, private telephone line to the White House, and his ranch was often the Johnsons' first stop when they returned to Texas. Vicky McCammon, the secretary who shared boat rides with Lyndon and Moursund, reported that their conversation often centered on "different money matters, television interests, just how the whole thing was going to be wrapped up." When the Johnsons invited Moursund to stay overnight at the White House, Lady Bird identified him as "the children's trustee," with whom she "had a lot of business to talk about."

Bird managed the guest quarters of the executive mansion like a busy small hotel. She assigned big names, such as philanthropist Mary Lasker, to the famed Queens' Bedroom suite or the Lincoln Bedroom. But personal guests—Johnson City neighbors, friends of Luci and Lynda, the family doctor, the Moursunds and the Bullions—slept in less impressive quarters on the third floor. The turnover in those rooms was so heavy, she marked her diary with an exclamation point when they were empty.

Her open-door policy contrasts sharply with that of Jacqueline Kennedy, who liked to restrict the upper floors of the White House to a privileged few. She valued her own privacy and wanted her children to feel free to play, out of sight of gawking strangers. She occasionally opened up the Lincoln Bedroom for a national hero like Charles Lindbergh, but she was also known to fib to keep people away. On at least one occasion she had the furniture shrouded to give the appearance of a paint job under way, providing her with an excuse for not accommodating a guest who had hoped to stay overnight.

In other ways, Mrs. Johnson resolved to define the job of first lady in her own terms, without feeling daunted by her predecessor's celebrity glamour and enormous popularity. Pity was not what Bird wanted. When offered sympathy for having to move in the shadow of the trend-setting Mrs. Kennedy, she was shocked, and replied, "Don't feel sorry for me. I still have my Lyndon."

The contrast between the two first ladies was immediately obvious in how they dressed: Jackie's designer outfits in runway model sizes made the shorter, older Bird look like a thrifty matron. During her thousand days in the White House, Jackie had added dozens of outfits, with five-digit price tags, to her already extensive wardrobe, while Bird, who disliked shopping, had to borrow black coats and dresses for the Kennedy funeral and for the mourning period that followed. Showing her limited regard for big-name designers, she admitted that one funeral outfit made her look "very Salvation Army but in a smart way, I hope."

Two months as first lady passed before Lady Bird finally found time to buy clothes for what was becoming a very busy schedule. Even then, she purchased only two new outfits and decided that "wrapped up" the matter until summer. Instead of adding to her wardrobe, she had old suits altered, and she updated her mink coat by shortening it, recycling the excess fur into a hat. She had lost weight in the stressful first weeks in the White House, and, reaching to the back of her closet, she found a gold and silver lamé dress that Lyndon had bought her in Paris. It finally fit.

First ladies typically take primary responsibility for parenting in the White House, especially if young children are involved, and Anne Morrow Lindbergh asked Mrs. Johnson how she planned to handle that. Bird's reply—that her two daughters could "count on her to be there for them"—was typical of her, dutiful and correct, but a world away from Jacqueline Kennedy, who maintained that if one failed at parenting, nothing else mattered. Michelle Obama's description of herself half a century later as "Mom-in-Chief" would have sounded as foreign as a Chinese proverb to Mrs. Johnson.

Very few presidential families deal easily with the explosion of publicity that their move into the White House ignites, and the Johnsons were no exception. Lynda, enrolled as a sophomore at the University of Texas in Austin, wanted to stay there, where she had pledged to a sorority and acquired a boyfriend, rather than live in the Washington fishbowl. Her mother disagreed. She recognized the White House provided a rare opportunity that few people have—to meet world leaders and national celebrities, to witness history in the making—and she wanted both daughters to take full advantage. When Lynda continued to resist the move, her mother suggested her UT roommate, Warrie Lynn Smith, come with her, and a deal was struck. By the end of January 1964, the two young women had settled into third-floor bedrooms and enrolled at nearby George Washington University. But Lynda made very clear she resented the change. She had been overruled by her parents, she told *The New York Times*, and had made the transfer under pressure.

Even with the entire Johnson family under the same roof, the daughters saw little of their parents. Lyndon's supercharged schedule meant he ate dinner late, often after 9 p.m. Even if they waited for him, they had limited opportunity to voice personal concerns or share their worries. He liked fast-paced talk, and Lynda complained it was "Lose your breath; lose your chance." The president routinely polished off a meal in less than twenty minutes, much of that time in conversation with a staff member or friends he brought with him. Lady Bird made a point of joining him at the table, no matter how late the hour, but she did not always wait for him to eat. She would sneak a plate earlier, and then play with her food while he ate. On the very rare occasion when she dined on her own, she felt like a "deserter."

The four Johnsons so rarely sat down together at the same table that the prospect of their doing so became a joke. When the White House photographer announced that he wanted to take some pictures of a relaxed presidential family, enjoying a quiet dinner together, the staff howled that he would never get the chance. The first lady finally managed to corral her husband and daughters for a film showing them lunching together, but the result was decidedly awkward. Sitting in the family dining room, at a perfectly set table, with Lyndon at the head and Bird on his right, the four exchange pleasantries that sound like those of strangers on a train. Then the president announces he has to leave, plants a kiss on each of the three women, and walks out. Instead of showing a warm, happy family, glowingly content to share time and thoughts, the few minutes of footage document detachment and discomfort.

That Bird was continuing to manage her children much like her television stations is illustrated in her telephone conversation with Lyndon on February 7, 1964. At 3:20 that afternoon, he phoned to tell her to prepare to leave for Texas around 6 p.m., a trip necessitated by the death of their dear friend Louise Kellam, wife of their business manager. The Kellams' daughter, Carolyn, was scheduled to marry a few days later, making Louise's death all the more tragic. Even though Bird was suffering a bout of influenza and diarrhea, she immediately started preparing to attend the funeral in Austin.

In working out travel plans, Lyndon inquired: "Taking any children?" and she shot back a resounding "No." Sounding a little disappointed, he signaled his willingness to accommodate them by saying tentatively, "They can go if they want to." But her mind was made up and she wasn't going to change it: "I just believe I won't take them." Although she called him "Darling" and "Love," the tone of the call is that of minor executives divvying up office assignments, and of the two, she sounds the more authoritative. In the parenting part of their partnership, she was calling the shots.

Later that afternoon, President Johnson phoned his wife again to invite her to the celebration of a big legislative victory. The Senate had just passed his tax bill, and Lady Bird figured in the triumph. He had put that measure high on his immediate to-do list and had urged Congress to honor the slain Kennedy's memory by passing it, along with a new civil rights law. But it was going to take more than sentiment for a dead president to get either bill through. The political mastermind in Lyndon told him to seek the tax reduction first because it would boost his chances in the upcoming presidential election, while a bitter debate over civil rights could bog down into a stalemate that left him looking weak.

In preparation for getting both measures (and others) through Congress, the Johnsons worked together to woo votes. Bird was not involved in the drafting of bills or in the intricate maneuvering that precedes passage—that was Lyndon's forte—but she was very much involved in the socializing that could convert a "No" vote to a "Yes." As a congressman's wife she had attended countless receptions where she was one of many, and she knew how good it feels to be singled out, as someone special, in a small group. When she and the president started planning the first-of-the-year parties they would give for legislators and their spouses, they decided to avoid mass gatherings and give several small receptions instead so they could greet each guest warmly by name and ask about the family.

As soon as the black mourning draperies on the White House came down, the tables in the State Dining Room went up, and the Johnsons issued invitations like a lobbyist dispenses booze—to effect a sale, promote an idea, make an ally. Two or three times a week, after a hard day in the Oval Office, Lyndon trooped back to the residence for handshaking and small talk. While he led a couple dozen elected representatives to the East Wing theater for more schmoozing or a short film, Bird escorted spouses to the second-floor family quarters. Many of the wives had lived in the capital for years but never been invited beyond the State Floor that every tourist sees. Bird knew they would be thrilled to see the private quarters, and they would remember who made that possible.

One small cluster of Washingtonians qualified for special attention from the Johnsons—the Kennedy loyalists who had stayed to work for LBJ. Many of them had once committed their futures to JFK, planning to see him through two terms in the White House and then continue the association at a public policy institute or in an academic setting. After his assassination, they found themselves cut loose, afloat, listening to Lyndon's pleas that they work for him. Part of his motive was simple continuity, but he also saw their presence as valuable validation of his succession.

Kennedy staffers were not easy to win over. They doubted Lyndon's commitment to their goals and made little attempt to hide their disdain for his style. His earthy vocabulary and outsize ego had continued to make him an easy butt for their jokes. Georgetown dinner parties relayed nasty gossip more rapidly than the parlor game "Telephone," and some of it reached the Johnsons. Lyndon fumed that, no matter what he did for them, he would never get the Kennedy crowd to like him; obtaining a fair hearing was out of the question. Bird also detected condescension in the treatment she received. She thought Ted Sorensen wrote excellent speeches, but behind the words he was "making fun of Lyndon and me."

Bird lost no time deploying her usual arsenal of hospitality and genial gestures to keep Sorensen and other JFK loyalists on Lyndon's team. On her fourth day in the White House, she invited Sorensen to dinner, along with Nancy and Pierre Salinger, the high-powered press secretary. Sorensen, who was busy writing Lyndon's first State of the Union message, came to the ranch over Christmas, and Bird set aside one of the guesthouses for the exclusive use of him and his three young sons.

After Sorensen quit in February, Bird kept plotting how to retain other Kennedy people. In a telephone call with Jack Valenti, a newcomer to Lyndon's staff, she explained that she thought small dinners, mixing people from both camps, could help. It was important to keep the numbers "kind of even-steven," so that JFK's aides would not feel overpowered "with Johnson." But she did not do well. The key players in the Kennedy White House she had singled out (Myer Feldman, Ralph A. Dungan, and Kenneth O'Donnell) were gone within the year, and Salinger dropped the bombshell about his departure within days of her talk with Valenti. This was one of those times when Bird's hard work and careful planning did not produce the desired results.

Mrs. Johnson did much better at keeping reporters on her side. Jacqueline Kennedy had antagonized journalists by treating them like nuisances. Although Jackie had pursued stories about politicians' families when she worked as a reporter herself (and had even managed an impromptu interview with Vice President Nixon's young daughters), she wanted reporters nowhere near her children when she became first lady. She routinely snubbed the "harpies" who ferreted out tidbits about her, and reminded her husband's press secretary that it was his job to keep reporters at bay.

Lady Bird Johnson never earned a cent as a working reporter, but she accepted the fact that public attention inevitably comes with holding office. She agreed with her press secretary, Liz Carpenter, that a first lady should "Be Available" and "Never Lie," and the two kept reaching out to journalists in hopes of obtaining positive coverage.

Immediately after the official mourning month ended, the first lady invited female reporters to the second floor of the White House. Several of those women were old enough to have attended Eleanor

Roosevelt's groundbreaking press conferences in the Treaty Room decades earlier, and Mrs. Johnson wanted to emphasize that her "informal meetings" were not going to produce the kind of controversy that surrounded those events. Mrs. Roosevelt had taken questions and sometimes scooped the president with her answers; Mrs. Johnson intended to duplicate the same openness but not upstage her husband. She was modernizing a very traditional role.

After leading sixty-five women reporters through the private quarters on January 10, Bird sounded pleased with herself. "Because I have lived openly and unafraid and quite candidly with people all my life," she added to her diary, "I found this press party pleasant. I like to show people my way of life." Jackie Kennedy thought it unseemly to guide visitors through one's bathroom, where they could check out the brand of toothpaste and the quality of the towels. But Bird didn't mind. Her one regret was having left out in plain sight the books she was reading, and she resolved to stow them away next time.

Her openness and authenticity was not catching—at least to Lyndon. From his earliest days in Congress, he had been wary of reporters. In an attempt to win them over, he shamelessly flattered and courted them, but as soon as he picked up even a hint of criticism issuing from their typewriters, he cut them cold, relegated them to his version of exile, and refused to furnish them with any news. As president, he continued those same self-defeating tactics, but with more miserable repercussions.

Dozens of reporters now depended for their jobs on how accurately they collected information about his decisions and actions and on how quickly they relayed that information to their editors. But he withheld news on appointments and travel arrangements, then taunted reporters about what they did not know. After he purposely misled them, resulting in inaccurate articles, journalists felt blindsided and tricked. He made them look incompetent or stupid, then gloated about outsmarting them.

Lady Bird is a living example of the famous St. Francis prayer—about knowing the difference between what can be changed and what cannot. She took her husband's childlike delight in secrecy as a given. It was part of his makeup for as long as she had known him, and being president of the United States was not going to change that. She also understood that his earthy humor and nearly perfect timing when telling a joke in private did not work with larger audiences or in front of TV cameras. To compensate, he turned excessively formal and reserved, trying to convey a dignity that was not part of his natural style. Rather than banter with the press and exchange witticisms, as JFK did so well, Lyndon became defensive when questioned on a sensitive subject.

Sometimes President Johnson sounded outright snarky, as the text of his press conference on January 25, 1964, shows. After ponderously defending his handling of the current uprising in Panama, he chastised reporters for prying into his private life, writing about his aged, deaf cousin, Oriole Bailey. He suggested they ask him more questions, then stonewalled when they brought up a subject he wanted to avoid, his relationship with Bobby Baker. Lyndon's answer: "I have said all I'm going to say on that."

No, Bird couldn't turn him into a star performer, but she could coach him on content and delivery. And she did. Her critique of the January 25 press conference is not available but a later one, on March 7, shows how cannily she could take him apart without riling his anger. First, she inquired if he wanted to hear her opinions now or later, and he meekly replied, like a student ready for the paddle, "Yes, ma'am, I'm willing now." She praised the parts where he gave a "good crisp answer" or showed a "pickup in drama and interest." But she tore him apart on eye contact and speed: "You were a little breathless and there was too much looking down and I think it was a little too fast." She noted a contradiction between what he was saying now and what he had said in the past. When she gave him a chance to defend himself, he made a brief attempt, protesting that he was pushed for time. But mostly he listened and acquiesced. How often she delivered such appraisals is not known, but the fact that this was among the telephone conversations that he recorded, without her knowledge, suggests that he did not mind that people recognize that she offered him advice and he took it.

Presidents' wives had always supervised the social side of state visits by foreign leaders—menus, entertainment, protocol—and employed a sizable staff to help them. But Lady Bird Johnson wanted to make a more substantive impression, one that enlarged and added to, rather than merely provided backdrop for, her husband's interaction with a foreign leader. Although she lacked Mrs. Kennedy's language skills and had to rely on translators, she prepared carefully for each visit, pinning up a map of the country, reading about its people and traditions, like a high school student cramming for a final exam.

Italy's president Antonio Segni was her first test, and she trooped down to Union Station to welcome him and his party. She found it easy to converse with the "elderly gnome, with spidery white hair and a gentle smile" and his "plump and gentle" wife. But Foreign Minister Giuseppe Saragat, who accompanied them, proved a bigger challenge: "I had to try a bit on that."

Entertainment at the state dinner for President Segni featured both Metropolitan Opera star Robert Merrill and a popular young group, Christy Minstrels. Bird loved the opera arias but decided she was just "too old" to appreciate the Christy Minstrels. "I love folk music," she recorded for her diary, "but the Hootnanny sort of throws me off." Paul Hume, music critic at *The Washington Post*, agreed with her and found Robert Merrill's opera arias more to his liking. Bird regretted she didn't have a chance to tell Merrill about how her mother had introduced her to "Scotti and Severini and Tetrazzini and Galli Curci and all of the Verdi things." At the Italian embassy the next day, President Segni offered some advice that she carefully recorded in her diary, although culinary sophistication never rated a high place on her list of priorities: a good chef is more important to the success of an embassy than a good ambassador.

After two months in the White House, the Johnsons had reason to feel good. Polls showed that four out of five Americans approved of the job the president was doing. The assassination was too fresh in people's minds for them to feel unqualified enthusiasm for LBJ, but his humble-sounding appeals and calls for action touched many. When he insisted he needed everyone's help, that this was a difficult time for the nation, he won over many who had formerly shown little affection for him.

Bird had just returned to Washington from a short trip to New York on February 26 to have more of her old clothes altered when she received the "big news" that the tax bill had "completely, irrevocably, finally" passed both houses of Congress and was ready for the president's signature. With only a quick change of outfit and a lipstick fix, she made it down to the East Room and found a seat in the back row before TV cameras started rolling. At 6:30 Lyndon announced to the nation what she called, "Victory Number One . . . the largest [reduction in income taxes] in the history of the United States." In praising senators who helped, he saved his "highest accolade" for Virginia Senator Harry F. Byrd, who had publicly opposed the tax bill but had not blocked it in the Senate Finance Committee, which he could have done, Lady Bird explained in her diary, for "God knows how long." As she listened to Lyndon purr proudly about his success, she admitted she felt good about how things were going. "I must say it's pleasant."

After signing the tax bill, the president decided to show his regard for JFK by going to Jackie Kennedy's residence in Georgetown and giving her the pens used in the ceremony. One or two pens would not suffice to convey his gratitude—he took four: one for Jackie, one for each of her children, and one for the future JFK presidential library.

Lyndon had previously reached out to the young widow, phoning her several times in December to say he wished he could make her happier. He called her "Honey" and "Darling" and repeatedly invited her back to the White House, threatening to spank her if she didn't come see him. Although Jackie accepted the president's calls and wrote to thank him and his family for their many kind gestures (including the fire engine they delivered for John Jr.'s Christmas), she refused to set foot in the executive mansion. The Johnsons had to go to her.

After the quick pen passing at Jackie's house, Lyndon and Lady Bird proceeded to the home of Jack Valenti, the advertising executive from Houston who had married Mary Margaret Wiley, Lyndon's secretary, and moved to Washington to join Lyndon's staff. At the Valenti home, the Johnsons found a more relaxed setting than at the Kennedy house. Mary Margaret grilled impromptu steaks; Lyndon fussed over three-months-old Courtenay Lynda, and Bird kept an eye on reporter Marianne Means, who joined the party. Famous as much for her looks and fetching ways as for her writing, Means was, Bird noted, "somebody that Lyndon and all men, in fact, have their eye on. . . . So I guess I'll have to look her over harder!" Means was known as "soft and cheerful and pretty," and rather than object to what appeared flirtatious behavior between her husband and the reporter, Bird reminded herself that Means's articles "about Lyndon have all been very favorable."

When Bird returned to the White House later that evening she could reread on the bedroom mantel the haunting reminder that her predecessor had put there: "In this room lived John Fitzgerald Kennedy with his wife Jacqueline" during the time he was "president of the United States." It was only ninety-three days since the horrific tragedy in Dallas, but Bird had already begun to define a new kind of first lady, very different from Jackie or, for that matter, most of the women who preceded her in the White House. Rather than act the fashion icon or very private helpmate, Bird intended to show how a spouse can be a full collaborator. She would continue to privately critique Lyndon's speeches and press conferences, publicly help him court legislators and the press, and act as his sounding board. On her own, she would travel to the nation's troubled spots to highlight problems and explore solutions. It was a tall order for a presidential partner, but the Texan in her understood that in some quarters a workhorse counted for more than a show horse.

13

TEAMING UP FOR
THE BIG WIN

AUGUST 25, 1964, was one of those dog days in Washington, when energy slumps as the temperature hovers near 90 and the gray sky threatens a drizzle. But Lady Bird Johnson was on high alert, not sure what bombshell Lyndon would drop next. The Democrats had already convened in Atlantic City, New Jersey, to select their presidential candidate, but the name at the top of their list was not co-operating. Daughter Luci and most of the president's staff had already arrived at the convention site and checked into their hotel suites, but Lyndon was refusing to join them. When he wouldn't even reveal a timetable for his arrival, Walter Jenkins, his chief aide, phoned him from convention headquarters to find out what was going on.

Just before noon that Wednesday, Jenkins reached an utterly dejected president who whined that he wanted out of the job because it was too much for him. With all "the responsibilities of the bomb and the world and the Nigras and the South," Lyndon told Jenkins, he had decided to let the Democrats choose a "better-prepared . . .

better trained . . . Harvard educated" man. With nothing going right for him, why fight? If newspaper editors were going to treat him so badly, ignoring his accomplishments and headlining his shortcomings, why prolong the agony? Maybe it was beyond the power of any "white southerner . . . to unite the nation now." He wasn't asking for a lot, LBJ complained, just "a little love."

Jenkins, knowing how useless it was to contradict his boss when he sounded this self-pitying, muttered non-committal phrases and let the whimpering run its course. Lyndon explained he had already written his withdrawal speech (except for the last sentence) and now he needed to decide where to deliver it. He had sounded out Bird and she thought he owed it to his supporters to make the trip to Atlantic City and face them directly. But he favored calling a few reporters to the White House and dropping his shocker right there in Washington.

After twenty-five years on Lyndon's staff, listening to his innumerable threats and mind changes, Jenkins still could not be sure what Lyndon was really thinking, and he phoned press secretary George Reedy, who was still at the White House, to find out what he thought. Reedy's rundown offered little comfort. A few hours earlier he had endured a long, excruciating walk around the South Lawn, his hammertoes making every step an effort, as he struggled to match the pace of the much taller Lyndon and, at the same time, process his ranting about the Democrats convened in Atlantic City: "Fuck 'em, they don't want me anyway. . . . I'm going to go up and fuck 'em. I'm going to tell them that I'm not going to accept the nomination." Reedy confessed to Jenkins that he could not be absolutely sure but this time Lyndon "sounded like he really meant it."

Baffled by what to do next, Jenkins then turned to "one person . . . of all the people . . . around [Lyndon who had the] ability to reason with him and be convincing." Jenkins called Bird. Lyndon's state of mind was no news to her. Although he had been holding a couple of meetings every day and was on the phone a lot, she had picked up signs that he was falling apart, and she was doing everything she could to keep him operational. When he had breakfast and dinner in bed, she was there, beside him, eating off a tray. She had walked with him on the South Lawn and consulted trusted friends and advisers about his condition. The previous day, she had met twice with Abe Fortas, who held no official position at the White House but remained one of the Johnsons' stalwart team. The second visit had lasted almost to midnight. She had also spent time with Dr. Willis Hurst, who had come to the White House, along with three other physicians, to examine Lyndon. What else could she do? "I do not remember hours I ever found harder," she confessed to her diary.

That sticky Wednesday, with everyone waiting to see when he would go to the convention in Atlantic City, she decided to use a tactic that had worked before. She wrote Lyndon a letter and left it for him to read while she and Lynda went for a walk on the White House grounds. Upstairs, in the president's bedroom, the shades were drawn, but Bird knew her husband was in there, refusing to "talk to anybody . . . wrestling with his own demons."

Eventually he took up her letter and read it, and within hours he was on his way to Atlantic City. But not until August 27, when he stood in front of hundreds of delegates to the Democratic National Convention and actually accepted their nomination, did she have clear proof of how he would answer her letter. She had often described her role in their partnership as offering him good judgment, although he didn't always accept it. This time he did, picking up her challenge to stay the course and run for a full term of his own. She later singled it out as an example of how she had influenced his presidency.

The letter was vintage Bird. Fully available in her published *White House Diary,* it began with flattery, telling her husband how great he was: "Beloved—You are as brave a man as Harry Truman—or FDR— or Lincoln."

Then she promised him things would get better: "You can go on to find some peace, some achievement amidst all the pain."

After stroking his ego further ("You have been strong, patient, determined beyond any words of mine to express. I honor you for it. So does most of the country.") She was not afraid to use a mild threat: "To step out now would be wrong for your country, and I can see nothing but a lonely wasteland for your future. Your friends would be frozen in embarrassed silence and your enemies jeering."

As for herself, he need not worry—she could take whatever came her way: "I am not afraid of *Time* [which had just published an unflattering article about her] or lies or losing money or defeat."

Knowing how her man resisted taking instruction from anyone, she left the decision entirely up to him. But she closed her plea with one final dose of adulation and support: "In the final analysis I can't carry any of the burdens you talked of—so I know it's only *your* choice. But I know you are as brave as any of the thirty–five.

"I love you always,

"Bird"

In designating those August hours as the hardest of that year, Bird was saying a lot, because she had some strong contenders for the title: the election year of 1964 was one of sleepless nights and hard choices. Along with big legislative victories, like the tax bill, came many disappointments, and during tough negotiations with railroad workers in April, she and Lyndon had talked "every night [about the negotiations] . . . and how much is hanging in the balance for him." It was clear to her that part of Lyndon wanted out of the presidency and he was looking for her help on that. On a day when they had been wakened by a phone call at 5:30 in the morning, he had started out the door and then come back to whisper in her ear, "Get me out of this, won't you?"

But she could not. After considering how an exit now might hurt "his image as a father figure to the nation," she felt obliged to urge him to "Stay on." No matter how much both of them wanted to find it, "There [was] no way out." They had endless talks on the subject, and during the Republican convention in mid-July, Lyndon wakened Bird at 4 a.m. to talk "in detail the problems, the pros and cons, the good points and the bad, of every decision that faces him with regard to this campaign. . . . So it was a wakeful night, with about two hours' sleep."

One big problem, beginning with President Kennedy's assassination, was figuring out how to move into his job with confidence, yet not look like a greedy usurper. As Lyndon and Bird served out what was left of JFK's term, they toggled between those opposite poles: paying careful respect to the Kennedy legacy while promoting themselves as able leaders of the nation. The martyred JFK, the iconic Jackie, and their two endearing children had captured the nation's love in a way few political families ever manage, and the Johnsons had the unenviable task of following them.

Lyndon had no guarantee that his party would choose him as their presidential nominee in 1964. He feared they might dump him in favor of one of the Kennedy crowd. Among the assassinated president's most grief-stricken supporters were some who talked of reclaiming the Oval Office, and his brother Robert appeared eager to lead them.

So it wouldn't do for either of the Johnsons to look too confident about their chances of remaining in a White House they had inherited rather than won on their own. Better to emphasize that their occupancy was only temporary and show respect for the man whose death had put them there. In public, Lyndon praised the leadership of JFK, and urged passage of the laws he had proposed. Bird made a point of not appearing to compete with Jackie, knowing she lacked both the interest and the preparation. In purchases for the White House family quarters, Bird held back, and she refused to upgrade the worn upholstery and draperies because, she explained, whoever moved in at the next election might not approve of her choices. She wouldn't even designate a special project for herself. When reporters asked what legacy she wanted to leave, she declined to be specific, saying only that her answer would be revealed in deeds, not words.

Privately, Bird kept evaluating Lyndon's performance and her own against what the Kennedys had done. After hearing her husband deliver a speech to a large crowd in Mississippi on February 27, she graded it a good B+ but lamented that it lacked "that singing quality of so many of Mr. Kennedy's." For herself, she recognized that she could not afford to ignore the value of Jacqueline Kennedy's White House restoration project. It had added gravity to Jackie's fashionista image and won her high marks with voters. Although Lady Bird did not share Jackie's attachment to historic buildings—she cared more about good reading lights—she resolved to pick up on the White House project where Jackie left off. On February 28, she went to Mrs. Kennedy's pink brick house in Georgetown for pointers on how to proceed. It was the kind of undertaking Bird dreaded because it resurrected old insecurities about her own provincial upbringing.

The prospect of meeting with the Committee for the Preservation of the White House on May 7 was even more daunting. Bird mused in her diary why a woman as confident as she in many matters shrank from any encounter with these arbiters of taste: "Why, when I'm not the least bit afraid of meeting the tycoons of business, or the titans of labor, or any other sort of people at home or abroad, should I look upon this [meeting] with such trepidation?" In addition to the White House committee members, she would have to face dozens of others invited to participate in the day's events: ultra-wealthy donors, with names like Loeb and Paley; super-pedigreed Americans like Charles Francis Adams; celebrity curators and decorators, including James Biddle, from the Metropolitan Museum of Art, and Mrs. Henry "Sister" Parish, who had counseled Jackie. It was not that Bird coveted what they had or were—she accepted the fact that they possessed a key to a world that was different from hers—but she knew they would be tempted to compare her with her stylish predecessor.

Bird prepared for the May 7 event for weeks and then, up to the last minute, kept looking for ways to make it flawless. At the morning session of the White House committee, she reviewed what had been accomplished and then triumphantly unveiled a Winslow Homer painting that had been "precipitously and happily dropped into our laps." At noon, she was still polishing the speech she would deliver to a larger assembly that afternoon. She had studied diligently with White House curator James Ketchum, and could talk knowledgeably about provenance and restoration techniques when she led her guests on a tour of the mansion. For a woman who admitted she had to learn the difference between a *bergère* and a *fauteuil*, it was a remarkable performance.

To maximize her effectiveness in the White House Lady Bird denied herself small pleasures, like reading the newspaper comics. That freed up time for speech making and for planning and taking investigative trips. Her solo journey to the poorest parts of Appalachia in January 1964 had given such satisfaction that she resolved to do more. She found it personally gratifying to travel on her own, without Lyndon's staff telling her where to go and what to say. When he set out on a five-state poverty tour in early May, daughter Lynda accompanied him while Bird stayed behind, conserving her energy for her own foray to Kentucky later that month.

Although the Kentucky trip required rising early and hiking along footpaths through one of the most economically depressed parts of the country, Mrs. Johnson loved it. Sitting alongside students in a one-room schoolhouse and washing her hands in the same zinc bucket they used brought back vivid memories of her own primary education in Karnack. For these youngsters, she had a special treat that was not available to country schools in Texas in her time: she threw the switch that turned on the first electric light their school had ever had.

Back at the White House that night, she ran herself a hot bath and thought back over the past few hours. Lyndon was already in Michigan, preparing to deliver a major salvo in the War on Poverty he had declared in January. In a speech entitled "The Great Society," he would outline his vision, the cornerstone of his bid for reelection. But Bird would not be there to hear him. Savoring thoughts about her own solo excursion to Kentucky, she ranked the day among her "ten best" since becoming first lady.

Bird still found public speaking challenging, requiring hours of work. Nonetheless, she doggedly accepted many of the invitations that came in. George Reedy noted she had an uncanny ability to size up an audience and tailor her remarks to fit, while Lyndon was prone to gaffes. On a swing through the Midwest, he affected a common touch by telling a group of Iowa farmers that he had to leave and go "slop the hogs." His press entourage joked afterward that his recipe for hog slop would start with champagne and contain "truffles and pâté de foie gras."

Among the most daunting speaking invitations Lady Bird accepted was one to address a gathering of illustrious New Yorkers at the newly opened Hilton Hotel on April 9, 1964. Nearly three thousand people would gather that day to celebrate the first anniversary of the Eleanor Roosevelt Memorial Foundation, and Mrs. Johnson dreaded the prospect of standing up in front of them. The program promised a star roster, including the legendary Marian Anderson reading from Eleanor Roosevelt's book *Tomorrow Is Now*, and Adlai Stevenson, orating "with his silver tongue." Bird braced herself and went. She had decided to do what she did best—recount in her own words her personal recollections—in this case of a woman she had known, Eleanor Roosevelt. Bird could be as tough on herself as on Lyndon but this time she gave herself a satisfactory rating: "I had acquitted myself well enough—something I seldom feel."

When Radcliffe College invited her to deliver the commencement address on June 9, she accepted, although she knew her presence at the podium would ignite comparisons between the exalted Seven Sisters colleges and her own alma mater, the University of Texas. Lyndon was famous for holding up the "Harvards" as specimens of sophistication and erudition, and Radcliffe, in those sex-segregated days, was the Harvard for women. Bird claimed she labored more diligently on this than on any of her previous speeches, and the result was exhilarating. *Life* magazine singled it out as one of the season's best. She had used the opportunity to encourage women graduates to involve themselves in the nation's political debates and to use both "energy" and "intellect" to help solve the nation's problems. After chatting with students and faculty following her talk, she returned to Washington, and although she would never get her husband to agree, she saw the gap between Karnack and Cambridge as definitely bridgeable.

Her upbeat mood got another boost on July 2. For nearly a decade, that date had marked a double milestone in the Johnson household: Luci's birthday and another year of Lyndon's surviving his 1955 heart attack, an event Bird singled out as the "severest trial" that she and Lyndon ever faced. Now, in their first White House year, the Johnsons added a third reason to celebrate the day. After the candles on Luci's favorite cake (lemon) were extinguished that afternoon, word came that the Civil Rights Bill, which was a crucial part of Lyndon's legislative agenda, had finally passed the last hurdle: the House of Representatives had voted overwhelmingly (289 to 126) in favor. In a burst of jubilation, the president announced he would go to the East Room at six that evening and sign the bill in front of television cameras, so the entire nation could watch. Just over a year had passed since President Kennedy introduced legislation to guarantee all Americans the right to be served in hotels, restaurants, theaters, retail stores, and similar establishments. President Johnson had engineered the passage of a broader version that gave more attention to schools.

Bird had sometimes doubted her husband could pull this off. A few months earlier, she had felt "shaky" hearing him come out so "forthrightly for the full Civil Rights Program" in Mississippi, where integration had been "a little bit on the token side." But she concluded he had been right to press his case there: "You might as well say it where it's hard to say." She had registered his defiant response to others who warned he was moving too fast on civil rights: "What the hell is the presidency for?" Now, as she watched him deliver "a marvelous televised statement" on the subject, her thoughts went back to the nights he spent on the office cot while he worked to get the 1957 Civil Rights Act through the Senate. Today was just "another step," she decided, in what looked like a long struggle.

As soon as he had penned his name on the Civil Rights Bill, Lyndon wanted to escape Washington and get an early start on the July 4 weekend at the ranch. Leaving Luci behind, under the supervision of Willie Day Taylor, the president and first lady climbed into a chopper on the White House lawn at 10:30 for the short trip to Andrews Air Force Base, where they boarded the JetStar that took them directly to the landing strip at their ranch. It would be midnight (Texas time) before she arrived, but Bird was animated "with that sense of adventure and youth and release . . . [on] one of those rare nights, starry in every way, when one does not think about tomorrow."

That lofty elation could not last—Bird knew—not with the next presidential election coming up fast. Immediately after signing the Civil Rights Act, Lyndon had become depressed. He had confided to aide Bill Moyers his fear that, with their endorsement of that measure, the Democrats had effectively relinquished the South to the Republican Party for the next fifty years. November would be the first test of his prediction.

With all her other worries, Bird had to keep an eye on her husband's health. It was the top item on her checklist in deciding whether she even wanted him to run. She had already sounded out the physicians whose opinion she valued most, the same two who had been treating him since his heart attack: Dr. Hurst and Dr. Cain. Before their examination of Lyndon in Washington on May 15, she scheduled her own conference with them at Huntland, where Lyndon had his heart attack and where she often went for some private time of her own.

By the time the doctors arrived at the Virginia estate, she had a nine-page, handwritten letter waiting for them, listing what she saw as the pros and cons of going for another term. She and Lyndon had been talking this over for a while, from every vantage point, and the letter summarized her thinking on the subject. The reasons for quitting were appealing: he would have more free time to do what he wanted, and he might possibly live longer. But the prospects for what might happen if he dropped out were frightening: questions might arise about "skeletons in the closet"; and, most pertinent to her, he risked falling into periods of "depression and frustration" as he watched someone else run the country.

The bottom line was that she wanted him to run. Although she included points he ought to include in announcing his withdrawal, she hoped he wouldn't use them. However, she made very clear that this should be his last hurrah. "February or March 1968," she wrote, would be the time to announce he was retiring. That was nearly four years away, and she didn't even know if "the Lord [will let] him live that long." If, as she fervently hoped, Lyndon did survive a full term, he would be sixty years old. By then, "the juices of life will be sufficiently still in him" and he would agree to leave politics behind. Then the two of them could "return to the ranch" and "live the rest of our days quietly."

When Lady Bird Johnson published her *White House Diary* after leaving Washington, she paraphrased only tidbits from that letter, but Lyndon, in his own *The Vantage Point*, published the full version. He wrote that he had talked over the pros and cons of a run with Lady Bird "of course," and that she had been gung ho. One line of her letter to him, omitted from her book, gave a key reason. Out of office he would feel frustrated and useless, drink too much, and look for a scapegoat. She did not want to be "it."

When physicians Hurst and Cain came to Huntland to talk with Bird, she solicited their advice in front of a blazing fireplace. Specifically, she wanted their opinions on how Lyndon could deal with the stresses of a four-year term. Dr. Hurst assured her that the 1955 heart attack did not doom her husband to the sidelines of public life. Dwight Eisenhower suffered his first heart attack on September 24, 1955, when he was sixty-four years old, Hurst reminded Bird, but Ike then won and served out a second presidential term before leaving the White House in 1961. He had suffered other ailments by 1964, but he was currently enjoying a comfortable, rewarding life with Mamie at their Gettysburg farm. He remained involved in public affairs, and was one of the first people Lyndon turned to for counsel after Kennedy's assassination. Reassured by what the doctors told her, Bird gave them her letter, with instructions to deliver it to Lyndon when they examined him the following day.

Even with his wife's endorsement, the president questioned whether he should run. Some days he was buoyantly confident, as if no one could beat him, but on others he foresaw a disastrous finale. When a Gallup poll reported that 77 percent of Americans liked what he was doing, he worried about what he had done to disappoint the other 23 percent.

A race riot, starting in New York City three days after he signed the Civil Rights Act, added to his anxieties. The uprising started in Harlem, where a white, off-duty police officer had shot a black fifteen-year-old dead, and quickly spread to Brooklyn's Bedford Stuyvesant section and then to Rochester, three hundred miles north. Individual narratives varied with the neighborhood but charges of excessive police force ran through them all. After reporting that angry protesters had hurled bottles and bricks, looted homes and stores, overturned cars, and set fire to buildings, *The New York Times* opined that the long hot summer had begun. Governor Nelson Rockefeller called up the state's National Guard to restore order in Rochester, and the worst of the rioting stopped. But questions remained about how such protests might alarm voters and siphon votes away from the president.

More devastating to Lady Bird was an outpouring of articles and books that summer that questioned her integrity, especially regarding the accumulation of the Johnsons' wealth. It was not yet required—or even expected—that presidential candidates would file a public report of their approximate net worth, and Lyndon had no intention of doing so. But that left *The Wall Street Journal* and other periodicals free to conduct their own investigations and publish their findings. Many of the articles reported stupendous gains in the Johnson holdings and attributed them not to old-fashioned hard and honest work, but to chicanery and favoritism, even outright illegal maneuverings. The most disturbing of the indictments, because it contained extensive, careful research, came from fellow Texan J. Evetts Haley, whose 35-cent edition of his little book sold more than seven million copies that summer. Haley's title left no doubt about where he stood on his subject: *A Texan Looks at Lyndon: A Study in Illegitimate Power.*

Haley's book might have been discredited as a petty assault by one Texan on another, but other journalists, highly respected, had already come to similar conclusions. *Wall Street Journal* reporter Louis Kohlmeier had spearheaded the attack with a series that began on March 23, with a front-page headline that zeroed in on Lady Bird: "The Johnson Wealth: How President's Wife Built $17,500 into a Big Fortune in Television." Although Kohlmeier's first piece credited Lady Bird's acumen and luck (instead of suggesting LBJ made nefarious interventions), his follow-up articles were not so kind. Some outlined how the president and first lady remained in close contact with the trustees who controlled their holdings, an obvious flouting of "blind" in their "blind trust," and an outright challenge to announcements coming from the White House that the presidential family no longer had any voice at all in the management of their broadcasting empire.

Wildly different numbers were tossed around about the extent of the Johnson wealth, and they alone were enough to arouse suspicion. How could a public official, whose salary was public knowledge, get that rich that fast? And whose numbers were correct? The accounting firm hired by the Johnsons, Haskins & Sells, reported the presidential family had total assets of less than $4 million, but one wag quipped that a similar accounting method would put the value of the island of Manhattan at a measly $24. Everyone agreed that whatever the exact number, Johnson holdings dwarfed what the Republican presidential nominee, Barry Goldwater, owned, reportedly little more than a modest house in Arizona.

By the end of July, the money story consumed inordinate public attention, and the first lady was central to the plot. Not only was she principal owner of a profitable broadcasting company but she also held title to Alabama land where renters lived in abject poverty. In May, two Republican congressmen had visited parts of Autauga and Chilton counties, near Montgomery, where Bird's property was located, and chided the presidential family "to put their own 'squalid' tenant houses in order before trying to establish a billion-dollar [national] program to combat poverty."

One of the investigating congressmen admitted he was "shocked" at the "squalor" of what he saw: "shanties" with broken windows, leaking roofs, and floors with holes big enough to see the earth down below. He counted eleven persons crowded into one tiny, dilapidated dwelling. Many Alabamians in that area lived in poverty, and the surrounding counties were not prosperous, but the Republicans deemed those tenants "on the Johnson land were the worst."

Voters across the nation registered outrage. One Delaware schoolteacher wrote the White House to ask how she should "explain Slum Lord Johnson" to her students. At first Bird struggled to defend herself, saying some of the tenant families had lived there for generations, virtually rent free, and making them move would be cruel. But of course that did not quell the criticism and Bird prepared to "batten down the hatches for a nasty storm." Lyndon advised her to hunker down and take it, like a "jackass in a hailstorm," and she opted not to issue any more public statements on the subject.

As stories about the family's wealth continued to pile up, the first lady worked with the president behind the scenes to combat the bad press. On Saturday afternoon, July 25, after learning that *Life* magazine was preparing its own exposé, they met with their political trouble-shooters, Clark Clifford, Walter Jenkins, Bill Moyers, and Cliff Carter, for a forty-five-minute, off-the-record strategy session. The following Monday, the president followed up with a call to media tycoon Henry Luce, chair of the corporation that owned both *Life* and *Fortune*. After chatting amiably about the general state of the nation, LBJ suggested that Luce encourage his reporters to widen their investigation of presidential wealth. Rather than settling for unsubstantiated gossip, they ought to talk with a "trusted person" (the president was ready to recommend one) because there was "a lot of politics" in what they were writing. It would also be a good idea, LBJ added, to take a closer look at Goldwater, whom Luce was supporting.

In trying to convince Luce that he was not a rich man, Lyndon used numbers that he said came from a "national auditing person," but they tended to be smallish. He, himself, was worth only a paltry $400,000—the rest belonged to Lady Bird and their two daughters. No one could accurately calculate the value of the broadcast empire without selling it, he claimed, but the yearly earnings averaged only about $162,000. As for the Alabama farmland, it barely yielded enough to pay the taxes on it.

All through the president's rambling explanation, Luce said very little, but his response came soon after, on August 14, when *Life* put a picture of a grim LBJ on its cover and began an unflattering series of articles on his career, summing up details of how he became a multi-millionaire and how badly he was performing as president. This was one time that Lyndon's persuasive power, often dubbed "the treatment," did not work.

No president's wife had ever faced such a searing attack on her finances. But then none of Bird's first lady predecessors had ever racked up such a fortune by her own making. Many had been wealthy, starting with Martha Washington, the "wealthiest widow in Virginia" when George married her, but Bird's inheritances had been modest. *Life* reporters Keith Wheeler and William Lambert decided that her net worth was the product more of her husband's interventions than of anything she did. According to *Life,* that intervention reached all the way back to her 1943 acquisition of KTBC, when Congressman Johnson had used favors, including a West Point appointment for a son of one of the principals, to wangle a good price on the station.

As for how the station prospered, *Life*'s Wheeler and Lambert came up against the same cold paper trail that other reporters found—no documentation of malfeasance existed. But the reporters concluded that Bird's "Midas touch" was only "legend." Although they found no hard evidence of Lyndon's intervention "by word or deed" in obtaining special treatment for any of her TV or radio stations, they strongly hinted that he had done so. The list of charges leveled against him, including hardnosed tactics on potential advertisers and out-and-out threats against competing stations, was simply too long to ignore. The article in *Life* suggested strongly that where there's smoke there must be fire, and stoked Lyndon's fears that he could lose the upcoming election, clearly the most important of his life.

Unfortunately, the outpouring of articles about money peaked in August, just as the Democrats were about to name their nominee, and had contributed to the president's reluctance to go to Atlantic City. He still feared as well that a spontaneous outburst of Kennedy support could undercut him. In looking over a proposed schedule of convention events, he had spotted a laudatory film about JFK and insisted it be relegated to the last spot on the program, after the nomination was securely nailed down.

But the convention in Atlantic City had a potentially more inflammatory issue, and it required immediate resolution. Two different sets of delegates demanded the right to cast Mississippi's sixty-eight votes at the convention, and someone had to decide between them. Members of the racially integrated Mississippi Freedom Democratic Party (MFDP) argued they were the rightful representatives, having opened the selection process to blacks, who had historically been shut out. The all-white delegation they were competing against resulted from a different election, officially sanctioned by the state's Democratic Party, but excluding black voters.

Lady Bird advised Lyndon that it should be the "legal delegation" that got seated. Her memo to him even outlined the points he should use to justify that decision: it would not do to bend to "emotionalism." Lyndon had already done a lot to make a more nearly equal playing field for blacks and he should vow to do more. But political parties had to operate within the laws on the books, and in this case, Bird argued, that meant seating the Mississippi delegation selected under current Democratic Party rules, notwithstanding the fact that under those rules black voters had been shut out.

Lyndon, more politically attuned than his wife, knew that a decision giving full victory to one side would infuriate the other; he had to come up with a compromise that gave something to both. By pressuring the MFDP to accept two at large seats at the convention, in lieu of the state's full sixty-eight, he tossed them a bone without seriously diminishing the clout of what Bird had called the "legal delegation." Although his argument, that this was the best that could be gotten, resonated with some of the would-be delegates from Alabama and Mississippi, others were so outraged by the decision that they decided to boycott the convention and go home. As the nominating process finally got started, hostility was obvious among Democrats inside the convention hall and outside. Who knew how that rancor would make itself felt in November?

With Lyndon's nomination tied up on August 27, the campaign against the Republican nominee, Senator Barry Goldwater, could begin. But Mrs. Johnson had already started her planning months earlier, and it centered on the part of the nation she knew and loved best: the South. It was exactly the region where the Republican nominee was running far ahead of Lyndon, who had, since signing the Civil Rights Act, become a reviled figure there. Back in Marshall, Texas, where Bird went to high school, he was being called a traitor.

Not all Southerners were so scathing in their judgments. Bird happily relayed the story of one African American woman who exuberantly greeted the passage of the Civil Rights Act by shouting, "I'll throw away the bottle." Pushed to explain, the woman, whose husband was a prominent educator, told about trips across the South where she found "Whites Only" signs on public toilets. She had started carrying a screw top bottle to relieve herself. With access to public accommodations now the law of the land, she could dispense with the bottle.

Bird knew Lyndon had the support of voters like that woman; the problem was to persuade white Southerners who abhorred his civil rights stand to vote for him. She also wanted to restore some dignity to Southerners. Tired of hearing them denigrated with "snide jokes" and mentions of "cornpone and red neck," she resolved to go there and prove that "as far as *this* President and his wife are concerned," the South was a valued part of the nation. She did not conceal her own convictions: "I know the Civil Rights Act was right, and I don't mind saying so." But she refused to disparage those who thought differently: "I'm tired of people making the South the whipping boy of the Democratic Party." She had beloved relatives in Alabama, and she still warmed to the slow rhythms of the lives they led, to memories of the generosity they once showed a motherless girl.

Bird recognized that she was better able to present Lyndon's case throughout the South than he. Voters were less likely to connect her to the Civil Rights Act, and they would see her as more human and approachable. Since she could count on the region's ideas about chivalry to women to limit hostility toward her, she would undertake what no presidential candidate's spouse had ever done—a solo campaign trip of her own. She called it a "journey of the heart," but it was actually a carefully calculated excursion to win votes.

Planning for a campaign swing through the South, on a train dubbed the Lady Bird Special, started in May, although Bird had been assessing her options for weeks. Whistle-stop campaigning had once been a staple of presidential campaigns, and Harry Truman had showed its effectiveness in 1948 when he came from behind to win a tough election. Truman had observed that trains chugged through small towns that had no airports, reaching communities where national candidates had never set foot, so he set out to reach them. In 1960, the Kennedys had ignored that counsel, preferring fast-moving planes and comfy hotel suites, but Lady Bird and Lyndon undertook their own whistle-stop campaign through the South, on behalf of the Kennedy-Johnson ticket. This time, in 1964, she was on her own.

The first lady had definite ideas about scheduling. She favored small towns "because I feel at home [there] and I want my speeches to make the people feel I am at home, too." But she would not limit herself to friendly territory or easy towns. "Anyone can get into Atlanta," she reminded Liz Carpenter, "[because Atlanta is] the new, modern South. Let me take the tough ones."

Staff scrounged through abandoned cars in rail yards to find a car with a platform at the back, so that Bird could greet people up close, as Truman had done. The Democratic National Committee paid the bills, but the first lady's office executed every small detail of the planning and preparation. Her staff pored over maps, made calculations about the best places to stop and about how much time to spend in each. She and Liz Carpenter compiled lists of local officials to contact and invite aboard the Lady Bird Special along the way.

As plans progressed, not a word leaked to the press. When the president was asked if his wife would campaign for him, he used one of his famous "Mother Hubbard" answers—covers everything and touches nothing—to keep the details secret a bit longer. She had campaigned in the past, he noted, and she would in the future. Behind the scenes, he enthusiastically supported her effort. When he learned that provisions were being made for an advance staff of only fifty, he instructed Carpenter to increase that number to seventy.

Not everyone in the West Wing shared his zeal. Kenny O'Donnell, a Kennedy holdover, struck Carpenter as "half laughing at the whole idea and obviously feeling that neither the South nor women were important in the campaign." Such disdain for women's efforts was old hat to Carpenter. Veteran of many campaigns, she knew that even the most politically astute females still found themselves relegated to the drudgery jobs, like "licking stamps and sealing envelopes. . . . [Then it was] back to the kitchen and the bedroom, girls, for four more years."

Not until everything was in place did the first lady contact leading figures in the states she planned to visit. With Liz Carpenter's help, she spent an entire day phoning governors and senators, one after another, to clue them in on her plans. After giving them the bare outline of her schedule, she solicited their suggestions on what to add, as if any leeway remained in the itinerary. Liz Carpenter insisted Mrs. Johnson had not "a phony bone" in her body, but when she started talking to Southerners, she just naturally included homey references to watermelon and honeysuckle. Only a hard-nosed opponent could turn her down when she began, in her most charming voice, "Guvnuh . . ."

The Lady Bird Special, its nineteen cars painted in patriotic red and blue stripes, left Union Station a little past 7 a.m. on October 6. A few minutes later, the president climbed aboard in Alexandria, slapping a White House seal of approval on the undertaking. He joined his wife's

campaign venture twice more, once at the midpoint in Raleigh, North
Carolina, and again at the jubilant conclusion in New Orleans. That
was just enough to express his support without diverting the focus
from Bird. Daughter Lynda accompanied her mother for the first two
days, and Luci replaced her sister for the last two days, as the train
moved through eight states, over 1,682 miles of track.

Dozens of staff, security workers, and journalists remained on board
for most of that time, and hundreds of guests climbed on and off as
the train moved through their hometowns. Curious crowds assembled
along tracks in places where celebrity sightings were rare. Residents of
tiny Ahoskie, North Carolina, marveled that this was their most exciting day since Buffalo Bill came to town.

In other areas, the reception was neither so kind nor enthusiastic.
Hecklers gathered, some wielding signs of support for Goldwater;
others, more menacing, warned, "Blackbird, go home" and "Fly away,
Bird." In Columbia, South Carolina, where a group of young men tried
to drown out the first lady with chants of "We Want Barry," the rest
of the audience hushed, curious to see how she handled disruptions.
Up there on her own, she had no speech coaches or political aides to
script her reply, but she answered with a calm logic that even the most
hostile onlookers registered. Holding up a white-gloved hand, she announced, "This is a country of many viewpoints. You've had your say
and now it's my chance for me to have mine."

Mrs. Johnson played her strongest card—her own Southern heritage—to convince voters of how much she shared with them. Faced
with dissenters' placards and chants, she reminded them that she
came from a town much like theirs; she had the same concerns and
spoke with the same accent. They might not agree with what she
said, but they understood what she was saying. With college-debating
precision, she ticked off her husband's accomplishments; with gracious good manners, she complimented local officials; with cheerful optimism, she predicted a better future for them all. Rather than

the scolding teacher from the North, she came across as the genial cousin who had moved away but remained attached to the people she had left behind. In Alabama, she spotted familiar faces in the audience and invited "Cousin Effie" and "Cousin Cox" up to the platform, to stand beside her. Who wanted to heckle a woman related to the family down the road?

Bird's rail car, adjacent to the platform car, was well equipped; she had her own chef, a private bathroom, and a parlor where she could chat with local dignitaries who came aboard to be photographed with her. Conditions in the other passenger cars were more primitive. Fifteen volunteer hostesses, in perky hats and blue dresses, managed the human traffic, but it was difficult, as dozens of reporters, security agents, and service workers vied for a dollop of space. In the absence of bathing facilities, body odors produced choruses of "I've grown accustomed to your smell," until Liz Carter booked a few hotel rooms in Tallahassee (and extra towels) so everybody could clean up.

Although Bird insisted that assassination was not part of her destiny, her security detail remained on guard. The volunteer hostesses listened for ominous talk, including threats against Mrs. Johnson, when they got off the train to mix with the crowds and pass out posters and other campaign items. A surveillance squad preceded the train to inspect the track, and in Florida, after a bomb threat was received, security agents insisted on carefully examining a long bridge before allowing the first lady's train to cross it.

At Bird's final stop in New Orleans on October 9, Lyndon met her with a big hug and warm praise. Behind the smile, one journalist friend detected a hint of jealousy. Lyndon had a long record of pushing her to excel, then showing some petulance when she upstaged him. He certainly sounded peeved in a telephone conversation with her on October 7. Evidently pleased with his TV appearance earlier that day, he phoned her to ask what she thought of it, and when she said she hadn't even watched it because she didn't know it aired, he exploded:

"Well, why the hell don't you find out? Why don't you find one of those eighty women you got with you to find out?"

Aides marveled at how calmly she took such outbursts, answering him with an acquiescent "Yes, dear," or a sympathetic comment about how hard he was working. His criticisms sometimes bordered on the ludicrous. Kenny O'Donnell, who noted Lyndon was constantly "up and down" during the 1964 campaign, reported he went so far as to accuse Bird of "working for Goldwater."

After four days of giving speeches and greeting countless individuals, Mrs. Johnson hardly had time to catch up on her sleep before she faced one of the biggest trials of the entire campaign year. She was at the White House and Lyndon was stumping in New York when both learned that Walter Jenkins, whom they loved like a blood relative, had been arrested in Washington on what was then called a "morals charge," but was actually a homosexual encounter with an indigent, aged war veteran in a public restroom.

At first incredulous, both Johnsons listened to the strong evidence and came up with separate explanations of what happened. They disagreed sharply on how they should respond. She insisted that only the strain of extreme fatigue could have caused Jenkins, a married father of six, to do anything to harm his boss's chances in the upcoming election. Lyndon believed the meeting was setup, a plotted conspiracy to discredit Jenkins and raise questions about his boss. Prior to the arrest, Jenkins had attended a *Newsweek* party to which the president had also been invited. Could Jenkins have been drugged, possibly with something intended for LBJ? The presence of three police officers in that public toilet on a weekday evening looked suspicious to Lyndon. Who had passed the word that Jenkins would be there?

Both Bird and Lyndon understood that voters would be alarmed to learn that the president's aide, who had access to top secret information and was privy to all his boss's contacts and scheduling, was vulnerable to blackmail. That Lyndon had employed that man for twenty-five years cast doubt on his judgment; that he should continue to rely on him was unthinkable. Yet both Johnsons valued loyalty above all else, and Walter Jenkins had epitomized the devoted employee. He had worked eighteen-hour days, canceled critical medical appointments whenever the president summoned him, and doggedly tackled all of LBJ's assignments, even those delivered in such condescending, abusive terms that Jenkins's face flushed red. The entire Jenkins family was close to the Johnsons. Walter's daughter Beth was one of Luci's best friends, and his wife, Margery, helped Bird with her speeches and had thoughtfully invited the Johnsons to dinner on the day they moved into the White House.

Bird was determined to put together a compassionate response that accommodated both loyalty and political necessity. A little past 9 a.m. on October 15, after having checked with legal advisers Abe Fortas and Clark Clifford, she phoned Lyndon and in her chairman-of-the-board staccato, told him that she thought they should do "two things": offer Walter the number two job at KTBC and issue a public statement of support for a man who had suffered a "nervous breakdown" because of an overly demanding schedule. When Lyndon objected to taking any action and warned her to "stay out of this," she remained firm and appealed to his survival instincts by cautioning that if he did not come to Walter's aid now, he risked alienating his entire staff. For nearly thirteen minutes, husband and wife argued about what to do. Even after he complained that a plane was waiting for him and he was already an hour behind schedule, she kept him on the line, trying to convince him that she was right.

While Lyndon continued to hold back, rejecting one option after another, she went into action. She wrote out her own statement and then turned to J. Russell Wiggins, editor of *The Washington Post*, to publish it. Wiggins singled out that day as proof that the first lady, whom many disdained as so under her husband's control she "would have followed [him] to the guillotine," was very much her own person. "My God, she was like a vessel under full sail," Wiggins said. "She came into that little blue room [upstairs at the White House] and she issued a statement declaring full loyalty to Walter Jenkins. She read it, and she said she wondered if we would print it."

The paragraph that Wiggins deemed "great . . . and we did print it, of course," read: "My heart is aching today for someone who has reached the end point of exhaustion in dedicated service to his country. Walter Jenkins has been carrying incredible hours and burdens since President Kennedy's assassination. He is now receiving the medical attention which he needs. I know our family and all of his friends—and I hope all others—pray for his recovery. I know that the love of his wife and six fine children and his profound religious faith will sustain him through this period of anguish."

Lady Bird Johnson was later questioned about how differently she and Lyndon had handled the Jenkins matter, and, as usual, she defended her husband. In 1999, in the last substantial interview she gave before suffering a debilitating stroke, C-Span's Brian Lamb asked her to explain why Lyndon had distanced himself from Jenkins while she had come to his aid immediately. In reply, Bird showed, even though her husband had been dead for a quarter century, that her loyalty to him remained as firm as ever. She admitted she was "sorry" that Lyndon had not spoken up to defend his friend. But, she noted, Lyndon was only a few days away from the most important election of his life. She omitted from the interview with Lamb how she had followed up with the Jenkins family, showing compassion while her husband kept his distance. A month after Walter's arrest, she visited the Jenkins home, although it was not easy. She described her time there as "a strange hour—very much the same and very different." She later offered the Jenkinses land on which to build a new house, and she engaged Walter to handle some of her personal accounts. But for her, the whole ordeal was one "of the two or three most painful things in my life—more painful than the death of many close to me."

On November 3, 1964, the Johnsons cast their ballots early in the day near the ranch, as was their habit, and then went to Austin to await returns at their favorite suite in the Driskill Hotel. Lyndon felt drained. When he spoke on the phone with Secretary of State Dean Rusk that afternoon, he confessed how low he had sunk: "I've had a headache . . . been in bed all day. I just kind of came off the mountain . . . just kind of feeling punchdrunk." By late evening, when the results started coming in, a crowd of friends, family, and staff had gathered in the Johnson suite, as everyone waited eagerly to see their hard work pay off.

Early numbers indicated that votes for LBJ would greatly exceed JFK's 1960 numbers. Even Lyndon's hero FDR never collected such an overwhelming endorsement. In the end, Lyndon swamped Goldwater, taking 61 percent of the popular vote. The electoral college gave him 486 votes, leaving only 52 to the Republican, who claimed (besides his home state of Arizona) five states in the Deep South. All five had been on the Lady Bird Special's route, but three other states also on that route (North Carolina, Virginia, and Florida) went for Lyndon.

It is impossible to know how many votes Lady Bird influenced, but her effort did not go unnoticed by other would-be first ladies. In Georgia, Rosalynn Carter, wife of future governor Jimmy Carter, watched the Lady Bird Special's progress carefully, and a decade later she started out on her own solo campaign to advance her husband's chances for the presidency. That a Southerner, like herself, had expanded so greatly the role of a candidate's spouse was remarkable, and Mrs. Carter later explained that when she reached the White House herself, she had selected Mrs. Johnson as "my favorite first lady."

Long after Rosalynn Carter had left Washington, her press secretary, Mary Hoyt, reminded readers of the *Los Angeles Times* that Lady Bird Johnson had changed the rules for candidates' spouses. Not every aspiring first lady would have the confidence (or willingness to devote the time and energy) to undertake the kind of outreach that Mrs. Johnson engineered, but she set a new standard for what could be done. Americans became accustomed to the fact that a candidate's wife would give speeches, hold her own press conferences, and fund-raise by herself to help propel her man into the White House.

A little past midnight on voting day in 1964, Lyndon Johnson impetuously decided to leave the Driskill and make a surprise appearance at the Austin Civic Center, where enthusiastic supporters had gathered. As he exited his hotel in a euphoric mood, a spontaneous assembly cheered him. Television cameras moved in to capture images of a man walking on top of the world. Minutes later, his mood shifted abruptly. On the way to the Civic Center, he happened to hear a radio announcement of his impending arrival. Enraged that his surprise had been spoiled, he lashed out at those he considered responsible and was particularly nasty to one press aide, who swore he had nothing to do with the leak. For the rest of the evening, Lyndon pouted, or, as his official diary noted, he was "quiet" on this, the night that should have been a high point of his life.

Bird is not on record as intervening that night to soothe the offended aide. She had worked hard in this campaign, and the August day when she persuaded her husband to get up out of bed and go to the Democratic convention stood out as the most trying. Now, as she faced four more years in the White House, she felt no sense of elation but only "a curious pall of sadness and inertia [which is] hard to shake." For nearly a week she did not make a single entry in her official diary, as she gave herself a break. After doing all that she could to produce a big win, she now had to prepare for the next four years.

Her mail showed that Americans were counting on her. Of the nearly two thousand letters that came into her office each week in 1964, most were invitations to speak or requests for a photo or autograph. But the others were what interested *New York Times* reporter Nan Robertson. They were the ones that addressed the first lady as presidential aide and appealed for her help—to get some legislation passed or to promote one cause or another. Her staff called them her "tell-it-to-the president" letters, and according to Robertson, Mrs. Johnson was receiving a lot of them because, unlike Jacqueline Kennedy, Mamie Eisenhower, and Bess Truman, she "has been and continues to be deeply involved in her husband's political life."

Not since Eleanor Roosevelt had a first lady been so enmeshed in a president's agenda or so featured in the public's expectations. Bird recognized her mandate. Now that Lyndon had won the big prize, the Oval Office in his own right, she would have to turn her attention to what she could accomplish in the upcoming term. She would have more time to tweak her side of their partnership.

14

LINCHPIN IN THE LAUNCH
OF THE GREAT SOCIETY

O N JANUARY 20, 1965, as thousands gathered on the side of the
Capitol and millions more tuned in on TV to watch the inauguration of Lyndon Baines Johnson, they got a surprise. For as long as
anyone remembered, a congressional aide had held the Bible for the
swearing in, so the incoming president could raise his right hand and
put his left hand on the Scriptures as he took the oath of office. But
on that sunny Wednesday, as Lyndon faced Chief Justice Earl Warren,
who would administer the oath, Lady Bird stepped forward to hold the
family Bible.

A Johnson spokesman informed reporters that Lyndon had told
his wife it would "mean a lot to him" if she took this new role in
the ceremony, and she had not objected. In her diary, she confessed
it was "sweet" of him to want her at his side at this special moment.
With Lyndon towering nearly a foot above her, she had to tilt her chin
sharply upward to fix her eyes squarely on his, while the congressional
aide, who had not been warned about the change, stood awkwardly

aside. In her buttoned-up American Beauty red coat and brimmed hat, she would appear in the same frame as Lyndon in nearly every photo of the event.

Bird's break with precedent that day might be written off as inconsequential, a trivial altering of an old ritual. But it was much more. It signaled the valuable partner role she played. Her strategic linchpin status in her husband's administration would be underlined time and again in the next four years as she served as sounding board, collaborator, and emotional stabilizer. Moreover, that change in the inauguration rite would become the new tradition, solid as steel half a century later. Even spouses of lesser public servants—mayors and governors across the nation—routinely take the same part as Mrs. Johnson did that day.

Anyone well acquainted with the Johnsons knew how much he depended on her. Those who had worked with him very long were accustomed to hearing, when a difficult matter had to be settled, "Ask Lady Bird." Or, when Lyndon was frazzled or tired, "Call Bird in here." Even when things were going well, he craved her company. His aide Joseph Califano Jr. reported how that dependence was demonstrated one night when he was finishing up the day's work with the president in his bedroom, during his rubdown. Drowsy from the late hour and the massage, Lyndon soon waved Califano out and called Lady Bird in. He "relished [her] pillow talk," according to Califano, "and was lonely when she was not there." If she had to be away overnight, he would invite an employee to sleep in her room, with instructions to leave the door open in case he called out for help.

As with most of his speeches, Lady Bird had had a hand in shaping the short but rousing inaugural speech, and at the end she rushed over to kiss him on the cheek and whisper in his ear that he had been "wonderful." Then she lost no time telling reporters which part "went straight to my heart." It was the phrase "always trying" from the president's description of the American spirit as one that never gave up: "always becoming, trying, probing, falling, resting and trying again—but always trying and always gaining."

Unfortunately, the high spirits of that day soon dissipated and Lyndon would require a much larger dose of Bird's cheerleading. After seeing the last out-of-town guests on their way and entertaining new vice president Hubert Humphrey and his wife, Muriel, at a cozy White House dinner on Thursday, Bird headed off to Camp David for some time with Lynda on Friday. Mother and daughter could finally enjoy a quiet dinner and a movie together. But not long after they went to bed, they were wakened by a phone call from Washington, telling them that the president had been rushed to Bethesda Hospital with influenza and a fever. The White House physician insisted there was no cause for alarm, and Bird, realizing how her middle-of-the-night rush back to her husband might raise fears that Lyndon was seriously ill, took a sleeping pill and went back to bed. But before noon the next day she was at her husband's side, and she checked into a hospital room near his. At the time of his heart attack ten years earlier, he had begged her to stay at his side, but they both knew there was no need for that reminder this time. Her calm soothing and competent supervision were essential to his convalescence.

The weeks before the inauguration had been mostly upbeat, although Bird had been "startled" to find Lyndon covered up with a blanket and asleep in his office on the afternoon of January 9. Deciding that "fatigue" was to blame, she had tempered her New Year's resolution to get him to shed twenty pounds and lose a few herself. He had sounded energetic and determined at his State of the Union address a few days earlier, when he unleashed a rash of proposals for the months ahead. Bird thought he might have included too much in his to-do list, but that was just the way he was. The Great Society programs he had unveiled the previous May would now take top priority, as he promised to move ahead on legislation that would have huge effects on the nation, drastically changing the playing field in education, civil rights, health insurance, and immigration.

With his hospitalization, all that would be put on hold, at least for a while. Even after doctors released him three days later, he continued to appear "washed out" and "depressed." She kept careful watch the following week as his lethargy and gloom continued to immobilize him. No one knew better than she, after so many years beside him, that Lyndon thrived on high activity. Getting him busy would provide the best medicine, but with a sick man, "How to fight it?"

His dejection reminded her of William Butler Yeats's poem "The Valley of the Black Pig," an apocalyptic account of doom and dread. Realizing what might lie ahead, she went out and bought funeral attire, which for a woman who hated to shop and had borrowed clothes for the official mourning period for President Kennedy was a huge step. Then, trying to put her deepest anxieties aside, she concentrated on Lyndon's physical comfort and recuperation. He would sometimes sweat through two or three sets of pajamas in a single night, and she made sure he always had a fresh supply.

When Lyndon was able to return to the office, for at least a few hours a day, Bird monitored his eating and rest. In her own version of Meals-on-Wheels for him, she would call one of his secretaries to check if he had eaten lunch, and then send Lynda with soup if he had not. When he stayed at his desk late into the evening, Bird phoned, sometimes more than once, to remind him that dinner was waiting. If that failed to move him, she walked over to the Oval Office and sat near his desk until he agreed to accompany her back to the residence for a meal.

In spite of everything she did, Bird observed an alarming lethargy in her husband's attitude and activity level in the early spring of 1965. He would start the day late, take long naps in the afternoon, and repeatedly call for his dogs to cheer him up. At the March 4 reception for members of Congress, he looked tired and confessed to his guests that the "Vietnam thing" was "wearing [him] down." His wife couldn't obliterate the worries of his job but she could try to boost his spirits by keeping his surroundings carefree and inviting his favorite people, like the Valentis or Bill and June White, as often as possible. When she had to be away, she made sure one of her daughters was available for "Daddy duty"—to provide company at mealtime and keep her posted on how he was doing.

When Mrs. Johnson recognized she was making little progress, she called for help from the two physicians she still trusted most. Dr. George Burkley, the White House staff doctor, had already examined the president multiple times, but she wanted the opinions of the two specialists who knew his medical history: cardiologist Willis Hurst and internist James Cain. They were the ones who had assured her Lyndon had sufficient stamina to endure the presidency, and now she wanted to hear what they had to say about periods in which he appeared unable to cope.

The president's official daily diary describes his appointment with the two doctors on March 13 as a "routine physical checkup," but their diagnosis was hardly routine—it was alarming. Although they found all his organs "sound," they warned the first lady that the presidency was putting a "heavy load of tension" on him, resulting in "this fog of depression." In the 1960s understanding of depression, before the role of body chemistry played much part, stress and grief were deemed the major culprits for initiating low moods, and healthy living was the usual prescription for recovery. Following the examination, the doctors counseled the cook on nutritional diets and emphasized to Lyndon the importance of exercise. But Bird had already been pushing both remedies, and nothing had helped. What else could she do?

Suddenly, his mood changed. Lyndon was in "great form . . . intensely active . . . loosed from the bonds of depression," Bird recorded in her diary. She didn't have a clue as to what caused the quick turnaround, or "quite what sprung him." A week later, as he continued to exhibit high energy, she speculated that he must have "given himself . . . a shot of adrenalin."

Lyndon continued to have exuberant periods, when he seemed pleased with himself and the legislation he ushered through Congress. He chose Hollywood settings for signing the most noteworthy measures into law, and Bird was usually there beside him to applaud. In early April, after Congress passed the $1.3 billion Elementary and Secondary Education Act, he could have just remained in the Oval Office to sign it or used a local institution for fitting backdrop. Instead, he returned to the tiny one-room schoolhouse in Texas where he had once sat on Miss Kate Deadrich's lap for reading lessons. Down the road from the LBJ Ranch and near the small frame house where his parents had started their married life, the small structure could not accommodate the swarm of well-wishers and journalists who turned out that Sunday afternoon. So the president sat outside in the sun, with the seventy-two-year-old Miss Deadrich, now the married Mrs. Loney, at his side. She beamed as television cameras recorded her most famous protégé signing a law providing a huge injection of money into education. Then he handed the pen to her.

Busloads of Lyndon's former students, together with their friends and families, had come all the way from Cotulla and Houston to applaud. Neighbors and relatives cheered the president, one of their own, as he proudly talked about what education had done for him. He was determined that others would have the same chance.

The Johnsons' high spirits lingered after the brief ceremony ended, and they hastened to enjoy a few hours together on their own. A short helicopter ride took them to a small boat on the nearby Llano River, where they lay on the deck, caught the red rays of the setting sun, and watched the familiar Packsaddle Mountain's silhouette sharpen against the sky. It was one of those times, when Lyndon was so upbeat, so lovingly attentive to Bird that she felt purringly content to lie quietly beside him. She spotted bluebonnets, a sure sign of spring, and Lyndon, still pumped up by the day's events, started talking about leaving politics and returning to teaching. It would be "heaven," he said with a sigh, to live and work in small-town Texas again.

Bird had never taken seriously his talk about leaving politics, which generally came in moments of defeat and disappointment. She fully expected him to stay "lashed to the mast until the last gasp of breath." But now, as he celebrated a major legislative triumph, his eyes sparkled and he talked "joyously" of retirement. Maybe this time he really meant it.

During the warm evenings that followed, after boating ended for the day and ranch jobs were postponed for the morrow, Lyndon took center stage and regaled his guests with stories full of "earthy and colorful and true and fresh" phrases that made Bird wish she had a tape recorder. She admitted some of his language could get a little rough, with mentions of body parts and toilet functions, but his audience howled in appreciation. This was the jaunty, hilarious Lyndon who delighted her when she first met him. Never one to tell jokes herself, she loved hearing him deliver side-splitters about some recent encounter or future plan. No one could outdo his graphic phrasing or the timing of his punch lines.

But she soon saw the other side of the relaxed, funny raconteur, as he slumped into hushed melancholy. Back in Washington, Bill Moyers, who worked every day with the president, noted that his often ebullient boss had become "deeply depressed," and it was an ongoing despair that left him "morose, self pitying, angry . . . tormented." Although the term "manic depressive" was thrown around a lot at the time, having been included in the first edition of the *Diagnostic and Statistical Manual of Mental Disorders* (*DSM*) in 1952, Moyers did not use it.

Nor did Dr. Willis Hurst use it, either then or later. In 1969, when he was asked outright if his famous patient was manic depressive, Hurst admitted that Lyndon had wide mood swings. He also acted inappropriately at times, according to Hurst, and like most "creative people. . . [tended to] display many emotions, ranging from anger, to humor, to unpredictability." Whether that constituted "abnormal" behavior, Hurst thought "very debatable," but he himself was not willing to say that Lyndon acted "outside the normal range."

It is important to note that both Moyers and Hurst pointed to Lady Bird as the key contact person on Lyndon's moods. Moyers went directly to her for an explanation of the president's dismaying, swift shifts. When he learned that she was way ahead of him, having already called in doctors to assess her husband's condition, Moyers decided to leave the matter to her. And wait.

For a portion of most days, Lyndon continued to work, if only to make a few phone calls or confer with an aide. He attended social events in crisp attire, kept appointments with legislators, and greeted foreign dignitaries on schedule. But between appearances, he withdrew, "lying in bed with the covers almost above his head." Bess Abell, the first lady's social secretary, told historian Will Swift, "I worked in the residence and I had a chance to see how depressed he became."

On good days, the president vigorously pursued his Great Society agenda, and by early May he was ready to highlight one of the linchpins: Project Head Start. Once again, he dramatized the event by choosing a special setting—the Rose Garden on Mother's Day—to unveil particulars of a program he saw as a major boost to busy mothers. Head Start was designed to help preschool children whose parents had not managed to nourish them in belly or brain. The youngsters lacked communication skills and exposure to the world around them, and many had never visited a zoo or been inside a post office. Head Start would begin that summer to try to narrow the gap between them and more advantaged children.

Lady Bird saw huge potential in this program and immediately signed on to help. She liked the idea of targeting children at an early age, before they even thought about dropping out or heard themselves labeled as delinquent. By reaching them, Head Start could affect entire families and break the dismal cycle that trapped generation after generation in poverty; it was a cycle, she thought, that bred dependence, anger, and hostility. The program's director, Sargent Shriver, was one of Bird's favorites from among the Kennedy crowd, and she labeled him a "superb salesman." At his invitation, she agreed to serve as Honorary Chair, despite her distaste for the title. Working Chair was more to her liking.

Throughout the spring and summer of 1965, as the president juggled foreign policy questions and a host of domestic issues, his mood continued to seesaw. On May 21, Bird noted in her diary that his "spirit is lighter and his face less weary." But three weeks later, on what she dubbed "Black Tuesday," his "dark countenance was dour and grim." She put part of the blame on the arts festival, which started as a White House celebration of American accomplishment but ended up making both Johnsons, especially the president, look bad.

Neither Lady Bird nor Lyndon felt secure in the highbrow art world in which the Kennedys thrived, and she shied away from using the word "culture." She made no apologies for her lack of expertise in art and music, and she encouraged others to find what "talks" to you rather than "make a fool" of one's self by "running after art for art's sake." But she enjoyed "what people create, if the book or painting says something to me," and she thought it appropriate to spotlight the nation's outstanding artists and writers. In early 1965, she happily signed on to help plan a White House Festival of the Arts to celebrate American writers, performers, and visual artists.

Squabbling started almost immediately about which artists deserved an invitation. Princeton professor Eric F. Goldman, a new addition to the White House staff as intellectual in residence, and Bess Abell, the first lady's social secretary, expressed heated opinions about the other's ability to judge such matters: Goldman said Abell talked about culture in a way that made him "wince," and the well-connected Abell countered that Goldman was clueless about how the capital worked.

By the time everyone agreed on a tentative guest list, the festival, set for mid-June, was only a month away, and some artists on the A-list, like Edmund Wilson and E. B. White, had made other commitments they did not wish to break. Robert Lowell, the poet, accepted but then changed his mind, fearing that his attendance would imply his approval of the president's decision to escalate the American military presence in Vietnam. Instead of withdrawing his acceptance quietly, Lowell wrote a letter for publication in *The New York Times*, explaining that he had declined the White House invitation because he viewed "our present foreign policy with the greatest dismay and distrust."

Other invitees began lining up behind Lowell, although not all of them rescinded their acceptances. John Hersey, author of the acclaimed book *Hiroshima*, decided he would take advantage of his featured place on the program and call attention to the horrors of war by reading from his book about the horrific suffering endured by Hiroshima residents after the atomic bombing of their city in 1945.

When Bird learned of Hersey's plan, she made clear to Goldman that neither she nor the president wanted Hersey reading anything about bombs and wars. Goldman warned her that any hint of censorship, when applied to an author of Hersey's stature, would generate loud and ugly publicity. But she stood firm. Goldman remained equally committed to his stand—he refused to cancel Hersey's invitation or issue any directive on what could or could not be read.

As the date for the arts festival approached, the president and first lady continued to respond to the unpleasant publicity around it in very different ways. He lashed out at journalists for attacking him— for dwelling on Vietnam and for undercutting every move he made there—and he barred offending reporters from covering the festival. As for his own participation, he played hide-and-seek, saying first he would attend and then he wouldn't. When he did show up, he used his brief remarks to deflate the honorees' egos. After mumbling some platitudes to a distinguished gathering primed to receive accolades, the president declared that this was *not* an assembly of the nation's "greatest artists" although in the minds of some, it might be. Then he stalked out.

Bird stoically attended the whole program, sitting in determined resignation through John Hersey's reading. When he punctuated his account of the appalling suffering at Hiroshima by directing meaningful glances at her, she resorted to her famous powers of self-remove to tune out. The "veil" came down, and when Hersey finished and people seated around her began to applaud, she kept her hands neatly folded in her lap and gazed straight ahead.

The president could be very testy on other fronts during the summer of 1965, grumbling to aides about minor inconveniences or lambasting them for failing to solve problems that were beyond their control. On the July 4 weekend at the ranch, he disgusted his guests at the lunch table. First he ridiculed a Secret Service agent's appearance and then he went after Bird. One of the lunch guests, Jeanne Murray Vanderbilt, realized others at the table were so embarrassed at the president's appalling treatment of his wife that they kept their eyes glued to their plates. But Mrs. Vanderbilt could not resist a quick glance, and she saw the first lady was staring straight ahead, as if she hadn't heard a word: "She didn't even blink."

Speechwriter Richard Goodwin described enormous physical changes in the president that summer as his moodiness and outbursts became more apparent: His "public mask . . . [began] to stiffen . . . the face seemed frozen, the once-gesturing arms held tightly to the side or grasping a podium." With scant or no reason, the president would change his mind, requiring Goodwin to rewrite speeches at the last minute. One especially troubling substitution occurred after Goodwin had crafted a bold statement for the president to deliver at the United Nations' twentieth birthday celebration on June 25. The first draft, emphasizing the need to limit atomic weapons, had apparently pleased the president, but then, after he heard that Robert Kennedy had recently spoken in the Senate on the same topic, he ordered a rewrite, with barely a mention of arms control.

Increasingly concerned about what he considered irrational shifts in the president's moods and behavior, Goodwin consulted with Bill Moyers, who had worked with his fellow Texan longer and was personally closer to him. Moyers had become accustomed to seeing Lyndon erupt in anger over some small mishap, like a telephone call that did not go through or a lunch plate that was not hot enough, but he had considered these outbursts harmless quirks or eccentricities. Now he was seeing something far more serious, and he confided to Goodwin that Secretary of State Dean Rusk had expressed similar doubts about the president's mental state. Moyers agreed with Goodwin that the flare-ups came more often now, and were more extreme and less rational.

Goodwin looked for clues in medical textbooks, and he talked with psychiatrists, who alerted him that he was describing a "paranoid" personality, who could function well for long, productive stretches, but could also show excessive reliance on secrecy and an inordinate need to control his surroundings. This type of personality, when bent on action, often produced remarkable results—like leading "a Senate or even an entire country."

As if to demonstrate the validity of the psychiatrists' descriptions, the president was astoundingly productive during the summer of 1965. Within the space of only one week, he signed two of the most significant acts of his generation. Each ceremony was accompanied with fanfare in a picture-perfect setting.

Bird participated in only one, the Medicare signing on July 30. Since Air Force One could not accommodate all those who wanted to accompany the president to the Truman Library in tiny Independence, Missouri, Air Force Two went also, with Lady Bird aboard, along with a contingent of aides, legislators, and reporters who were eager to witness the event. Back in November 1945, President Truman had proposed to Congress a national program of health insurance under Social Security, but Southern legislators, including Texas congressman Lyndon Johnson, stymied passage. In the interim two decades, Lyndon's public position on the subject had shifted, and now in what *The New York Times* described as a "moving tribute" to Truman, he took the signing of Medicare to him. The eighty-one-year-old Truman, retired a dozen years, found it hard to find words to convey his gratitude for the presidential visit and attendant fuss: "It's an honor that I haven't had done to me—[for] quite a while."

In typical Johnson fashion, the visit ended so quickly the Trumans barely had time to register it. The president and first lady landed in Kansas City at two in the afternoon and, together with their entourages, immediately boarded buses to go to neighboring Independence where runways were too small for their planes to land. On the stage of the very modest Truman Presidential Library, LBJ dwarfed the frail HST. After signing Medicare into law, Lyndon handed the first pen to Bess Truman (the second went to Harry) and rushed out so he and his party could be airborne again by 4:30 to the LBJ Ranch.

But it was a very brief stay. In those first days of August, when many Americans were enjoying family vacations, the Johnsons gave themselves little time off. By Wednesday, Bird had checked into the Carlyle Hotel in New York, to clothes shop with daughter Lynda while eighteen-year-old Luci remained in Washington on "Daddy duty." It fell to her to accompany him to Capitol Hill on August 6 to sign the Voting Rights Act, a breakthrough measure giving the federal government authority to monitor elections and punish states that did not treat all voters fairly on balloting day.

The first lady did not linger in New York. After trying on fall outfits that Friday morning, she made a quick trip to the Connecticut estate of Joseph Hirshhorn to see his collection of sculpture and paintings. But Bess Abell, who accompanied her, kept an eye on the clock, and by 5:30 the first lady was airborne for Washington. Intent on escorting her husband to a restful weekend, Bird was in the Oval Office by 7:40. She had to wait while he finished some phone calls, but she had him on a helicopter by nine, headed to Camp David.

Cabins at the presidential retreat could accommodate a large party, and Lady Bird filled them that weekend with more than a dozen people to serve Lyndon's various needs and provide diversion: men he could relax with (boyhood friend Bill Deason and journalist Bill White); staff he could work with (George Reedy and speechwriter Horace Busby); Hollywood producer and bigtime contributor to the Democratic Party Arthur Krim and his attractive young wife, Mathilde, whose German accent ("Now A'tur, I t'ink . . .") Lyndon found amusing. Bird fed Lyndon's soul (inviting Dr. George Davis to conduct a religious service on Sunday) and his eyes with comely reporters Marianne Means and Cissy Morrissey (of *Life*). For forty-eight hours, the president enjoyed a secluded, circumscribed world where he could take to his bed whenever he wanted. He could enjoy a game of dominoes with Deason or an extra scotch with a lineup of women who could have passed for contestants in a beauty competition.

The weekend proved a short respite. Any satisfaction derived from the upbeat Voting Rights ceremony on Friday evaporated the following Wednesday when word came that rioting had broken out in Watts, a low-income section of Los Angeles. Headlines across the country reported that African Americans were attacking police officers, looting stores, and burning cars. The Johnsons did not need an editorial in *The New York Times* to make them see the irony: Watts, one of the places where residents stood to gain most from the Voting Rights Act, greeted it with violence. Lyndon was mystified. How could African Americans, whom he had sought to help with his War on Poverty programs, be anything but grateful? He concluded his enemies must have orchestrated the riots. He suspected the media of poisoning minds with exaggerated reports and suggested Watts residents had been incited to lawlessness by someone out to get him— "probably the Kennedys."

As word of the violent protests spread, Lady Bird kept glued to the work to be done, upholding her end of the Great Society initiative. While the president cruised down the Potomac with thirty-five visiting ambassadors, she proceeded with previously scheduled visits to check out two Head Start centers. The program was less than three months old, but, as the Honorary Chairman, she wanted to assess its effectiveness at two very different sites: highly urbanized Newark, New Jersey, where enthusiasm for Head Start had been obvious from the beginning, and rural Lambertville, Pennsylvania, where she viewed pockets of poverty that brought back memories of her own childhood, in the "backwoods of East Texas or Alabama." As she met what seemed to her dazed and frustrated parents, the real "impact of Head Start" struck her. "I do not want to turn America over to another generation as listless and dull as many of these parents looked."

After starting her day at seven, she had completed her Head Start visits and was bracing to greet hundreds of guests at a reception at the New Jersey governor's mansion when Lyndon phoned with one of his abrupt schedule changes. Instead of the quiet evening in Washington she had been anticipating, they were going to leave for the ranch. That meant she would not get to bed until after 2 a.m. Although she registered a gentle objection to what she called "not-so-restful news," she did not attempt to change his mind, certainly not at a time like this when he was wrestling with bad news from the West Coast.

During the night, rioting in Los Angeles escalated, but there was not a sign from the LBJ Ranch that anyone was taking note. The president spent much of the weekend driving around the fields and boating on a nearby reservoir that had been named Lake Lyndon B. Johnson. Lady Bird uncharacteristically left those four days blank in her diary, but the president's diary shows she was extremely busy looking after him. She accompanied him on long walks and entertained his favorite friends (including Jesse Kellam and the Valentis) at poolside dinners. Especially soothing to a beleaguered president was a visit to his nearby birthplace, which his wife had been carefully restoring as a tourist site. She took him there on Sunday and he went back on his own the next day.

What the president was not doing was taking phone calls from his legislative liaison, Joe Califano, back in Washington. Califano needed desperately to speak with the president about how to respond to the situation in Watts, which had grown increasingly violent and ugly. Before it ended, thirty-four people would die and more than a thousand were treated for injuries. Califano wanted instructions about calling up the National Guard. Should the White House issue a statement? But a president famous for staying virtually attached to a phone, with one under the dining room table and another in a nearby tree whenever he went outside, was not picking up the receiver. Not until Saturday evening, nearly forty-eight hours after leaving Washington and after newspapers reported the violence was spreading to white neighborhoods, did LBJ finally speak with Califano.

On Sunday morning the president issued a statement calling for calm, but his earlier failure to communicate fit into a larger pattern of not facing up to circumstances, of not always reacting with the utmost integrity and urgency. Califano had been in Washington long enough to hear the litany of complaints against his boss for fudging on numbers (such as his net worth), denying relationships (saying he hardly knew Bobby Baker when all the capital considered theirs a father-son relationship), and tilting the truth when it came to troop buildups in Vietnam. A joke had begun circulating about how to assess the president's veracity: "When he pulls his ear lobe, scratches his chin, he's telling the truth. When he begins to move his lips, you know he's lying."

That duplicity had shown itself way back in his courtship letters, and Bird had learned to factor it into any of her dealings with him. Like a mischievous little boy, he enjoyed delivering the unexpected, and he would withhold information and then spring it when it suited him. Adept at adjusting, Bird took every schedule change or new revelation in stride, making the necessary accommodation without objection.

Lady Bird's father, the tall, commanding T. J. Taylor, became her template for what a man should be. (Courtesy of the LBJ Library)

At age three, when her mother was still alive, Claudia Taylor wore the latest children's fashion. (Courtesy of the LBJ Library)

Lady Bird's childhood home stood out as one of the most elegant houses in Harrison County, Texas. (Courtesy of the LBJ Library)

At age seven, Lyndon Baines Johnson already showed the confidence of a first-born son, groomed to take charge. (Courtesy of the LBJ Library)

His four younger siblings—Lucinda, Josefa, and Rebekah on his right and Sam Houston on his left—later complained that Lyndon liked to boss them around. (Courtesy of the LBJ Library)

The humble Johnson homestead, near Stonewall, Texas, furnished cramped quarters for a growing family. (Courtesy of the LBJ Library)

Bird Taylor, who hated being photographed, made sure to wear a dress that Lyndon liked for this picture she had made for him in October 1934. (Courtesy of the LBJ Library)

Although she came to dislike flying as an adult, Bird Taylor, shown here with neighbor Dorris Powell, found air travel "exciting" in her youth. (Courtesy of the LBJ Library)

(*Top*) Bird initially detected a trait she didn't like—arrogance—in this 1934 photo of Lyndon. But she revised her judgment, deciding his pose justifiably signaled confidence and pride. (Courtesy of Bachrach Photography)

(*Bottom*) Although most of his courtship letters to Bird ran on for pages, Lyndon kept this one short, concentrating on how bad he felt and how much he needed her. (Courtesy of the LBJ Library)

(*Top*) Other photos of their honeymoon in Mexico showed such an erotic charge between Lyndon and Bird that she suggested the negatives should be destroyed. But this one survives. (Courtesy of the LBJ Library)

(*Bottom*) Rather than remain in Texas in 1935, while Lyndon worked in Washington, Bird went with him and became his invaluable, but unpaid, assistant in the capital. (Courtesy of the LBJ Library)

Using the movie camera that Lyndon gave her for Christmas, Bird started documenting his appearances and recording his opponents' speeches in the 1941 Senate campaign. (Photo by *Austin-American Statesman*/Courtesy of the LBJ Library)

Helicopters were still a rarity in 1948, but Lyndon relished the mobility this one gave him and the attention it attracted to his Senate campaign. (Courtesy of the LBJ Library)

By the end of the grueling run-off primary in 1948, both Bird and Lyndon were exhausted, ready to see more of their young daughters. (Courtesy of the LBJ Library)

Just down the road from Lyndon's birthplace, the LBJ Ranch became the family's "heart's home" in 1952. (Courtesy of the LBJ Library)

Lady Bird thought it sad that Lyndon, as president, had more time for toddler Courtenay Valenti, shown here during a meeting of the National Security Council, than he ever had for his own daughters when they were her age. (Photo by Yoichi Okamoto/ Courtesy of the LBJ Library)

The birth of Luci's son, Patrick Lyndon Nugent, just before her father met with Soviet Premier Alexei Kosygin in New Jersey, provided LBJ with the opportunity to greet his guest by announcing he had just become a grandfather. (Photo by Yoichi Okamoto/Courtesy of the LBJ Library)

Weeks of careful planning preceded Lynda Bird's marriage to Charles Robb in December 1967, the first White House wedding of a president's daughter in more than fifty years. (Photo by Yoichi Okamoto/Courtesy of the LBJ Library)

As the bride's parents danced at the Robb wedding, they reminisced about the "awful purple dress" Lady Bird had worn to her own wedding. (Photo by Yoichi Okamoto/ Courtesy of the LBJ Library)

During her final months in the White House, Lady Bird worked hard to record, in both still and motion pictures, details of her family's tenure. In the only Christmas they spent there (1968) they hung stockings and opened gifts in the Yellow Oval Room. (Photo by Jack Kightlinger/Courtesy of the LBJ Library)

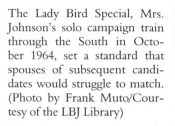

The Lady Bird Special, Mrs. Johnson's solo campaign train through the South in October 1964, set a standard that spouses of subsequent candidates would struggle to match. (Photo by Frank Muto/Courtesy of the LBJ Library)

Seasoned journalist Liz Carpenter operated as the first lady's right-hand aide, scheduling her appearances, handling publicity, and helping her write speeches. (Photo by Frank Muto/Courtesy of the LBJ Library)

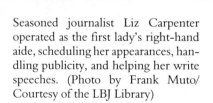

When the Johnsons were flooded with mail after the assassination of President Kennedy, Lady Bird enlisted her friends to help write the replies. (Photo by Cecil Stoughton/Courtesy of the LBJ Library)

Walks on the South Lawn of the White House gave the president and first lady time to confer. (Photo by Mike Geissinger/Courtesy of the LBJ Library)

When the Senate Ladies Red Cross Unit honored First Lady Jacqueline Kennedy at a lunch, Lady Bird Johnson, a longtime member, accompanied her. (©Bettmann/Corbis)

Lyndon Johnson relied on his wife to extend a warm welcome to all visitors to the ranch and to keep one delegation occupied while he conferred with another. (Courtesy of the LBJ Library)

Although she rarely traveled with her husband outside the United States during his presidency, Mrs. Johnson was pleased to assist at his arrival in Ohakea, New Zealand, in 1966. (Photo by Frank Wolfe/Courtesy of the LBJ Library)

Shown here meeting with Secretary of Defense Robert S. McNamara, Ambassador
Llewellyn Thompson, and President Johnson (back to camera) in 1967, Lady Bird
observed that men's discussions were often more interesting than those of women.
(Photo by Yoichi Okamoto/Courtesy of the LBJ Library)

Lady Bird Johnson noted that her husband liked to have beautiful young
women, like Mathilde Krim, around him. (Photo by Mike Geissinger/
Courtesy of the LBJ Library)

When he signed an important law, President Johnson summoned Lady Bird
to participate in the ceremony, and for those victories in which she had played
a part, he made sure she received one of the signing pens. (Photo by Yoichi
Okamoto/Courtesy of the LBJ Library)

President Johnson, shown here with Abe Fortas, was often described as domineering when he towered over lesser men and women, but Bird admired the self-assurance he conveyed. (Photo by Yoichi Okamoto/ Courtesy of the LBJ Library)

In delicate situations or when he wanted to polish the impression he was making, Lyndon Johnson would enlist Lady Bird to speak for him. (Courtesy of the LBJ Library)

After Lyndon's death, Mrs. Johnson was finally able to indulge in private travel without the obligation to make an official appearance. Venice, which she explored with her daughter Luci in 1975, was one city she did not like. (Courtesy of the LBJ Library)

To make up for the lack of attention she had shown her own daughters when they were young, Lady Bird made a point of planning, financing, and enjoying extravagant trips with her grandchildren. Here she poses with Jennifer and Lucinda Robb in Alaska. (Courtesy of the LBJ Library)

Though classmates at the University of Texas in 1934, Walter Cronkite and Claudia Taylor Johnson did not get acquainted until he was a famous broadcaster and she was the president's wife. When the widowed Lady Bird rented a vacation house on Martha's Vineyard, Cronkite was one of the neighbors she enjoyed seeing. (Courtesy of the LBJ Library)

Members of the most select sorority in the world, former first ladies rarely criticized one another, and they often crossed party lines to express admiration. Left to right: Nancy Reagan, Lady Bird Johnson, Rosalynn Carter, Betty Ford, and Barbara Bush in 1994. (Courtesy of the LBJ Library)

As her husband's most trusted adviser, Mrs. Johnson knew how to phrase
her counsel in ways that would not antagonize or upset him—she called it
"infiltration." (Photo by Yoichi Okamoto/Courtesy of the LBJ Library)

Claudia T. Johnson, as she always signed business documents,
liked to mull over her options before making a decision. Here
she is shown at a board meeting of the LBJ Foundation in 1981.
(Photo by Frank Wolfe/Courtesy of the LBJ Library)

But reporters assigned to follow the president and report his movements were less tolerant. Having to leave on a few minutes' notice for 90-degree Texas when they had to come to work dressed for 50-degree Washington was no fun. Nor was explaining to their families why they would have to miss a weekend event they had promised to attend.

Any leak about a pending matter could lead to cancellation of the action and a vicious verbal attack on the person deemed responsible. In one instance, after the president decided on a new ambassador, word got out, and Lyndon struck his name from the list, saying: "I wouldn't appoint him to dog catcher now." When press secretary Bill Moyers tried to mollify reporters by giving out information he had not been authorized to release, the president denounced him as a traitor. Aide Jack Valenti observed that Lyndon got so angry when he lost control of his news coverage, he was fit "to crawl the walls of the White House."

That was the year—1965—when the media started referring to a credibility gap, between the president and the people, but no such phrase fastened on Lady Bird. Her press secretary, Liz Carpenter, maintained that she and her boss had, from the start, agreed that reporters deserved open and honest treatment. The first lady (or her representative) would answer all questions, or, if they could not, they would explain why. As a result of her openness, Mrs. Johnson had few enemies in the press.

Nor did she seem bothered by unflattering accounts published about her. The August 28, 1964, issue of *Time* had put her picture on the cover and described her as decidedly lacking in physical beauty: "Her nose is a bit too long, her mouth a bit too wide, her ankles a bit less than trim . . . and her voice [sounds] something like a brassy low note on a trumpet." The quotes of those who knew her during high school and college were vicious. One classmate remembered her as a perennial wallflower, who was "never accepted into our clique," so pathetic that the other female students felt obliged to press their brothers into escorting her to school dances. Even the formerly loyal Gene

Boehringer chose to highlight Bird's frugal streak for *Time* rather than the adventuresome spirit she had once admired.

Mrs. Johnson knew her true value could not be measured in a popularity poll—but in an assessment of how she helped Lyndon work "to the best of his ability and to make some steps forward." He could be incredibly insensitive, as Joe Califano, a Brooklyn-born Harvard man, found out on his first day working in the White House. It was midsummer, and Califano appeared in a light-colored poplin suit, only to find everyone else wearing dark blue or black. Rather than keep quiet and assume Califano would register the gaffe on his own, the president embarrassed him by yelling, in front of others, that he looked like an "ice cream salesman." The next time Lyndon belittled Califano, Bird was there to intervene. After the president compared Califano's necktie to a "limp prick" and started to retie it, the first lady interjected one of her gentle reproaches: "Maybe Joe likes his tie the other way, darling."

The first lady engineered more significant interventions, impressing her husband's aides and endearing her to them. Always on the watch for rifts developing between her husband and his associates, she would attempt to bring the two sides back together. She could be subtle in her fence-mending, and Califano admitted it took him some time to decipher her strategy. After she had invited him to dinner more than once and he had refused, she became more forthright about her motive. He had been delivering one catastrophic announcement after another to the president, and the first lady, having noticed, warned him: "You know Lyndon sometimes can confuse the messenger with the message and I wouldn't ever want that to happen to you." Touched by her concern, Califano accepted her invitation, and then noticed at dinner how she showered him with compliments about the great job he was doing. She coaxed Lyndon into a jovial mood by lifting her usual ban on dessert and then passed him the candy dish (although she did draw the line at smoking).

That mixing of the personal with the professional, always a hall-mark of the Johnsons' marriage, became more marked and significant in their White House years. Bird had always run an "open house" for employees at all hours and for family in all seasons, and with the added perks of the presidency she could increase the numbers. She made sure to include a few relatives and longtime friends at every state din-ner, so that her brother Tony and Karnack neighbors got the thrill of meeting world leaders. At events outside the White House, both the first lady and the president were quick to invite friends along. Their trip to New York City the first weekend in October 1965 provided yet one more example of the seamless life they lived. They used the signing of an important law as an opportunity to reconnect with loyal friends, spend time with family, and strengthen political alliances.

Neither Bird nor Lyndon had any personal connection to Ellis Is-land immigrants—their families had settled in the colonies before the United States existed. But the Johnsons recognized the poignant sym-bolism of his highlighting a new immigration policy while standing in the shadow of the Statue of Liberty, with Emma Lazarus's words about "huddled masses" above him. Bird realized others thought it "corny," and she knew that one unfriendly congressman, well aware of Lyndon's cinematic choices for important announcements, had sin-gled out this very place as over-the-top. But she wrote defiantly in her diary, let them "make the most of it! . . .The ceremony was a jewel of an hour that I won't forget."

The day the president signed the act, Sunday, October 3, illustrated how easily the Johnsons mixed family and neighbors with world lead-ers. They started the day at the White House, with a late breakfast and then church services nearby, where they encountered old friends who were visiting Washington. Spontaneous as always, Lyndon invited the two couples to come to the White House for lunch, and without even asking them, he sent for their suitcases so that they could accompany him and Mrs. Johnson to New York City that afternoon. When one of the guests confessed she had not packed a coat, the first lady lent her one, and by the time their helicopter landed on Liberty Island, huge crowds had gathered.

As Lyndon stood tall in front of them, the Manhattan skyline behind him, flags snapped in the wind and Anna Moffo, the operatic soprano, sang "America" in tones that made spines tingle. Bird admitted her eyes went "from Lyndon's face to the flag, to the great old statue, [and] I was caught up in the magnificent drama of the moment. It was good history and good theater and there was many a wet cheek in that crowd." Erich Leinsdorf, the renowned orchestra conductor (who was now with the Boston Symphony), had a special reason to be on Liberty Island that day—to thank the former congressman from Texas who had come to his aid in 1938, when he risked being forced to return to his native Austria because of visa problems.

After the signing ceremony ended, the presidential entourage moved from Liberty Island to the Waldorf-Astoria on Park Avenue, and although the setting shifted from a site reminiscent of "huddled masses" to one tinged with gold, the ecumenical theme continued. New York was preparing for the arrival the next day of Pope Paul VI, who was making the very first papal visit to the Western Hemisphere. Luci, who had just converted to Catholicism on her eighteenth birthday the previous July, was eager to meet the head of the world's Roman Catholics, and she came to the city with her boyfriend, Patrick Nugent, for the occasion. Luci maintained that she abandoned the Protestantism of her parents (the Disciples of Christ of her father and the Episcopalianism of her mother) in a search for ritual and meaning more resonant with her; she had not meant it as a rebuff or a denial of anyone. But Bird viewed the decision as a rejection of the family, and she wrote in her diary about the day of Luci's conversion ceremony: "We went in [to the church] as four and came out three."

That October 1965 weekend in New York softened the first lady's attitude on religious differences. On Sunday evening Dorothy and

Arthur Goldberg, who had recently become the U.S. ambassador to the United Nations, hosted a large dinner, with a star-studded guest list including Rockefellers, Roosevelts, and Kennedys. When the host repeated an old Hebrew prayer, asking for "wisdom for the leaders of the nation," Bird could see its similarity to "passages of the Episcopal prayer book," and she concluded it had been a memorable weekend, "even for the most Protestant of us."

That would be her last burst of jaunty enthusiasm before reality set in. Lyndon was set for another medical procedure, and that always called for her full-time surveillance. For more than a month she had known that Lyndon was going to undergo gall bladder surgery, but he had insisted on keeping it secret, and she had not even told her closest staff, Liz Carpenter and Bess Abell, who did her scheduling and made most of her arrangements. Only when she returned to the White House on Tuesday, October 5, a few hours before he was scheduled to enter the hospital, did she let them know. Then she turned her full attention to seeing that his hospital suite provided all the comforts he required.

For a commander-in-chief who thrived on issuing imperatives, it was exasperating to don an ill-fitting hospital gown and take orders from nameless nurses. Add the discomfort of serious surgery and the hurt delivered by a suspicious press, and you have a very disgruntled patient. When recovery turned out to take longer than anticipated, Lyndon became more truculent than usual. The press reported, erroneously, that he was being treated for something far more serious than his gall bladder, possibly another heart attack or pancreatic cancer, and his fractured credibility left him ill equipped to rebut the claims.

Presidential press secretary Bill Moyers tried to allay suspicion by releasing detailed medical reports and frequent updates on the patient's activity and recuperation. Lyndon, attempting to do him one better, provided the image that came to characterize the worst side of his presidency. While still at the hospital, he met with reporters and, according to *Time* magazine, pulled up his blue sport shirt to "let the whole world inspect the ugly twelve-inch seam under his right rib cage" where the doctors had stitched him back together.

Cartoonists had a bonanza as they tried to outdo each other in conveying his boorishness. One showed him preparing to greet Britain's Princess Margaret, his shirt raised to expose the gory scar; the caption was an aide's warning that viewing of scars would have to wait until after he had been formally introduced to his royal guest. Lyndon recognized he had gone too far this time, and he explained to reporters that he hadn't meant to be crude. But it was too late.

Hearing a national snort of derision aimed squarely at him, Lyndon fell into a deep funk. When he had to return to the hospital a few weeks later for more surgery to repair the scar and remove a small growth in his throat, his spirits sank further. His thoughts turned increasingly to death and the fact that the men in his family did not live much beyond sixty. He was fifty-seven. Americans deserved a more vigorous leader, he decided, not one likely to die in office. He started hinting that he would resign, and only twelve months after boasting of how many Americans voted for him, he had his secretary type up a letter asking Vice President Humphrey to take over the Oval Office.

With her husband appearing as besieged as "a man on whom an avalanche had suddenly fallen," Bird decided that the "black beast of depression [was] back in our lives." She kept hoping he would get better if only she could manage to "buy a little time." At least she could stay close at hand, ready to cajole and placate. When he became rebellious and finicky about who sat at his table for the state dinner for Princess Margaret, she kept coming up with different combinations until he finally acquiesced and ended the phone conversation with "I love ya." For small gatherings in the family dining room, she made sure that no one she invited would make any mention of gall bladders or Vietnam.

White House staff remarked on the calming influence she had on Lyndon. When he exploded in anger, she gingerly edged up to him, in a version of what she called "infiltration," and began her soothing, nonconfrontational suggestions with, "Now, Lyndon . . ." Bill Moyers quipped years later: "Who knows how many disasters were averted by her uttering those two words, 'Now, Lyndon . . .' "

During a visit to the LBJ Ranch in 1965, speechwriter Richard Goodwin was sitting at the pool when Lyndon launched into one of his tirades about how all his critics were communists and about how he was going to go down in history as the president who lost Southeast Asia. He went on and on about how communists already controlled the three major networks and dozens of other communications outlets. According to Goodwin, he even named names: "Walter Lippmann is a communist and so is Teddy White. And they're not the only ones. You'd all be shocked at the kind of things revealed by the FBI reports." While Goodwin and the other guests sat in stunned silence, the president became "more intense." Then Bird leaned over and "tenderly patted his hand," causing the anger to dissipate and the tension "to seep from his body."

"Now, Lyndon," she began, "you shouldn't read [the FBI reports] so much." When he bristled and asked why not, she explained in serene tones, "Because they have a lot of unevaluated information . . . accusations and gossip which haven't been proven." According to Goodwin, Lyndon looked less than convinced, but for the moment he seemed mollified.

Although 1965 had several low points, Bird included it in what she called a time of "wine and roses," and in many ways it was. The president had managed to get through Congress some breakthrough, nation-altering legislation. He was being heralded as outstripping his own hero, having done, according to Senate majority leader Mike Mansfield, "more than FDR ever did or ever thought of doing." She could take pride in the quiet, linchpin role she had played.

But as the year came to a close, it was clear that behind the satisfied glow of achievement lay disappointment and frustration. The president was facing huge problems and finding decisions increasingly difficult to make. What stood most prominently as the buffer between him and his "Valley of the Black Pig" was Bird. She was, and had always been, his emotional keel. But things could get worse, she knew, and they did.

15

---⟡⟡⟡---

BEAUTIFICATION: A LEGACY OF BIRD'S OWN

S NOW HAD begun falling outside when Lady Bird Johnson entered the Queens' Sitting Room late in the afternoon of St. Patrick's Day, 1965. The day had started with a mixture of fog and drizzle, and by 5 p.m., when her meeting was due to start, darkness nearly shrouded the White House. She had conferred that morning with her philanthropist friend, Mary Lasker, and now wanted to hear from half a dozen others. As everyone stood around, greeting one another and chatting, faint sounds of singing wafted in from the Lafayette Park side, and the first lady turned to her newly hired aide, Sharon Francis, to ask what was going on outside. Francis, who was nearest the window, pulled back the curtain and replied, "They're singing, 'We Shall Overcome,' and they're kneeling in the snow."

The room went dead silent, as everyone waited to see how the first lady treated this poignant appeal for help. It was ten days after Bloody Sunday, the violent confrontation on an Alabama bridge between civil rights activists and their opponents, who remained staunchly committed to racial segregation. President Johnson had, just that morning, proposed to Congress legislation that would become the Voting Rights Act of 1965. But without any further acknowledgment of the chanters outside, Bird started her meeting. As talk about cleaning statues and planting flowers proceeded, the elegant Queens' Suite might as well have been thousands of miles away, in Buckingham Palace.

It was not that Lady Bird Johnson lacked sympathy for those kneeling in the snow, but she had called together specialists to talk about an entirely different subject, and she was not one to be diverted from a purpose. One of what her friend Marny Clifford had labeled "pigeonholes" in her mind took top billing that afternoon, and her uncanny ability to keep projects separate from each other was never more apparent. Concern for Lyndon, his health and his career, was not a pigeonhole—it overlay everything else—but on this particular day in March 1965, she was concentrating on a project distinctly hers, one that resonated deeply with her but related only peripherally to Lyndon.

It was important, Mrs. Johnson often said, to find something for one's self, an interest or project that made the "heart sing," and the dedication had to be authentic. Eric Goldman, the historian involved in the Johnsons' first White House years, went to her for support on a library project he was promoting because he knew she was an avid reader. Although she rarely referred publicly to what she was reading, because she did not want to offend authors by mentioning some and not others, books were definitely part of her every day. To Goldman's surprise, she turned him down on the library project, with the explanation: "I haven't been in a library since I left college. This is not *me*." What *was* "me" was her deep, intense love of nature, which had provided a valuable refuge during a pathetically lonely childhood.

Like the mother she had barely known, Bird found the highest beauty and the deepest tranquillity out of doors, and now, from her White House podium, she could encourage others to explore the sights that had enriched her life—the verdant forests, rocky outcroppings, and blankets of wildflowers that calmed and soothed her, even in the most troubling times. This would be her legacy, something apart from Lyndon's, and she would make no apology for taking time from other work to give it its due. It is an aspect of her marriage often overlooked, in the typical portrayal of her as entirely geared to her husband's needs and demands.

Before unveiling any beautification goals, Bird carefully did her homework and assessed the political implications. Any venture of hers could not contradict or interfere with the president's policies. She had watched Eleanor Roosevelt strike out on her own, drawing a younger and more liberal following than FDR did. Although Bird admired Mrs. Roosevelt's courage, she rejected her example. Any member of Bird's fan club would have to root for Lyndon, too.

The president had already set up a Task Force on the Preservation of Natural Beauty in 1964, and Interior Secretary Stewart Udall credited Lady Bird with influencing her husband "to demand—and support—more far sighted conservation legislation." That task force, chaired by Harvard professor Charles Haar, received an "open sky" assignment, reaching all the way from "natural parks and society" to the "quality of urban life." But the task force had a deadline only two months hence. Lady Bird operated more deliberately. No sixty-day rush jobs for her. First, she wanted to quiz experts, evaluate previous efforts, and mull over lists of people willing to help her.

High on that list was Mary Lasker, and within days of the November 1964 election Bird reached out to her. A few years older than the Johnsons, Lasker (born in 1900) had already impressed both of them with her energetic devotion to a cause. Always perfectly coiffed and stylishly dressed, she needed no reminder from Lyndon to freshen her lipstick. The ambitious Midwesterner had set out after college (art at Radcliffe, literature at Oxford) to join the New York art world, and at her first job she met up-and-coming artist and gallery owner Paul Reinhardt. In 1926 she married him. Divorced eight years later, she married an even more promising go-getter, Albert Lasker, in 1940. An executive with Lord & Thomas in Chicago and a virtual icon in the advertising world, he was credited with making orange juice a staple on every breakfast table in America. Mary Lasker soon adopted her husband's interest in marketing, and she applied her art training to the design of packaging for Lucky Strike cigarettes.

By the late 1940s, the Laskers were less interested in making money than in spending it on what had become their shared mission. Although the link between cigarette smoke and cancer had not yet been publicized, they transferred their promotional skills to finding funding for medical research. With adequate resources, they argued, cures could be found for the big killers of their time—cancer and heart problems. The overly optimistic Laskers even set a deadline for reaching their goal—the year 2000.

After Albert Lasker died of cancer in 1952, his widow pursued their objective with renewed zeal. Realizing private contributions would never suffice to pay for the necessary research, she turned to Washington where, in 1958, Senate Majority Leader Johnson looked like her most promising ally. He had survived a major heart attack himself, and his mother had just died after suffering from multiple medical problems. Even so, Lyndon quaked at the size of Lasker's request, and both of them knew she would have to settle for less. On hearing that she was asking for $565 million, equivalent to about $3 billion in 2014 dollars, he asked, "Isn't that too much?" and she replied, "Not if you want to live."

By 1960, he was the one who needed help—from her. After his presidential ambitions met a frigid reception in New York City, he asked her to intervene with her influential friends and put in a good word for him. He told her that Eleanor Roosevelt and Dorothy Schiff, owner of the *New York Post,* were very wrong in thinking he was "anti-Negro and . . . anti–civil rights. . . ." Lasker agreed to speak with both women, but she reported back that she had not made a "dent" on either one. In fact, Roosevelt and Schiff thought she was "crazy" to believe Lyndon harbored any genuine interest in civil rights.

Stuck in the stagnant trough of his vice presidency, Lyndon was of little use to Lasker, who turned to Lady Bird. Invited to The Elms for lunches and dinners, Lasker pronounced her hostess "absolutely charming," and each event "very well done, very well organized." Although the New York art maven and the wildflower enthusiast from Texas would appear to have little in common, something clicked between them, and Mrs. Johnson described Lasker as "very dear to me."

When Lyndon snapped back into action after President Kennedy's assassination, Lasker was one of the first people he called. She joined the small group, including Abe and Carol Fortas, who gathered at The Elms on Sunday evening, November 24, to talk about Lyndon's priorities as president. Lasker had recommendations ready for the new first lady as well, but it was too early, and the energetic New Yorker had to sit by and watch as Mrs. Johnson "just marked time."

The legitimacy conferred by the 1964 landslide election lifted Bird's diffidence. Now she was ready to tackle some of the projects Lasker had listed. They included improving "the appearance of the vast federal highway system . . . the beauty of our cities, and . . . the health of the people." Lasker recommended starting with roadways, which had expanded enormously as a result of the Highway Act of 1956, providing billions of dollars for a sprawling interstate network. Even a high-flying multimillionaire like Lasker had to travel by automobile sometimes, and she complained of being a "victim . . . [of] totally treeless and hideous [roadsides, including the] New Jersey Turnpike." Illinois was just as guilty, with "thousands of miles . . . of highway, totally without trees, which makes driving there a pain." In striking contrast, the Taconic Parkway near Lasker's New York City home base had been "beautifully landscaped," and she held it up as a model for the entire nation.

Mrs. Johnson also solicited ideas from Arizonan Stewart Udall. He had remained as secretary of the interior after Kennedy's death and found himself more personally attuned to the Johnsons, with their Westerners' proud ties to land and open spaces, than to the sea-loving JFK. At forty-four, Udall boasted an enviable record. An athlete who helped integrate his college cafeteria before the law mandated it, a decorated World War II veteran who came home to earn a law degree, and a three-term veteran of the House of Representatives, he unveiled his concerns for the environment in a book, *The Quiet Crisis*, published in 1963. Written while he held a day job in the president's cabinet, *The Quiet Crisis*, along with Rachel Carson's *Silent Spring*, published the previous year, put a staggering price tag on the overuse of natural resources: increased pollution and decreased open spaces would create an environment in which birds could no longer sing.

In spite of his own national perspective, Udall advised the president's wife to use her clout on a project close to home—Washington, D.C.—and turn it into an attractive "garden city" with tree-lined streets and flowering parks. Hundreds of thousands of tourists visited every year, Udall noted, and they left Washington with memories of a gritty, shabby metropolis, so inferior to the grand capitals of Europe. Jokes about Washington's sorry state had circulated for years, among them President Kennedy's quip that it was a city that combined Southern efficiency with Northern charm.

For more brainstorming, Lady Bird turned to Libby Rowe, a friend since the 1930s, whom President Kennedy had appointed to the National Capital Planning Commission, charged with sprucing up Washington. Rowe, who had a broader concept of environmental issues than Lasker, encouraged Mrs. Johnson to think beyond plantings and statues and do something for those neighbors of hers who lived in wretched poverty only blocks away from the White House. First ladies since Dolley Madison had been taking some part of the city under their wing, heading charitable organizations looking out for orphans or others in need, but only Ellen Axson Wilson, the first wife of Woodrow Wilson, had zeroed in on a specific local problem—housing. As a result of her lobbying, Congress passed a housing act with her name on it after her premature death in 1914.

Upgrading the nation's capital had never been high on the agenda of the wife of Congressman/Senator/Vice President Johnson. Nor had charitable work for the city's African American residents. With the exception of Lyndon's eighteen-month stint with the National Youth Administration in the 1930s, the couple had lived part of every year in Washington, where Lady Bird could have volunteered at a soup kitchen or joined a local garden club. But she, like most congressional wives, remained focused on her family's needs: managing moves between Washington and the home district; keeping multiple households running smoothly; entertaining in a style befitting a legislator. The Senate Wives' Club, where Bird rarely missed a Tuesday meeting, rolled bandages while exchanging travel tips and other useful information. The only garden she worked in Washington was in her own backyard. Now, as first lady, she enlarged her scope, and with the encouragement of Lasker, Udall, Rowe, and others, formed the Committee for a More Beautiful Capital.

Lyndon also qualified as a new convert to conservationists' ranks. In 1958, when Congress considered rewarding states that limited billboards, Senator Johnson voted "nay," and it is not clear that his wife even knew the matter was under discussion. The following year Lyndon again sided with the billboard industry in a debate on the placement of outdoor signs. Lady Bird had driven the route between Texas and Washington too many times to count, and she credited those trips with fueling her aversion to highway advertising. But she had been raised with a healthy respect for the bottom line, and billboards were clearly valuable to those who wanted to tout their product to motorists as well as to those who rented them the space to do so.

By 1965, Mrs. Johnson altered her view, and in fairness to her, so did many other Americans who converted their own personal love of nature into a cry for legislation to protect it. Rather than crediting herself with initiating the change in attitude, she explained that she had just "jumped on a moving train," propelled by the arguments of Rachel Carson, Stewart Udall, and others.

But there is absolutely no question that Mrs. Johnson's interest in the subject was authentic. Her cousin, Patsy Chaney, was one of several people who reported that the only time they ever saw her really angry was when she witnessed an assault on the landscape. Chaney remembered returning to the ranch with Lady Bird and catching sight of a crew cutting down a particular variety of cypress that is difficult to grow in the Hill Country. Visibly agitated, Bird couldn't wait to get to a phone. When she connected with the person responsible, she tore into him and made her objection very clear.

Thomas Donahue, who came to Texas to be interviewed by the president for a job in the Labor Department, reported a similar outburst on a cold December day while Lady Bird was driving him and Ambassador Llewellyn "Tommy" Thompson around the ranch. When she spotted a broken irrigation tube that was spraying cold water on a tree, icing it up and killing it, she grabbed the car phone and "really tore [the ranch hand responsible] up for destroying that beautiful tree . . . ripped" him out. Then, remembering that she had two passengers in the car, she switched to a more affable "tone . . . much more measured and controlled." It was enough to convince Donahue that she possessed "a lot of steel," and her dedication to conservation was not just a posturing for publicity.

Equally committed to environmental concerns was Laurance Rockefeller, who became one of her staunchest allies. After President Eisenhower selected him in 1958 to chair a commission to evaluate the nation's outdoor recreation resources, he sank almost $800,000 of his own money into the effort. The report of his commission was grim. By the year 2000, he argued, Americans would be working shorter days, almost entirely indoors, and would want more parks and athletic fields, hiking trails and bike paths, within easy reach of the cities where they lived. But who would provide these? It was not a matter of charity, Rockefeller noted—"just plain good business."

Lady Bird Johnson officially kicked off her environmental campaign on February 5, 1965, by dedicating one of what had become an ongoing series of Women's Doer lunches to the topic of beautification. Her husband was still recovering from the flu that had hospitalized him on January 24, and his mood was very low, but along with careful monitoring of him, she crammed her appointment book with enough interviews to attract considerable attention to her project. *U.S. News & World Report* published a lengthy favorable article on her in the February 22 issue. A couple of weeks later, James Perry wrote a glowing piece in *The National Observer,* describing her concern as genuine and her power as considerable. Mrs. Johnson had, Perry wrote, as much influence as "any First Lady we've seen in this century."

Her beautification team split almost immediately into factions. Those dubbed the "nationals" wanted to focus on parks and highways across the country, while the "locals" insisted on spending their energy and funds right there in Washington, D.C. A second rift, within the "locals" camp, pitted the "daffodils and dogwood set," who saw their mission as planting trees and polishing statues, against the ghetto reformers, who thought it more pressing to improve living conditions in the slums. The nation's capital was clearly a divided city, with a wide chasm separating the rich from the poor into what historian Lewis L. Gould would later describe as the "two Washingtons."

By the March 17 meeting, when Bird heard the civil rights chanters outside, she had already decided that her beautification agenda would range wide, to include national parks and highways, as well as Washington's ghettos, parks, and monuments. She knew she would need a lot of help to do all that. Besides asking her current staff to work extra hours, she recruited new talent for the East Wing. Press secretary Liz Carpenter, intent on putting the first lady on the front page, hired

Cynthia Wilson, with a master's degree in journalism from the University of Texas, to write catchy press releases and do advance work on the first lady's trips.

Just how many people worked on Mrs. Johnson's project is difficult to say, because she "borrowed" experts from various departments, sometimes for short stints and other times for years. That meant the first lady's office did not have to pay them—they continued to collect their salaries from their employer of record. Udall had recruited Sharon Francis, an enthusiastic environmentalist, soon after she graduated from college, and she helped him write his book. But when the first lady initiated her beautification campaign it was Francis, still collecting her paycheck from the Interior Department, who dedicated herself full time to Mrs. Johnson, assisting her in spinning out ideas, drafting speeches, and forging ties with conservation groups across the country. Nash Castro, who, as an employee of the National Park Service, had supervised sites from Mount Rushmore to the Rocky Mountains, was now regional director for Washington, D.C., and he became one of Mrs. Johnson's most valuable sources of information and aid (while still an employee of the Park Service).

Besides those who were paid, an army of volunteers signed up to help. On her own time, Lee Udall, wife of the interior secretary, organized a speakers bureau, composed of Senate and cabinet wives, to help the first lady fulfill the many requests that came in. Using kits of background information prepared by Sharon Francis and Liz Carpenter, the surrogates fanned out to audiences that Mrs. Johnson could not reach on her own. Not since Eleanor Roosevelt had a first lady headed a publicity machine of her own, and Mrs. Roosevelt's was neither so extensive nor so efficiently run.

Nobody liked the term "beautification," and Lady Bird ordered it used as little as possible because it sounded "cosmetic and trivial and . . . prissy." It lacked precision, and some Americans connected it to beauty salons rather than landscapes. When Jane Freeman, wife of

Agriculture Secretary Orville Freeman, was introduced in Alaska as a member of Mrs. Johnson's beautification team, a woman in the audience queried her about "the latest hair styles" in the rest of the country. At another event, one of the first lady's stand-ins was asked: "Do you just do Mrs. Johnson's hair or do you do Lynda's and Luci's too?"

But "beautification" remained the label of choice because no one came up with anything better. "Conservation" and "Environmental Beauty" sounded too old-fashioned and stodgy for the dynamic program Bird envisioned. For her, what would later be called "green" issues did not deal with cosmetic, prettifying extras to life. She would always connect spots of soul-feeding serenity with what made life worth living.

Mary Lasker wanted to forget about the ghettos, because, she said, it was useless to build playgrounds for people who wouldn't take care of them. Bird disagreed. Professor Haar's task force had ignored the capital's poor neighborhoods, but she thought it important to engage the people who lived there. After escorting committee members on a tour of Greenleaf Gardens, a public housing area in Southwest Washington, she told Stewart Udall that nothing the committee did would mean anything unless "people in these neighborhoods can see the challenge and do the work in their own front yards."

Among her strongest allies on the "people" side of beautification was African American Walter Washington. Born in Georgia and raised in upstate New York, he quickly earned a respected place in the can-do circles of the nation's capital. At age fifty, he headed the National Capital Housing Authority, and his marriage to Bennetta Bullock, daughter of a prominent Washington minister, guaranteed him entrée to a network of influential blacks, including one who described him as "a smooth briefcase operator who had learned the white man's game and was excellent at it." Walter Washington was Bird's personal guide through the capital's black neighborhoods and, seeing how she worked, he became an admirer. He noted how quickly she absorbed details, how easily she greeted crowds, and how eagerly she took on the grimmest problems.

In May 1965, President Johnson hosted a Conference on Natural Beauty to follow up on his task force's recommendations. Mrs. Johnson, although never a member of that task force, had a starring role at the conference, delivering the keynote speech on May 24. When rain threatened to cut short an outdoor session, the garrulous president invited everyone inside the White House where he rambled on about many matters, including his plan to send four highway beautification bills to Congress the next day.

The conference disappointed many who wanted much stricter regulation of highway advertising, but it underlined both Johnsons' genuine commitment to the cause. As Henry L. Diamond, a young associate of Laurance Rockefeller, told historian Lewis Gould years later, "The word went out" that both the President and first lady "cared." It remained to see if they could steer the relevant legislation through Congress.

At the same time she was moving full speed ahead on environmental issues, Lady Bird engaged in another project that had nothing to do with nature (although plenty to do with beautification). Working with S. Dillon Ripley, the energetic secretary of the Smithsonian Institution, she helped bring the enormous Joseph Hirshhorn collection of paintings and sculpture to Washington. Some of it went into the White House collection, but the bulk of it became a museum of its own within the Smithsonian, whose leadership Ripley, a renowned ornithologist, had taken on in 1964. He had vowed to expand and invigorate the stodgy institution, and in his twenty-year tenure, he would add nine new museums, including the National Air and Space and the National Museum of African Art. On the first of the nine, the Hirshhorn Museum and Sculpture Garden, he turned to the first lady for essential help.

Joseph Hirshhorn, an immigrant to the United States from Latvia, had acquired a fortune by investing in uranium and other precious metals, and he had used his millions to build one of the world's premier privately held art collections. As he approached his seventies, word went out that he was looking for a place to deposit his art treasures, and multiple offers came in. Israel wanted the collection, and London's Tate Gallery proposed building a magnificent Taj Mahal–type structure to house it near the Thames. Other bids came from Pasadena, California, and from New York governor Nelson Rockefeller, who suggested Hirshhorn's art would enhance his state university's collection.

To outdo all that competition and bring the collection to Washington, Lady Bird used her most self-effacing, solicitous manner. She admitted to Hirshhorn, known as the "Medici from Brooklyn," that she knew little about modern art, and she invited the connoisseur and his new, much younger wife, Olga, to lunch at the White House. Several weeks later, on a hot August day, Mrs. Johnson trooped up to his Connecticut estate with her brother Tony and walked through Hirshhorn's garden. Its modern sculpture, including creations of Giacometti, Calder, and Rodin, rivaled that of a world-class museum. After admiring the art, Bird expressed surprise that two of her favorite French painters, Matisse and Degas, had also sculpted. But it was the paintings inside Hirshhorn's country house that she really coveted. The Eakins portraits struck her as "commanding . . . [with] something of the quality of the Flemish masters," and she concluded that any one of them would look very good in either the Green Room or the Red Room of the White House.

Bird issued more invitations to Hirshhorn, who brought his lawyers to broker a deal that suited him. The Smithsonian was bound by a rule, imposed by Congress, that none of its museums would be named for a living human being. Hirshhorn wanted to break that rule. If the president could convince Congress to humor Hirshhorn on this, he was ready to donate thousands of artworks and set up an endowment to provide for their maintenance. Congressional approval and the necessary paperwork for the Hirshhorn Museum and Sculpture Garden went smoothly, but groundbreaking for the startling modern edifice did not occur until January 1969, only a few days before the Johnsons retired to Texas. Not until 1974 did the museum open.

The first lady had won over Hirshhorn as she had so many others with her affable manner and lack of artifice. Impressed by her humble admission that she was "prepared to learn [about art]," Hirshhorn told his biographer, "That was honest and I respected her." When the acquisition was announced, Smithsonian director Ripley acknowledged that Bird was the "decisive factor" in making it happen: "Hirshhorn is crazy about her and the president."

Proud as Bird was of her role in bringing Hirshhorn's collection to Washington, she gained far more recognition for beautifying the streets of the capital. When Mary Lasker donated nine thousand azaleas to prettify Pennsylvania Avenue, Bird's committee found the money to have them planted. The first lady's efforts made her a hero to local residents, and decades after she moved back to Texas, taxi drivers would point to the capital's flowering parks and say, "Lady Bird Johnson did that."

The Highway Beautification Act of 1965 carved Bird into the national consciousness in even larger letters, but that effort evoked criticism, involving her in one of the very few controversies surrounding her name. Considering her aversion to airing differences in opinion, it is remarkable that she pursued a plan to get rid of billboards. Virtually no one opposed planting flowers, but the billboard lobby was powerful and well financed, representing both builders and advertisers. The Outdoor Advertising Association of America had already sent lobbyists to state capitals to fight against any restriction at all on the size or placement of their signs. Bird knew that the billboard association had potent allies in Congress; her husband had once been one of them. Now she was taking the other side, and some of her aides feared she was initiating a battle she couldn't win.

Bird proceeded with her usual low-keyed, well-mannered tactics. Privately, she phoned congressmen to make her case, and she invited their kin to tea. She saw that every White House guest list had its share of conservation activists and she made sure they had a chance to talk with the legislators who remained undecided. When journalists wrote favorable articles or newspapers ran kind editorials, she sent thank-you notes, an obvious ploy to encourage more good publicity.

But passage of the Highway Act, which provided for relocating junkyards as well as limiting billboards, still looked doubtful, and Liz Carpenter turned to the president for advice. He instructed the plump press secretary to put on her tightest girdle and best perfume and go talk individually with three recalcitrant House members whose votes were needed for passage. When she won over two of them but failed to convince the third, he suggested how to increase the pressure. The obstinate congressman had just procured a plum of a military installation for his home district, and the president told Carpenter to remind the congressman that military bases can be given and they can be taken away.

The Outdoor Advertising Association and the White House eventually hammered out a compromise bill to put before Congress. It banned billboards, but not in "areas of commercial and industrial use." That left a huge loophole, of course, since "commercial and industrial use" could be interpreted very broadly. Now the House and Senate would have to pass the bill.

The final vote in the House was set for October 7, the same day as one of the biggest social events of the season—a Salute to Congress at the White House that evening. The party was scheduled to start at the State Department with a program, then move to 1600 Pennsylvania Avenue for festive imbibing. When a contingent of congressional wives, dressed in their party best, arrived on Capitol Hill about 7 p.m. to join their husbands for what they thought was going to be a celebratory evening, they were told they had to wait. On the House floor, a lively debate on the Highway Beautification Act was still under way, and the legislators had been warned not to leave until it passed. President Johnson had sent word via his aides: "You know I love that woman and she wants that highway beauty bill and by God we're going to get it for her."

Buses hired to transport legislators and their spouses around D.C. that evening stood empty on Capitol Hill as Republicans proposed amendment after amendment to water it down. With the votes already lined up among Democrats, it was going to pass in some form, but in the process the Republican minority meant to dilute its provisions and ridicule its backers. The first lady came in for special mockery. Robert Dole, Republican congressman from Kansas, suggested striking "Secretary of Commerce" in the bill and inserting "Lady Bird," to imply that an overly aggressive, nonelected woman was now dictating policy. One of Dole's fellow Republicans brandished a picture that he suggested the president use as backdrop when he signed the anti-billboard measure into law: it showed a roadside sign advertising Lady Bird's broadcasting company.

At the White House, the food-and-drink tables were set up and the entertainers ready to perform. But the only guests present were cabinet members and other Washingtonians not involved in the House debate. Not until 10 p.m., when the Republicans called it quits, did the Highway Act pass. House members and spouses who still had the stamina could finally start partying.

The president and first lady stayed only a few minutes to greet the late arrivals. For the preceding weeks, while wrangling over the bill continued, the Johnsons had been guarding their secret about Lyndon's upcoming gall bladder operation. Now, with approval in both houses of Congress secure, they could proceed. Within an hour of the House vote, Lyndon had checked into the Bethesda Medical Center, where he would undergo surgery the next day. His signature on the

Highway Beautification Act would have to wait until after he was released from the hospital two weeks later.

Although the 1965 Highway Beautification Act would be further
diluted in subsequent legislation, its initial passage permanently associated Lady Bird with the anti-billboard fight. In one of his most
famous cartoons, Bill Mauldin showed her driving through unspoiled
forest, and the caption, implying she had assumed too much power,
was: "Impeach Lady Bird." Mrs. Johnson, who knew Supreme Court
Justice Earl Warren was currently under attack and threatened with
impeachment because of his liberal decisions, was delighted. She wrote
gleefully in her diary: "Imagine me keeping company with Chief Justice Warren!"

While the results fell short of her goals, Lady Bird Johnson showed
how a president's wife can leave a legacy of her own without subtracting
anything from her husband's achievement. Hers was an example that
each of her successors for the next fifty years would try to match. Each
took a project of her own, although it would be difficult to argue that
they all equaled her genuine enthusiasm, efficient management, and
continued involvement after leaving the White House. For Pat Nixon
it was volunteerism; for Betty Ford, the Equal Rights Amendment and
dance; for Rosalynn Carter, mental health reform; for Nancy Reagan,
"Just Say No to Drugs"; for Barbara Bush, literacy; for Hillary Clinton, health care reform; and for Laura Bush, literacy programs. One of
the first questions Michelle Obama had to answer after her husband
entered the 2008 race for president was: What will be your project if
you become first lady? The answer came after the election: an anti-
obesity campaign for juveniles and support for military families.

On that March 1965 day, when civil rights activists knelt in the snow,
chanting "We Shall Overcome," Sharon Francis thought she saw a tear
roll down the first lady's face. But before she could be sure, Mrs. John-

son called the beautification meeting to order, right on schedule. It had been fifty years since Minnie Pattillo Taylor introduced her daughter to the solace of nature's beauty, and now that daughter was not about to miss her chance to pass on to others what made her "heart sing." In the process, she also changed what Americans expected of their president's spouse.

16

WAR CLOUDS

W HEN LADY BIRD Johnson looked back on her White House time and divided it into two distinctly different periods, the first of "wine and roses" and the second, "pure hell," it was the Vietnam War that produced the "pure hell." Criticism of the president's war decisions caused deep anguish in the White House and threatened to blot out gains already made toward the Great Society and forestall new programs. Lyndon Johnson sometimes came near tears while witnessing the body bags of fallen soldiers being unloaded at Union Station, but he kept sending more young men to take their places. Although he agonized about the deaths, he could not justify reversing the buildup of troops. Frustrated, unhappy with himself and with the world around him, he became even more difficult to live with. Lady Bird had a long record of stepping in when he faltered or drew back, and she felt she had made a difference more than once. Could she be of any help now?

A U.S. strategy for Southeast Asia was already in place in November 1963 when the Johnsons moved into the White House, and the president's top foreign affairs advisers, mostly holdovers from JFK, advocated continuing it. To bolster South Vietnam's independence and help it resist pressures to unite with communist North Vietnam, the United States had agreed to supply weapons and a core of "advisers" to train local soldiers. At the same time, Americans would assist in showering South Vietnam villages with "imaginative propaganda" about how much better life would be for them if they remained outside the communist bloc. Although directed by military generals in an "advisory" capacity, the policy did not, in the parlance of today, put any American "boots on the ground" in Vietnam.

That suddenly changed. Eight months after President Johnson moved into the Oval Office, Congress wrote him a blank check to "take all necessary action" to protect American forces abroad. The red letter day was August 4, 1964, a date that Lady Bird would never forget. Nor would others. Long after Lyndon's death, when Steven Stucky and Gene Scheer were commissioned to write an opera to commemorate the centenary of his birth, they titled it simply *August 4, 1964*.

The first lady does not appear in the opera, but in real life she was right there, doing "rather trivial things" while knowing it was a "momentous day" and that "great decisions [were] being shaped . . . by the man closest to me." After registering the "extraordinarily grave" expression on the face of foreign affairs adviser McGeorge Bundy when she met him by chance in the hallway, she concluded, "We might have a small war on our hands." As she worked her way through the day's appointments, going to her hairdresser, conferring with her tailor, and welcoming visitors for afternoon tea, she kept wondering what Lyndon and his three top advisers (Bundy, Secretary of Defense Robert McNamara, and Secretary of State Rusk) were discussing and why their regular Tuesday lunch went on so long. In spite of her worry, she managed a two-hour nap in the afternoon, showing she could "relax at the most amazing times . . . almost as though you'd have to wake me up in order to get me to the execution on time."

That evening big black limos kept dropping off congressional leaders and military advisers outside the Oval Office, and after thirty years in politics Lady Bird Johnson needed no one to spell out for her the seriousness of the situation. This was going to be another of those days when dinner had to wait. In fact, she did not get her husband to the table until nearly 11 p.m.

August 4, 1964, was the day President Johnson received reports on two unrelated but tragically significant incidents: an attack on an American military ship in the Gulf of Tonkin off the coast of Vietnam, and the discovery in an earthen dam in Mississippi of the bodies of three civil rights workers who had been missing for seven weeks. Either calamity was of the magnitude to consume the president's full attention, but on this hot Tuesday, he had to deal with both, juggling phone calls and in-person consultations with dozens of people. In between discussions with legislators and foreign policy advisers on how to respond to the attack in the Gulf of Tonkin and ward off further strikes, he made his most painful phone calls, offering condolences to the families of the young, martyred civil rights workers. In the opera *August 4, 1964* voices of two grieving mothers mix with those of Secretary of Defense McNamara and President Johnson in a cacophony of misery and despair.

Lyndon Johnson acted more decisively in the event than in the opera, and sought congressional approval to proceed as he thought appropriate. Although the Gulf of Tonkin Resolution (passed on August 7) would later haunt him and embarrass those who supported it, it caused little comment at the time. Only two senators, neither particularly influential with his colleagues, voted against what one of them, Ernest Gruening of Alaska, called a misguided license to send Americans to fight a war in which the United States had no business. Other senators who would later become outspoken critics of the president's actions (William Fulbright, George McGovern, and Frank Church) all voted in favor of the Gulf of Tonkin Resolution.

They had been persuaded by Lyndon's call for authority to strike back at what he termed "open aggression on the high seas against the United States of America."

During the next few months, the president rejected suggestions of Senator Gruening and others that he should hold back. Instead, he did just the opposite, turning what had been a limited initiative into full-scale war, an "Americanized" war, that lacked allies' support and became increasingly unpopular at home. As his critics multiplied, his frustrations grew, and his behavior, formerly viewed as inappropriate but harmless, now became incredibly bizarre and worrisome.

Katharine Graham, publisher of *The Washington Post*, gave one example. At a surprise anniversary party that Lyndon gave for Bird, he was very grumpy, and then called Graham and Abe Fortas into his bedroom to rant at them for not supporting him on a recent appointment. So far, nothing unusual, but then the president started taking off his clothes, shedding first his jacket, then tie and shirt. As he began unzipping his pants, Mrs. Graham found herself "frozen with dismay" and thinking: "This can't be me being bawled out by the President of the United States while he's undressing." When he abruptly commanded her to "Turn around," she obeyed, and his harangue continued while she faced the wall. At his second order to "Turn around," she was relieved to see him in pajamas, and at the very first lull in his tirade, she and Fortas beat their retreat.

On another occasion, the president dumbfounded reporters who pressed him to explain why he was escalating the war in Vietnam. Unzipping his fly and taking out "his substantial organ," he shouted at them: "This is why!"

Accounts like these continued to surface after LBJ left the White House, inviting academics and psychologists to consider what effect, if any, his mental state had on his decision making. Two traits in particular were singled out—his insistence on secrecy and his tendency to blame his failures on a conspiracy of others. The title of D. Jablow

Hershman's 2002 book left no doubt about the author's point of view: *Power Beyond Reason: The Mental Collapse of Lyndon Johnson.* Using a term popular during Lyndon's lifetime but later replaced by bi-polar, Hershman described Lyndon Johnson as manic depressive.

Hershman never treated or even met Lyndon Johnson, who had been dead a quarter of a century when Hershman published his book. But the continuing debate over LBJ's handling of the Vietnam War had focused renewed attention on his mental state, and interviews with LBJ staffers after he died tended to back Hershman up. Harry McPherson, who served throughout the Johnson presidency, remembered the month of February 1965 as the most "dismaying" period in the White House, because LBJ was what "an analyst would call manic depressive." Secretary Vicky McCammon noted that the president's moods were extreme—either he was "very up and monopolized all conversation" or "very down" and sat mute. Press secretary George Reedy complained that LBJ walked "on air" one minute and then was ready to "slash his wrists" the next. Reedy said he described these extreme swings to physicians who assured him that the president was "manic depressive."

Robert E. Gilbert, who has written and lectured widely on the mental health of U.S. leaders, concluded that Lyndon Johnson's insecurities provoked such erratic behavior, especially in regard to Robert Kennedy and other critics of his Vietnam policies, that the nation suffered as a result. Gilbert went further, and using diagnostic criteria of the American Psychiatric Association, he argued that throughout his long political career, "Lyndon Johnson exhibited behavior patterns that conform to those associated with a 'narcissistic personality.'" According to Gilbert, narcissistic personality types, while under stress, can show many paranoid features, and America paid a price for Johnson's temperamental outbursts, excessive secretiveness, fear of losing control, and outlandish suspicions. But Gilbert was lavish in his praise of President Johnson's domestic policies, which he judged "perhaps as extraordinary as [those] of Franklin D. Roosevelt, making him one of the most effective legislative leaders in American history." Echoing Dr. Willis Hurst, who had noted what "a very great asset" Lady Bird was to her husband, Gilbert labeled her a "key helper . . . a central figure in [the Johnson] Administration."

But how did she do it? Besides trying to monitor her husband's diet and exercise she had a litany of morale boosters. One of her frequent refrains, when Lyndon was too discouraged to get out of bed, was that all he had to do was put "one foot in front of the other and do the best you can." She surrounded him with people he enjoyed and could be counted on to flatter and boost his ego. And she was a genius at mending the fences he tore down, soothing the feelings of those he ridiculed and disparaged.

Eric Goldman, the Princeton professor who worked closely with the first lady's office, listed an arsenal of tools Mrs. Johnson employed to clean up her husband's messes. After he had insulted someone, word would get back to her, often via Lyndon himself. She would make a phone call, sometimes to the spouse of the offended party, perhaps mentioning the incident, perhaps not, but cooing in her most amiable tones how much the Johnsons valued a friendship such as theirs. She followed up with more substantial appeasements, such as an invitation to the ranch or an intimate dinner at the White House. Goldman rated her instincts as nearly infallible in such matters—and far-reaching. Lyndon would go over a dinner guest list, striking out names on the basis of his most recent clashes and peeves. But she would unerringly put back the names of those who needed special consideration.

Bill Fisher, a Navy photographer assigned to the White House, gave a specific example of how Mrs. Johnson worked to undo the president's harsh words. Fisher was at the ranch one of those perfect Sunday mornings in spring when the first lady suggested he go to a nearby field and photograph the bluebonnets. A short time later, as Fisher and an associate were busy taking pictures, a helicopter came to summon them back to the ranch, where they found a very angry president. He had been looking for the photographers and not found them where he thought they ought to be. Fisher was dismayed by the inconsistency. The president was right there when Mrs. Johnson's discussion with Fisher took place, and he had registered no objection. Now Fisher was angry—he felt he was being punished unfairly. It remained for Bird to do what she had been doing for years. She didn't contradict her husband in front of anyone, but she made a point of telling Fisher later, in private, that she was sorry for getting him into trouble and she thanked him profusely. In a sentiment echoed by most people who knew her, Fisher concluded: "I would walk over hot coals for her."

Mrs. Johnson was less successful at helping her husband navigate difficult foreign policy decisions. In their three decades of marriage, she had sometimes managed to "influence" him or pass on what she considered "good judgment." But under the barrage of criticism regarding Vietnam, she felt overwhelmed, the questions seemed too big. As she lived every day "against the backdrop of air strikes by our planes in Vietnam," she watched Lyndon move "in a cloud of troubles, with few rays of light."

The antiwar protest that had begun with a few disaffected youths had mushroomed into a huge movement that united people of different ages, politics, professions, and places. On June 5, 1966, *The New York Times* took three pages to publish an advertisement with the names of more than 6,400 educators and other professionals who were appealing to President Johnson to withdraw troops from Vietnam. Some of the service men and women who had returned from duty in Vietnam registered their disapproval by forming Vietnam Veterans Against the War. Rallies to register antiwar sentiment were organized all across the country, and U.S. embassies in London, Paris, and Rome reinforced security to protect their staffs from assault by antiwar protesters

Although Mrs. Johnson prided herself on an ability to ferret out a tranquil spot in even the most turbulent waters, she admitted she was stymied now: "It's like shooting the rapids, every moment a new struggle, every moment a new direction—trying to keep the craft level and away from the rocks, and no still water in sight." She felt herself "swimming upstream against a feeling of depression and relative inertia." Struggling to free herself and take control, she lamented: "I flinch from activity and involvement and yet I rust without them." Lyndon's description of their dilemma lacked her eloquence but matched her desperation: "I can't get out [of Vietnam]. I can't finish it with what I have got. So what the hell can I do?"

Lady Bird saw their predicament as a uniquely troubling challenge for her husband. "It was just a hell of a thorn stuck in his throat," she later told historian Robert Dallek. "It wouldn't come up; it wouldn't go down . . . It was just pure hell." Starting preschool programs and formulating environmental measures made sense; she could get excited about either one of those because "Win or lose, it's the right thing to do." But on Vietnam there was no "reassuring, strong feeling" about what was right. "So uncertainty . . . we had a rich dose of that." Lyndon described their quandary in less elegant terms, telling aide Bill Moyers that he was accustomed to looking "for the light at the end of the tunnel." But in this case, "Hell, we don't even have a tunnel; we don't even know where the tunnel is."

Mrs. Johnson may have lacked a tunnel but she had resources, and she enlisted them all. When she ventured outside and encountered angry signs and shouts, she relied on her famous ability to shut out what she did not want to see or hear. Her myopia helped, making it hard to read all but the biggest lettering on the signs. Even when physical assault seemed a real possibility, she proceeded. On her trip to give conservation speeches on the campuses of Williams College and Yale University in October 1967, she encountered crowds that her aide Cynthia Wilson thought looked like they might physically attack the first lady, but Mrs. Johnson gave no indication she even saw them. She just kept walking, eyes straight ahead, remaining "amazingly calm."

It was no secret that Jacqueline Kennedy had escaped Washington woes with trips to exotic places, riding elephants with her sister in India; swimming with daughter Caroline off Italy's Amalfi coast; cruising in the Greek islands with European jet-setters. But Lyndon Johnson frowned on his family indulging in expensive vacations abroad, even if paid for out of their own pockets. So the extended international travel that Lady Bird had relished during her husband's vice presidency was almost entirely eliminated now. Her official trips as first lady, such as representing the president at the funeral of a Greek monarch, did not count as time off. Not when Secret Service agents surrounded her, reporters scrutinized every facial expression, and European royalty weighed in on whether she removed the correct glove at the proper moment. She needed an escape, a place to unwind, and she orchestrated one such trip in June 1965, while her husband wrestled with Vietnam problems.

On that Caribbean outing, she took along Herman Wouk's newly published *Don't Stop the Carnival*, about living it up on a sunny, laid-back island, and she included only a tiny work assignment for herself. To justify spending taxpayers' money and appease Lyndon, she promised to deliver the commencement speech at the University of the Virgin Islands. With that obligation out of the way, she proceeded to enjoy the sea and sun on the island, St. John, with her brother Tony and his wife, Matianna. Bird, slim in a two-piece, powder blue bathing suit, mugged for her home movie camera and strutted like a winner at the Miss America contest. Her security detail kept a polite distance while she and her closest aides, Bess Abell and Liz Carpenter, cavorted in the sand. The first lady donned snorkel gear and a slicker before scampering to a little boat waiting to take her to a secluded cove. She laughed so hard, her face screwed up, squeezing her eyes shut.

But such ventures beyond U.S. borders were rare. The first lady found some relief from the cares of her job at the LBJ Ranch, and she started whittling out more time to spend there. After an action-packed day of greeting hundreds and giving a major speech in Lincoln, Nebraska, on June 15, 1966, she let her staff and accompanying reporters return to Washington while she headed to the ranch. She remained there for nine days. Sounding like a kid let out of school, she penned in her own hand her diary entry for June 18: "drove myself" around the ranch, "watched 'Gun Smoke,'" and "read."

Back in Washington, the president was distraught. On top of all his other disappointments, one of his beagles had been killed the day Bird left, right there on the White House grounds, accidentally run over by one of the chauffeurs. Staff had been so reluctant to tell him, they sent Lynda Bird to relay the sad news. But even revelation of tragedy did not induce Mrs. Johnson to rejoin her husband. She wanted some time for herself, to savor "supper alone at pool" and the pleasure of going to bed "early."

While she was in Texas, the president alternated spurts of buoyant, high spirits with troughs of brooding discontent. His secretaries recorded jovial bantering between him and congressional leaders at one meeting; a subsequent photographic session erupted in laughter. He hosted a stag dinner for more than one hundred in honor of King Faisal of Saudi Arabia. But on unscheduled evenings, LBJ moped and fidgeted, trying to figure out "what to do tonight." On June 18, he phoned his secretarial pool more than once, asking if the weather looked good for a boat ride. Unable to come up with a plan, he took a nap. By a little before 8 p.m., he was on the phone again, lining up companions for a dinner cruise on the Potomac. Quiet time with only a good book for company, or watching an old movie with one of his daughters, did not suit his high-octane style. To put the pressures of his job out of mind, he needed an audience, an extremely appreciative one, and that usually meant a congenial mix of high-powered, sympathetic males and attractive, complaisant females. On June 18 his first call went to

Eloise Thornberry, wife of the judge who once represented Lyndon's old congressional district.

To relieve the pressure of their jobs, both the president and first lady looked for small diversions while on duty in Washington. Lyndon liked to turn one workday into two: after getting to his office, he typically stayed until late afternoon, then had lunch, took a nap, and started again. After a shower and full change of clothes, he would continue until nine or so in the evening. Under the high tension surrounding Vietnam decisions, he turned one nap into two, and routinely summoned a masseur for a rubdown before bedtime. By 1966, Bird was incorporating the same relaxation techniques, naps lasting sometimes two hours and a daily massage. During one twenty-four-hour period, she summoned the masseur twice.

For exercise, which their physicians encouraged, both the president and first lady walked on the South Lawn, often together, and she dutifully took herself to the Executive Office Building for a measured thirty minutes of bowling. Since these were often spur-of-the-moment decisions, she didn't have time to book anyone to join her, and she never liked to plan ahead anyway—Lyndon could call for her at any time and expect her to show up in a matter of minutes. With the White House pool at her disposal, she might have indulged in solo swims, one of her favorite forms of exercise, but the cost of getting her hair done deterred her. "It takes $8 to make me presentable to the public after I have had a swim," she noted in her diary.

As Lyndon's anxieties ballooned, he spent fewer hours in the Oval Office and more in the pool. In the first frenetic months of his presidency, he typically dressed for work before 9 a.m. so he could cram breakfast meetings with legislators in between conferences with aides and photo sessions with foreign dignitaries. Now, in a besieged White House, he dwelt longer on the morning papers. Day after day, he did not leave the residence until nearly noon. His calendar is dotted with "swim," even on weekday mornings at eleven, when most busy executives stayed at their desks.

Bird felt guilty spending time away from her overwhelmed husband, but she did it anyway. After a July 4, 1965, weekend at the ranch, she stayed behind while he returned to the White House to host a dinner for Australian prime minister Robert Menzies. The next evening, when Lynda Bird phoned her father from Wyoming, where she was vacationing, she thought he sounded "lonesome," and she immediately sent out an SOS to the person who could help: "You know, Mother, he's never the same without you." Although Bird stood her ground and refused to budge, she wrote in her diary, "I felt selfish, as though I was insulating myself from pain and troubles down here." In a touch of defiance, she added: "I do know I need [time alone at the ranch]." Not until the next day did she phone her husband.

The president assuaged her guilt a bit by joining her at the ranch the following weekend, and he engaged some of his favorite people—Jack and Mary Margaret Valenti, secretary Vicky McCammon, and aide Joe Califano—to help him have fun. When he ushered them onto his boat on Saturday evening, Bird joined the party. But she brought her own circle of congenial company—a group from Karnack who were trying to buy the Brick House, where she was born, and turn it into a historical site. In the midst of so many disappointments and trials, it must have been gratifying to know that her hometown wanted to recognize her by turning her birthplace into a tourist site, although they were unsuccessful. The Brick House remained the private residence of her stepmother Ruth and of Ruth's heirs.

As the anti-Vietnam protests escalated, the Johnsons turned more inward, taking a measure of satisfaction in seeing movies about themselves. When they first moved into the White House, they used the East Wing theater to watch Hollywood's latest releases, but by 1966, they showed a preference for more familiar subjects. The first lady had enlisted presidential aide Harry Middleton to give a professional touch to the documentary films that Navy photographers made about the president and his family. Some sounded like newsreels, reporting on travels and meetings. Others showed family fun—pictures of Luci and Lynda and their friends. All were flattering. Rather than the TV documentaries on body counts in Vietnam, the Johnsons saw tranquil pictures of people and places they loved. They watched *The President's Country*, full of ranchlands and lakes, more than a dozen times, and the White House projectionist, who served several presidential families, noted that the Johnsons were unusual in how much they liked watching themselves.

Courtenay Lynda Valenti, the curly-headed toddler daughter of Mary Margaret and Jack Valenti, became a featured player in the Navy photographers' films because she was one of the president's pet diversions. She had the ability, Bird noted, to keep Lyndon "in the palm of her small cherub hand." He would phone the Valenti home, sometimes twice a day, just to hear her babble, and he included her on Potomac cruises even when her parents couldn't come. After he permitted her to climb on his lap during a meeting of the National Security Council and tweak his nose, journalists scrambled for more information on the child, and Maxine Cheshire of *The Washington Post* requested a picture of her. She didn't get it.

Neither of the president's daughters had ever provided the same escape as Courtenay, and Bird lamented that it was "almost sad" that in his mid-fifties Lyndon had more time for another child than he ever had for his own. The negligence was not a fault, however, as far as Bird was concerned. She thought he "was cut out for destiny and doing anything less would be a waste." She would have to handle for both of them "the troubles that came along."

Those troubles included dealing with the needs of their two very different daughters: the solid, "reliable, planning-ahead" Lynda and the unpredictable Luci, a "lark," who met "each day on tiptoe." The bubbly, younger daughter had struggled to get passing grades at school, while Lynda excelled. But in the spring of 1964, as a sophomore in high school, Luci began treatment with Washington optometrist Dr. Robert A. Kraskin, who diagnosed an eye coordination problem and prescribed eye exercises. Her grades quickly improved, as did her attitude. She had always been outspoken about her objections to her father's job and how it impinged on her life—separating her from both parents for long periods and showering her with unwelcome scrutiny. But once in the White House she appeared more amenable to the demands of a politician's life, and Lady Bird marveled at the change: "You might as well try to bottle sunshine as to suppress her." Luci shared her father's love of animals, and after the death of one of his favorite beagles, she picked up a stray at a Texas gas station and it quickly became his treasured companion, Yuki. In times of despair, when he asked staff to "call in the dogs" for a little diversion, it was Yuki he wanted to see.

Lynda shared many of her mother's interests—in history and theater—but lacked her press savvy and social skills. After grousing about living in the White House for the spring semester of 1964, she returned to her sorority house in Austin the following September and finished college at the University of Texas. When she came east for vacations, she occasionally accompanied her mother to a local art gallery or on shopping excursions to New York, where the two liked to end the day with a Broadway show. But on her solo trips, Lynda annoyed the press by refusing requests for pictures and interviews. Bird admitted Lynda could be "impossible" at times, and worried that she was missing out on "the world" and the chance "to taste it all."

With such diverging personalities, it is not surprising the two sisters fought a lot—or as their mother put it, they failed to show much "mutual appreciation." After Luci's conversion to Roman Catholicism, Lynda objected that she "looks down" on the rest of the family, judging them inferior for choosing to remain Protestant. Luci complained about her sister's inability to "reach out to other people," and when *Women's Wear Daily* gave all three Johnson women bad marks for how they dressed, Luci blamed Lynda's "bobby socks and loafers" for the humiliation.

The Johnson White House years coincided with tumultuous changes in both daughters' lives. After announcing and then breaking her engagement to a young man from Comfort, Texas, Lynda became involved in a highly publicized romance with Hollywood actor George Hamilton, then met and married White House aide Chuck Robb, and gave birth to a daughter. In just two years, July 1965 to June 1967, Luci converted to Catholicism, married Pat Nugent, and gave birth to the Johnsons' first grandchild.

The normal anxieties of early adulthood were underscored for the Johnson daughters by the intense publicity and Secret Service surveillance they received. Luci complained, "I had just gotten my driver's license and my first car and all of a sudden I had a twenty-four-hour chaperone." What remained strictly family business in other households—youthful romances, wardrobe mistakes, honor rolls, career choices—made national news when a daughter of the president was involved, and neither the daughters nor their parents were happy with the result. Lyndon found fault with much of what they did. He objected to how Lynda dressed and instructed her to go out and buy some good clothes and send the bill to him. After an article appeared about a projected trip to Europe, he was livid. When Katie Louchheim mentioned to Liz Carpenter that she found Lady Bird "rushed . . . helpless and disturbed," Liz shot back, "What would you be, if you had a husband who constantly raised hell with you about your two daughters' difficult behavior?"

When eighteen-year-old Luci announced in late 1965 that she wanted to marry Midwesterner Pat Nugent, she set off a string of worries and problems for her parents. First, that she was too young. Bird was hardly in a position to object to short courtships—hers lasted only a few weeks. But she had been nearly twenty-two years old, with two university degrees in hand, when she married Lyndon; Luci had only high school and a few nursing school classes. Bird had tried to expose both daughters to career women with exciting jobs in some "wicked and delightful city" like Rome. But neither one showed much interest in "leading the sort of life" that Bird had imagined for herself after college. She had wanted them to "taste the cream of life and fall in love a dozen times" before marrying anyone.

But here Luci was, setting her wedding date for August 6, 1966, when she would be barely nineteen. Loud objections suddenly surfaced, objections that would never have arisen concerning the offspring of less famous parents. It seemed that even the slightest acquaintance expected an invitation, and Washington's Immaculate Conception Catholic Church, although large, could not accommodate them all. Katie Louchheim complained that she was one of those left off the list, even though she had generously offered to put up some of the bride's out-of-town guests.

While agonizing over the particulars of a wedding—attendants' gowns and flowers and food at the reception—Luci faced a barrage of criticism. One busybody suggested it was insensitive to choose a date that much of the world associated with the American bombing of Hiroshima in 1945. Luci countered that perhaps December 7, the anniversary of Pearl Harbor, would have been preferable. Labor union leaders objected that the bridal gown lacked a union label; and when an airline executive offered to provide air-conditioning for the church, the president had to refuse the offer—because the airline's workers were currently on strike. The Immaculate Conception church became so overheated that August Saturday that the bride's sister fainted. Rather than a happy family milestone, the Nugent wedding was a mixture of calamitous events, and Bird was happy to escape to Huntland, the Virginia estate of her friends Alice and George Brown, when it was over.

That same summer saw Lynda dating George Hamilton, the tall, perpetually tanned movie star with facial features resembling those seen in shaving cream ads. Five years her senior, Hamilton had been around Hollywood long enough to know something about makeup and fashion, and he started encouraging Lynda in a remarkable make-over. She had tended to be overweight and once quipped that her "awkward age" extended from "five to twenty-five," a statement her mother deemed "a ridiculous exaggeration." But Bird did admit that Lynda "was a fat little girl for quite a number of years," and blamed herself: "I'm afraid I'm the one who gets the black marks for that."

Lynda had started taking off excess weight in her sophomore year in college, and her much publicized romance with Hamilton gave her the chance to show off her lithe figure in sleeveless sheath dresses in Jackie Kennedy size. In an AP photo of a beaming, elegant Lynda beside Hamilton at a social event in Los Angeles, she bore a striking resemblance to Audrey Hepburn. Bird's home movies caught the grinning couple lounging at the ranch pool, and although she thought Hamilton overrated, with "a few too many women crazy about him," she liked his effect on her daughter. "Excitement is a new mood for Lynda," Bird wrote in her diary, "and it becomes her. She looks radiant, happy, in the swift current of her life."

On October 3, 1967, Bird was at the ranch, happily arranging her collection of Doughty birds on shelves and thinking about the time when she and Lyndon would live full time in that house, when she received a phone call that sent her rushing back to the capital. It was from Dr. Hurst and he needed to see her—about Lyndon. Three hours later she was on the JetStar, headed east. When her plane landed in Washington just before midnight, Dr. Hurst was there waiting, and as he rode with her in the backseat of her soundproof limo to the White House, he updated her on the president's condition.

Hurst had been treating Lyndon long enough to feel he could size up his condition pretty quickly, without an extended examination. Just by looking at him, assessing his color and energy level, and talking with the staff who saw him every day, Hurst felt confident of his diagnosis, which he would then substantiate with the tests and measurements commonly used in physical examinations. The doctor had already stopped at the White House twice that year, and although others commented that the president looked excessively tired, Hurst did not agree with them. This time was different—he saw reason for alarm. His most famous patient looked fatigued; energy depleted; mood glum. The prescription that Hurst knew worked best—attention from Lady Bird—had to be increased in dosage.

As the doctor and first lady rode together that night through Washington streets, he advised her to spend more time with her husband, monitor his rest and diet more closely, help him through this rough period. It was a rare case of Bird being told she was falling short of expectations, and her first reaction was to pull down the famous psychic veil and shut out what she was hearing. When Hurst saw that she was not listening to a word he said, he called her on it and she immediately "jolted herself back into this world and she apologized profusely." Although it was well after midnight when she got to bed that night, she was in her husband's bedroom by 7:45 the next morning.

In the months that followed, her juggling act—preserving her own sanity and helping her beleaguered husband—grew more difficult as antiwar rallies multiplied. No U.S. city showed deeper anger and hostility toward the president than the capital. "Washington was burning, [with] endless protests," one of Bird's aides remembered, and the first lady could not look outside her window without seeing them. Mothers who had never demonstrated for any cause showed up with their daughters at the Women Strike for Peace march on the Pentagon in February 1967. A few months later, another women's march turned violent after security officers ordered the demonstrators to keep their distance from the White House. In October 1967, an estimated 100,000 gathered at the Lincoln Memorial, and nearly a third of that number remained for a march on the Pentagon, where they camped overnight to underscore the strength of their dissent.

Bird's dream of leaving the White House in a blaze of achievement had vanished, as the behemoth of Vietnam quashed hopes for a grand legacy. She is not on record as challenging at the time her husband's decision to expand the fighting in Vietnam, but evidence accumulated later indicates she may have had misgivings about the course he chose. In a March 1967 entry in her White House diary, not open to the public until 2014, she questioned the wisdom of "looking for communists under every bed." Long after leaving the White House she told an interviewer that a president needs some momentous justification for leading a nation into war, "like Pearl Harbor or the Alamo," a justification her husband clearly never had.

Even while her husband was still alive, she questioned the validity of the "domino theory," which drove his decisions on the war. And she did it in front of a witness. Aaron Asher, the editor who worked with Lyndon on his book, *The Vantage Point*, in 1971, had once been an antiwar protester, and he had continued to question what really lay behind the dogged persistence to stay in Vietnam when so much of the evidence indicated victory could never be won.

When Asher learned that President Nixon was planning to reverse American policy and turn the war back to the Vietnamese, he decided to ask what ex-President Johnson thought about that. Would it work? "Of course not," Lyndon replied very emphatically. And then he proceeded to outline the disastrous future he foresaw: the "incompetent" South Vietnamese military will "lose Vietnam," giving the communists the chance to overrun the Philippines and invade Hawaii. He ended his monologue with the dire prediction that his grandson would one day have to fight in Asia. Asher found himself speechless, wondering if LBJ could "really believe all that?" Then Bird spoke up, and in her soft, deferential way, asked, "But, Lyndon, don't you think that they, the Vietnamese, if they take over, will have so much on their plates that like the Russians and their détente, they'll turn inward?" Asher admitted that he was so "fearful of being in the middle of a domestic explosion," he excused himself and left the room. But he later regretted that decision, realizing that it was "possible that this had not been the first time the Johnsons, in the privacy of their home, had disagreed about the war."

Throughout her long marriage, Bird had admitted to helping her husband navigate through serious illnesses and draconian choices, but she had not claimed any credit for influencing his thinking on Vietnam. She had once explained that she had not felt "big enough" for that. But her comment in front of Asher doesn't sound like that of a woman who didn't try.

17

OUTLANDISH LBJ

L YNDON WAS A big-time flirt for as long as Bird knew him. He
called most women "Honey" and showered them with buttery
compliments, like those that gained him an extra piece of pie from the
mothers of his boyhood friends back in Johnson City. In the White
House, he greeted female staff with head-to-toe appraisals and questions about how each had spent the previous evening. His banter—
about the boyfriend of one or the new hairstyle of another—turned
what should have been a professional relationship into a confusing
intimacy that mixed paternal concern with Don Juan overtures. He
rewarded his favorites with expensive shoes and jewelry, and if that
did not ignite jealousy, his proffer of a seat beside him on Air Force
One surely did. Someone suggested the first lady post a warning for
the secretarial pool: "You can play with Lyndon, but you cannot take
him home with you."

With a husband whose interest in other women was so fully documented, Lady Bird would have looked foolish trying to disprove it.
Yet the honesty with which she acknowledged his wandering eye produced the most damning charges against her. Even her most ardent

fans expressed dismay that she failed to show more backbone—assert her own dignity and rein him in. Quick to entertain at her table the women whose names had been linked to his, she heartily complimented them on their looks and cleverness, even hosted them on overnight stays.

What *was* she thinking? Why *did* she do it? Those were virtually the only questions that visibly raised her ire, as Texan journalist Jan Jarboe Russell learned during interviews in the late 1990s. After Mrs. Johnson spent amiable hours with Russell, who was preparing to write an article about her, the meetings suddenly stopped. Russell's queries on the subject of Lyndon's philandering had made the ex–first lady very angry. Her voice turned uncharacteristically shrill, and she lashed out: "When people ask me these sort of things, I just say, 'Look to your own lives. . . . Fix yourselves, and keep your problems to yourself.' "

Lyndon's high-spirited physicality fueled rumors about his sex life. He wound his arms around male and female alike, and since pre-1970s women were less likely than subsequent generations to object to a hand brushing a breast or lingering on a buttock, he got away with it. A member of Mrs. Johnson's White House staff wrote many years after leaving Washington that President Johnson "enjoyed his physical power. What I experienced nearly every time I saw him was a squeeze on the butt, or putting his arm around my wrist and pulling me to his side. These were definitely sexual expressions, but he wasn't trying to take the next step [and I] interpreted his gestures as a natural exuberance, not a threat I had to repulse."

In other cases, the evidence is more substantial and the goal clearer. Early in his presidency, he warned reporters that they should take no notice of "me coming in and out of a few women's bedrooms while I am in the White House. . . . That is none of your business." And he bragged about the number of his sexual partners, quipping that he had had more women by chance than JFK had had on purpose. Aides became accustomed to that braggadocio, and although he avoided names, his behavior (which included frequent private sessions with one woman or another) provided enough supporting evidence to lend credence to his claims.

Harry McPherson, who worked closely with him for more than a decade, insisted Lyndon was not priapic, using and then discarding women for his own pleasure; he genuinely cared for the women he wooed. Unlike JFK, who explained that "if he did not have a woman every three days, he would have a terrible headache," LBJ formed relationships that lasted over time.

One woman whose relationship did last many years stands out from all the others, and might well have presented a genuine threat to the Johnson marriage. Texan Mary Margaret Wiley, who had taken a job in Lyndon's Washington office in 1954 before she graduated from UT, quickly became a mainstay in his work and personal life. She traveled with him on both business and pleasure trips and even lived for a while in the Johnson home. Lyndon's on-and-off aide for many years, Joe Phipps, later wrote that Wiley was performing "all the wifely chores" that had previously fallen to Bird. But Phipps insisted the relationship was not intimate and that gossip to the contrary was "vicious."

At Washington dinner parties that Bird attended with Lyndon or hosted at home, Wiley's name was often paired with that of Bob Waldon, a bachelor newly arrived in Washington. But in December 1961, a different man started showing up as Wiley's escort—Jack Valenti, a forty-year-old advertising executive from Dallas, who had met Wiley while working for Lyndon in the 1960 campaign. By the spring of 1962, he was Wiley's regular date for dinners at the Johnson homes, both at the ranch and at The Elms.

In mid-May, Valenti's status suddenly changed when the vice president announced to his staff that Mary Margaret was quitting her job to marry Jack. Events surrounding this decision suggest that it was made with difficulty. George Reedy, who shared a flight with the Johnsons and Mary Margaret at that time, recalled, "Well, believe me, we celebrated my father's death with more hilarity than was exhibited on that trip." Although a new secretary, Marie Fehmer, had been hired to take her place, Mary Margaret stayed with the Johnsons until five days before the wedding. On Friday, June 1, the vice president of the United States walked Mary Margaret down the aisle at St. Ann's Catholic Church in Houston, while her father sat in a nearby pew. (Mary Margaret was Episcopalian but Jack's Sicilian mother wanted a Catholic wedding.) Bird and Lyndon attended the lunch following the nuptials and presented the couple with an "antique silver tray."

Although Mary Margaret Valenti was no longer their employee, she continued to be a featured player in the Johnsons' lives. Only four weeks after her wedding, she flew to Washington without Jack to spend time with them. She subsequently accompanied them to Jamaica, where they all met Princess Margaret and her husband, Antony Armstrong-Jones. In October, Mrs. Valenti joined the vice president on his speech-making jaunts to California and Hawaii, and she spent considerable time at the ranch.

Jack Valenti gradually began doing less advertising work in Houston so he could make himself useful to the VP, and he showed a dogged loyalty that quickly propelled him into the Johnsons' innermost circle. He was at LBJ's side at a governors conference in Florida and also at the opening session of the Senate on September 18, 1962. Both Valentis were in the Johnson delegation to the Dominican Republic in February 1963, and to the Vatican in June for the funeral of Pope John XXIII.

By summer 1963, the now visibly pregnant Mrs. Valenti and her husband were such frequent guests at the ranch that Bird included them in nearly every family event. On July 1, they helped comfort the vice president when one of his dogs died, and they assisted in his plan to surprise Luci on her "sweet sixteen" birthday with a shiny Corvair Monza convertible. On November 1, 1963, Mrs. Valenti gave birth to a daughter, Courtenay Lynda, in Houston, but two weeks later she and Jack were back at the ranch, driving around the fields with the vice president. Lyndon may have lost a secretary but not the companionship and whatever moral support and satisfaction the relationship with Mary Margaret brought him. The Valenti family continued to figure in the Johnsons' life all during the White House years, joining them for Sunday lunch in the residence and for weekends at Camp David.

Naturally, rumors flew and jokes proliferated about the real relationship between the president and his former secretary. But then, speculation about Lyndon's sex life had figured in descriptions of him for a very long time. When he first arrived in Washington, his co-workers did not detect signs of the sexual conquistador in him—he was too busy chumming up to superiors and exerting power over his colleagues. Part of his ambitious play for advancement included squiring the wives of important men around the dance floor, but no one took that for anything other than courting favor with the husbands. By the late 1930s, however, evidence accumulated, both in Washington and Texas, that he had little regard for monogamy.

The women whose names were linked to his came from his closest circle—wives of fellow legislators and aides, family friends, journalists, and secretarial staff. His wife could hardly avoid the women mentioned—she saw them every day—at political gatherings, in his office, in their homes or hers. Snubbing them or treating them ungraciously could have backfired, reverberating through Lyndon's office. So she incorporated them into her day without showing an ounce of bad will; she was particularly gracious to Mary Margaret, even driving out to the airport at midnight to pick her up in Washington when she returned from a speech-making trip with Lyndon.

Friends mused that a look of sadness sometimes crossed Bird's face when she encountered blatant evidence of her husband's attention to other women, but she quickly rallied to the task at hand and hid whatever disappointment she felt. Marie Fehmer, Lyndon's secretary for many years, told Randall Woods, professor of history at the University of Arkansas, that she once accompanied Mrs. Johnson to Lyndon's California hotel, where they found Mary Margaret's lingerie strewn about his room. Calmly and without comment, Bird began gathering up the panties and bras, and then she "went out of her way to be nice" to Mary Margaret.

No shortage of women competed for Lyndon's attention. Winsome journalists crowded around the president, illustrating the truth in Henry Kissinger's famous comment that power is a potent aphrodisiac. When *Time* magazine reported on the 1964 Easter vacation of the Johnsons at the ranch, it made it sound like everybody was living it up. The headline, "Mr. President, You're Fun," appeared to be a quote from Hearst reporter Marianne Means, who had cooed that in his ear while fastening her "baby-blue eyes" on him as he drove her around in his Lincoln Continental. One of the other female reporters in the car explained that Lyndon had just shown them his prize cattle and given them "a very graphic description of the sex life of a bull." Coincidentally, that same issue of *Time* carried a full-page advertisement, encouraging readers to notice how it's always the most exciting people who drive Lincoln Continentals.

Lady Bird had already noted Means's powers of attraction a few weeks earlier when she accompanied Lyndon to Means's Washington home to join a gathering she described as "a younger crowd, including lots of Roosevelts." Bird extolled the hostess as "absolutely ravishing— like a mermaid . . . in a blue-green iridescent sequined [gown] that fit her like her skin—low neck, low back."

For a woman like Bird, who started life as the daughter of a gruff shopkeeper in a gritty Texas town, the chance to mix with sequined mermaids, movie stars, and bona fide Roosevelts was as exciting as extramarital affairs were commonplace. Her father's reputation as a ladies' man survived him in Harrison County. Bird made no secret of her preference for big, macho men like her father, and staffer Horace Busby concluded it was impossible to fathom her outsized attraction to Lyndon without understanding her deep attachment to T.J. She admired kindly, mild men, such as Adlai Stevenson, but was not physically drawn to them and could not understand why so many other women were. Liz Carpenter admitted her own tastes differed, and she said she would be delighted to have Stevenson "put his shoes under my bed any night."

Although Lady Bird Johnson and Jacqueline Bouvier Kennedy differed in many respects, they were a lot alike in their thinking about men. Each idolized her own notoriously philandering father. In their impressionable early years, both women learned that the "manliness" of their beloved fathers did not include monogamy, and, wedding vows notwithstanding, "faithful" was not part of the marriage bargain. Lady Bird implied as much in her comment to Jan Jarboe Russell, and Mrs. Kennedy's friend, the author Edna O'Brien, reported in her memoir that Jackie "skimmed over" JFK's infidelities when talking about the magnetism of the Kennedy men.

In comparing the philandering of LBJ and JFK, Theodore Sorensen, who worked for both men, noted that Johnson flaunted his extramarital relationships while Kennedy went to great lengths to keep his hidden, especially from his wife: he took pains not "to confront, humiliate, hurt or anger Jacqueline with public misconduct." Sorensen admitted he did not know how much Jackie knew or suspected about her husband's relationships with other women. "Nor do I know," he wrote, "whether she would have responded to her husband's womanizing with the same philosophical acceptance as Lady Bird Johnson."

After Jackie's death, evidence surfaced that she knew a lot. A letter that came to public attention in 2014 indicated she was fully aware of JFK's voracious sexual appetite before she married him in 1953. The previous year she had written to an Irish priest in Dublin, the Reverend Joseph Leonard, that John Kennedy resembled her father in his transitory interest in women: "loves the chase and is bored with the conquest—and once married needs proof he's still attractive, so flirts with other women and resents [his wife]. I saw how that nearly killed Mummy."

As first lady, Jackie occasionally alluded to her husband's philandering and at least once angrily objected to having to face one of his sex mates. When she spotted a certain "blonde bimbo" in a reception line, she "wheeled around in fury" and lambasted one of her husband's aides: "Isn't it bad enough that you solicit this woman for my husband, but then you insult me by asking me to shake her hand!" Jackie subsequently regained her composure and greeted the woman politely, just as Lady Bird would have done. On another occasion, Jackie pointed to one of her husband's assistants and said, in French, to a French newsman: "This is the girl who supposedly is sleeping with my husband."

In the wake of the assassination, most books on the Kennedys portrayed their marriage as fairyland perfect, but the chimera of Camelot lifts with hindsight. Jackie was often away or found ways to distance herself from potentially embarrassing scenes. Accounts proliferated of JFK's "after-hours" parties, especially in the summer when husbands, whose wives were vacationing elsewhere, felt free to squire other women to the president's soirees. When Marilyn Monroe delivered her notoriously suggestive rendering of "Happy Birthday, Mr. President," at a large fund-raiser in Madison Square Garden in May 1962, it was televised, and columnist Dorothy Kilgallen described the performance as "nothing less than making love to the president in the direct view of forty million Americans." But Jackie was not among the forty million—she had gone horseback riding in Virginia, taking daughter Caroline with her.

After Jackie's death in 1994, Mimi Beardsley Alford and Helen Chavchavadze both revealed details of their own intimate encounters with President Kennedy. Alford was a young intern at the White House in 1963, and the book she published half a century later, describing her bedroom meetings with President Kennedy, sounds a bit like the dallying between President Bill Clinton and Monica Lewinsky. Chavchavadze's association with JFK, as she described it to biographer Sally Bedell Smith, was more substantial. The affair had begun before the 1960 election and continued after his inauguration, when he invited Chavchavadze "from time to time for intimate evenings when Jackie was away." Although Chavchavadze admitted she never was sure what Jackie knew and always "felt ambivalent [about the relationship] and wanted to end it," she could not. Jack was "irresistible."

In appearing not to notice what was going on, Jackie Kennedy followed a long line of first ladies who kept mum about their husbands' other women. Rather than derail a political career, Ellen Axson Wilson, the first wife of Woodrow Wilson, even incorporated her husband's "other woman," Mary Peck, into the Wilson family circle and invited her to meet with the Wilson daughters in the White House. Florence Harding died without ever facing journalists' questions on the subject of her husband, Warren's, philandering, but her rivals supplied ample evidence of his wandering eye. In 1927, Nan Britton published a book, *The President's Daughter*, claiming that her liaison with Warren had produced a child. Four decades later, newly discovered letters between Warren and his Marion, Ohio, neighbor (and his wife's close friend) Carrie Phillips revealed details of an extramarital relationship extending over many years. When those letters were fully opened to researchers in 2014, they left no doubt that Mrs. Phillips and Warren Harding liked to exchange sexually explicit messages, including pet names for private body parts.

Lady Bird Johnson was too young to observe either Florence Harding or Ellen Wilson firsthand but she saw Eleanor Roosevelt plenty of times, and it is unlikely that she did not hear about FDR's relationship with Lucy Mercer. Eleanor had discovered it back in 1918, when she accidentally opened letters between the two lovers. Although the liaison was not documented in print until years later, it rocked the

Roosevelt clan at the time, and Eleanor's cousin Alice Longworth liked to tattle mercilessly about Eleanor's marital troubles. So any congressman's wife who lived in Washington as long as Lady Bird Johnson did would have picked up hints about Mercer, who, as the widowed Mrs. Rutherfurd, resumed visits with Franklin in the White House. Regardless of when she heard about it, Lady Bird's reaction is a matter of record: she dismissed the affair as only "a fly on the wedding cake."

By the 1960s, tidbits about the private lives of the nation's leaders started turning up in tabloids, alongside gossip about movie stars and big-time athletes. Mamie Eisenhower got a taste of the coming change when photos of her husband, the Allied commander in Europe in World War II, showed him smiling broadly at the side of his willowy, winsome, young driver, Kay Summersby. Rumors of a romance spread, and Harry Truman, president at war's end, told a biographer that Ike had intended to divorce Mamie and marry Summersby. Although Truman's claim is not entirely accepted by historians, speculation about Ike's relationship with Summersby was still floating around Washington after he became president in 1953. Reporter Ruth Montgomery, preparing an article about Mamie's first year in the White House, broke an old unwritten rule and asked the first lady directly about her husband's relationship with Summersby. Mamie quickly dismissed any possibility of impropriety, because, she said, "I know Ike." Lady Bird Johnson, a senator's wife at the time, may have hoped she could treat speculation about Lyndon's other women just as breezily.

But she was wrong. As media competed among themselves to feed a public hungry for salacious details about their leaders, LBJ, unlike JFK, was eager to accommodate them. He permitted news cameras to follow him as he drove around the ranch or lounged on a lake boat with one or more attractive woman at his side. For years, he had been nurturing stories about his huge sexual appetite, and now he had a bigger audience eager to hear about it. Aide Horace Busby provided one example, describing how he had observed from the backseat of a car how Lyndon drove with one hand and used the other to go "under the . . . skirt" of the woman seated between him and Bird. Other staff and advisers who stayed overnight at the ranch hinted at heavy use of the back stairs, which connected Lyndon's office with second-floor bedrooms where female guests and secretaries slept. Ann Brinkley, wife of TV commentator David Brinkley, was among those who reported they had to rebuff Lyndon's overtures.

With a record as public and blatant as that, Lady Bird had to find her own accommodation with the role of transgressed wife. She could not rely on the examples of previous first ladies. The stances they had used to protect themselves from scandal and appear sophisticated and classy (Jackie Kennedy), shrewdly political (Ellen Wilson and Florence Harding), admirably involved in more serious issues (Eleanor Roosevelt), or harmlessly naive (Mamie Eisenhower) would not work for Mrs. Johnson.

To Lady Bird's advantage, she had decades of experience dealing with a womanizing husband before she got to the White House. As long as she had known him, he had hired secretaries who could double as Hollywood extras. No "tired old maids" for him. As a young congressman, he had shocked residents of his congressional district by appearing to be intimately involved with the females on his staff. He posed for campaign photos alongside the most glamorous of them and made little attempt to hide the fact that he enjoyed afterwork hours with them. Marietta Brooks, head of the Women's Division in one campaign, refused to travel with him. In Washington, the word spread, and Helen Thomas, who took her first newspaper job there in 1942, immediately observed that Congressman Johnson "liked women."

What had been only insignificant local rumor gained importance as he climbed the legislative ladder. He seemed to relish including sexual references in his everyday conversation, and he even alluded to intimate relations with his wife. In one press conference, with Bird present, he announced that his sleep had been interrupted the previous night by some "vigorous activity." He winked, to make sure reporters got his point, and then invited them to verify his story with Lady Bird.

The "sexual gorilla" image he liked to project tempted press and aides to put a tag of suspicion on every interlude he spent in the company of a sole female. And there were plenty. On Air Force One, he would lock himself in his private compartment with a secretary, even with his wife aboard. His official diary records dozens of forty-five-minute sessions in the Oval Office with only one woman present. He did make one concession to propriety, according to a White House employee. After Lady Bird walked unannounced into the Oval Office and found him on the sofa with one of his secretaries, he had an alarm system installed to alert him to her arrival.

Lyndon's reputation as a Don Juan has to be viewed alongside other evidence that he respected smart women. During his first White House year, he exhorted his cabinet to promote more women, and he issued a specific goal of fifty for them to reach. He later explained the fact that his administration did not do better than it did because so many of the women refused to serve, citing family responsibilities or timidity or personal preference for not taking a demanding job.

One of those who turned him down was his old friend Mary Lasker, whom he had tried to cajole into serving as ambassador to Finland. Even though he promised considerable latitude in the job (he told her she could come back home to the United States as often as she liked) she refused, saying she had no taste for the diplomat's life, or what she called being an "actress."

The president had better luck getting a female ambassador to Luxembourg. He had leaned on Secretary of State Dean Rusk to name

Patricia Roberts Harris, saying, "These women—I want to move them up." Although only forty years old, African American Harris already had national name recognition (she had seconded Lyndon's nomination at the 1964 convention) but Rusk hated to lose her on the home front, and he told the president she would be more valuable as deputy legal adviser in Washington. Not until LBJ persisted, saying an ambassadorial post conferred exceptional international recognition, did Rusk name her and she accepted.

Who can decipher LBJ's real motivation for advancing women's careers? Esther Peterson, the shrewd labor specialist who became his special assistant for consumer affairs in January 1964, credited Lady Bird's influence. But the president's long-standing comfort with striving women like his mother may well have played a part, too, as did his desire to win women's votes.

Some of those jobs for women in the Johnson White House came with a sexual component included, as journalist Grace Halsell learned. Hardly an ingenue Texan when first spotted by the president, Halsell was forty-two years old and had been supporting herself her entire adult life by writing. An alumna of Columbia University and the Sorbonne, she moved easily between journalism and freelance editing, and she blithely left a job with the "best [boss] I ever had," oilman Earl Baldridge, because she wanted to travel in Asia. After returning to the United States and joining the Washington bureau of *The Houston Post*, she was part of a pack of reporters covering an event on the White House South Lawn on the afternoon of October 3, 1964. The president singled her out, shouting, "Come over here! You are the prettiest little thing I ever saw."

He soon dismissed the other reporters and escorted Halsell to the Oval Office where he plied her with trinkets—a bracelet, key chain, and paperweight, all with the LBJ monogram. When she stood up to leave, he, too, was suddenly "on his feet, propelling me to a sofa," Halsell wrote; she had already realized he "did not want to engage my mind." This was part of a power play, to feel he was a "bigger man" because he had a "small creature, a pretty little thing" at his side.

The scene that followed bordered on the ludicrous—and Halsell described it as "Gary Cooper without a script." The most powerful man on earth suddenly went shy, tongue-tied. Then he blurted out one of the "oldest, most hackneyed" come-ons that worldly-wise Halsell had ever heard: "Tell me all about yourself." Aware of his interest in livestock, she began talking about her deceased father, a Fort Worth cattleman who had written several books about cowboys and the Chisholm Trail.

But Lyndon was not into books right then. According to Halsell, he took her hand in his and with great solemnity declared, "I wish I could have been your father." The fifteen-year-difference in their ages hardly suggested a parent-child relationship, but Halsell realized he wanted "to see himself as older, wiser, a mentor." That was part of his need to protect and dominate lesser, female figures. The meeting lasted less than fifteen minutes, and the president's official diary listed it as a discussion of Oveta Culp Hobby, owner of the *Houston Post*, for which Halsell worked at the time.

When Halsell showed up for a job interview weeks later, she expected the same grilling on competence and experience as a male interviewee faced. But the questions the president posed convinced her that he wanted a personal relationship with his female employees; he viewed their after-work lives as relevant to their employment, part of their curriculum vitae. He inquired about Halsell's love life, her personal problems, and why she had "never had children."

Horace Busby had warned Halsell that the president, although fully informed about her writing credentials, would try to add her to his secretarial pool. She was pretty, and the president surrounded himself with pretty secretaries, "more for display than passion." He liked to tutor them on makeup and wardrobe, and in the process he sought to create the perfect female specimen, his "Aphrodite or Galatea" to make him feel good about himself.

After learning that Halsell did not take dictation, the president hired her as an aide, responsible for churning out pithy, short speeches on his achievements and scanning newspapers for favorable editorials. The resulting press packets, which she sent over to Capitol Hill for inclusion in the Congressional Record, struck her as sad evidence of a pathetic man. Here he was, a world leader, but he still required constant reassurance of his worth.

Although Halsell remained on his staff until 1968, she deplored his treatment of women and judged him a terrible boss. He instructed his aides to hire women with "good behinds" so he could "enjoy" their rears as they left, in case he had not fully registered their precise measurements when they walked in. He commented on Halsell's clothes and warned her one day: "If you wear a tight dress like that, you are going to get your bottom pinched." He inserted sexual innuendo into the most innocent relationships, and when Halsell went to lunch at a Washington restaurant with a male colleague, the president tracked them down and called three times, implying they were having lunch-time sex or what he called "a matinee." He even implied he wanted a matinee of his own, phoning Halsell days later with instructions to get "rested up . . . hair fixed real pretty . . . get perfumed up."

As for why he carried on with other women in front of his wife, Halsell had a theory: "The more he belittled [Lady Bird], the more 'man' he perhaps imagined himself to be." Sometimes floundering in the face of big decisions, he could feel upstaged by a self-controlled, disciplined wife. That Bird loved him dearly made her the perfect target for his darts. And he certainly knew how to launch them. Halsell noted that whenever she and the president walked into the first lady's line of vision, he would take one of Halsell's hands firmly in his, implying an intimacy that never existed.

———————

The list of women reporting Lyndon's sexual advances and proposi-
tions is so long as to suggest he might have thought a woman would
feel offended if he did not try. Nora Ephron, the sassy dramatist, noted
after reading the many accounts of JFK's trysts that she must have been
the only White House intern he did not hit on. Lyndon had a similar
reputation. His seasoned secretaries (such as Mildred Stegall and Juanita
Roberts) were not on his playmate list, but most of the younger ones reported how he hinted at wanting—or outright invited them into—a sexual relationship. The very proper, religiously observant Marie Fehmer,
his secretary from 1962 to 1969, revealed that he offered to set her up
in a New York apartment if she would agree to bear him a son. Doris
Kearns (later Goodwin), the White House fellow who worked with him
on his memoir and later wrote a book about him, acknowledged that he
had broached the subject of marriage with her, too.

Lyndon Johnson's presidential diary is full of names of beautiful women who passed through the Oval Office, swam in the White
House pool, slept in the executive mansion's guest quarters, sometimes night after night, and spent weekends at Camp David. But, with
one exception, none has published a tell-all account of a sexual relationship.

The exception is Madeleine Duncan Brown, an advertising sales-
person, whose 1997 book, *Texas in the Morning,* details a twenty-year-
long affair with Lyndon that she said began in 1948 and produced a
son two years later. Only twenty-three when she met him, she was
so awed by the "fierce, dynamic energy . . . [of the] handsome . . . six
feet, five [*sic*] inches tall" senator that she could hardly talk. But she
regained enough composure to accept every invitation she received to
spend time with him, invitations usually delivered via Jesse Kellam,
who as head of KTBC had business dealings with her employer, Glenn
Advertising.

When Brown told Lyndon she was pregnant, he was furious, and called her a "goddamn dumb Dora." But after the baby was born (and named Steven Brown, taking the surname of Madeleine's husband, from whom she was separated), Lyndon generously provided funds, she claimed, with largess funneled through Dallas attorney Jerome T. Ragsdale. Although shocked by Lyndon's threats that she should keep quiet about their relationship or "your ass will be in a hell of a lot of trouble," Brown accepted his terms, which she listed as including a six-room house, live-in maid, sheaf of credit cards, and a monthly stipend.

In Brown's very last meeting with Lyndon, an entirely platonic encounter in August 1969, she tried to persuade him to recognize Steven as his son, but she reported that the "crumpled, overweight, haggard-looking" ex-president balked: "I'm sorry. I just can't go public with this. I've got the girls to consider and Bird. I have hurt them enough."

Although Brown first spoke publicly about the affair in a 1982 interview, she did not mention the paternity issue until five years later, when she was diagnosed with a serious illness and wanted to set the record straight with her son before she died. Steven Brown subsequently sued for a $10.5 million share of Lyndon's estate, causing *People* magazine to publish an article on the Lyndon-Madeleine relationship in 1987. But Steven died (of lymphatic cancer) in 1990 without collecting.

Even after Madeleine Duncan Brown published her book, full of tantalizing details about steamy couplings and pet names (he was her "Sandow," a currently famous bodybuilder), Lady Bird maintained there was no credible evidence for an affair between the two. But historians took special note of one letter Brown reproduced in her book, a letter from attorney Jerome Ragsdale, written soon after Lyndon's death and promising to "continue with the financial arrangements that Lyndon provided for you and Steve . . . [with additional funds] if you need." Biographer Randall Woods is among those who tend to credit Madeleine Brown's account.

Even after Lyndon ridiculed them or treated them unkindly, his secretarial pool and female staffers supplied him with loving attention and admiring support beyond what any one woman could offer. Tallish Vicky McCammon, who began working for him in 1962, said he told her she looked like an ox when she wore big prints, but she still named her first son for him. Other female employees agreed that an insult from Lyndon felt like a compliment. One new hire from Texas reported that she had been excited about going along with the president and his female entourage on a night out. She dressed carefully in what was then her Sunday best, and only years later, as a chic Washington matron, did she realize she probably looked "tacky . . . [as if she came from] Walmart." At evening's end, as his limousine stopped to let her out, she overheard him say, "Can't somebody teach that girl how to dress?" Rather than feeling offended or hurt, she was elated that he had noticed her and that he cared.

Lyndon needed a bevy of beauties around him, and Bird made room for all of them, including Mathilde Krim, the blond scientist with beauty to match her brains. Born in 1926 in Como, Italy, she had earned an Italian science degree and a Swiss doctorate before moving to Israel to conduct medical research at the Weizmann Institute. In 1957 she met and married a Weizmann board member, American Arthur Krim, a forty-seven-year-old entertainment lawyer who had not yet produced the Hollywood blockbusters that would earn Oscars in the 1970s, but was already extremely wealthy. After briefly trying a bicontinental partnership, the couple settled on New York's Upper East Side.

As Arthur Krim became an increasingly important contributor to the Democratic Party, he grew friendly with top-rung politicos, and after a Madison Square Garden birthday bash in 1962, President Kennedy spent time at the Krim apartment on East 69th Street. Vice President

Johnson accompanied Kennedy and met the diminutive Mathilde, whose long reddish blond hair and round face made her look younger than her thirty-five years. By 1966, the Krims had entered the top tier of Johnson guests. Arthur, who chaired the Finance Committee of the Democratic Party, and Mathilde spent so much time at the White House that one source reported they kept a room there. They had also purchased land near the LBJ Ranch and built a home of their own, convenient for spontaneous visits with the Johnsons. Arthur occasionally stayed on the third floor of the White House but more often his wife was there alone. Even when Bird was back in Texas, Mathilde Krim, whose only official title was member of the President's Committee on Mental Retardation, stayed at the White House, and the first lady appeared not to mind. She wrote in her diary on one occasion "the fact that [Mathilde's] so pretty is a pleasure for [Lyndon]." A year later, Bird wrote: Lyndon "likes to have the prettiest woman beside him. Today it is Mathilde Krim."

Bird's home movies show a high-spirited, athletic Mathilde Krim cavorting near the pool at the ranch, scaling a windmill, and attempting upside-down balancing acts—in full view of a smiling, appreciative Lyndon. On Saturday afternoon May 21, 1966, when the president was taking a beating from the press on Vietnam, Mathilde spent time alone with him and then joined his party at Camp David. Bird cooperated in lining up other people who could make her husband forget his problems that weekend, a group that included Bill and June White, Jack and Mary Margaret Valenti, Marianne Means, and Vicky McCammon. On Sunday, the president moped in his pajamas all day, but by 6:30 that evening he had a circle of doting females (including Mathilde Krim) around him in the Aspen Cabin living room, while Lady Bird took the male guests bowling. It was another example of what one of those women later cited as an example of Mrs. Johnson taking "time off."

Speculation about Lyndon's sexual conquests included humorous word play and some denials. After NBC's Nancy Dickerson, one of the first female correspondents on network news, accompanied Lyndon on an overnight trip, Walter Cronkite (of CBS) quipped that the president had "gone to bed and Dickerson is covering him." To set the record straight, Dickerson later wrote in her memoir, *Among Those Present*, that there had been talk about her and Lyndon but she wanted the truth known: "sex had nothing to do with it." Though Lyndon "might talk about sex, it was mostly just that—talk." She admitted he had propositioned her, but not very convincingly, as he paced around a Chicago hotel room in his pajamas and she sat there listening, with curlers in her hair. To add to the incongruity of it all, she knew Bill Moyers was just outside the door, waiting for Lyndon.

Rumors of Lyndon's relationships with a long list of other women, from secretaries to socialites, would shape public opinion of Lady Bird until the day she died. Because of her apparent complaisance in his outlandish behavior, whether real or feigned, she looked more like an accomplice than a victim. She refused to play the part of wronged wife, and others agreed she did not deserve that tag. Nancy Dickerson, who as a reporter covering the White House and a close friend of Mrs. Johnson was in a position to know, insisted that in Lyndon's female lineup, Lady Bird "had no peer; she knew it, he knew it and so did everybody else." That was evidently Bird's view, too. She liked to say, "I had a great love affair. No matter what, I knew he loved me best."

Bird had plenty of signs that Lyndon loved and respected her. Associates noted how often he would place a guiding hand at her back and how his eyes lit up when she entered the room. He bought her thoughtful gifts and inscribed new books with the pet name he had used for her during their courtship. Although she cut corners on the rest of her wardrobe, she spent freely on party dresses and would sometimes interrupt a meeting her husband was conducting to seek his approval of her latest purchase. As she preened in a ball gown and he registered his delight, she basked in it, Liz Carpenter observed, "like a magic wand passed over her."

18

———◦◦◦———

WRAPPING UP "OUR" PRESIDENCY

I T MIGHT have looked to outsiders like a long, relaxed weekend at the ranch for the president and first lady, but it was anything but. Within hours of arriving there on September 7, 1967, they had summoned two of their time-tested advisers, John Connally and Jake Pickle, for what was going to be some very heavy decision making. For much of Friday afternoon, Lyndon rode around the ranch with the two men, going over his thoughts and theirs on the subject top on his mind: to run or not to run again in 1968 and when he should make that decision public. Pickle, who was facing his own reelection for Congress the following year, was dismayed that Lyndon might drop out, thus affecting Pickle's chances. Connally, who favored retirement, suggested an early announcement, possibly within the month, to allow the Democratic Party plenty of time to groom a successor.

About seven that evening Lyndon called for Bird, saying he had been "waiting" for her all afternoon, and she put on a robe, sausage curlers still in her hair, and joined the trio. Having discussed the matter with her all summer, Lyndon already knew she was hell bent on wrapping up what she called "our presidency" and retiring to Texas. Back in May she had told him that the idea of another campaign struck her as unthinkable as an "open-ended stay in a concentration camp." Now she restated that objection just as emphatically to Connally and Pickle, explaining that she "simply did not want to face another campaign, to ask anybody for anything."

In addition to her dread of another energy-draining campaign, she had a nagging fear that Lyndon's health would not hold up for four more years. He would be sixty years old at the start of a new term, and the men in his family had a record of dying early. An even more frightening prospect than death was the possibility that this man of "roaring energy" would find himself physically or mentally incapacitated, unable to fulfill the demands of the job. This would be, she admitted, "unbearably painful" for him to recognize and for her to watch.

In the tense atmosphere surrounding her argument for not running, she delivered one line that got a laugh out of all three men: "If we ever get sick, I want to be sick on our own time." Then, with her sausage curlers still in place, she ordered supper trays for the four of them, and they sat down to eat, knowing that the final decision would be Lyndon's. All they could do was wait.

Nine months earlier, the year had gotten off to a very gloomy start. Bird had developed the habit of scanning a room during Lyndon's speeches, "picking out friend and foe and question mark," and at the annual State of the Union address on January 10 the "foes" were very evident. She observed the "stoney" face of Senator Robert Kennedy and noted that he had applauded only once, with "two or three light claps like a seal in a circus." After the speech, she invited a few from the friends list to the White House, but their presence failed to cheer her up. Only days earlier, she had confessed to her diary: "Now is indeed the 'Valley of the Black Pig.'. . . A miasma of trouble hangs over everything."

That was the same day—January 5, 1967—that *The Washington Post* published an article about a nasty encounter between the president and the painter Peter Hurd that had occurred more than a year earlier. Now, just when everything else seemed to be going wrong, the Hurd story was out there for everyone to read.

Both Lady Bird and Lyndon had liked Hurd when he came to sketch the president for a *Time* magazine cover in late 1964, and they chose him to do Lyndon's official portrait for the White House collection. After Hurd accepted the commission, he and his wife joined the Johnsons several times for overnight stays at Camp David and the Texas ranch, so that the artist could work from a life model. The president tended to fall asleep during the sessions, which he likened to taking "castor oil," but afterward he and Bird would invite the Hurds to join them for congenial dinners and long walks.

It was the delivery of the completed portrait in October 1965 that soured the relationship. Eager to get the subject's reaction, the Hurds flew to Texas to present it to him in person. Lady Bird sat them down first for a pleasant lunch with Lyndon, and then the four of them went into the office wing of the ranch house for the unveiling. Lyndon took one look and blurted out that it was "the ugliest thing I ever saw." Taken aback, Hurd asked what kind of picture the president preferred, and Lyndon, with icy politeness, reached into a drawer and took out a Norman Rockwell drawing. Hurd thought it "damn rude" of the president not to acknowledge the many hours of hard work he had put in, and Bird, seeing the artist's disappointment, tried to soothe his feelings and placate him. She "could not have been kinder," Hurd later told *The New York Times*, but she found the episode so grim she hoped never to face a similar exchange if she "lived to be 1000." The Hurds did not stay for dinner.

The portrait went home with its creator, and nothing more was heard of it—until Maxine Cheshire published a full account in the society pages of *The Washington Post* in January 1967. Newspapers across the country picked up the story, and some of them put the "ugliest thing I ever saw" quote in large headlines, making Lyndon look exceptionally vain (since others judged the portrait favorably) and buffoonish (confusing a tempera portrait of Hurd's quality with a Rockwell magazine illustration). Cartoonists lampooned the president on both counts. In February, Chicago's Richard Gray Gallery opened an exhibit of paintings, sculptures, and drawings of the president that made Hurd's rendering look flattering. An article in *The New York Times*, "Chicago's Art World Takes Aim at Johnson," explained how the Richard Gray collection mocked LBJ's competence and his appearance. One showed a potbellied Indian on a tired horse at the brink of a canyon, with the title: "End of the Trail." Another pictured a fat centaur, with the tag line, "Ladybird's Johnson."

Up against that kind of ridicule, the Johnsons each responded in characteristic mode. Lyndon sank into a swamp of self-pity, lambasting reporters for treating him unfairly; she, recognizing that a childish "I don't want it, I don't like it" did not play well, especially out of the mouth of an unpopular president, came up with two specific objections to Hurd's work. It was too big (four feet wide) to fit well with other portraits in the White House gallery of presidents, and the composition was off, she argued: Hurd had upset the balance of the painting by making the background of the Capitol building too "brilliantly illuminated." After dictating an announcement that included those two points, she vowed to keep quiet and let the story play itself out.

If the president had enjoyed a more amiable relation with the press, he might have engineered some sympathetic coverage for himself. But just at the time the "ugliest thing I ever saw" headlines appeared, he was initiating yet another press secretary, the fourth since taking office. After Pierre Salinger, a holdover from the Kennedy administration, resigned in early 1964, George Reedy, who had been a newspaperman before he started working for Senator Johnson in 1952, took the job. Bird liked Salinger but never warmed to Reedy, whom she described as "sloppy fat and drank too much." But the fairness in her admitted that he did have a "splendid mind and wrote well" and that the advice he gave Lyndon was always on the mark. By the summer of 1965, Reedy felt overwhelmed by the struggle to keep the voracious press happy. As media reports on Vietnam grew increasingly critical of the president, Lyndon decided to ease Reedy out, and his need for extended medical leave, to recover from treatment for his hammertoed feet, provided the opportunity.

Reedy's departure opened the press slot for the much younger, more enthusiastic Bill Moyers, who had known both Johnsons for a decade and had developed an almost son-parent intimacy with them. While sleeping in their basement on 30th Place, he had overheard much of what went on between husband and wife, and one night was wakened by Lyndon's angry shouts on the floor above. After the decibels dropped a bit, Bird came tiptoeing down the basement stairs, and Moyers, thinking she was coming to check on him, called out, "I'm all right." "Oh," she replied, "I was just coming to tell you that I am, too."

Bird had been enthusiastic about Moyers taking the press secretary slot, but he fared no better than Reedy in a job that was becoming a practice in cover-ups. When reporters pressed him for facts—about the president's travel plans or Vietnam casualties—Moyers found it impossible to satisfy both the journalists and his secrecy-obsessed boss. When he revealed just a bit more than the president wished, he gained points with reporters but received a stiff reprimand from Lyndon, who accused him of excessive self-promotion. Bird, who liked Moyers, admitted that word of a rift between the two men fell "like a stone on my heart." After little more than a year on the job, the exhausted Moyers announced he was taking his ulcer-ridden body to Long Island, New York, where he would become publisher of *Newsday.* His defection infuriated the president, who put Moyers on his not-to-be-recognized list, unworthy of further notice. The name that dotted the White House daily diary hundreds of times before 1967 now never appeared.

Anyone who dared refer to Moyers received an icy stare—or a broken phone connection as the receiver slammed down. Like his mother, Lyndon punished people by freezing them out.

Although Moyers left Lyndon's employ, he did not lose Bird's friendship. She continued to see him until her death, and he was one of those who eulogized her at her funeral. She had recognized the complicated relationship between him and Lyndon as just what it was: a back-and-forth of "I love you" one day, and "No, I don't" the next, a relationship "more needful" on Lyndon's part than on Moyers's. For herself, no such games were necessary.

Moyers's replacement, George Christian, another Texan, began handling the president's press relations in February 1967. A more seasoned newsman than his predecessors, Christian was more like Lady Bird. He understood that he could not always please everyone and that his boss could be maddening at times—with his constantly changing plans and fixation on secrecy. When Christian had to tell reporters that a trip was on—only hours after telling them it was off—he expected to be lambasted—and he was. But he had a thick skin, and he treated reporters as colleagues rather than trying desperately to gain their friendship, as Lyndon did.

With that more laid-back attitude, Christian retained the press secretary job longer than any of his predecessors, and he was still there, alongside Liz Carpenter, who masterminded Lady Bird's press, when the Johnsons left Washington. Christian stood up for Carpenter when the president tried to rein her in. Although she might be too folksy or brash for some people and she had a corny penchant for heavy Texas touches, Christian saw her as savvy and inventive at getting excellent coverage for the first lady. That's the way Bird saw her, too.

Christian and Carpenter came up against a big challenge in 1967 when William Manchester's book about the assassination of JFK finally came out. It made both Johnsons look pushy and unsophisticated. Lady Bird had cooperated with the author, sitting with him for two arduous hours in 1964, to talk about how she remembered that tragic day in Dallas. In a race against other authors hoping to turn out quick books on the same topic, Manchester worked hard, and in spite of hospitalization for "nervous exhaustion," he had a draft of *The Death of a President* ready by February 1965. It would be much longer, however, before Lady Bird learned exactly what he had written.

After his editor at Harper & Row circulated the manuscript to readers in the Kennedy camp (including Richard Goodwin, Arthur Schlesinger Jr., and Ethel Kennedy), word got back to the Johnsons in mid-1966 that they were not going to be happy with what Manchester had written about them. Even Lyndon's admirers described him as sometimes suspicious, devious, and domineering, but Manchester, in the draft that was circulating, went further, depicting an indecipherable human being, for whom the "shortest distance between two points was a tunnel." Rather than call Lyndon a low-class liar, which is what he meant, Manchester described him as looking like he came out of a Grade D movie and being a "practitioner of political tergiversation." Prodded by his editors to be kinder, the author excised his most damning judgments but left enough examples of Lyndonesque behavior to make him sound like a backwoods oaf. Bird did not fare much better. Manchester described her as weak and spineless, wholly subjugated to a loutish husband. After the JFK assassination, she had said to her regret that she was sorry it happened in Texas, and now that inept remark appeared in Manchester's book for everyone to read. To her, it seemed the book was part of "a planned wave of attacks" aimed to undercut her and Lyndon.

Wrangling about the book's content continued as the Kennedys worried that its negative treatment of LBJ might backfire, and he would take out his anger on Robert Kennedy and squelch his chances for the presidential nomination in 1968. Finally, as what some of Lyndon's critics gloated would be a Christmas present to him, the book came out, and *Look* magazine, one of the nation's largest, started publishing the juiciest segments in four installments, beginning January 1967.

Finding herself included in so many of the attacks against her husband, Mrs. Johnson obviously felt justified in talking about *our* presidency and wanting to end it. In the radical fringes of antiwar protest, she was garnering blame, entirely baseless, for the continuing war in Southeast Asia. As one American serving in Vietnam later explained: "I believed, as did many other soldiers, that dear ole Lady Bird had some, probably substantial interest in our TV/radio stations in Vietnam. So it was no surprise that this horrible war was prolonged by one Lyndon Baines Johnson." While she may not have heard that kind of unsubstantiated gossip, she undoubtedly knew about the satirical play running at the Village Gate in New York's Greenwich Village. Titled *MacBird!*, it compared Lyndon's assumption of power to Shakespeare's Macbeth. In this version, Duncan (now O'Dunc, speaking with a Boston accent) is brutally murdered by power-thirsty MacBird (Texas accent), egged on by his ambitious wife, Lady MacBird. The play ran for nearly a year, from February 1967 until January 1968, and Mrs. Johnson's picture appeared on publicity posters as the infamous harridan.

The closing date of *MacBird!* coincided with more reports of the first lady under fire. She had been scheduling Women Doers' lunches every three months or so since the vice presidency days, and the topic for this one, on January 18, 1968, was crime, a subject she had been "itching" to consider for a while. The routine for these meetings was fairly simple. A couple dozen women, selected because of their achievement in the area of concern, were invited to lunch in the second-floor dining room, where they were recognized for their work and given a chance to discuss it with the other guests. With crime as the topic, Bird had no reason to expect this lunch would be any different from the polite and pleasant Women Doers' lunches that preceded it.

As he often did, the president dropped by to greet the first lady's guests and say a few words to each one, including on this day African

American cabaret star Eartha Kitt, who cordially shook his hand. After he left, the three honorees made their remarks and Bird opened the floor for questions, as she always did. But the amiable, polite mood in the room suddenly shifted. Eartha Kitt stood up, and with her eyes flashing and her voice shrill, she accused her hostess of being completely clueless about the real causes of crime and ignorant of the culture of violence and drugs that appealed to so many young Americans. It was the disaffection with the Vietnam War, Kitt argued, that caused people to turn to drugs and crime. Her angry outburst so alarmed staffer Sharon Francis that she prepared to move in and protect Mrs. Johnson in case Kitt physically attacked her.

The other guests froze in their places, trying to figure out what had ignited this vehement eruption. Liz Carpenter wondered if Kitt had lost control because she was ill. Then Elizabeth Hughes, wife of the New Jersey governor and the mother of sons fighting in Vietnam, spoke up, drawing a distinction between war and crime in the streets. African American Bennetta Washington, wife of Walter Washington, assured Kitt that she "knew a little bit [about anger] too," but the women were not gathered that day to vent anger: "We are here to release these energies in constructive rather than destructive channels." Then Lady Bird, in measured tones, tried to defend herself. She admitted she lacked Kitt's experiences but she, nonetheless, hoped the country was moving toward solutions.

Mrs. Johnson's calm response received little comment in newspaper accounts—virtually all attention focused on Kitt's attack. Her outburst resonated with those who believed that inner-city black youths were being used as cannon fodder in a war that middle- and upper-class youths found ways to avoid, and this Woman Doers' event became the most publicized of all those that Lady Bird hosted. The "Kitt lunch" was a painful reminder that a first lady collects blame for her husband's unpopular policies, and she will be the target for frustration coming from unpredictable quarters.

In the ever darker Valley of the Black Pig, Lady Bird's determination to leave Washington hardened and the president's frustrations showed in his belligerent bad-boy behavior. Much as she loved him, she continued to be shocked by some of his acting out, and she was not alone in failing to see how a grown man could throw such childish tantrums. When a drink was not to his liking, he threw it against a wall, and he registered his objection to a dish of food by spitting out a mouthful onto an aide's plate. He hectored employees to do his bidding, oblivious to whether or not the task lay within that employee's control.

Bill Fisher, one of the Navy photographers who often accompanied the president, realized, as others did, that it was useless to protest these commands, no matter how unreasonable. The best response was simply "I'll take care of it" and then pass the request on to someone else. Fisher found that tactic useful one day aboard the president's plane, as he walked down the aisle and was intercepted by LBJ, who was eating his lunch. "This chili's too hot," he groused at Fisher, who replied, "I'll take care of it" and walked to the back of the plane to relay the message to the chef. When asked if the president meant "too warm" or "too spicy," Fisher replied, "How the hell should I know? I'm just the photographer." As he walked away, he heard the chef murmur, "I'll take care of it." Bird, who was often the one who had to "take care" of things, never claimed to understand her husband's bizarre behavior, and she once confided to Bill Moyers: "I'm more bewildered by Lyndon than he is bewildered by himself."

While Lyndon weighed running again in 1968, Lady Bird continued to put long hours on the job. On June 9, 1967, she set off on a four-day visit to New England where she stopped at the John Adams house in Quincy, Massachusetts, and the Calvin Coolidge birthplace in Vermont. She collected an honorary doctorate at Middlebury College and visited the home of Laurance Rockefeller, where she enjoyed after-dinner recreation in her host's private bowling alley. With those obligations behind her she headed for Texas to await the birth of her first grandchild. It was one of two bright spots in that dismal year. Luci and Pat Nugent had settled in Austin, and Lady Bird arranged her schedule so she could be with them well in advance of her daughter's June 17 due date. It was not until early morning on June 21 that the young couple set out for the hospital, with the excited grandmother-to-be in another car right behind them. By 7 a.m. when nurses informed her that Luci had delivered a healthy baby boy, twenty-one inches long with gray eyes, Lady Bird, who had suffered through multiple miscarriages herself, could hardly believe the news. She was thrilled that her daughter had such an easy time and equally pleased to learn that the baby would be named Patrick Lyndon.

The new grandfather, scheduled to start meetings a day later with Soviet premier Alexei Kosygin in Glassboro, New Jersey, seized on the baby's birth to form a bond with his Soviet counterpart. He had not known how to greet Kosygin, then remembered he had a grandchild, and so Lyndon's first words to Kosygin were, "My daughter just made me a grandfather." It was a cordial opener to what became an amicable, if unproductive, meeting between the two leaders. When Lyndon received word that Kosygin's daughter would accompany her father, he immediately summoned Lady Bird to join the Glassboro party, and she reluctantly left her newborn grandson to do so. Within hours of the president's call, she was on her way, accompanied by Lynda, with gifts in hand for the Soviet leader and his daughter. By Sunday afternoon, all four women were strolling amicably along a New Jersey beach.

After doing her part to contribute to what became known as "the Spirit of Glassboro," the first lady retreated to Texas, where she resumed visits with Luci and the baby and worked with architect Roy White on an addition to the ranch house. When Lyndon phoned from Washington, she heard the "loneliness in his voice and the desire just to talk to me." Although he did not say it, she knew he wanted her beside him, and she felt guilty, "torn between doing what I was doing, which must be done, and being with him." But she did not budge. She still had nearly eighteen months in the White House and, although the two of them had talked the subject over, she did not know if he would call it quits even then. But she was proceeding with her preferred scenario, preparing for full-time retirement to her "forever home" in Texas. She was making lists of which of her own furniture she wanted taken from the White House and what she would have to buy. Wherever she was, the requirements for her bedroom remained the same: a canopied bed, plenty of bookshelves, a fireplace, and a beautiful view.

The second family milestone to break the misery of those last two White House years was the marriage of Lynda Bird. After her period of dating George Hamilton and other high-profile men, she began seeing Chuck Robb in the summer of 1967. An "all-American boy" who, except in looks, bore no resemblance to Hamilton and his café society friends, Robb received an instant seal of approval from her parents, especially from Bird, who knew Robb as an affable military aide at the White House and an excellent bridge player.

As Mrs. Johnson prepared for the December 9 wedding, Vietnam hung, like a nasty veil, over everything the family did. Even with nearly half a million American troops in the war zone and rising casualty figures every day, stalemate prevailed, victory nowhere in sight. General William Westmoreland, commander of U.S. forces in Vietnam, underscored the tense atmosphere by his presence at the White House—he slept several nights in a bedroom above the president's. Bird could see her husband was exhausted, and she had to fit parties in both Washington and Texas into his already packed schedule. As she struggled to combine the duties of first lady and mother of the bride, combining sittings for the portraitist Elizabeth Shoumatoff with fittings for the big day, she could see her husband was wrestling with uncertainty and despair.

Lynda's wedding day started gloomy, with skies overcast in Washington, but inside 1600 Pennsylvania Avenue there was such a buzz of activity that the grayness outside was easily forgotten. Under the direction of social secretary Bess Abell, the family quarters of the White House had been converted into what looked like a busy hotel, with Bird's regular hairdresser, Jean Louis, and two assistants busily shaping bridesmaids' tresses into bouffant swirls. Bird started the day early, with a last-minute consultation with Lyndon on the day's schedule. Then the happy parents summoned the bridal couple to the Queens' Suite to receive their wedding gift. As Lyndon handed over a U.S. Savings Bond, Bird thought him full of "tenderness and understanding."

The bride's long-sleeved dress of white silk-satin was chosen to stand the test of time, and Bird hoped to see it one day on a granddaughter. A little bow-knot pin, from the 1820s, was sewn inside it, providing the "something old"; a handmade handkerchief from a great-grandmother was the "something borrowed," and at the hem, embroidered in blue, was a marking that only a handful of wedding gowns have the right to use: after the bride's name and the date, "The White House."

Canon Gerald McAllister had come from Mrs. Johnson's St. Barnabas Episcopal Church in Fredericksburg, Texas, to perform the ceremony. Four generations of the Robb family, including Chuck's grandmother and her great-grandchildren, attended the event, and after the ceremony they assembled in the Oval Room for a group picture. Nash Castro, who had worked closely with Bird on beautification and was about Chuck Robb's height, stood in for him as a marker, and it was, Castro later recalled, the only time he ever saw Bird lose her temper. When the president walked in, holding his favorite dog, Yuki, wearing a red blanket with "Congratulations" sewn in sequins, the first lady lost no time in setting her husband straight. She stepped out of her place in the first row and pointing her finger in his face announced,

"That dog is not going to be in this picture." Without a word, the president passed off the dog to someone else, and took his designated place.

As it turned out, that wasn't the only time Bird and Lyndon differed that day. At 8:45, he abruptly left the party, taking Luci, Pat, their little boy (who was being called Lyn), and a couple dozen others with him on his flight to Texas. The remaining guests were still dancing and drinking, but he had had enough, and he was not about to curb his restlessness even for his daughter's wedding. Bird had gotten a whiff of his plan that morning, and while she knew he needed a rest, she had to admit it would be a "disappointment" to see him go, leaving her to face only "supper upstairs after Lynda and Chuck have gone." She managed to join him at the ranch two days later, but only briefly because he soon took off on a whirlwind of speaking engagements. In spite of the warning issued by Dr. Hurst in October, that Bird ought to spend more time with her husband, this was a couple seeing less and less of each other.

When the president was alone at the White House, he tried to line up his favorite people to keep him company at mealtime. He so dreaded loneliness that he asked Vicky McCammon, who had quit as his secretary when she married, and her husband, Simon McHugh, to sleep over in Bird's bedroom one night. Bird made it back to Washington in time to see him light the national Christmas tree on December 15, but seventy-two hours later he was gone again without her. He had put together a group of congenial friends and advisers (wealthy industrialist and philanthropist Charles Englehard and his wife Jane; Jack Valenti; and National Security Advisor Walt Rostow) to accompany him to Australia for the funeral of Prime Minister Harold Holt and then to a round of talks on Vietnam. Funerals always depressed him, and he announced as soon as he entered the plane that he was very tired—he had not slept for three nights and planned to go straight to bed. That proved an empty threat as he signed documents, conferred with advisers, and chatted with his guests.

By trip's end, he made headlines as the first U.S. president to circle the world while in office. But he came back exhausted, as Lady Bird and both daughters noted when they got out of bed before daylight and went down to the South Lawn to welcome him home on Sunday, December 24. He had done his Christmas shopping—toys for his baby grandson and an array of brass trays and silver bracelets for others—on a refueling stop in the Azores, where a local military post opened in the middle of the night to accommodate him.

The president had missed his wife's fifty-fifth birthday, and it would be tempting to think that while he was circling the globe with friends, she was pining away, feeling neglected back in Washington. In fact, she kept herself merrily occupied the entire time he was gone, doing what she couldn't fit in when he was there. She went Christmas shopping with Lynda, wrote captions for the photo album she was preparing as her special gift to him, and entertained people she really wanted to see at dinner. Liz and Les Carpenter joined her, along with Bess and Tyler Abell, for a viewing of the not-yet-released-to-the-public movie *The Odd Couple*, and both daughters sat with her for the film *The President's Analyst* and for recorded segments of *Gunsmoke*. The exuberance with which she and her daughters welcomed the president at his predawn arrival, taking turns "hugging and kissing him," suggests that, much as Bird had relished some R & R of her own, she was now ready to resume her role as nurturer-in-chief.

Lyndon's State of the Union address was set for January 17, 1968, and that was one of the occasions Bird had suggested for him to announce whether or not he would run in November. In an early draft of his speech, she saw that a sentence promising to retire was included, but she doubted he would use it because "his mind was lashed [to the job], as though to a Siamese twin." On the night of the speech, as she sat in the first row of the Visitors Gallery in the House of Representatives, listening to him summarize for the umpteenth time his views on Vietnam, she still did not know how he would conclude. Would he promise to retire, as she hoped? Or wait? After speaking defiantly about not cutting back—neither in Vietnam nor on his poverty and environmental programs—he closed with the standard "God bless . . ." Then she knew he was not yet ready to leave all this behind him.

Sunday, March 31, 1968, marked the beginning of the end. The day started early at the White House, when the president and first lady went down to the South Lawn in their bathrobes at seven to greet Lynda. She had taken the overnight flight, the red-eye, from California after seeing her husband off to Vietnam. Looking like a wraith, she seemed tired and full of complaints about how people had pushed and shoved her around at the site of the troop departure. Finally, she blurted out the question that was being asked all across the country: "Why do we have to be in Vietnam?" She showed her father a letter she had received from a woman whose husband had been killed in Vietnam, just hours before he was due to come home. "If that happens to Chuck," Lynda warned, "I will never forgive you." Bird admitted she had not seen such pain in her husband's eyes "since his mother died."

By 9:30 that morning, Lyndon was working with speechwriter Horace Busby in the Treaty Room, and secretary Marie Fehmer was typing up a fresh copy each time the wording changed. The president's speech, to be delivered on television at nine that evening, had been scheduled to announce a bombing halt in Vietnam, but now it was being revised to include a final sentence promising not to run again. The volume of vitriol against his current Vietnam policy, the prospect of antiwar Democrats wresting the nomination from him, and pressures from within his own family and staff had heaped together on the no-run side of the scales. It was time to quit.

After church that Sunday morning, the president stopped by the Humphreys' apartment to update the vice president, who was about to leave on an official visit to Mexico. Back at the White House, Lyndon read an early version of his line about not running again to house guests Arthur and Mathilde Krim, who urged him not to use it. When Lynda and Luci heard about their father's decision, they became "emotional, crying and distraught." They had wanted an end to the war, not to his presidency, and felt his retirement announcement would look like desertion of the men and women who were fighting. Bird passed her daughters' objection on to Lyndon, but he had already checked with General Westmoreland, who had assured him his withdrawal would not "affect the morale" of the troops. Bird thought Lyndon looked at her "rather distantly" as he said, "I think General Westmoreland knows more about it than [Luci and Lynda] do."

A parade of visitors moved through the second floor of the White House that Sunday afternoon: Walt Rostow, looking "gray and weary," Soviet ambassador Anatoly Dobrynin; old friends Clark and Marny Clifford. Bird kept busy, ordering more sandwiches and drinks as the numbers grew, but she was counting the minutes until she could go to the Oval Office at nine that evening and hear what Lyndon said. Just before the camera lights went on, she walked up to his desk and delivered the advice she reserved for his most important addresses: "Remember—pacing and drama." Taking her seat, she still could not be sure what Lyndon would say. Not until he looked directly into the camera with the red light and announced, "Accordingly, I shall not seek . . ." then uttered the phrase she had penciled in after the final typing, "and I will not accept . . ." did she finally know.

During the rest of the chaotic evening, disbelieving staff and friends poured into the White House from around the city. The switchboard lit up with calls from across the nation, including one from Bill Moyers on Long Island. Mary Lasker appeared to be crying, and others looked stunned. Only the president seemed really upbeat. When aide Tom Johnson, no relation, arrived at 11 p.m. with thirty-five reporters in tow, Lyndon was warning friends to brush up on their dominoes and telling his former secretary Vicky McCammon (now pregnant) that his real motivation for retiring was to have more time for baby-sitting. Lynda, who had curtailed her foreign travel while her father was in the

White House, inquired in jest if she could finally go to London. She suggested her mother consider a trip to the Greek islands.

If Bird hoped the announcement would give her permanent solace and Lyndon a respite, she was disappointed. The following Thursday evening, while Lyndon prepared to leave for Hawaii and yet another conference on Vietnam, and as Bird donned her red chiffon evening gown for a Democratic leaders' dinner, Lynda rushed into her mother's room to say "Dr. King's been shot." For Bird, the evening immediately took on a "nightmare quality." Lyndon, still in the Oval Office, began shaping a speech to the nation, pleading for calm and deploring the tragedy of a violent death for a man who had been the strongest voice of nonviolence. Bird changed to at-home clothes and, hearing televised predictions of rioting and unrest in the big cities, started canceling plans for the upcoming trip she had dubbed "Texas Trails." She had wanted to show foreign journalists, who saw a lot of big urban centers but missed the gems of small towns, the out-of-the-way places she loved best. Now the idea of celebrating nature while cities were burning seemed very inappropriate.

Within forty-eight hours, several of the nation's major cities exploded, with the most devastating damage in Chicago, Washington, and Baltimore. As Chicago's West Side smoldered in fires along a twenty-eight-block stretch of Madison Street, insurance companies estimated that property damage claims would run into millions of dollars. To limit the mayhem, the Army readied fifteen thousand troops to go wherever they were needed most. Another 5,500 Army and National Guardsmen were assigned to patrol Washington, D.C., making this deployment the largest number of troops ever called out up to that time to deal with civil disturbances in the United States.

While Lyndon grappled with how to curtail the rioting, he used its fallout to obtain legislation he wanted—a Fair Housing bill. Often called the Civil Rights Act of 1968, it prohibited discrimination (in race, color, national origin, religion, sex, familial status, or physical disability) in the sale or rental of housing. Two years earlier the president had proposed a similar measure but Congress refused to act. Now the political climate had changed, and only one week after the assassination of Dr. King, the Fair Housing Act passed.

Bird was not in Washington to see her husband announce victory this time. She had decided to go ahead with her Texas Trails venture, leading more than three dozen journalists from thirteen countries, along with some of their American colleagues, through "historic towns and blooming fields of wildflowers." Spring was her favorite time of year—she said she came alive then—and she wanted to show "foreign writers that there *are* places in this country which are not aflame with hatred and riots."

By the time she returned to Washington, the rioting had abated, and she could drive around the capital to assess the damage. She and her beautification colleagues noted with satisfaction that the areas where they had worked with local residents remained surprisingly unscathed. Bird had marked one big Giant supermarket in a low-income area with a plaque designating it part of her "Beautification Project" after store officials planted flowers and trees in the area and then hired local teenagers to care for them. Now, in contrast with other parts of Washington that had been charred, the Giant stood unharmed. Her aide Sharon Francis had defended using funds in ghetto areas when others argued that money should not be wasted on "black people [who] were unreliable and . . . didn't care for things . . . [and would just] tear it up." Now Francis felt vindicated, as she noted that "no parks, no trees [in areas where the beautification committee invested] were damaged whatsoever." The first lady's work paid off "when Armageddon came."

As her last day in the White House approached, Mrs. Johnson bade affectionate good-byes to her staff. It would be their faces she missed, she assured them, not the material perks of the 134-room mansion or the convoy of cars and planes that ferried her around. She penned a poignant letter to White House Curator James Ketchum, telling him that she hoped other families would enjoy the stately old mansion as much as she had. Ketchum, who had worked with her on cataloguing paintings, knew that she sometimes tuned out of mundane housekeeping conversations that bored her and started whistling to herself. Now both she and Ketchum understood she wanted more time for whistling.

At 11 a.m. on an icy, gray January 20, 1969, Lady Bird Johnson took her seat beside Pat Nixon for a ride that both had eagerly anticipated, but for different reasons. As they were chauffeured from the White House, where they had coffee, to Capitol Hill, where Richard Nixon would be inaugurated the nation's thirty-seventh president, the two women, both born the same year, could look back over decades spent in the shadow of their ambitious husbands, who now rode ahead of them in a flagged limo. Bird and Pat had met countless times, at the Senate Wives' Club and various Washington receptions. Both knew how to mouth pleasantries without saying much. When their car stopped, reporters aimed their flashbulbs at Pat as she and Bird headed to the office of Margaret Chase Smith. As the sole female senator, Smith could provide a place for the women to do a last-minute check of hair and lipstick. In the VIP parade to the east side of the Capitol, where the inauguration would take place, Pat walked alone, taking her featured spot in the front row, while Lady Bird accompanied Muriel Humphrey, whose husband would also be out of a job at noon, to an inconspicuous seat off center. But the outgoing first lady could not fail to note that Pat Nixon, in her bright red coat and fur hat, followed the example set four years earlier—and held the Bible for the presidential oath taking. How quickly that role had become an accepted part of the ritual.

After the ceremony, the Johnsons went to the home of Clark and Marny Clifford, where they were honored at a lunch, and then they boarded Air Force One, with daughter Lynda and her three-month-old baby, Lucinda, to return to Texas. By the time they landed in Austin, where the air felt much kinder than Washington's near freezing temperatures, it was nearly dark. Lyndon said a few words to well-wishers who had gathered, and then, as the Johnsons boarded the smaller Jet-Star for the final short leg of the trip, Bird spotted a tiny slice of new moon, which anointed this homecoming as a real renewal.

By 9:10 that evening Bird would be in bed at the ranch. As she thought back over her time in the White House, she drew on a favorite poem to describe her feelings. The lines she selected came from "The End," by the British author Adela Florence Nicolson, writing under the pen name Laurence Hope. Rather than dwell on the morbid, opening lines about disappointment and despair that Nicolson published not long before she committed suicide at age thirty-nine, Bird singled out two soothing lines in a middle stanza:

I seek, to celebrate my glad release,
The Tents of Silence and the Camp of Peace.

Having wrapped up "our" presidency, Bird was ready to celebrate, but whether she would find a "camp of peace" remained to be seen.

19

CALMING ANCHOR FOR
A "HOLY TERROR"

T HE HOUSE the Johnsons retreated to on January 20, 1969,
looked pretty much as it would decades later when it operated
as a national historic site, available for any tourist to walk through. Not
nearly sleek or fancy enough to merit a spread in *Architectural Digest,* it
reflected the unmistakably different tastes of its two occupants. The
well-worn slipcovers and jumble of furnishings suggested a practical
resident, more tuned to personal comfort than to decorating trends.
Stitching on one sofa pillow proclaimed defiance: "This is my ranch
and I can do as I damn please." To the right of the fireplace, the only
portrait in the living room featured an unsmiling Sam Rayburn, who
had been dead for seven years. Only a home with a high political index
would display the likeness of a man known chiefly for presiding over
the House of Representatives. Large copper pots from France on the
hearth and naïf Mexican paintings on the wall contrasted sharply with
the triplet of TV monitors along one wall, making very clear that two

very different personalities inhabited this space—one firmly rooted in the United States, the other looking outward.

Lady Bird had meticulously, and with some trepidation, prepared for the day when her workaholic husband no longer had a job. Again and again, through their years together, most notably after his heart attack in 1955, she had recognized how he thrived on work—it kept him going. Vacations made him testy, impatient, and she could count on the fingers of one hand the times she and their daughters had enjoyed a trip with him that did not revolve around business. That's why she had insisted he run again in 1964—she dreaded the prospect of an unemployed, bored husband who drank too much and then looked around for someone to blame for his sorry state. Who made a better scapegoat than a wife? She dreamed of a time when the two of them could put political cares aside and enjoy leisurely walks along the lanes and drives across the fields, maybe even some travel abroad. But the gnaw of those other fears gave her pause. It would take more than his beloved ranch to keep him happy, and if the two of them were going to have any pleasure out of these so-called golden years, she would have to augment her soothing nurturing and find ways to keep him busy. She would also need to find new projects for herself, including, above all, a way to burnish his legacy.

On the Johnsons' first night out of office, dozens of local residents gathered in the hangar behind the ranch house to applaud their return, and after greeting many of them by name, Lyndon and Lady Bird disappeared into the house. With temperatures hovering near 70, she did not need to light the fireplaces, but she had lined up friendly, smiling faces to add a dose of cheer. In addition to daughter Lynda, dinner guests included movie mogul Arthur Krim and his wife, Mathilde; ranch manager Dale Malechek; and three secretaries whose long, committed service made them virtually family: Mary Rather, Yolanda Boozer, and Juanita Roberts. Not much chance of a lull in conversation at that table.

Before leaving Washington, the Johnsons had made enough commitments to keep them both busy for a while. They had signed with Holt, Rinehart & Winston to write "his and her" White House memoirs, the first presidential couple to do so. The combined book advances for the two of them exceeded $1 million, and all of it would go to the building and operation of the new LBJ Library.

Although she had virtually no precedent to guide her, Lady Bird immediately set to work on her volume. Eleanor Roosevelt had chronicled her White House time in "My Day" newspaper columns, and she had written several books about various periods of her life. But Bess Truman and Mamie Eisenhower did not follow her lead—they preferred to let others recount their lives. Even Jacqueline Kennedy, who once worked for a newspaper and eventually took a day job helping other celebrities write their stories, never wrote her own. Helen Taft, the first presidential wife to publish a book about herself, might have served as Mrs. Johnson's model, but more than half of Taft's 1914 memoir, *Recollections of Full Years,* dealt with the time *before* her husband became president, when the couple lived in the Philippines.

The success of Lady Bird Johnson's *A White House Diary*, with its careful use of language and revealing anecdotes, made hers an example subsequent presidents' wives would follow. Of the next seven first ladies, only Pat Nixon relied on a family member to write her life; the others all had their memoirs ready for printing soon after their respective terms ended: Betty Ford, *The Times of My Life* (1978); Rosalynn Carter, *First Lady from Plains* (1984); Nancy Reagan, *My Turn* (1989); Barbara Bush, *A Memoir* (1994); Hillary Rodham Clinton, *Living History* (2003); and Laura Bush, *Spoken from the Heart* (2010).

Within hours of the JFK assassination, Lady Bird started making notes for her book, and although she later explained she had intended to write just for her children and grandchildren, that seems unlikely, considering the time and effort expended. Her English teacher back at St. Mary's had fueled her interest in writing, and now she was in a position to produce a book that people would want to read. One of the first pieces of equipment she bought after becoming first lady was a small tape recorder, which she tried to use each day for describing the people she met and what happened around her. She evidently kept the project secret from all but her closest staff, and depended on her personal secretary, Ashton Gonella, to clip articles from newspapers and magazines to flesh out her accounts. In July 1965, when President Johnson ordered a cutback in the number of periodicals that his office paid for, Gonella registered an objection. She needed those publications for the "private and confidential" project that the first lady had undertaken, and if the president wouldn't pay for them, then the first lady would have to. Those articles, along with scraps of notes, names of guests, menus, and other reminders, went into big brown envelopes, each marked by date, to be used for what would become Lady Bird's *A White House Diary*.

When in Washington, the first lady's favorite spot for dictating to her "talking machine" was the little sitting room on the southwest corner of the second floor, where she still had furniture from The Elms. She felt comfortable with those familiar pieces—the blue velvet sofa, the French armchairs flanking the fireplace, the mahogany desk. Depending on where she sat, she could gaze south toward the Washington Monument or into the Rose Garden, with the windows of her husband's Oval Office just behind it. Her preferred time for dictating was early evening, after staff had all left, before Lyndon came back for dinner—a treasured interlude she designated "my time." At the ranch or on the road, when a succession of days remained jam-packed, she had to rely on those big brown envelopes to jog her memory a week or more later.

Turning those hours of taped observations into a printed book required discipline, but she found the task appealing. "I *like* writing," she wrote, "fearful labor though I sometimes find it—I like words." Never much of a typist, she relied on secretaries to transcribe the tapes she had made, and then used her trusty Gregg shorthand to add details in the margins and correct transcription errors. (Unfortunately, the shorthand she learned in the 1930s was not always decipherable to archivists and biographers who later struggled to figure out what she wrote.) She prided herself on finding the perfect phrase and on learning new words (such as "ineluctable") to convey exactly what she wanted to say.

By the time she left Washington she had a suitcase full of tapes, some of them not yet transcribed. Eventually they would yield 1,750,000 words, enough to fill a shelf of fourteen volumes if printed out verbatim. The many typists who struggled with transcribing did not always understand her accent, and they made some atrocious errors. LBJ archivist Claudia Anderson, who worked closely with Mrs. Johnson in the last years of her life and was familiar with her style of speech and writing, was so surprised at what she read in one transcript that she went back to check the recording. A careful listening showed that Mrs. Johnson had *not* described a woman as looking like a "bowl of jelly" but as a "Botticelli."

As Lady Bird faced the prospect of sifting through those hundreds of thousands of words to pick what she wanted included in *A White House Diary*, she found herself reminded of William Faulkner's reaction to his editor's slashings: "You are killing my darlings." But she plowed ahead, and with the help of experienced editor Margaret "Maggie" Cousins, she finished the job in eighteen months. Cousins, also a Texan, was seven years Bird's senior and superbly qualified to collaborate on the project, having made a name for herself in New York as editor at Doubleday and as the author of *The Life of Lucy Gallant*, the basis for a movie starring Jane Wyman. Cousins spent months in Austin to get the manuscript ready for the printer by August 15, 1970, in time for Christmas sales.

The ex–first lady's book quickly hit *The New York Times* Best Seller list, where it remained for thirteen weeks, while the author appeared with popular TV interviewers, including British celebrity-host David Frost. *McCall's* magazine added to the hype by carrying excerpts of *A White House Diary* in its fall issues. Reviewers criticized the book's length (806 pages) and its surfeit of details on *kinde* and *kuchen,* but they appeared awed by the first lady's energy. Jean Stafford wrote in *The New York Review of Books*, "The velocity at which Mrs. Johnson flew makes the hardiest Bird-watcher giddy."

While his wife became a celebrated author, Lyndon dithered and dallied at writing his book. He had other commitments, including interviews with Walter Cronkite (scheduled to pay him $300,000, which would also go to the presidential library). But the ex-president wasn't faring well with Cronkite either. After spending days with the veteran newsman, talking about the Kennedy assassination and Vietnam and civil rights, Lyndon had been irked by how his comments were edited. He objected that the seven one-hour segments that the Cronkite team turned out had twisted and distorted his views. Once again, the media had shortchanged him, and he grouched to staff that he wasn't getting credit for all those good laws he had gotten passed.

It wasn't that Lyndon worked alone, stricken by writer's block and cut off from records he needed to tell his story. He had brought with him to Texas a team of aides (Harry Middleton, Robert Hardesty, and William Jorden) and a huge personal archive of memos, scheduling books, and photos to prod his memory. But words did not come. Hardesty suggested he talk into a tape recorder while driving his convertible, top down, across the fields, and pay no mind to documents flying in the wind. But Lyndon remained as tongue-tied with the recorder as with the pen. Harvard grad student Doris Kearns, who first met the president while she was a White House fellow, spent weekends and vacations at the ranch, listening to his reminiscences and trying to get them on paper. Kearns and Hardesty both urged him to use the earthy vocabulary and down-home phrases that amused his friends. But he balked, saying he wanted to sound dignified and "presidential," not boorish and crude. Still hobbled by the old dichotomy that defined his youth, when he wavered between the models offered by the dignified Baineses on his mother's side and the rowdy ranch hands on his father's side, he returned one section to Kearns with instructions: "For Christ's sake get that vulgar language of mine out of there. What do you think this is, the talk of an uneducated cowboy? It's a presidential memoir, damn it, and I've got to come out looking like a statesman, not some backwoods politician."

The Vantage Point: Perspectives of the Presidency, 1963–1969, finally appeared one year after Bird's *Diary*, in October 1971, and *The New York Times* added to the buzz it caused by running a dozen pre-publication installments, each focusing on a different topic. Lyndon had not finished in time for the book party scheduled for him in August, and he had to placate autograph hounds by signing books that others had written about him. But on November 7, he had stacks of *The Vantage Point* ready when a large crowd assembled at the LBJ Library, eager to shake his hand and consider buying an autographed copy.

Unlike Lady Bird's book, this one pleased virtually no one. Jewell Malechek, the ranch manager's wife, captured the gist of the general disappointment when she observed that it "would have been more exciting if he had written it like he talked." Veteran journalist David Halberstam, reviewing *The Vantage Point* in *The New York Times*, mused that one of the most fascinating figures of the time, a complex leader who shifted and changed, a president who "as a study in political psychopathology . . . is probably without peer" had produced a dull and disappointing book. He had "tidied up" his life, made it "antiseptic." The one quote that stood out in Lyndon's book as both revealing and authentic was the one from Bird in 1964, when she had counseled him to run because he would become a miserable human being if he didn't have something to do.

That prediction was right on the money. The initial reports on LBJ's retirement were fairly rosy. A *New York Times* article described a contented, exuberant ex-president who looked like "a kid kicking off his shoes at the first sign of spring . . . whooping it up on horseback among his Herefords, chasing deer in his Lincoln Continental convertible, romping with his dogs and grandchildren on the lawn . . . going to supper in leather-trimmed gabardine." But the reports from those around him were much less jolly. Family, who sat with him at breakfast, and staff, who tried to keep him focused on writing his memoirs, saw sadness and gloom. Jewell Malechek described him as the moodiest man she ever met.

Since she lived nearby and helped out at the ranch, Mrs. Malechek had ample opportunity to observe the ex-president in retirement, and she reported he was restless and dissatisfied, changing his mind endlessly and making life difficult for everyone around him. On a short helicopter ride to San Antonio, she had offered to comb his hair before landing. No matter how hard she worked, with brush and spray, odd strands kept popping out, and he became so distraught he started to cry. It took Bird's soothing reassurance that everything would be all right as soon as they landed to get him to stop. Wicky Goldschmidt, who had known the Johnsons since the 1930s, reported that in a visit to the ranch she and her husband found Lyndon in a "deep depression." Staffer Bob Hardesty noted that Lyndon was being his "normal manic depressive self."

Ranch hands found Lyndon's volatility exasperating, and the extravagant gifts (including brand-new automobiles) that he gave them did not compensate for his imperious commands and unreasonable requests. He continually updated the workers' to-do lists, bombarding them with orders to check on a particular heifer or mend a small patch of fence when they were already overloaded with more urgent assignments. Acting like a white-collar executive supervising a team of salesmen, he requested end-of-the-day written reports and memos, which weary ranch hands were loath to deliver. Dale Malechek, on his boss's explicit orders, spent thousands of dollars on a prized breeding bull, and after the animal died following a single mating, Lyndon complained that he was eating the most expensive sausage in Texas.

When frustrated aides and co-workers sought guidance from Lady Bird on how to tolerate Lyndon's abusive treatment, she counseled them to look on the mood changes and perverse demands as "one great adventure." She used her time-tested remedy, inviting guests she thought would lift her husband's spirits, and in cases where she could, she stepped in to soften her husband's brusqueness and offensiveness. Sometimes she registered a small victory. Secret Service agent Jim Hardin remembered that while he was driving the retired Johnsons to Austin one day, Lyndon kept issuing instructions from the backseat: to drive faster or slow down, to pass the truck ahead or stay in lane. At first, Bird, seated beside Hardin, tried to rein her husband in with a soft "Lyndon, please," but when that didn't work, she raised her volume and in firm tones told him to stop. Hardin noted that Lyndon "quieted right down."

For five years, Lyndon Johnson had been the most powerful man on earth, and now he couldn't even control his ranch workers or his drivers. He had been sorely reminded of his diminished status at the launching of Apollo 11 in Florida in July 1969. Relegated to a hot seat in the bleachers, he watched while the assembled crowd's attention focused on Vice President Spiro Agnew, an upstart on the political scene. He won his first election in 1962, and that had been to the relatively insignificant job of county executive, in Baltimore, Maryland. As LBJ sat by, largely ignored, he had a painful lesson in how quickly celebrity status fades.

Power brokers rarely sought out ex-president Johnson for his counsel, and they showed little gratitude for the advice he offered them. When President Nixon's adviser on foreign affairs, Henry Kissinger, trooped down to Texas, he found a long-haired, sagging-in-the-face smoker who kept calling him "Dr. Schles-ing-er." It had been an old tactic of Lyndon's to demean a person by mangling his name, and close associates maintained he was just employing his craftiness on the unsuspecting Kissinger. But Kissinger went away from the meeting convinced that Lyndon was "crazy." Other Nixon associates backed Kissinger up, and chief-of-staff Bob Haldeman concluded after talking with ex-President Johnson that he was "psychopathic." But he hadn't lost his bawdy sense of humor. When queried about attending the 1972 Democratic nominating convention, he replied why he would feel foolish there: "The only thing more impotent than a former president is a cut dog at a screwing match."

Lyndon had not ditched his old habit of harboring old grudges and forming new ones. Aide Tom Johnson first met Lyndon when he came to Washington as a White House fellow in 1965, and he followed him to Texas in 1969. When Bill Moyers published his book *Listening to America* in 1971, Tom Johnson and his wife, Edwina, wanted to host a celebratory party for Moyers in Austin. Tom phoned Lyndon to say that he and Lady Bird were the very first ones to be invited, but the phone went dead at the first mention of Moyers's name. To underscore his displeasure with Tom, Lyndon stopped speaking to him, too, put him in the same "freeze out" as Moyers.

If the relationship between the two men had been purely social, the break might have mattered less, but Tom held a high-level job in the Johnson business. He could not continue working for a man who refused to acknowledge his existence. So Tom did what Lyndon's associates had been doing for years—he went to Bird for help. Soon Lyndon was talking to Tom again, and the younger man learned how the rapprochement had been achieved. Bird had reminded her husband: "The fact that Tom is loyal to Bill Moyers doesn't mean he isn't loyal to you."

Other ruptures were harder to repair. Lyndon's younger brother, Sam Houston Johnson, erratic and alcoholic, had always depended on his brother and sister-in-law to see him through hospitalizations, scrapes with scandal, and spotty periods of employment. Now, with

Lyndon out of the White House, he published a book, revealing what he thought about his super-successful sibling. Sam Houston emphasized Lyndon's obsession with secrecy and his mood swings to the point that some readers, including Lyndon, thought the former president sounded mentally ill. Another banishment followed, and this one, exiling his own brother, lasted until Lyndon's death.

The ex-president still relished evidence that his female entourage adored him, and he was still buying intimate attire to flatter them. When Bird inadvertently opened a box delivered to the ranch and found a lavender bikini, definitely not her size, she passed it to him, with the observation, "It must be for one of your lady friends." He ordered clothes for his wife, too, but he could be imperious and rude in his pronouncements about what he wanted her to wear. One outfit made her look fat, the other too short, so that even his largesse translated into insult. She could still talk back to him if the occasion warranted, as one her friends observed. Late to church one Sunday morning, Lyndon was following Bird through the kitchen when he observed a run in her stocking and told her to go change. She retorted, "Too late now, Lyndon," and kept walking. But few of his demands were so easily dismissed, and she admitted that he had become "a holy terror."

Travel on her own, although she had enjoyed precious little of it, had always provided Lady Bird with some escape, and now that her husband was no longer in public office, she could consider trips abroad. Only eight months after leaving the White House, she and Lynda took advantage of their new freedom as private citizens—they left their husbands and little Lucinda behind while they explored the South of France. Charlotte Curtis, society reporter for *The New York Times,* noted that the Johnson women happily rubbed shoulders with princes, dowagers, and the dashing ballerino Rudolf Nureyev on the Côte d'Azur, although they seemed less thrilled with a performance by nude dancers. Lynda perked up at the idea of buying gambling chips in

Monte Carlo, and told Curtis, "My mother never let me do anything like this before."

But leaving an unhappy Lyndon behind was not something Bird liked to do, and after her splurge in the South of France, she limited herself to trips to Mexico with him. Since their 1934 honeymoon, they had relished short sojourns south of the Rio Grande, and now, in re-tirement, they could stay longer. They lingered a month in February, relaxing at former president Miguel Alemán's beachfront villa in Aca-pulco or at one of the more secluded ranches that he, in partnership with Lyndon, owned in the interior, more rugged parts of Mexico. But old habits don't suddenly vanish with retirement. Lyndon still needed an audience, and preparation for those trips included rounding up friends to go with him, along with bottled water, groceries, and Cutty Sark. Lyndon's super-powerful shower heads were always part of the packing, along with the latest movie releases—to re-create the com-forts of home. During the day he played golf by his own rules, which permitted him but not others to retrieve balls from the rough, smooth out the grass around a hole, and alter stroke counts. In the evenings, he could still keep guests riveted with stories about what happened or might have happened once upon a time in Texas politics.

At the top of the Johnsons' plans for retirement was the library that would house their records and document their achievements, and they wanted it to be the biggest, best organized, most visited presidential library of all. Planning had started years earlier, and Lady Bird had broken her vigil by Lyndon's hospital bed after his 1965 gall bladder surgery to tiptoe out of his room before daylight and join their archi-tect friend Max Brooks on a tour of some of the nation's most dazzling new buildings. She found little to like in Philip Johnson's State The-ater at New York's Lincoln Center, but she warmed to Eero Saarinen's dormitory at Yale, and she loved the Beinecke Library that Gordon Bunshaft of Skidmore, Owings & Merrill had designed to house rare manuscripts in New Haven. Bunshaft was known for widely different creations, specifically suited to site and use, and his blueprint for the Hirshhorn Museum, sometimes described as looking like a space ship on legs, did not appeal to Mrs. Johnson. But his view that a presidential library should fit the man reflected her thoughts perfectly. Bunshaft explained: "I thought the President was really a virile man, a strong man with nothing sweet or sentimental or small about him, and he ought to have a vigorous, male building. And we've got a vigorous male building [in the LBJ Library]. I don't know if you'd do a building like that for President Roosevelt."

Choosing Bunshaft was just the beginning of decision making, and Mrs. Johnson took a hand in virtually every segment of the planning. She visited the Truman and Eisenhower libraries to observe how they worked. All four of the presidential libraries in operation at the time (Herbert Hoover, Franklin Roosevelt, Truman, and Eisenhower) were located in the respective presidents' hometowns, and Lady Bird immediately saw the downside of sending archives to sleepy little places like Independence, Missouri, or West Branch, Iowa. Much better to locate the Johnson library in a sizable city, preferably on university grounds, where it would be easily accessible to scholars doing research and to vacationers tempted to wander through its exhibits of memorabilia.

After eliminating Lyndon's alma mater in small San Marcos, Lady Bird zeroed in on Austin, home to her cherished University of Texas. As UT officials put together a package of enticements, they worked directly with her because they knew how much confidence her husband placed in her judgment. William W. Heath, who negotiated for the university, credited her as the primary factor in all major decisions and in getting her husband's approval: "we felt like she could sell [LBJ] on whatever joint idea she and the rest of us came up with better than we could."

Rather than a single structure, Lady Bird envisioned a complex, with a School of Public Affairs in a separate building alongside the taller, more impressive library. UT's Austin campus would have to acquire several acres to accommodate what Bunshaft proposed, and that meant dealing with dozens of landowners, including some who were not eager to sell. The National Archives, responsible for staffing and running presidential libraries, had not yet put limits on how big each could be, and Lady Bird was restrained only by how much private donors, footing the costs of building, would ante up. Deep-pocketed Johnson supporters stepped forward, and the result was a building to dwarf all presidential libraries in operation at that time—ten stories high. After spending a lot of time examining different kinds of stone for it, she settled on travertine, which she described as "sheer beauty" compared to "cold" granite.

In meeting after meeting, Lady Bird participated in discussions about lighting, placement of exhibits at eye level, and how to hang documents without damaging the library's polished walls. She ruminated over the number of entrances the building should have and how to display the shelved boxes of documents. She had herself raised in a crane to check out the view she would have from her office on the top floor, and she contacted relatives, both hers and Lyndon's, to urge them to contribute photos, family Bibles, and other memorabilia to document the couple's story. To file the thousands of letters and memos, she wanted attractive red buckram boxes. The color turned out to be a bad choice, as archivists learned later when a water main break in one area flooded a few shelves and the red dye discolored precious documents. But the bright boxes did enliven what would otherwise have looked like the boring, neutral tones of most scholars' shelves.

Lyndon spent far less time on such details—his interventions centered less on practical matters than on being sure his side of the story came out. In the replica of the Oval Office, he wanted visitors to hear a recording he made, explaining how very hard he had struggled with decision making in the White House. He was still looking for understanding and approval—what he had described as "just a little love."

He had another office, for his post-presidential use, with bulletproof windows, down the hall from the Oval Office replica, and a helicopter landing pad on the building's roof to provide quick access. But he preferred working at the ranch in the big wood-paneled room with comfortable, worn chairs and a mishmash of desks and books.

The modest private suite that the Johnsons set aside for themselves at the Lyndon Baines Johnson Library and Museum looked like what an unpretentious CEO might use for his business entertaining. It didn't even have a bedroom for sleeping over. Guests entered via a small anteroom lined with photos, gifts, and other reminders of the Johnsons' long political partnership. In the suite's one large room, which served both for sitting and dining, a wall of windows provided an expansive view of Austin's skyline. The bathroom did have one quirky Lyndonesque touch—its five powerful shower heads were strong enough to knock a frail person over.

The library's gala opening in May 1971 attracted an all-star lineup, including President Nixon. During the festivities, Lyndon, whose reputation for paranoia and secrecy remained intact, provided the day's shocker when he announced that he wanted the library to be a model of transparency, to show him "with the bark off." That blustery promise would later be contradicted (by those who insisted he instructed them differently) and countermanded by those bent on protecting him. But it provided the justification in the early 1990s for a crucial decision to open the revealing recordings he had made during the presidency. That cache of thousands of conversations, in the president's own inimitable language, produced invaluable documentation to anyone studying the Johnson years.

Both Lady Bird and Lyndon made other decisions, besides location, to maximize the library's use. Unlike other presidential archives, the LBJ Library did not charge admission—at least as long as its endowment could fund the extensive exhibits and events offered. She did not live to see that policy changed, on what would have been her one hundredth birthday, but nothing about her life suggests she would have objected. She had always been a stickler for seeing that income balanced outgo. Visitors continued to find ample, free parking nearby. As if he and Bird had not already provided sufficient enticement to visit the library, Lyndon once proposed making loudspeaker announcements to football fans who packed the stadium nearby: if anyone needed a drink of cold water or a toilet, the library was there for them to use.

By the end of 1971, with the library open and both their books published, the Johnsons had to decide what to do with the rest of their lives. Their White House successors would engage in a variety of post-presidential ventures, including extremely profitable speech making, managing international relief efforts, and monitoring human rights abroad. But the Johnsons opted to follow the example of the Trumans, continuing to do what they had liked doing before: spending leisure hours in the company of old friends, trying to find enjoyment in the people and places they already knew.

When Mrs. Johnson was offered a seat on the Board of Regents of her alma mater, she refused at first, not wanting to make any commitments beyond those she already had. But Lyndon upbraided her, reminding her how often he had been turned down by busy people, especially women. So she relented and agreed to serve a six-year term, beginning in 1971. Her co-regents noted that she came well prepared for every session, and she spoke her mind on subjects that mattered to her. As chair of the Academic Committee, she championed extending courses in the health sciences, and later described her service on the board as the pinnacle of her public service life. It was, notably, the only significant achievement that she could claim as strictly hers.

Bird still gave the occasional speech on conservation, and she funded a contest on highway beautification in Texas. The $1,000 prize went to the highway employee who had done the most to upgrade the state's roadsides. The annual award ceremony, held at the ranch, was a festive affair with food and drink, and Lyndon joked that he made a point of attending because it was one of the few chances he had to see his wife give away any of her own money.

On the private side, Bird began devoting more time to her daughters, who had merited only the bottom of the page on her White House daily diary. By January 1969, each had produced one child. Rambunctious Lyn Nugent, at two and a half, was a household favorite, since Lynda Robb's Lucinda, at three months, was still too young to play. In 1970, the Johnson daughters added two more baby girls: Nicole Marie Nugent and Catherine Robb. The Nugents had settled in Austin, but the Robbs remained in the East, moving from rented quarters in Arlington, Virginia, where they started married life, to a ten-room house in Charlottesville when Chuck Robb enrolled in law school at the University of Virginia in the fall of 1970.

Bird doted on her grandchildren, showering them with the attention she had not had time to give her daughters in their early years. But LBJ, with more empty hours than ever, was only a "sometimes" grandfather. Visitors to the ranch watched him relax by horseplaying on the lawn with Lyn, but his granddaughters did not inspire the attention he had lavished on Courtenay Valenti. He was chronically tired, disgruntled by inactivity, and it would take more than an amusing child to lift him from his melancholic lethargy. He had spots of exuberance, when he went with Luci to root for UT at football games, but his predominant mood was low. He would sit for hours and "just stare at the ceiling." He let his hair grow long, gained thirty-five pounds, and resumed chain-smoking, a habit ditched after his 1955 heart attack.

Well aware that he was approaching the age at which his father died, Lyndon started thinking more about how he would be remembered. His birthplace, down the road from the ranch house, and his boyhood home in Johnson City, twelve miles east, had already been designated as national historic sites, and Bird had spent a lot of time selecting the exhibits and working with the guides. He liked to drop in unannounced at both places, disarming tourists with a personal anecdote or two. He sometimes lingered at the family cemetery down the road from the ranch to mull over the names on the tombstones and look at the spot waiting for him.

Morbid or exuberant as he might turn on any of these excursions, they were playtime compared with the dollar decisions he made, tidying up money matters. Mrs. Johnson evidently let him take charge on this, probably glad to have him occupied. During his presidency, when neighbor A. W. Moursund acted as a trustee of the Johnson investments, the broadcasting business had yielded about $1 million each year, and Moursund had invested those earnings in land, buildings, and banks, which he bought in his own name or that of someone else in order not to implicate the president. Moursund made complicated trades, so that he ended up the owner of record on deeds and shareholder lists, when the property actually belonged, in whole or in part, to one of the Johnsons. In a curious deal in 1965, Moursund acquired 1,600 acres of California land for what appeared to be the amazing price of $10. After 1969, when Moursund was no longer a trustee, the Johnsons' holdings mushroomed, and one historian estimated that their net worth doubled in the four years after they left Washington. That included stock and ranchlands and businesses across several states, from Oklahoma and Kansas to the West Coast, but Moursund's fair share of it all would be very difficult to figure out.

As Lyndon converted real estate and equity into cash, he and Moursund, one of his oldest, most trusted friends, had a falling-out. The neighbor Bird once described as "hard to imagine life without" became persona non grata with Lyndon. Neither man revealed the details of their disagreement, and Lyndon offered only the cryptic: "We decided to split the blanket," to explain the break. The two men did not speak for the remainder of Lyndon's life, although Bird's friendship with A.W. and his wife continued.

Lyndon's health took a bad turn in April 1972 while he and Bird were visiting the Robbs in Charlottesville. He had been treated earlier that month in San Antonio after suffering chest pains, and the Charlottesville doctors deemed it wise to put him in an intensive care unit at the University of Virginia Hospital and keep him under careful watch. But Lyndon, never an easy patient, quickly became edgy, and that led, as it usually did, to action. Fearful he would die far from home, he engineered his own escape from the hospital. Three days after he had been checked in, startled nurses in Charlottesville noticed unusual activity in his suite one night, and they called the hospital director, who was off the premises. He arrived to find an empty wheelchair in the parking lot, a stark reminder that Lyndon Johnson still liked to take charge.

Two more weeks in San Antonio's Brooke Medical Center followed for Lyndon, and during that time he suffered a brief burst of extra heartbeats that prompted calling Dr. Hurst to come from Atlanta. This episode initiated a period of painful angina, and for the remaining months of his life, Lyndon suffered severe chest pains that kept him close to the Texas ranch.

The Robb family visited over Labor Day weekend, but what should have been a low-keyed reunion turned into near tragedy when two-year-old Catherine almost drowned. She had crawled under a rope around the pool and was floating faceup when her mother spotted her and summoned help. After a Secret Service agent administered mouth-to-mouth resuscitation, the child was taken to a hospital where she was kept overnight before being released.

At the same time the Johnsons' young granddaughter came shockingly close to death, Lyndon was showing signs of reckoning with his own mortality. On September 20, when he returned to Brooke Medical Center to give a speech, he titled it, "As the Days Dwindle Down." As he spoke of the "green leaves of summer" turning to "brown" and the "chill winds of winter . . . [starting] to blow," it was clear he was talking about more than seasonal changes. "Before we are ready for the end to come, the year will be gone." Friends observed he moved more slowly now, relied on others to drive him around, and popped nitroglycerin pills for pain.

Within days of that speech, LBJ arranged for a portion of the broadcasting empire to be sold to the *Los Angeles Times-Mirror* for $9 million. His wife and daughters received the bulk of the money ($4.9 million to Bird and $1.3 million to each of the daughters) and they continued to own a string of radio stations. The LBJ Ranch, restored to the acreage it boasted when Lyndon's father was forced to give it up in the 1930s, was not sold. Bird, who singled it out as the place "where the best years of my life were spent. I can't imagine living anywhere else," would have hated to leave it. She often boasted she and Lyndon could ride for hours across that land and feel "at utter peace." By transferring the ranch to the National Park Service, with a provision that Bird could live there until her death, the Johnsons enjoyed tax advantages while guaranteeing Bird's continued enjoyment.

Jan Jarboe Russell, the Texas reporter who interviewed several people who worked for or socialized with the Johnsons during the post–White House years, concluded that Lyndon was utterly dependent on Bird. She was "so clearly in charge of the day-to-day management of his life that some former staff members got to the point that they did not want to be alone with Johnson unless Lady Bird was with him." Without her, he was "impossible: depressed one minute, raging the next." As his wife had predicted, he drank too much and seemed frustrated by his diminished powers and physical infirmities. George Christian, who returned to live in Austin after serving as the president's press secretary, underscored Lyndon's reliance on Bird: "I don't know what he would have done without her. She held him together. She held all of us together."

By November 1972, when Richard Nixon won reelection, Lyndon's increasing frailty was apparent to all. He slept with an oxygen tent beside him and downed the ever-present nitroglycerin pills. Doctors advised him to skip a civil rights symposium at the LBJ Library on December 11–12, but he insisted on going, even though Central Texas was suffering through a record-breaking cold spell. Temperatures descended to a frigid 20 below zero, a record that stood forty years later, and ice and snow added to the hazard of travel. While other conferees were delayed (and even those living only a few minutes from the library had trouble making the trip), Lyndon moved by snowmobile and car over the seventy miles to arrive in time to give the keynote address. It was a glorious last stand, requiring enormous effort. Hubert Humphrey, who was in the audience, thought Lyndon looked ashen gray and seemed to lack the stamina to finish his remarks. But he persisted, and after apologizing for what remained undone, he delivered a soaring call to action: "I'm kind of ashamed of myself that I . . . couldn't do more. . . . We know there's injustice . . . intolerance . . . discrimination and hate and suspicion. But . . . we have proved that great progress is possible . . . and if our efforts continue . . . we shall overcome."

That exertion cost him—he needed two days in bed to recover, but then he sparked on good days and starting talking about ambitious plans for the coming year. He told aides he wanted to invite world leaders to the ranch. The first name on his list was Israeli prime minister Golda Meir, who had already agreed to add Texas to her itinerary after a visit to the Nixon White House in February.

On December 22, Bird celebrated her sixtieth birthday, and Lyndon went out of his way to make it a festive occasion. His August birthday had always required big-time preparation, with a long list of guests and considerable feasting, drinking, and gifting. But her birthday, coming so close to Christmas, often got swallowed up in holiday entertaining and was observed on the run. This time Lyndon invited a dozen special friends and arranged a luxurious buffet. Privately, he asked one of the guests to see that all her future birthdays were as special as this one. His deep and genuine affection for her is often overlooked in the many accounts that emphasize the verbal abuse he handed out. Those outbursts make shocking reading, but they should be balanced alongside the many examples of his caring and genuine appreciation. "He very much loved her, turned on, and enjoyed her," one of the staff observed. Helen Thomas, the veteran capital reporter, added that he had conveyed those feelings to Bird, who knew "he loved her . . . knew he couldn't exist without her." When a friend reminded him that the best decision he ever made was to marry Bird, Lyndon emphatically agreed, "Don't think a day doesn't pass that I don't know that."

Exactly a month after Bird celebrated her sixtieth birthday Lyndon died. She thought him unusually quiet that morning, but it was Monday and she had work waiting for her in Austin. Leaving Jewell Malechek to look after him, Bird left. Lyndon, who had never conquered his fear of being alone, lunched by himself and then went to his bedroom to nap. A short time later he called for help, but by the time a Secret Service agent arrived, he was lying on the floor, his face deadly gray.

When the call reached Bird, telling her that Lyndon was being taken to the Brooke Medical Center, she immediately boarded a helicopter to meet him there. By the time she landed in San Antonio, at the site where he had given his "Days Dwindle Down" speech four months earlier, it was too late. He had already been pronounced dead. She had weathered many of Lyndon's hospitalizations, seen him through major heart attacks, gall bladder surgery, and more minor illnesses than she could count. This time she had not been there to try to pull him through, and she regretted that "very much." To the security agent who told her "This time we didn't make it," she replied stoically, "Well, we expected it."

Mrs. Johnson oversaw the funeral arrangements with a decisiveness that suggested she had only to pull outlined instructions out of her desk drawer. Mindful of how much he loathed being alone, she asked friends to stay by his coffin overnight. By 1 p.m. the next day, the doors of the LBJ Library opened and mourners who had waited in line for hours started filing up the wide marble steps and past the body, which was flanked by a full honor guard. By late afternoon, nearly eight thousand had moved past the flag-draped coffin, and others continued the show of respect throughout the night.

Much of the nation's attention that evening focused not on ex-President Johnson's death but on a televised speech of President Nixon. In a coincidence so fraught with irony it challenges credibility, he announced that an agreement had finally been reached to "end the war and bring peace with honor in Vietnam." And that announcement came at the very same time that the man who tried time and again to achieve the same settlement was being prepared for burial in Texas.

By the morning after Nixon's speech, when the coffin of Lyndon Johnson was flown to Washington for a ceremony in the Rotunda at the Capitol, seventeen thousand people had paid their respects. These attendance figures came from library director Harry Middleton, who explained he felt obliged to keep a count because "I know that somewhere, sometime, President Johnson's going to ask me how many showed up."

After a funeral service at the National City Christian Church in Washington, the body was returned to the ranch. A thunderstorm delayed the flight and snarled news feeds from the burial scene, jumbling delivery of the details. But by nightfall on January 25, 1973, as the rest of the nation mulled over the peace agreement that had eluded him, Lyndon Baines Johnson was interred in the family cemetery within sight of where he was born.

Less than a month earlier, on December 26, the nation had lost its only other living ex-president when Harry Truman died, and now two widows, who between them had wrestled with first lady obligations for a total of a dozen years, struggled with grief. A generation younger than eighty-seven-year-old Bess, Bird lost her husband when she was only sixty. The two women shared fierce loyalties to their respective mates and a dogged affection for their native regions; they had entered the White House in extraordinary circumstances, resulting from a president's sudden death, and each found herself compared to the iconic first lady who preceded her.

Bess had an advantage over Bird. Both their husbands had faced outsized ranks of detractors during their White House years, but "Give 'em hell, Harry" had two decades of retirement to dispel the critics' sting while chants deriding "LBJ, LBJ . . ." still rang in people's ears. Bess's Harry had become almost lovable, his gaffes far enough in the past to be excused or forgotten. But the transgressions of Bird's Lyndon were still fresh in people's minds, and showed up in the eulogies to him. Syndicated columnist James Reston noted the man's many contradictions: "Both the glory and the tragedy of Lyndon Johnson was that he believed utterly in the romantic tradition of America in the Congress and the church, in that order; in Main Street and Wall Street, in the competitive state and in the welfare state—in all of it part of the time and some of it all the time." For decades after Lyndon died, historians would continue to marvel at the complexity of the man. Columnist Russell Baker concluded he was a "human puzzle," too complicated for anyone to understand. Bill Moyers described him as "thirteen of the most exasperating men I ever met." Bird preferred to highlight the joy in his life, and at the time of his death, she reminded journalist Norma Milligan of *Newsweek*, "Ah, but didn't he live well."

Bird Johnson made few excuses for the inconsistencies in her husband's choices, and she set no limits on her devotion to him. She knew she owed him: "Lyndon pushed me, he drove me, at times he humiliated me, but he made me become someone bigger and better than I would have been." She had far more than that with him—the love of her life beside her and the realization that he relied on her as on no one else. Their daughter Lynda underscored that dependence when she observed, "The Lord knew what he was doing when he took

Daddy first because I don't think Daddy could've gotten along without Mother." Bob Hardesty, who worked with Lyndon right up to the end, wrote of Bird: "She tempered his rashness with a sense of calm, penetrating judgment that he had long since come to depend on. It would be too much to say that without Lady Bird Johnson there would have been no Lyndon Johnson—but it would have been a far different Lyndon Johnson than the one we came to know."

20

FLYING SOLO

Long after Lyndon's death, Barbara Walters went to Austin for another interview with Lady Bird Johnson. Decades had passed since the *Today* show encounter when Walters popped her question about Lyndon's womanizing, and she had taken some flak for it. Mrs. Johnson had not objected but some of her friends told Walters they found the question "impertinent" and "rude."

Now, with two more decades of widowhood behind her, Lady Bird was going to get another question from Walters that related to Lyndon, and it didn't come in the form of a compliment. How did she feel, Walters wanted to know, about her long marriage to a man who expected her to wait on him "hand and foot." Why didn't she object when "he bellowed, 'Bird, get in here.'" The thoughtful answer came back as sage and smoothly as the one about his wandering eye: "It was a different world then," Bird explained. "That was your husband. You lived his life." A woman had her "own life, yes," but her most personal interests and deepest pleasures had to wait. They were "put on the shelf" for later. To guarantee that her explanation did not register as regret, she added, "and many things I have done since his departure were on that shelf."

Lady Bird Johnson had thirty-four years after Lyndon's death, slightly more than a third of her long life, to explore those postponed pleasures. Her friends observed that she seemed more easygoing, having shed the worry about what her unpredictable husband might do next. Although she maintained that she loved every minute of her time with Lyndon, it is impossible to ignore the fact that she drastically altered her life after he was gone. She became much more her own person, showing enormous zest for travel to faraway places, forming tighter connections with her daughters and their families, enjoying friends who were hers but had never been (or had ceased to be) his.

"Politics was Lyndon's life," Bird liked to say, and "38 years were enough." But having shared that life so long, she could not immediately wean herself from the intrigue and maneuvering in the nation's power center. Her Virginia-based daughter reported that Bird would phone to check up on the latest gossip from Capitol Hill. When Lynda's husband, Charles Robb, ran for lieutenant governor of Virginia in 1977, Bird pitched in to help in one more campaign. "When it gets as close as your son-in-law, you can't say no," she explained.

It was to Lyndon that Bird owed her only national title—first lady— and, as Betty Ford once observed, that was a job that diminishes but never ends. When subsequent presidents invited Mrs. Johnson back to Washington, to receive an award or participate in an event, she eagerly accepted. By the time the Clintons invited her to join other VIPs and help celebrate the two hundredth birthday of the White House in 2000, her hair had grayed and height had shrunk from the five foot four she registered as first lady. But she put on the brown fur-cuffed Victor Costa gown she had already worn to her eighty-seventh birthday party and went.

Her celebrity status still tickled Lady Bird, and she perked up at the sight of fans. Her friends tried to head them off, fearing they would become a burden, but she was always gracious. When busloads of curious tourists drove past the LBJ Ranch, she interrupted whatever she was doing to go outside and give them a big smile and friendly wave. In Austin restaurants, when a stranger approached her to exchange a few words, she cordially took time to chat.

Beneath the gray hair and ladylike composure, signs of the spunky young Bird Taylor still sparked, as a University of Texas professor observed. Seated next to her at a small dinner party, he listened as another guest at the table described in graphic detail a new X-rated movie. Bird listened intently, and then leaned over and asked the professor, "What was the name of that film?" On a trip to New York City, she happened to eat breakfast in the same hotel restaurant as a motley group of young men, wearing assorted costumes reminiscent of bygone centuries. The group recognized her immediately and asked her to pose with them for a photograph. Ever affable, she consented, then inquired who they were. Told that they were a popular disco group performing as "The Village People," she smiled and, turning to the friend who accompanied her, said, "Well, I wonder if we just made the cover of their next album."

A first lady reveals a lot about herself by how she chooses to spend her "ex" years. Does she continue her leadership role on a national stage, or even enlarge upon it as Betty Ford did with her eponymous treatment centers? Or does she jettison her first lady project, as Nancy Reagan did with "Just Say No to Drugs"? If she survives her husband long enough to compile a record of her own, does she change course, as Jacqueline Kennedy Onassis did with a new husband and a career in publishing? Much depends on how much time a first lady has on her own: Eleanor Roosevelt survived Franklin by seventeen years, and quickly achieved "First Woman of the World" status.

Bird had double that time to polish her legacy, and besides her highway beautification agenda, she had another project up there on that shelf that she wanted to tackle. In what she called her "last hurrah," a birthday gift to herself, to celebrate her seventieth in 1982, she started a National Wildflower Research Center in Austin. Out of her own pocket, she donated $125,000 and sixty acres of land, as "rent for the space I have taken up in this highly interesting world" and then appealed to others to contribute to an endowment, which eventually totaled $700,000. Friends encouraged her to think on a grander scale, with more ambitious goals and aggressive fund-raising, but T. J. Taylor's daughter, even at seventy, liked to cap her risks.

The Wildflower Center, renamed the Lady Bird Johnson Wildflower Center on her eighty-fifth birthday, had the acres and resources to conduct research and answer questions from all over the world about which plants thrived under what conditions. It created model backyard gardens and instructive exhibits for school groups, demonstrating that some wildflowers thrive in even the harshest climates and the poorest soils. Up until a few weeks before she died, Mrs. Johnson continued to visit the center, joining the 100,000 tourists who showed up there each year. She communicated, if only with a smile or a wave, with employees and sightseers, even when she required a wheelchair to move, an oxygen tank to breathe, and a companion to compensate for her failing eyesight.

Before she started the Wildflower Center, the ex–first lady signed on to another project to spruce up Austin. Its Town Lake had long provided a waterway for Texans to boat and swim, and its banks had been a favorite path for bikers and hikers. Beginning in the spring of 1972, she joined the effort to make the area around the lake more attractive and user-friendly, with a variety of blooming trees that she could reel off by name ("redbud, crepe myrtle . . .") lining its hike and bike trail. When Austinites tried to show their gratitude by renaming Town Lake for her, she objected, and only after she died did it become "Lady Bird

Lake." No statues or big plaques are there to mark her involvement. Apparently, none is needed.

Wherever she went, Secret Service agents accompanied her, 365 days a year, whether she stayed at the ranch, visited one of her daughters, or traveled abroad. Because she rarely received serious threats after Lyndon's death, economy-minded critics suggested that Secret Service protection was an unnecessary public expenditure. But the woman notoriously frugal with her own money was not inclined to cut costs here. She registered her objection to giving up her guards, many of whom had been with her for decades and had become almost like family. By the time she died, she had received more years of Secret Service coverage than any figure in U.S. political history.

Secret Service agents who accompanied her on world travels sometimes took their spouses along (at Mrs. Johnson's suggestion but not at her expense or that of the government) and they had an eye-opener time. Stay-at-home Lyndon never wanted to go anywhere, but as soon as Lady Bird had the opportunity, she set out to explore the world, places she had been whisked through as an official visitor: Europe, Asia, and Africa. The first summer after Lyndon's death, she started with London, and in subsequent years managed to crowd several European capitals into one trip. She always took a few family members or old friends along, and sometimes living conditions were chaotic. Lynda Robb revealed that her mother rented a house in France's Dordogne, oblivious to the fact that seventeen people might find it inconvenient to share a single bathroom. But could Lynda even imagine her father in the Dordogne?

Lyndon's deep disdain for East Coast liberals had not rubbed off on his wife, and in 1981 she started spending part of every summer on Martha's Vineyard, where she rekindled her relationship with Jacqueline Kennedy Onassis. Forever linked in history by an assassin's bullets, the two women had seen little of each other since Mrs. Kennedy left Washington, but on the Vineyard they arranged to get together.

The following summer Bird wrote Jackie to say that her previous stay on the Vineyard had provided such pleasure, she was coming back and had rented a "grandchildren proof" house for the month of July so Luci could bring her children, now numbering four. Would Jackie like to come to the birthday party Bird was throwing for Luci's forty-fifth on July 2? Although Jackie couldn't make it, she replied that it was "sweet of you to ask me" and in other circumstances, "I'd love to." The two ex–first ladies continued to remember each other at Christmas with boxes of pecan pralines (from Bird) and books (from Jackie).

Their final meeting was in the summer of 1993, when Bird accepted Jackie's invitation to a boat outing. The weather turned stormy, and they had to switch to lunch at Jackie's new house. Afterward, Lady Bird wrote that everything about the visit pleased—the "delicious meal, your guests, particularly Maurice Tempelsman [Jackie's longtime companion], the good conversation." Bird "loved the house. It sits on the Island so 'at home' with its surroundings, almost as if it grew out of the land." Nine months later, Bird made the effort—assisted by walking cane and the arm of a Secret Service agent—to attend Jackie's funeral at St. Ignatius Loyola Roman Catholic Church on New York's Park Avenue.

As Mrs. Johnson's frailties became ever more apparent, she scaled back her role in the family businesses. She had already brought in an outsider, Dallas lawyer Richard Hull, to restructure her financial empire in 1990, and after the LBJ Holding Company was formed, Claudia T. Johnson sat on the board, attending meetings until she turned eighty-nine.

With a substantial portfolio throughout her widowed years, Lady Bird Johnson could have afforded about any Austin house she fancied, but she continued using the modest apartment she had shared with Lyndon atop the Texas Broadcasting offices. Finally, in 1987, after recognizing that she needed more space to entertain her brood of grandchildren and their friends, she started house hunting. She took an immediate liking to an unpretentious ranch-style home on a quiet, untraveled street in the hills to the west of the city, and she summoned daughter Luci, who had remarried and moved to Toronto, to help assess it. Luci immediately nixed the idea of purchase, pronouncing the house too small. Her mother's Secret Service detail required more space than 2505 Camino Alto provided, and the 1960s structure had no outstanding architectural detail to recommend it. Although mother and daughter had remarked on the property's Madrone tree, one of Bird's favorites, Luci advised her to keep looking.

A few days later, the daughter received a follow-up call from her mother, announcing that she had found the perfect house. When Luci heard it was the same little ranch-style that she had already vetoed, she objected: "But I thought we agreed that all it offered was a view of Austin and a Madrone tree." Lady Bird replied, "I decided that was all I need," and she bought it.

In fact, 2505 Camino Alto, nestled into a hill on a one-and-one-quarter-acre lot, accommodated all her needs and far more vegetation than a single Madrone tree. The hollowed out space beneath the main floor had enough footage for Secret Service agents and a large family room. On the entry-level floor, Bird had her essentials: a small office for herself, living and dining rooms for entertaining, and a bedroom with a fireplace and lots of bookshelves. Through the wall of windows on one side of the house she could look down on her alma mater, and watch its tower light up in signature orange after every football victory.

At the ranch, where Lady Bird spent her weekends, she had restored the house to the cozy, user-friendly dwelling of the pre-presidential years. Out went the desks from Lyndon's huge office, and in came comfortable sofas to turn it into a family room. She had a Jacuzzi installed just outside her bedroom so that on warm nights she could sit with her guests in the gushing water, stare at the stars in the sky, and talk about what was currently playing on the Broadway stages of New York.

With more time of her own, Lady Bird became a devoted, doting grandmother. The Johnson daughters produced a total of seven children between 1967 and 1978 and to them all, Bird was simply "Nini." She often said the best gift one can give is the gift of memory, and she made a point of lavishing extravagant trips on her "grands," the kind of travel that left precious memories but had not been on her calendar when her own daughters were young. Not a big spender before, she was now booking her grandchildren into the luxury hotels of Europe, setting a standard, Lynda Robb noted, that the children's parents would have trouble matching.

By the time she neared eighty, Lady Bird Johnson found it increasingly harder to reach her widow's shelf of deferred pleasures. Decreased energy, failing eyesight, and a succession of minor illnesses slowed her step. After leaving Washington, she had resumed driving herself, at least on local roads around the ranch. But that stopped one Sunday morning when her Secret Service detail observed her driving more erratically than they thought prudent. They insisted she leave the driving to them. For a woman who had owned her first car at thirteen and considered driving as natural as walking, it was a painful reminder of diminishing options.

In 1993, Bird had a small stroke, and it was obvious by that time she was losing her eyesight. When macular degeneration made reading difficult, she turned to audio books, including the Harry Potter series, so she could keep up with what young people were reading. But she still kept her bedroom bookshelves stocked with the printed versions—books on travel and gardening, autographed gifts from authors, biographies, and more than one first lady's story, including Eleanor's *On My Own*, and Joseph Lash's book about ER, *The Years Alone*.

More physical failings followed that first stroke and she received a pacemaker in 1998, underwent cataract surgery in 2001, and was hospitalized for repeated falls and various maladies. In 2002, the year that should have seen her jubilantly celebrate a ninetieth birthday, she suffered a devastating stroke that left her unable to walk and form intelligible words. It was, one of her trusted friends explained, a "mild stroke in a bad place." While Lady Bird retained full comprehension and delighted in hearing one of her great-grandchildren read from *Little House on the Prairie*, she could only smile and nod to signal her response. Full-time caretakers got better at deciphering her requests, and daughter Luci tried to translate her garbled phrases. But Bird found the loss of words extremely frustrating. At first she attempted speech therapy but then, her friends noted, she seemed to give up. She could still smother her great-grandchildren with hugs and kisses and beam proudly as one of them played a guitar for her, but the woman famous for saying "I love words" now had none left.

At the dinner table, where Bird still insisted on a single conversation at any one time, she was the first to laugh at jokes. Although she had to depend on others to order her food for her, she continued to frequent Austin restaurants, where bearded truck drivers, looking much like those who had once shouted Lyndon down, came up to thank her for what she had done for Texas. Across the nation, those who remembered her only as the wife of an unpopular president may still have disparaged her Southern drawl, but closer to home she qualified for sainthood, widely loved for her civility and for her environmental work.

Bird hoped to live until 2010, when her estate would no longer incur federal taxes, but she didn't make it. She died on July 11, 2007, at 2505 Camino Alto, and the Madrone tree in her yard expired soon after.

Her funeral service at Austin's mammoth Riverbend Centre (capacity five thousand) was an outpouring of love and admiration. Representatives of eight presidential families besides her own (Kennedy, Nixon, Ford, Carter, Reagan, Bush 41, Clinton, and Bush 43) filled the front rows, but the eulogies came, not from the notables, but from her female descendants and closest male friends.

Much of what they said centered on her solo, widowed years: Granddaughter Lucinda Robb Florio described her as "the least needy, quietly confident person" she had ever known; granddaughter Nicole Nugent Covert listed the ways the great-grandchildren remembered and loved her. Bill Moyers, in his eulogy, reached back to her earlier years when, during some of the nation's most tumultuous times, she remained a beacon of courage and civility. Harry Middleton emphasized she was a "whale of fun," with a sense of humor that made light of those who had dogged her earlier years. He related how, during the vacations he shared with Mrs. Johnson on Martha's Vineyard, she kept him busy, rushing from one party to another. One evening, midweek, as they made their way from a cocktail party to a dinner, she turned to him and said, "I don't know why I'm doing this." Then, she corrected herself: "Well, I do know. It's because I didn't say, 'Hell, no, I won't go.' "

At that funeral, Lyndon's name was barely mentioned.

ACKNOWLEDGMENTS

———◦◦◦———

D URING THE six years I have worked on this book my debts to
family, friends, and complete strangers have piled up. Mentioning some of them here is only token recognition of what I owe
them all.

When Lady Bird Johnson began planning for the LBJ Library in
1965, she visited the presidential libraries in operation at the time and
then vowed to outdo them all. Half a century later, her resolve still
shows in the expertise, dedication, and generosity of everyone who
works at the LBJ Library in Austin. While pursuing my research there,
funded in part by a Moody grant from the LBJ Foundation, I found
the staff extremely helpful. I benefitted especially from the counsel
of Claudia Anderson, formerly curator of Mrs. Johnson's papers, and
Barbara Cline, the current curator. Margaret Harman, in AV, guided
me through the library's huge collection of photographs and videos.
After I was thousands of miles away, the staff continued to answer my
many queries, and both Laura Eggert and Nicole Hadad cheerfully
supplied me with oral histories that I could read off-site.

Writing may be a lonely business, but I am fortunate to have the
continuing support of dozens of fellow biographers. The Women
Writing Women's Lives seminar and its small offshoot, the Narrative

Writing Group (currently consisting of Pat Auspos, Barbara Fisher, Ruth Franklin, Dorothy O. Helly, and Melissa Nathanson), have been central to my writing life for more than two decades. The Gotham Bio Group (Kate Buford, Ina Caro, Gayle Feldman, Anne Heller, Justin Martin, Carl Rollyson, Stacy Schiff, and Will Swift) formed just as I was starting this book, and I have learned a lot from these prolific biographers. Kate Buford and Will Swift, who read the entire manuscript, suggested additional lines of inquiry, and Will turned over to me his own extensive research on the Johnsons. Lewis L. Gould, presidential historian and author of two books on Mrs. Johnson, replied quickly to my every query and gave me a trove of research materials he had ferreted out, including copies of the court records of the divorce of T. J. and Minnie Taylor. Professor Gould then read and commented on an early version of the manuscript. Others who read portions of one draft or another and offered suggestions were: Evelyn Barish, Carol Cavallo, Jane Clancy, Robert E. Gilbert, Myra Gutin, Carol Hebald, Dona Munker, Nancy Kline, and Julie Pycior. Elizabeth Hansen carefully photographed for me Mrs. Johnson's unpublished diary when it became available just as I was ready to publish. On her own time, Ruth Briggs, a volunteer at the Harrison County Historical Society in Marshall, Texas, sleuthed out information on Mrs. Johnson's youth, including her high school essays and early photos.

Many people who knew the Johnsons or their milieu were still available for me to interview when I began this book in 2009, and I was able to confer with more than sixty of them. Some of those exchanges were brief telephone conversations; others were face-to-face interviews lasting an entire day. A few consisted entirely of emails. All were valuable. Bess Abell drove over icy roads to pick me up and take me back to her picturesque Merry-Go-Round Farm for lunch and a long talk; Sylvia Bishop interrupted her quilting at the Karnack Baptist Church social center to reminisce about the very young Lady Bird she knew in East Texas. Their firsthand accounts, along with the accounts of those whose names follow, were invaluable in understanding the relationship of Lady Bird and Lyndon Johnson, neither of whom I had the chance to meet: Christina Anderson, Bonnie Angelo, Pace Barnes, Victoria Barr, Gail Beil, Phillip Bobbitt, Ruth Briggs, Mary Acheson Bundy, Michael Bundy, Joseph Califano Jr., Christy Carpenter, Rosalynn Carter, Nash Castro, Patsy Derby Chaney, Ramsey Clark, Sheldon Cohen, Lou Hill Davidson, Thomas Donahue, Bill Fisher, Betty Sue Flowers, Sharon Francis, Michael L. Gillette, Helene Lindow Gordon, Lucianne Goldberg, Ashton Gonella, Libby Cater Halaby, Charles Haar, Coleen Hardin, Harvey Herbst, Olga Hirshhorn, Shirley James, Luci Baines Johnson, Edwina and Tom Johnson, Marjorie G. Jones, James Ketchum, Sally Newcomb MacDonald, Margaret McDermott, Harry McPherson, Marcia Maddox, Jewell Malechek Scott, Larry Temple, Harry Middleton, Betty Monkman, Celia B. Morris, Cokie Roberts, Clarissa Rowe, Jim Rowe, Mary Jane Saunders, Patsy Steves, Larry Temple, Helen Thomas, Betty Tilson, Mary Margaret Valenti, Alfred Vanderbilt, Heidi Vanderbilt, Jeanne Murray Vanderbilt, Cynthia Wilson, Jim Wilson, Mark Young, and two others who preferred to remain off the record.

I started this project with a huge advantage—access to thousands of printed pages in Robert Caro's four volumes, Robert Dallek's two volumes, and the books of John Bullion, Randall Woods, and Joseph Califano Jr. I was fortunate to be able to speak or exchange emails with all of these authors.

Susan Rabiner, my agent, has been an enthusiastic supporter and shrewd promoter since we first met more than thirty-five years ago, when she showed me the wisdom of writing about a subject I didn't want to tackle. She is tough and blunt, but her dedication to her authors is boundless, and she has helped shape this book from the very beginning. She led me to Priscilla Painton, who turned out to be the ideal editor for me at Simon & Schuster because she held back as I found my way through the huge archive on the Johnsons and then, with the expertise of a seasoned editor, kept prodding me and pointing the way to write the best book I could. The entire S&S team has been more supportive than I had any reason to expect. The enthusiasm of Vice President and Publisher Jonathan Karp spread to others. Editorial Assistant Sophia Jimenez carefully ushered *Lady Bird and Lyndon* through the intricacies of publishing in the digital age, and the thorough and diligent copyeditor, Fred Chase, saved me from many errors.

During my work on this and previous books, my Italian husband, a classical musician, has developed a greater interest in American history than either he or I anticipated. He has become adept at helping me sift through deed records in county courthouses, locate tombstones in overgrown cemeteries, and set up interviews on five continents. For all this and much, much more, I dedicate this book to Livio Caroli, whom I met entirely by chance on a Venice vaporetto a long time ago.

NOTES

---◎◉◎---

Abbreviations Used in the Notes

AWHD Lady Bird Johnson, *A White House Diary* (New York: Holt, Rinehart & Winston, 1970).

Courtship Letters *Dear Bird: The 1934 Courtship Letters*, LBJ Presidential Library, Austin Texas.

CTJ Claudia Taylor Johnson

HM LBJ Library Video, Lady Bird Johnson's Home Movies.

LBJ Lyndon Baines Johnson

RTCM Recordings and Transcripts of Conversations and Meetings, LBJ Presidential Library, Austin, Texas.

WHD Lady Bird Johnson, White House Diary, LBJ Presidential Library, Austin, Texas.

Prologue

2 *"neglected"*: WHD, January 5, 1965, Box 2.
2 *"regal"* . . . *"all the way"*: *AWHD*, pp. 599–600.
3 *"magic"* . . . *"Pied Piper"*: WHD, April 15, 1964, Box 1.
3 *"looked just like my nose looks"*: WHD, February 17, 1967, Box 4.
3 *"firm and clear"* . . . *"Her mother and I"*: *AWHD*, p. 600.
4 *"pure hell"*: Michael Beschloss, *Reaching for Glory: Lyndon Johnson's Secret White House Tapes, 1964–1965* (New York: Simon & Schuster, 2001), p. 426.
4 *"vast array of cameras"*: WHD, December 9, 1967, Box 5.
5 *"a swirl"* . . . *"awful purple dress"*: WHD, December 9, 1967, Box 5.
5 *"most satisfying"*: WHD, December 10, 1967, Box 5.

1: Bird Learns to Fly

7 *"How did you handle your flirt and ladies' man husband"*: Barbara Walters interviewed Lady Bird Johnson on NBC's *Today* show; quotes are taken from *The New York Times* article on the interview, February 21, 1974, p. 21.

8 *"T. J. Taylor owns everything"*: Karnack resident Sylvia Wisdom Bishop to author, March 16, 2011.

9 *"stressful"*: Jan Jarboe Russell, *Lady Bird: A Biography of Mrs. Johnson* (New York: Scribner, 1999), p. 31.

9 *"the meanest man in Autauga County"*: Randall B. Woods, *LBJ: Architect of American Ambition* (New York: Free Press, 2006), p. 92.

11 *"white trash"*: Russell, *Lady Bird*, p. 36.

12 *"two thousand miles"*: *Taylor v. Taylor*, Divorce papers, Harrison County Courthouse, Marshall, Texas.

13 *"5 weeks"*: Ibid.

13 *"nervous trouble"* . . . *"quiet country home"*: Ibid.

13 *"valuable . . . real and personal property"*: Ibid.

14 *"judgment by default"*: Ibid.

15 *"deemed more respectable to assign credit to the nurse"*: Michael L. Gillette, *Lady Bird Johnson: An Oral History* (New York: Oxford University Press, 2012), p. 8. This was told to Gillette in private and does not appear in Mrs. Johnson's oral histories, which are online.

15 *"wacky"*: WHD, August 19, 1965, Box 3.

16 *"slacker"*: Same term used by two different sources in describing what Minnie Taylor said: Transcript, Dorris (Mrs. Hugh) Powell, Oral History Interview II, April 18, 1978, by Michael L. Gillette, Internet Copy, LBJ Library, p. 7. Transcript, Eugenia Boehringer Lasseter, Oral History Interview I, March 10, 1981, by Michael L. Gillette, Internet Copy, LBJ Library, p. 3.

17 *"I've been with a black woman"*: Woods, *LBJ*, p. 93.

17 *"pushed her down"*: Ibid., p. 94.

19 *"the will of God"*: Gillette, *Lady Bird Johnson*, p. 18. This phrase also appears in the Charles Guggenheim documentary film, *A Life: The Story of Lady Bird Johnson* (directed by Charles Guggenheim, produced by Guggenheim Productions, Washington, D.C., 1992).

20 *"my daily companion"*: *Lady Bird, Naturally*, a documentary, produced by KLRN, San Antonio, Texas, 2001, and available from Lady Bird Johnson Wildflower Center.

21 *"It did not come with the genes"*: Lynda Johnson Robb, speaking at First Lady Conference, Grand Rapids, Michigan, April 20, 1984.

21 *"passive"* . . . *"sights on being more like my father"*: Merle Miller, *Lyndon: An Oral Biography* (New York, G. P. Putnam's Sons, 1970), p. 51.

22 *"wouldn't share an account with the Angel Gabriel"*: Bess Abell to author, December 16, 2010.

23 *"had resources most people don't have"*: James Ketchum to author, April 14, 2011.

23 *"veil"* . . . *"Southern thing"*: Sally Newcomb MacDonald to author, March 31, 2012.

23 *"She put on her mask and let the world go by":* Harry Middleton to author, June 7, 2010.

23 *"psychic leave":* Doris Kearns Goodwin, *Lyndon Johnson and the American Dream* (New York: St. Martin's, 1991), pp. 83–84. This second edition has a new foreword; the original was published under the author's maiden name, Doris Kearns, in 1976.

24 *"She had her own car":* Sylvia Wisdom Bishop to author, March 16, 2011.

24 *"Yes, in a coarse and crude sort of way":* Russell, *Lady Bird*, p. 63.

25 *"because of sympathy":* Copy of Claudia Taylor's high school essay, in the Collections of the Harrison County Historical Museum, Marshall, Texas, supplied to the author by Ruth Briggs and quoted by permission of Janet Cook.

26 *"Don't just say 'a man is cruel'":* Harry Middleton, *A Life Well Lived* (Austin: Lyndon Baines Johnson Foundation, 1992), p. 59.

27 *"I loved the theater":* Transcript, Claudia "Lady Bird" Johnson, Oral History Interview XXXVII, Internet Copy, LBJ Library, p. 10. Also in Gillette, *Lady Bird Johnson*, p. 253.

27 *"the most exciting ride of my young life":* Russell, *Lady Bird*, p. 60.

2: Mama's Boy

29 *"Then I came along":* Doris Kearns Goodwin, *Lyndon Johnson and the American Dream* (New York: St. Martin's, 1991), p. 22.

29 *"I'd Rather Be Mama's Boy":* Alfred Steinberg, *Sam Johnson's Boy* (New York: Macmillan, 1968), p. 15.

29 *"In the rambling old farm house":* Rebekah Baines Johnson, *A Family Album* (New York: McGraw-Hill, 1965), p. 17. This is a published version of the family history Rebekah Johnson put together for Lyndon at Christmas 1954.

30 *"dominant force":* Ibid., p. 29.

30 *"call me lucky":* Ibid., p. 28.

31 *"think and to endure":* Ibid.

31 *"severe and sudden financial reverses":* Ibid., p. 29.

33 *"Red Warriors":* Ibid., pp. 74–75.

33 *"personable young man":* Ibid., p. 24.

33 *"a girl who really liked politics":* Ibid., p. 30.

34 *"We didn't really know about it at the time":* Transcript, Josefa Baines Saunders, Oral History Interview I, December 28, 1964, by Juanita Roberts, Internet Copy, LBJ Library, p. 2.

34 *"shuddered over the chickens":* Rebekah Baines Johnson, *A Family Album*, p. 30.

34 *"rambling farmhouse":* Ibid., p. 17.

35 *"Lyndon may have been born in a log cabin":* Harvey Herbst to author, October 6, 2011.

35 *"Dr. John Blunton of Buda":* Rebekah Baines Johnson, *A Family Album*, p. 17.

35 *"extremely beautiful woman" . . . "embarrassed and ashamed":* Transcript, Virginia Foster Durr, Oral History Interview I, by Mary Walton Livingston, October 17, 1967, Internet Copy, LBJ Library, pp. 12–13.

37 *"typical manic's career"*: D. Jablow Hershman, *Power Beyond Reason: The Mental Collapse of Lyndon Johnson* (Fort Lee, NJ: Barricade, 2002), p. 22.

39 *"laughable"*: Ronnie Dugger, *The Politician: The Life and Times of Lyndon Johnson* (New York: W. W. Norton, 1982), p. 89.

40 *"always bossy"*: WHD, December 12, 1966, Box 4.

43 *"May the Lord keep Watch"*: Transcript, Juanita Roberts, Oral History Interview I, April 28, 1965, by Eric F. Goldman, Internet Copy, LBJ Library, p. 13.

46 *"the man who started the fire under me"*: Robert Dallek, *Lone Star Rising*, p. 72.

3: Getting Out of Karnack, with the Right Man

50 *"Well, let's hope we did"*: Transcript, Sharon Francis, Oral History Interview III, June 27, 1969, by Dorothy Pierce McSweeney, Internet Copy, LBJ Library, p. 35.

52 *"magic place"*: PBS documentary, *Lady Bird Johnson*, produced by MacNeil/Lehrer Productions and KLRU, Austin, 2001, Transcript, Part I.

53 *"a romantic newspaperman"*: Transcript, Claudia "Lady Bird" Johnson, Oral History Interview III, August 14, 1977, by Michael L. Gillette, Internet Copy, LBJ Library, p. 14. Also in Michael L. Gillette, *Lady Bird Johnson: An Oral History* (New York: Oxford University Press, 2012), p. 34.

54 *"Navajo parties"*: Jan Jarboe Russell, *Lady Bird: A Biography of Mrs. Johnson* (New York: Scribner, 1999), p. 80.

54 *"never amount to anything"*: Transcript, Emily Crow Selden, Oral History Interview, January 10, 1980, by Michael L. Gillette, Internet Copy, LBJ Library, p. 11.

54 *"That one's not for you"*: Transcript, Claudia "Lady Bird" Johnson, Oral History Interview III, August 14, 1977, by Michael L. Gillette, Internet Copy, LBJ Library, p. 40. Also in Gillette, *Lady Bird Johnson*, p. 42.

55 *"oil men"* . . . *"Casino de Paree"*: Courtship Letters, Lady Bird Taylor to Lyndon Johnson, September 20, 1934.

56 *"lady friends"* . . . *"his domestic life"*: Transcript, Claudia "Lady Bird" Johnson, Oral History Interview IV, February 4, 1978, by Michael L. Gillette, Internet Copy, LBJ Library, p. 13. Also in Gillette, *Lady Bird Johnson*, p. 49.

56 *"the gentlest of men"*: Inscription on T. J. Taylor's gravestone, Algoma Cemetery, Marshall, Texas.

57 *"forget we've got him"*: Courtship Letters, Lady Bird Taylor to Lyndon Johnson, September 30, 1934.

58 *"stem-winding, arm-swinging speech"*: Transcript, Welly K. Hopkins, Oral History Interview I, May 11, 1965, by Eric F. Goldman, Internet Copy, LBJ Library, p. 4.

59 *"That's one of the most brilliant men"*: Transcript, Sam Fore, Dan Quill, Oliver Bruck, and William S. White, Oral History Interview I, January 20, 1965, by Douglass Cater, Internet Copy, LBJ Library, p. 1.

59 *"children"*: Transcript, Estelle Harbin, Oral History Interview, November 10, 1977, by Michael L. Gillette, Internet Copy, LBJ Library, p. 16.

60 *"charm":* Ibid., p. 25.

60 *"he had something":* Transcript, Sam Fore, Dan Quill, Oliver Bruck, and William S. White, Oral History Interview I, January 20, 1965, by Douglass Cater, Internet Copy, LBJ Library, p. 26.

60 *"didn't know what he wanted to be":* Robert A. Caro, *The Path to Power* (New York: Alfred A. Knopf, 1982), p. 229.

61 *"came on strong":* Transcript, Claudia "Lady Bird" Johnson, Oral History Interview IV, February 4, 1978, by Michael L. Gillette, Internet Copy, LBJ Library, p. 19. Also in Gillette, *Lady Bird Johnson,* p. 51.

61 *"the moth in the flame":* Transcript, Claudia "Lady Bird" Johnson, Oral History Interview IV, February 4, 1978, by Michael L. Gillette, Internet Copy, LBJ Library, p. 21. Also in Gillette, *Lady Bird Johnson*, p. 52.

62 *"best side":* Transcript, Claudia "Lady Bird" Johnson, Oral History Interview IV, February 4, 1978, by Michael L. Gillette, Internet Copy, LBJ Library, p. 20. Also in Gillette, *Lady Bird Johnson*, p. 52.

62 *"very much a gentlewoman":* Transcript, Claudia "Lady Bird" Johnson, Oral History Interview IV, February 4, 1978, by Michael L. Gillette, Internet Copy, LBJ Library, p. 22. Also in Gillette, *Lady Bird Johnson*, p. 53.

63 *"an eagerness about his face":* Transcript, Cecille Harrison Marshall, Oral History Interview I, February 19, 1976, by Michael L. Gillette, Internet Copy, LBJ Library, p. 13.

63 *"mule":* Transcript, Claudia "Lady Bird" Johnson, Oral History Interview XX, February 20–21, 1981, by Michael L. Gillette, Internet Copy, LBJ Library, p. 35. Also in Gillette, *Lady Bird Johnson*, p. 189.

63 *"rather overpowering"* . . . *"aging duchess":* Transcript, Claudia "Lady Bird" Johnson, Oral History Interview IV, February 4, 1978, by Michael L. Gillette, Internet Copy, LBJ Library, p. 25. Also in Gillette, *Lady Bird Johnson,* p. 54.

64 *"You've brought home a lot of boys":* Notes to CTJ interview with Ruth Montgomery, July 3, 1963, p. 14, in Lewis Gould Papers, Box 1, at LBJ Library. Also in Gillette, *Lady Bird Johnson*, p. 55.

4: More than "Electric Going"

65 *"so rich":* WHD, August 24, 1965, Box 3.

65 *"very close": AWHD*, p. 604.

66 *"the excitement of Lyndon mounting"* . . . *"one of the strangest, most off- key": AWHD*, p. 605.

68 *"hard"* . . . *"how satisfying and gratifying":* Courtship Letters, Lyndon Johnson to Lady Bird Taylor, September 11, 1934.

69 *"indifference":* Courtship Letters, Lyndon Johnson to Lady Bird Taylor, September 15, 1934.

69 *"definitely just how and where you stand":* Courtship Letters, Lyndon Johnson to Lady Bird Taylor, September 15, 1934.

69 *"Nobody in Marshall knows":* Courtship Letters, Lady Bird Taylor to Lyndon Johnson, September 17, 1934.

70 *"electric going":* Michael L. Gillette, *Lady Bird Johnson: An Oral History* (New York: Oxford University Press, 2012), p. 50.

70 *"simple things":* Courtship Letters, Lady Bird Taylor to Lyndon Johnson, September 13, 1934.

70 *"blue and depressed":* Courtship Letters, Lyndon Johnson to Lady Bird Taylor, September 29, 1934.

70 *"own perseverance":* Courtship Letters, Lyndon Johnson to Lady Bird Taylor, September 30, 1934.

70 *"moodiness":* Courtship Letters, Lyndon Johnson to Lady Bird Taylor, September 30, 1934.

70 *"always feeling blue":* Courtship Letters, Lyndon Johnson to Lady Bird Taylor, October 2, 1934.

70 *"never sure, never contented"* . . . *"Again I repeat":* Courtship Letters, Lyndon Johnson to Lady Bird Taylor, September 23, 1934.

70 *"who loved me":* Courtship Letters, Lyndon Johnson to Lady Bird Taylor, November 8, 1934.

70 *"to nurse me":* Courtship Letters, Lyndon Johnson to Lady Bird Taylor, October 10, 1934.

70 *"help me to climb":* Courtship Letters, Lyndon Johnson to Lady Bird Taylor, September 26, 1934.

70 *"Mix some 'I love you' in the lines":* Courtship Letters, Lyndon Johnson to Lady Bird Taylor, September 23, 1934.

71 *"right this minute I'd rather see you":* Courtship Letters, Lady Bird Taylor to Lyndon Johnson, September 21, 1934.

71 *"best letter you have written":* Courtship Letters, Lyndon Johnson to Lady Bird Taylor, September 26, 1934.

71 *"one by one"* . . . *"new hope, new interest"* . . . *"just thrilled"* . . . *"to death":* Courtship Letters, Lyndon Johnson to Lady Bird Taylor, September 26, 1934.

71 *"real"* . . . *"inward feelings 'silly,'"* . . . *"depressed":* Courtship Letters, Lady Bird Taylor to Lyndon Johnson, October 11, 1934.

71 *"too sentimental":* Courtship Letters, Lyndon Johnson to Lady Bird Taylor, October 14, 1934.

71 *"For weeks I've only half heartedly done anything":* Courtship Letters, Lady Bird Taylor quotes Lyndon in her letter to him, October 19, 1934.

71 *"Stop it, dear!":* Courtship Letters, Lady Bird Taylor to Lyndon Johnson, October 19, 1934.

72 *"I'm very unhappy tonight":* Courtship Letters, Lyndon Johnson to Lady Bird Taylor, October 19, 1934.

72 *"four or five years":* Courtship Letters, Lyndon Johnson to Lady Bird Taylor, October 20, 1934.

72 *"dear Bird":* Courtship Letters, Lyndon Johnson to Lady Bird Taylor, October 23, 1934.

72 *"No, honey":* Courtship Letters, Lyndon Johnson to Lady Bird Taylor, October 27, 1934.

72 *"sick little man":* Courtship Letters, Lyndon Johnson to Lady Bird Taylor, October 10, 1934.

73 *"real friends":* Courtship Letters, Lyndon Johnson to Lady Bird Taylor, October 5, 1934.

73 *"something awful might happen to us"* . . . *"forsaken"* . . . *"one thing I won't do":* Courtship Letters, Lady Bird Taylor to Lyndon Johnson, October 18, 1934.

73 *"I simply will not let it":* Courtship Letters, Lady Bird Taylor to Lyndon Johnson, October 4, 1934.

73 *"I think its [sic] plain silly":* Courtship Letters, Lady Bird Taylor to Lyndon Johnson, September 24, 1934.

73 *"my little radio writer":* Courtship Letters, Lyndon Johnson to Lady Bird Taylor, September 29, 1934.

73 *"sharpened [Lyndon] up":* Gillette, *Lady Bird Johnson,* p. 68.

74 *"I love you [but] I don't know":* Courtship Letters, Lady Bird Taylor to Lyndon Johnson, September 26, 1934.

74 *"Darling, don't you see":* Courtship Letters, Lady Bird Taylor to Lyndon Johnson, October 17, 1934.

74 *"poor lamb"* . . . *"Whenever do you play?":* Courtship Letters, Lady Bird Taylor to Lyndon Johnson, September 17, 1934.

74 *"hundred kisses":* Courtship Letters, Lady Bird Taylor to Lyndon Johnson, September 26, 1934.

74 *"Why you are all my laughter and my light":* Ibid.

74 *"gay life beyond the 'provinces'"* . . . *"very happy, nor content":* Courtship Letters, Lady Bird Taylor to Lyndon Johnson, September 27, 1934.

74 *"so cosmopolitan":* Courtship Letters, Lady Bird Taylor to Lyndon Johnson, September 20, 1934.

75 *"richest, raciest conversations"* . . . *"about what we're going to plant":* Ibid.

75 *"I don't want to wait":* Courtship Letters, Lyndon Johnson to Lady Bird Taylor, September 27, 1934.

75 *"Better than [on] a birthday":* Courtship Letters, Lady Bird Taylor to Lyndon Johnson, October 9, 1934.

75 *"creditable":* Courtship Letters, Lady Bird Taylor to Lyndon Johnson, October 10, 1934.

75 *"there are so many Crows":* Courtship Letters, Lady Bird Taylor to Lyndon Johnson, October 13, 1934.

76 *"so of course":* Courtship Letters, Lady Bird Taylor to Lyndon Johnson, October 16, 1934.

76 *"so terribly close!":* Ibid.

76 *"go traveling around a few months":* Courtship Letters, Lady Bird Taylor to Lyndon Johnson, October 17, 1934.

76 *"frightens me":* Ibid.

76 *"from caring deeply about people or things suddenly":* Ibid.

76 *"New York [job] offer":* Courtship Letters, Lady Bird Taylor to Lyndon Johnson, October 19, 1934.

77 *"Lyndon, please tell me as soon as you can":* Courtship Letters, Lady Bird Taylor to Lyndon Johnson, October 22, 1934, No. 2.

77 *"outcome":* Courtship Letters, Lyndon Johnson to Lady Bird Taylor, October 21, 1934.

77   *"I've an awful inferiority complex":* Courtship Letters, Lady Bird Taylor to Lyndon Johnson, October 6, 1934.

77   *"shirt sleeves with your arms on the desk":* Courtship Letters, Lady Bird Taylor to Lyndon Johnson, October 10, 1934. This photo is on the LBJ Library website with the Courtship Letters.

77   *"And you do look very arrogant there!"* . . . *"proud, sure look out of your eyes":* Courtship Letters, Lady Bird Taylor to Lyndon Johnson, October 21, 1934.

77   *"special delivery":* Courtship Letters, Lady Bird Taylor to Lyndon Johnson, October 8, 1934.

78   *"dreadful":* Courtship Letters, Lady Bird Taylor to Lyndon Johnson, October 17, 1934, No. 2.

78   *"If you don't love me enough now, you never will":* Transcript, Claudia "Lady Bird" Johnson, Oral History Interview V, April 1, 1978, by Michael L. Gillette, Internet Copy, LBJ Library, p. 8. Also in Gillette, *Lady Bird Johnson*, p. 58.

78   *"slow, considered sort of person":* Transcript, Claudia "Lady Bird" Johnson, Oral History Interview IV, February 4, 1978, by Michael L. Gillette, Internet Copy, LBJ Library, p. 19. Also in Gillette, *Lady Bird Johnson*, p. 51.

78   *"hate":* Courtship Letters, Lady Bird Taylor to Lyndon Johnson, November 8 or 9, 1934. (On Hotel Monteleone stationery, New Orleans.)

79   *"want":* Courtship Letters, Lady Bird Taylor to Lyndon Johnson, November 11, 1934.

79   *"break"* . . . *"both mentally and physically":* Ibid.

79   *"I want to rush on home"* . . . *"be gay":* Courtship Letters, Lady Bird Taylor to Lyndon Johnson, November 13, 1934.

80   *"beautiful negligee":* Transcript, Claudia "Lady Bird" Johnson, Oral History Interview V, April 1, 1978, by Michael L. Gillette, Internet Copy, LBJ Library, p. 11. Also in Gillette, *Lady Bird Johnson,* p. 60.

80   *"Fix everything":* Transcript, Daniel Quill, Oral History Interview, May 10, 1965, by Eric Goldman, Internet Copy, LBJ Library, p. 4.

81   *"mile a minute":* Transcript, Cecille Harrison Marshall, Oral History Interview I, February 19, 1976, by Michael L. Gillette, Internet Copy, LBJ Library, p. 14.

82   *"four or five bottles of sparkling burgundy":* Transcript, Henry Hirshberg, Oral History Interview, October 17, 1968, by Dorothy Pierce, Internet Copy, LBJ Library, pp. 8–9.

82   *"Lyndon and I committed matrimony last night":* Transcript, Eugenia Boehringer Lasseter, Oral History Interview I, March 10, 1981, by Michael L. Gillette, Internet Copy, LBJ Library, p. 11.

82   *"Bird Taylor":* Marriage certificate is online with Courtship Letters, LBJ Library.

82   *"Claudia Bird":* Announcement of marriage, in Reference File of Lady Bird Johnson, folder on Marriage, LBJ Library.

82   *"as long as our money lasted":* Transcript, Claudia "Lady Bird" Johnson, Oral History Interview V, April 1, 1978, by Michael L. Gillette, Internet Copy, LBJ Library, p. 16. Also in Gillette, *Lady Bird Johnson*, p. 62.

83   *"loads of flowers":* Transcript, Claudia "Lady Bird" Johnson, Oral History Inter-

view V, April 1, 1978, by Michael L. Gillette, Internet Copy, LBJ Library, p. 18. Also in Gillette, *Lady Bird Johnson*, p. 62.

83 *"protective tariffs"* . . . *"increasing paternalism of our government"* . . . *"Do you like to argue"*: Courtship Letters, Lady Bird Taylor to Lyndon Johnson, October 4, 1934, No. 2.

84 *"best secretary that a congressman ever had"*: Transcript, Claudia "Lady Bird" Johnson, Oral History Interview V, April 1, 1978, by Michael L. Gillette, Internet Copy, LBJ Library, p. 5. Also in Gillette, *Lady Bird Johnson*, p. 68.

5: Becoming a Priceless Political Partner

85 *"go to hell"* . . . *"Just remember"*: Transcript, Claudia "Lady Bird" Johnson, Oral History Interview IX, January 24, 1979, by Michael L. Gillette, Internet Copy, LBJ Library, p. 8.

86 *"ass"*: Transcript, Ervin "Red" James, Oral History Interview, February 17, 1978, by Michael L. Gillette, Internet Copy, LBJ Library, p. 39.

86 *"next to death's door"*: Transcript, W. Sherman Birdwell Jr., Oral History Interview IV, February 15, 1979, by Michael L. Gillette, Internet Copy, LBJ Library, p. 17.

87 *"Cut out the damn noise"*: Transcript, W. Ervin "Red" James, Oral History Interview, February 17, 1978, by Michael L. Gillette, Internet Copy, LBJ Library, p. 16.

89 *"sheer heaven"*: Transcript, Claudia "Lady Bird" Johnson, Oral History Interview VI, August 6, 1978, by Michael L. Gillette, Internet Copy, LBJ Library, p. 10. Also in Michael L. Gillette, *Lady Bird Johnson: An Oral History* (New York: Oxford University Press, 2012), p. 69.

89 *"romantic and charming"*: Transcript, Claudia "Lady Bird" Johnson, Oral History Interview VI, August 6, 1978, by Michael L. Gillette, Internet Copy, LBJ Library, p. 14. Gillette, *Lady Bird Johnson*, p. 70, has a slightly different version of her description of the house. Here she is quoted as saying that it was "thoroughly romantic, and I was utterly charmed by it."

89 *"dull little place"*: Transcript, Claudia "Lady Bird" Johnson, Oral History Interview VI, August 6, 1978, by Michael L. Gillette, Internet Copy, LBJ Library, p. 42. Also in Gillette, *Lady Bird Johnson*, p. 74, where she says they rented it for five years.

92 *"adviser . . . brain trust"*: Transcript, Claudia "Lady Bird" Johnson, Oral History Interview VI, August 6, 1978, by Michael L. Gillette, Internet Copy, LBJ Library, pp. 11, 42. CTJ calls Wirtz their "brain trust" on p. 42. First part of quote is also in Gillette, *Lady Bird Johnson*, p. 74.

92 *"We have to have ten"*: Transcript, Claudia "Lady Bird" Johnson, Oral History Interview VI, August 6, 1978, by Michael L. Gillette, Internet Copy, LBJ Library, p. 37. Also in Gillette, *Lady Bird Johnson*, p. 75.

93 *"Mrs. Johnson, you're going to have to make up your mind"*: Transcript, Claude C. Wild Sr., Oral History Interview, October 3, 1968, by David G. McComb, Internet Copy, LBJ Library, p. 6.

93   *"quite young"*: Ibid.

93   *"did not want women in politics"*: Transcript, Claudia "Lady Bird" Johnson, Oral History Interview VI, August 6, 1978, by Michael L. Gillette, Internet Copy, LBJ Library, p. 44.

94   *"spoke first, last and the loudest"*: Dallek, *Lone Star Rising*, p. 150.

95   *"with anything you can"*: Ibid., p. 161.

97   *"ask questions"*: Bill Moyers's eulogy at funeral service of Mrs. Johnson, July 14, 2007. Access at www.c-span.org/video/?199909-1/lady-bird-johnson -funeral-service.

98   *"listened to me"*: For her account of how she infiltrated, see Transcript, Claudia "Lady Bird" Johnson, Oral History Interview XIX, February 6–7, 1981, by Michael L. Gillette, Internet Copy, LBJ Library, pp. 47–48. The phrase "listened to me" is in PBS documentary, *Lady Bird Johnson*, produced by Mac-Neil/Lehrer Productions and KLRU, Austin, 2001, Transcript, Part 3.

98   *"nights of elation"*: Transcript, Claudia "Lady Bird" Johnson, Oral History Interview X, January 25–26, 1979, by Michael L. Gillette, Internet Copy, LBJ Library, p. 1.

99   *"very stimulating"*: Transcript, Claudia "Lady Bird" Johnson, Oral History Interview XI, January 27–28, 1979, by Michael L. Gillette, Internet Copy, LBJ Library, p. 10.

100   *"Remember that I am for you"*: Dallek, *Lone Star Rising*, p. 176.

100   *"free ride"*: Transcript, Claudia "Lady Bird" Johnson, Oral History Interview IX, January 24, 1979, by Michael L. Gillette, Internet Copy, LBJ Library, p. 8.

100   *"I never saw anything like it"*: Merle Miller, *Lyndon: An Oral Biography* (New York: G. P. Putnam's Sons, 1980), p. 74.

101   *"few times in my life"*: Transcript, Claudia "Lady Bird" Johnson, Oral History Interview X, January 25–26, 1979, by Michael L. Gillette, Internet Copy, LBJ Library, p. 15.

6: Network Builder

103   *"so enthusiastic and sweet"*: WHD, August 1, 1967, Box 5.

104   *"Things are Happening"*: Courtship Letters, Lady Bird Taylor to Lyndon Johnson, September 27, 1934.

104   *"beyond the provinces"* . . . *"life with a Capital L"*: Courtship Letters, Lady Bird Taylor to Lyndon Johnson, September 20, 1934, and September 27, 1934.

105   *"go crazy"*: Virginia Foster Durr, *Outside the Magic Circle: The Autobiography of Virginia Foster Durr*, ed. Hollinger F. Barnard (Tuscaloosa: University of Alabama Press, 1985). A note at the beginning by Studs Terkel quotes Virginia Durr as saying a Southern white woman brought up in good circumstances has three choices: act the genteel lady, go crazy, or rebel and leave.

105   *"loved . . . trips"*: Transcript, Claudia "Lady Bird" Johnson, Oral History Interview X, January 25–26, 1979, by Michael L. Gillette, Internet Copy, LBJ Library, p. 2.

106   *"social-economic bent"*: Miller, *Lyndon*, p. 64.

107   *"were the people who were going to do it"*: Ibid.

107   *"You didn't bother much about the food"*: Transcript, Claudia "Lady Bird" Johnson, Oral History Interview X, January 25–26, 1979, by Michael L. Gillette, Internet Copy, LBJ Library, p. 2.

107   *"I like mules"*: Transcript, Clifford and Virginia Durr, Oral History Interview, March 1, 1975, by Michael L. Gillette, Internet Copy, LBJ Library, p. 9.

108   *"Father of Social Security"*: Wilbur J. Cohen, "E. E. Witte (1887–1960): Father of Social Security," *Industrial and Labor Relations Review* 14, no. 1 (October 1960), p. 7.

109   *"Carol, with her cigar"*: WHD, January 24, 1964, Box 1.

109   *"narrow little staircases"*: Transcript, Claudia "Lady Bird" Johnson, Oral History Interview IX, January 24, 1979, by Michael L. Gillette, Internet Copy, LBJ Library, p. 16. Also in Gillette, *Lady Bird Johnson*, p. 91.

109   *"Dark didn't catch us"*: Transcript, Claudia "Lady Bird" Johnson, Oral History Interview VIII, January 23, 1979, by Michael L. Gillette, Internet Copy, LBJ Library, p. 15. Also in Gillette, *Lady Bird Johnson*, p. 99.

112   *"I was happily provincial"*: Transcript, Claudia "Lady Bird" Johnson, Oral History Interview VIII, January 23, 1979, by Michael L. Gillette, Internet Copy, LBJ Library, p. 21.

113   *"foggiest notion"* . . . *"with the kind of energy"* . . . *"to feed the pigs"*: Transcript, Erich Leinsdorf, Oral History Interview, March 18, 1969, by Joe B. Frantz, Internet Copy, LBJ Library, p. 2.

113   *"fascinating characters of the New Deal"*: Transcript, Claudia "Lady Bird" Johnson, Oral History Interview X, January 25–26, 1979, by Michael L. Gillette, Internet Copy, LBJ Library, pp. 1–2.

114   *"remarkably durable"*: *AWHD*, p. 486.

114   *"most undeviating liberal voice"*. . . *"his retirement last week"*: *Time*, November 24, 1975.

114   *"there's only 86 pounds of her"*: WHD, January 24, 1964, Box 1.

117   *"I saw a young man"*: Robert A. Caro, *The Path to Power* (New York: Alfred A. Knopf, 1982), p. 477.

117   *"invented"*: Dorothy Lane, "The Alice Glass Story," in Student Papers of Professor Lewis Gould, LBJ Library. Lane also wrote the entry for Alice Glass Kirkpatrick for *The Handbook of Texas*, published by the Texas State Historical Association, but there she omitted the reference to Manners but names the other husbands. According to Lane, Glass married Richard J. Kirkpatrick in 1959, and he died in 1974, but she continued to use the name Alice Kirkpatrick until her death in 1976. Accessed August 31, 2013, www.tshaonline.org/handbook/online/articles/fki55.

118   *"velvet warmth"*: Transcript, Claudia "Lady Bird" Johnson, Oral History Interview XX, February 20–21, 1981, by Michael L. Gillette, Internet Copy, LBJ Library, p. 16.

120   *"I just go along with Mr. George"*: Anne Morrow Lindbergh, "As I See Our First Lady," *Look*, May 19, 1964, p. 105.

120   *"Pappy O'Daniel"*: LBJ Library Video, Lady Bird Johnson's Home Movies, HM3, Senate Campaign, 1941.

121 *"living among people"*: Transcript, Claudia "Lady Bird" Johnson, Oral History Interview XIII, September 2–3, 1979, by Michael L. Gillete, Internet Copy, LBJ Library, p. 18. Also in Gillette, *Lady Bird Johnson*, p. 118.

121 *"It was all right we lost"*: LBJ Library Video, Lady Bird Johnson's Home Movies, HM3, Senate Campaign 1941.

121 *"in the right place at the right time"*: Ibid.

121 *"Lyndon Johnson's wife"*: Jonathan Daniels, *White House Witness, 1942–45* (New York: Doubleday, 1975), p. 58.

7: CEO and Finance Manager

125 *"It may take everything we have"* . . . *"Well, it's your money"*: Transcript, Leonard Marks, Oral History Interview I, June 15, 1970, by Joe B. Frantz, Internet Copy, LBJ Library, p. 3.

126 *"for medicine"*: Pre-Presidential Papers of LBJ, Folder on Public Activities—Biographical Information—Navy, January 18, 1942, LBJ Library, Box 74.

127 *"I am working without pay in the office"* . . . *"awful bald and ugly"* . . . *"I'm contributing my time"*: Transcript, Claudia "Lady Bird" Johnson, Oral History Interview XVI, January 29–February 3, 1980, by Michael L. Gillette, Internet Copy, LBJ Library, p. 3. A slightly different version of her point about her volunteer status appears in Michael L. Gillette, *Lady Bird Johnson: An Oral History* (New York: Oxford University Press, 2012), p. 126.

127 *"substance [of my life], the real thing"*: Transcript, Claudia "Lady Bird" Johnson, Oral History Interview XVI, January 29–February 3, 1980, by Michael L. Gillette, Internet Copy, LBJ Library, p. 1.

127 *"full time job now"*: Lady Bird Johnson to Miss Ella Powell, Marshall, Texas, April 13, 1942, Pre-Presidential Papers of LBJ, LBJ Library, Box 74.

129 *"I get right ashamed"*: Letter, "Ray [of the Austin Post Office]" to Lyndon Johnson, March 24, 1942, Pre-Presidential Papers of LBJ, House of Representatives, 1937–49, LBJ Library, Box 37.

130 *"We rely on a net-work of friends"*: Lady Bird Johnson to Miss Ella Powell, Marshall, Texas, April 13, 1942, Pre-Presidential Papers of LBJ, LBJ Library, Box 74.

131 *"mortified and embarrassed"*: Lady Bird Johnson to Charles Green, editor of the *Austin American-Statesman*, April 13, 1942, Pre-Presidential Papers of LBJ, House of Representatives, 1937–49, LBJ Library, Box 37.

131 *"I wish you'd drop me a line"*: Lady Bird Johnson to Buck Hood, February 26, 1942, Pre-Presidential Papers of LBJ, House of Representatives, 1937–49, LBJ Library, Box 37.

131 *"mission for the President"*: Lady Bird Johnson to M. H. Reed. March 16, 1942, Pre-Presidential Papers of LBJ, LBJ Library, Box 74.

131 *"serving his country"* . . . *"besides [it's] untrue"*: Ibid.

131 *"a little bit too close"*: Transcript, Claudia "Lady Bird" Johnson, Oral History Interview XVI, January 29–February 3, 1980, by Michael L. Gillette, Internet Copy, LBJ Library, p. 9.

133 *"bang-up job"*: J. J. "Jake" Pickle to Chief [LBJ], May 3, 1942, Pre-Presidential Papers of LBJ, House of Representatives, 1937–49, LBJ Library, Box 37.

134 *"hold down a job"*: PBS documentary, *Lady Bird Johnson*, produced by MacNeil/ Lehrer Productions and KLRU, Austin, 2001, Transcript, Part 2.

134 *"I want that house"*: John Connally, *In History's Shadow: An American Odyssey* (New York: Hyperion, 1993), p. 71, gives a slightly different version of Bird's outburst and tells how Connally replied to LBJ.

135 *"I'm not much of a housekeeper"*: Transcript, Claudia "Lady Bird" Johnson, Oral History Interview XXIII, September 5, 1981, by Michael L. Gillette, Internet Copy, LBJ Library, p. 45.

139 *"whole crowd"*: Mrs. Johnson reminisces about this in her diary entry of November 8, 1967, after attending a party for daughter Lynda and her fiancé, Charles Robb. WHD, Box 5.

140 *in one of his short appearances*: LBJ Library Video, Lady Bird Johnson's Home Movies, HM12, The Johnson Family 1945–1946.

140 *"drinks, sandwiches and talk"* . . . *"How she handled that I don't know"*: John L. Bullion, *In the Boat with LBJ* (Plano, Texas: Republic of Texas Press, 2001), p. 10.

142 *"like a Daddy to me"*: Dallek, *Lone Star Rising*, p. 266.

142 *"This is not a circus, you know"*: Transcript, Claudia "Lady Bird" Johnson, Oral History Interview XIX, February 6–7, 1981, by Michael L. Gillette, Internet Copy, LBJ Library, p. 12. Also in Gillette, *Lady Bird Johnson*, p. 169.

8: Crucial Campaigner and Marketer

144 *"errand boy for war-rich contractors"*: Dan Briody, *The Halliburton Agenda: The Politics of Oil and Money* (Hoboken, NJ: John Wiley & Sons, 2004), p. 128.

144 *"not a bit timorous"*: Transcript, Claudia "Lady Bird" Johnson, Oral History Interview XXI, Internet Copy, LBJ Library, p. 44.

145 *"Thou Shalt Not Bear False Witness"*: *Caldwell News and Burleson County Ledger,* in advertisement that appeared on July 5, 1946, p. 8.

145 *"with slanderous yellow sheets"*: L. Patrick Hughes, "Waging War with the Regulars: Lyndon Johnson's 1946 Renomination Battle." Accessed November 22, 2014, www2.austin.cc.tx.us/lpatrick/his2341/Waging_War_With_Regulars .html. Originally published in *Locus,* 1992.

146 *"kind of a slur"*: Transcript, Claudia "Lady Bird" Johnson, Oral History Interview XIX, February 6–7, 1981, by Michael L. Gillette, Internet Copy, LBJ Library, p. 42. Also in Michael L. Gillette, *Lady Bird Johnson: An Oral History* (New York: Oxford University Press, 2012), p. 176.

146 *"His body finally reached the point of exhaustion"*: Transcript, Claudia "Lady Bird" Johnson, Oral History Interview XX, February 20–21, 1981, by Michael L. Gillette, Internet Copy, LBJ Library, p. 10.

146 *"nervous exhaustion"* . . . *"bad"*: Robert A. Caro, *Means of Ascent* (New York: Alfred A. Knopf, 1990), p. 140.

146 *"six weeks or two months"*: Transcript, Claudia "Lady Bird" Johnson, Oral History Interview XX, February 20–21, 1981, by Michael L. Gillette, Internet Copy, LBJ Library, p. 10.

147 *"semi-valet"*: Transcript, Margaret Mayer Ward, Oral History Interview I, March 10, 1977, by Michael L. Gillette, Internet Copy, LBJ Library, p. 4.

147 *"Bird, where are you?"*: Bill Moyers's eulogy at funeral service of Mrs. Johnson, July 14, 2007. Access at www.c-span.org/video/?199909-1/lady-bird -johnson-funeral-service.

147 *"my lover, my friend, my identity"*: Jan Jarboe Russell, *Lady Bird: A Biography of Mrs. Johnson* (New York: Scribner, 1999), p. 185.

150 *"just a beautiful cloak model"*: Sally Denton, *The Pink Lady: The Many Lives of Helen Gahagan Douglas* (New York: Bloomsbury, 2009), p. 80.

151 *"if the gentleman from Mississippi is addressing me"*: Helen Gahagan Douglas, Transcript, Oral History Interview I, November 10, 1969, by Joe B. Frantz, Internet Copy, LBJ Library, p. 38.

151 *"gentlewoman from California"*: Ibid, p. 39.

151 *"lived together"*: Ingrid Winther Scobie, *Center Stage: Helen Gahagan Douglas, A Life* (New York: Oxford University Press, 1992), p. 172.

152 *"Lyndon Johnson—US Senator"*: LBJ Library Video, Lady Bird Johnson's Home Movies, HM5, LBJ Senate Campaigns 1941 and 1948.

153 *"Johnson City Windmill"*: Robert Dallek, *Lone Star Rising*, p. 304.

153 *"before you entered the race"*: Joe Phipps, *Summer Stock: Behind the Scenes with LBJ in '48* (Fort Worth: Texas Christian University Press, 1992), pp. 236–37.

154 *"terribly interested"*: Transcript, Jacqueline Cochran, Oral History Interview I, April 7, 1974, by Joe B. Frantz, Internet Copy, LBJ Library, p. 11.

156 *"He was depressed"*: Transcript, Claudia "Lady Bird" Johnson, Oral History Interview XXII, August 23, 1981, by Michael L. Gillette, Internet Copy, LBJ Library, p. 34. Also in Gillette, *Lady Bird Johnson*, p. 207.

156 *"I said I would rather fight and fight"*: Transcript, Claudia "Lady Bird" Johnson, Oral History Interview XXII, August 23, 1981, by Michael L. Gillette, Internet Copy, LBJ Library, p. 34. Also in Gillette, *Lady Bird Johnson*, p. 207.

157 *"violin string"*: Gillette, *Lady Bird Johnson*, p. 227.

158 *"Straight Shooter"*: LBJ Library Video, Lady Bird Johnson's Home Movies, HM15, 1948 Senate Campaign Spots.

158 *"climbed to the mountain"*: Ibid.

9: "A Wonderful, Wonderful Wife"

160 *"dropping out altogether"*: Sarah McClendon, with Jules Minton, *Mr. President, Mr. President!: My Fifty Years of Covering the White House* (Los Angeles: General Publishing Group, 1996), p. 272. McClendon confirmed this account elsewhere, and her daughter, Sally Newcomb MacDonald, confirmed these details to author, March 31, 2012. Copy of telegram could not be located at LBJ Library.

160 *"a wonderful, wonderful wife"*: Transcript, Frank "Posh" Oltorf, Oral History Interview I, August 3, 1971, by David G. McComb, Internet Copy, LBJ Library, p. 31.

161 *"for the last several nights"*: Transcript, Horace Busby, Oral History Interview

V, August 16, 1988, by Michael L. Gillette, Internet Copy, LBJ Library, pp. 23–24.

162   *"No mount is free once the bit is in his mouth":* Dallas Morning News, March 10, 1949.

163   *"everything":* Transcript, Kathleen Louchheim, Oral History Interview I, April 1, 1969, by Paige E. Mulhollan, Internet Copy, LBJ Library, p. 19. Although her oral histories are labeled "Kathleen Louchheim," her papers at the Library of Congress are labeled, "Katie Louchheim."

163   *"I don't know":* Ibid., p. 20.

164   *"heart's home":* Hal K. Rothman, *LBJ's Texas White House: "Our Heart's Home"* (College Station: Texas A&M University Press, 2001).

165   *"almost orphans in a sense":* Transcript, Marie Fehmer Chiarodo, Oral History Interview II, August 16, 1972, by Joe B. Frantz, Internet Copy, LBJ Library, p. 12. Fehmer Chiarodo confirmed the phrase as used by interviewer Joe Frantz.

165   *"they don't understand him":* Transcript, Marie Fehmer Chiarodo, Oral History Interview II, August 16, 1972, by Joe B. Frantz, Internet Copy, LBJ Library, p. 12.

165   *"whip outfits":* Lyndon Johnson to Lady Bird Johnson, May 12, 1952, Reference File, Folder, Letters of Lady Bird Johnson and Lyndon Johnson, LBJ Library.

165   *"got her feelings hurt":* Ibid.

166   *"I hadn't been as good a mother as I should":* Transcript, Claudia "Lady Bird" Johnson, Oral History Interview XXXV, March 8, 1991, by Michael L. Gillette, Internet Copy, LBJ Library, p. 5.

167   *"spasmodic, uncontrollable movements, jerkings":* Ibid., p. 14.

168   *"special care and attention"* . . . *"quite all right again":* Ibid., p. 15.

168   *"impatient"* . . . *"mad":* Ibid., p. 14.

168   *"more or less":* Transcript, Claudia "Lady Bird" Johnson Oral History Interview XXVIII, March 15, 1982, by Michael L. Gillette, Internet Copy, LBJ Library, p. 2.

169   *"It's hard enough for me":* Luci Baines Johnson, speaking to Harry Middleton's class, LBJ Library, March 22, 2011.

170   *"looseness":* Robert A. Caro, *Master of the Senate* (New York: Alfred A. Knopf, 2002), p. 433.

170   *"If there was a man to be picked up":* Ibid.

170   *"bedeviled with drink and too much medication":* Transcript, Claudia "Lady Bird" Johnson, Oral History Interview XXXII, August 3–4, 1982, by Michael L. Gillette, Internet Copy, LBJ Library, p. 7.

170   *"in very bad shape":* Ibid.

172   *"deserved credit for effective attention":* Louis M. Kohlmeier, "The Johnson Wealth: How President's Wife Built $17,500 into Big Fortune in Television," *Wall Street Journal,* March 23, 1964.

173   *"Young-Man-Going-Places":* Dallas Morning News, October 21, 1949.

173   *"ate, slept and dreamed strategy":* Ibid.

173   *"The Frantic Gentleman from Texas":* Saturday Evening Post, May 19, 1951.

174   *"History Makers":* U.S. News & World Report, December 31, 1954, p. 48.

174 *"Knowland and Johnson in '56?":* Patrick McMahon, "Knowland and Johnson in '56?," *American Mercury,* October 1954, p. 38.

174 *"antagonizing the press":* Katie Louchheim, Papers, Manuscript Division, Library of Congress, Washington, D.C., Box 77, January 28, 1951.

175 *"operations and ailments . . . no one will do it better":* Katie Louchheim, Papers, Manuscript Division, Library of Congress, Washington, D.C., Box 77, no specific date but is in Folder 6, January–April 1955, p. 48.

175 *"for poise and peculiar beauty":* Katie Louchheim, Papers, Manuscript Division, Library of Congress, Washington, D.C., Box 77, no specific page but is in Folder 6, January–April 1955.

175 *"gallivanting":* George Dixon, *New Orleans Times-Picayune,* May 26, 1953.

176 *"Texan Who Is Jolting Washington":* Newsweek, June 27, 1955, p. 24.

176 *"Who Will Run Congress":* New York Times Magazine, January 2, 1955.

177 *"keep going":* Transcript, Frank "Posh" Oltorf, Oral History Interview I, August 3, 1971, by David G. McComb, Internet Copy, LBJ Library, p. 30.

177 *"Doctor, let me ask you something":* Ibid., p. 32.

177 *"I just want to tell you what I want":* Ibid., p. 31.

10: Struggling with Balance and Momentum

178 *"got frantic":* Transcript, Sarah McClendon and Sally O'Brien, Oral History Interview I, February 16, 1972, by Joe B. Frantz, Internet Copy, LBJ Library, p. 8.

179 *"Texas kids"* . . . *"didn't know or care":* Sally O'Brien MacDonald to author, March 21, 2012.

179 *"Remember you are loved . . . hokey":* Ibid.

180 *"a real mother":* Luci Baines Johnson, speaking on PBS documentary, *Lady Bird Johnson,* produced by MacNeil/Lehrer Productions and KLRU, Austin, 2001, Transcript, Part 2.

180 *"not have hesitated":* Lewis L. Gould, biographer of Edith Roosevelt, speaking at National Archives, Washington, D.C., November 2, 2013. Professor Gould confirmed this quote in an email to author.

180 *"mean as a snake":* Joanna Sturm to author, October 20, 1994.

181 *"deprived of [Bird's] presence and her motherhood":* Transcript, George Reedy, Oral History Interview VIII, August 16, 1983, by Michael L. Gillette, Internet Copy, LBJ Library, p. 94.

181 *"go ahead with the blue":* Merle Miller, *Lyndon: An Oral Biography* (New York: G. P. Putnam's Sons, 1980), p. 181. A slightly different version of this quote appears in *Newsweek* article by Samuel Shaffer, November 7, 1955.

181 *"Honey, everything will be all right":* Transcript, Walter Jenkins, Oral History Interview XIV, July 19, 1984, by Michael L. Gillette, Internet Copy, LBJ Library, p. 5.

181 *"gray as pavement":* Lady Bird Johnson, "Help Your Husband Guard His Heart," Cleveland *Plain Dealer,* February 12, 1956.

182 *"stay here":* Ibid.

182 *"Heart Attack Drops Johnson from White House Hopefuls"*: Nashua *[New Hampshire] Telegraph,* July 6, 1955, p. 7.

182 *"I'll never get a chance to be President now"*: Booth Mooney, *LBJ: An Irreverent Chronicle* (New York: Thomas Y. Crowell, 1976), p. 198.

183 *"quiet, long, lonesome, sad"*: Transcript, Mary Rather, Oral History Interview I, December 10, 1974, interviewed by Michael L. Gillette, LBJ Library, p. 6. Quoted by permission of Nancy Kumpuris.

185 "kicked back" . . . *"a bandaged right eye"*: LBJ Library Video, Lady Bird Johnson's Home Movies, HM26, Friends visit the LBJ Ranch, Fall 1955.

185 *"time of their life"*: Transcript, Mary Rather, Oral History, I, December 10, 1974, interviewed by Michael L. Gillette, LBJ Library, p. 17. Quoted by permission of Nancy Kumpuris.

185 *"perched on the bed"*: Katie Louchheim, Papers, Manuscript Division, Library of Congress, Washington, D.C., Box 77, Journals, family and general correspondence, Folder 7, May–December, 1955, p. 134.

186 *"My Heart Attack Taught Me How to Live"*: Lyndon Johnson, *American Magazine,* July 1956, p. 15. An earlier article, "My Heart Attack Saved My Life," by Samuel Shaffer in *Newsweek,* November 7, 1955, quotes LBJ as claiming that he has slowed his pace, is living "more sensibly," likes to play dominoes with his daughters, read books, and listen to music.

186 *"her devotion and intelligence and diligence . . . I've never seen anybody go after something"*: *Dallas Morning News,* August 25, 1955.

187 *"Now I think that's enough of that, Lyndon"*: Harvey Herbst to author, October 6, 2011.

187 *"cry for about two hours"*: Booth Mooney, *The Lyndon Johnson Story* (New York, Farrar, Straus, 1956) p. 154.

187 *"gone sour"*: Katie Louchheim Papers, Manuscript Division, Library of Congress, Washington, D.C., Box 77, Folder 8, January–April 1956.

187 *"he's somewhat unbalanced"*: Ibid.

188 *"two or three most powerful men in the Democratic Party"*: Cleveland *Plain Dealer,* May 10, 1956. The same article ran four days later in *Seattle Daily Times.*

188 *"Lady Bird Likes Job in Senate"*: *Dallas Morning News,* August 13, 1956.

190 *"a chain"*: *AWHD,* p. 174.

190 *"Wife of Senate Majority Leader Highly Efficient"*: *New Orleans Times-Picayune,* December 8, 1957.

190 *"poised and sure"*: Katie Louchheim, Papers, Manuscript Division, Library of Congress, Washington, D.C., Box 78, Folder 3, January–June 1959, p. 20.

191 *"If only people knew"*: Ibid., p. 13.

191 *"personally my most joyous [years]"*: Transcript, Claudia "Lady Bird" Johnson, Oral History Interview XL, August 1994, by Harry Middleton, Internet Copy, LBJ Library, p. 40.

191 *"cried and cried and cried"*: Ibid., p. 26.

192 *"cute-as-a-button secretary"*: *New Orleans Times-Picayune,* December 14, 1959.

193 *"'divorce' his wife"*: Herbert Parmet to author, May 15, 2010.

193 *"by the pool"*: Portland *Oregonian,* July 26, 1959.

194 *"Will One of These Five Be First Lady?"*: *Newsweek,* February 15, 1960, p. 54.

194 *"Human Dynamo"*: *Newsweek,* February 22, 1960, p. 29.

ii: Outshining Her Husband

195 *"Never . . . a strong hold for us":* Transcript, Claudia "Lady Bird" Johnson, Oral History Interview XLIII, November 23, 1996, by Harry Middleton, Internet Copy, LBJ Library, p. 13.

195 *"Marie Antoinette in the tumbrel":* Harry Middleton, *A Life Well Lived* (Austin: Lyndon Baines Johnson Foundation, 1992), p. 79.

196 *"If the time had come when I couldn't walk unaided":* New York Times, November 5, 1960, p. 15 of continuation of page 1 article, "Jeering Texans Swarm Around Johnson and His Wife on Way to Rally." Photo has protester's sign, "Let's Beat Judas." Chants quoted in article are "Let's Ground Lady Bird" and "Yellow Thorn of Texas."

196 *"Things will never be the same":* Bill Moyers's eulogy at funeral service of Mrs. Johnson, July 14, 2007. Access at www.c-span.org/video/?199909-1/lady -bird-johnson-funeral-service.

197 *"not worth a bucket of warm spit":* Obituary of John Nance Garner, *Time,* November 17, 1967. *Time* attributes the quote to Garner but others suggest he may never have said it. See Patrick Cox, "Not Worth a Bucket of Warm Spit," History News Network, August 20, 2008. Access at www .historynewsnetwork.org/article/53402.

197 *"sonny boy":* Robert Dallek, "My Search for Lyndon Johnson," *American Heritage,* September 1991, p. 87.

198 *"very insecure, sensitive man with a huge ego":* Randall B. Woods, *LBJ: Architect of American Ambition* (New York: Free Press, 2006), p. 380.

198 *"Uncle Cornpone" . . . "Little Pork Chop":* See "JFK and the Death of Liberalism," *American Spectator,* May 31, 2012. William F. Buckley Jr. referred repeatedly to LBJ as "Uncle Cornpone" in his "Dispatches from Atlantic City," *National Review,* September 8, 1964.

199 *"pregnant and helpless" . . . "Why don't you call reporters in":* Transcript, Elizabeth Carpenter, Oral History Interview I, August 27, 1968, by Joe Frantz, LBJ Library, p. 31.

199 *"hunting dog":* Jacqueline Kennedy: Historic Conversations on Life with John F. Kennedy, Interviews with Arthur M. Schlesinger Jr., 1964 (New York: Hyperion, 2011), p. 85.

199 *"so calm":* Transcript, Jacqueline Kennedy Onassis, Oral History Interview I, January 11, 1974, by Joe B. Frantz, Internet Copy, LBJ Library, p. 13.

200 *"great demand as a speaker":* Barbara A. Perry, *Rose Kennedy: The Life and Times of a Political Matriarch* (New York: W. W. Norton, 2013), p. 240.

200 *"carry a women's audience":* Ibid., p. 241.

201 *"tall cotton" . . . "not quite up to me":* Ibid.

201 *"horns or tails":* Carol Lawson, "Liz Carpenter: Back on the Trail Again," *New York Times,* July 26, 1987, discussing Carpenter's recent book, *Getting Better All the Time.*

201 *"practically sat on them":* Transcript, Elizabeth Carpenter, Oral History Interview I, August 27, 1968, by Joe Frantz, LBJ Library, p. 25.

202 *her father's will:* In Lewis Gould Papers, LBJ Library, Box I, Folder 4: T. J. Taylor's will provided that his widow, Ruth, receive the house and furnishings, auto, and domestic property. Next, T.J. gave to the two children of Tommy, who had died in 1959, "all of my real estate situated in Marion County, Texas," and some other property in Harrison County; to son Antonio he gave all real estate in Cameron County; to daughter "Claudia Taylor" he gave "lot and improvements thereon [brick building]" located in Mauldin, Missouri; to grandson T. J. Taylor III (son of Tommy) he gave half of all his cattle; to Tommy's daughter, Susan, $5,000, which was less than he provided for the Methodist Church ($6,000).

202 *"eaten up and eroded":* WHD, June 30, 1964, Box 2.

202 *$1,500 a year in rent:* Documented in Lewis L. Gould Papers, LBJ Library, Box I, Folder 4.

203 *"Mogul emperor":* Dallek, *Lone Star Rising*, p. 587.

203 *"bawled her out"* . . .*"The whole thing was so revolting":* Transcript, George E. Reedy, Oral History Interview XVII, June 11, 1985, by Michael L. Gillette, Internet Copy, LBJ Library, p. 45.

203 *"a bunch of goddamn, son-of-a-bitching bastards":* Ibid., p. 44.

204 *"Lady Bird carried Texas":* Transcript, Elizabeth Carpenter, Oral History Interview I, August 27, 1968, by Joe Frantz, LBJ Library, p. 30.

205 *"where I came from":* "The Home: Ormes and the Man," *Time*, November 17, 1961.

206 *"rich Turk's harem":* Hal K. Rothman, *LBJ's Texas White House: "Our Heart's Home"* (College Station: Texas A&M University Press, 2001), p. 100.

207 *"Life in a Goldfish Bowl":* Vice President's Daily Diary, June 8, 1962, LBJ Library.

207 *"awfully good":* Transcript, George Reedy, Oral History Interview XVI, September 13, 1984, by Michael L. Gillette, Internet Copy, LBJ Library, p. 46.

207 *"If ever a woman transformed herself":* Mooney, *LBJ*, p. 236.

208 *"thoroughly, visibly and persistently miserable":* Transcript, Jack Valenti, Oral History Interview I, May 25, 1982, by Sheldon M. Stern, for the John F. Kennedy Library, Internet Copy, LBJ Library, p. 5.

208 *"the great adventure of our lives"* . . . *"You'll be flying with Lady Bird":* Transcript, Elizabeth Carpenter, Oral History Interview I, August 27, 1968, by Joe Frantz, LBJ Library, p. 22.

209 *"dumped right down in the middle":* Transcript, Elizabeth Carpenter, Oral History Interview III, May 15, 1969, by Joe Frantz, LBJ Library, p. 3.

211 *"We've come a long way":* Ashton Gonella to author, June 29, 2010.

211 *"We may never pass this way again":* Bess Abell, quoting CTJ on their August 1962 trip to Middle East. Access at www.lbjlibrary.org/lyndon-baines -johnson/lady-bird-johnson/rembrances-of-lady-bird-johnson.

211 *"waggish"* . . . *"fat":* Katie Louchheim Papers, Manuscript Division, Library of Congress, Washington D.C., Box 78, Folder 5, March–December 1962, p. 13.

212 *"looked absolutely gross":* Robert Dallek, *Flawed Giant: Lyndon Johnson and His Times, 1961–1973* (New York: Oxford University Press, 1998), p. 44.

212 *"I don't give a fucking damn":* Dallek, *Lone Star Rising*, p. 13.

212 *"deeply fatigued":* Vice President's Daily Diary, August 27, 1962, LBJ Library.

12: Presidential Partnering

215 *"We just wish Bird could be President"*: Rollin Shaw to author, March 30, 2012.
This account was corroborated by Rollin Shaw's husband, Frank Shaw, on
October 18, 2014.

216 *"Lyndon's living and working"*: *AWHD*, p. 35.

216 *"never tried to influence"*: Maurine Beasley, *The White House Press Conferences of
Eleanor Roosevelt* (New York: Garland, 1983), p. 128.

217 *"out of the same mind"*: WHD, January 27, 1964, Box 1.

218 *"American women have been partners"*: Anne Morrow Lindbergh, "As I See Our
First Lady," *Look,* May 19, 1964, p. 105.

218 *"as if I'm on stage"*: Ibid., p. 102.

219 *"busy as cats on a hot stove"*: WHD, February 25, 1964, Box 1.

219 *"I wish to heaven I could serve Mrs. Kennedy's happiness"*: Ruth Montgomery,
"What Kind of Woman Is Our New First Lady?," *Good Housekeeping*, March
1964, p. 32.

220 *"salt in your eye"*: WHD, December 7, 1963, Box 1.

221 *"Who is Oswald?"*: Sheldon Cohen to author, May 20, 2011.

222 *"different money matters"*: Transcript, Victoria [McCammon McHugh] Murphy, Oral History Interview I, June 6, 1975, by Michael L. Gillette, LBJ
Library, p. 32. Quoted by permission of Victoria Murphy.

222 *"the children's trustee"*: *AWHD*, p. 69.

223 *"Don't feel sorry for me"*: Bill Moyers's eulogy at funeral service of Mrs. Johnson,
July 14, 2007. Access at www.c-span.org/video/?199909-1/lady-bird-johnson
-funeral-service.

223 *"very Salvation Army"*: WHD, March 11, 1964, Box 1.

223 *"wrapped up"*: *AWHD*, p. 58.

224 *"count on her to be there for them"*: Anne Morrow Lindbergh, "As I See Our First
Lady," *Look*, May 19, 1964, p. 110.

224 *"Lose your breath"*: Video interview with Johnson daughters, moderated by Bob
Scully, 2003, at LBJ Library Media Center.

225 *"deserter"*: WHD, October 6, 1966, Box 4.

225 *"Taking any children?"*: Telephone conversation between Lyndon Johnson and
Lady Bird Johnson, February 7, 1964, Citation #1926, WH6402.08, RTCM,
LBJ Library.

227 *"making fun of Lyndon and me"*: WHD, February 15, 1964, Box 1.

228 *"kind of even-steven"*: Telephone conversation between Lady Bird Johnson
and Jack Valenti, March 9, 1964, Citation #2438, WH 6403.07, RTCM, LBJ
Library. Conversation is also reported in Michael Beschloss, *Taking Charge:
The Johnson White House Tapes, 1963–1964* (New York: Simon & Schuster,
1997), p. 279;

228 *"Be Available" . . . "Never Lie"*: *AWHD*, p. 15.

229 *"informal meetings" . . . "Because I have lived openly and unafraid"*: *AWHD*, p. 37.

230 *"I have said all I'm going to say on that"*: Jack Raymond, "Johnson Parries Queries
on Baker," *New York Times*, January 25, 1964.

230 *"Yes, ma'am, I'm willing now"*: Telephone conversation between LBJ and

Lady Bird Johnson, May 7, 1964, Citation #2395, WH6403.05, RTCM, LBJ Library. Also in Beschloss, *Taking Charge*, p. 272.

231   *"elderly gnome"* . . . *"I had to try a bit on that"*: WHD, January 14, 1964, Box 1.

231   *"too old"* . . . *"Hootnanny sort of throws me off"* . . . *"Scotti and Severini and Tetrazzini"*: WHD, January 13, 1964, Box 1.

232   *"big news"* . . . *"Victory Number One"* . . .*"I must say it's pleasant"*: *AWHD*, p. 75.

232   *"somebody that Lyndon and all men"*: WHD, February 26, 1964, Box 1.

233   *"In this room"*: Carl Sferrazza Anthony, *As We Remember Her: Jacqueline Kennedy Onassis in the Words of Her Friends and Family* (New York: HarperCollins, 1997), p. 192.

13: Teaming Up for the Big Win

235   *"the responsibilities of the bomb"*: Telephone conversation between Walter Jenkins and Lyndon Johnson, August 25, 1964, about 11:23 a.m., Citation #5177, WH6408.36, RTCM, LBJ Library.

236   *"Fuck 'em, they don't want me anyway"*: Transcript, George E. Reedy, Oral History Interview XXVI, November 16, 1990, by Michael L. Gillette, Internet Copy, LBJ Library, p. 7.

236   *"one person"*: Transcript, Walter Jenkins, Oral History Interview I, August 14, 1970, by Joe B. Frantz, Internet Copy, LBJ Library, p. 46.

237   *"I do not remember hours I ever found harder"*: *AWHD*, p. 192.

237   *"talk to anybody"*: Transcript, Claudia "Lady Bird" Johnson, Oral History Interview XXXVII, August 1994, by Harry Middleton, Internet Copy, LBJ Library, p. 15. Also in Michael L. Gillette, *Lady Bird Johnson: An Oral History* (New York: Oxford University Press, 2012), p. 369.

237   *"Beloved"*: *AWHD*, p. 192.

238   *"every night"*: WHD, April 21, 1964, Box 1.

238   *"Get me out of this, won't you?"*: WHD, June 19, 1964, Box 2.

238   *"his image as a father figure to the nation"*: WHD, June 11, 1964, Box 2.

239   *"There [was] no way out"*: WHD, July 5, 1964, Box 2.

239   *"in detail the problems"*: *AWHD*, p. 178.

240   *"that singing quality of so many of Mr. Kennedy's"*: WHD, Feb. 27, 1964, Box 1.

240   *"Why, when I'm not the least bit afraid"*: *AWHD*, p. 135.

241   *"precipitously and happily dropped into our laps"*: *AWHD*, p. 134.

242   *"ten best"*: *AWHD*, p. 140.

242   *"slop the hogs"* . . . *"truffles and pâté de foie gras"*: Transcript, George E. Reedy, Oral History Interview XVII, June 11, 1985, by Michael L. Gillette, Internet Copy, LBJ Library, p. 4.

242   *"with his silver tongue"*: *AWHD*, p. 104.

242   *"I had acquitted myself well enough"*: *AWHD*, p. 106.

243   *"energy"*: *AWHD*, p. 160.

243   *"severest trial"*: WHD, July 2, 1965, Box 2.

243   *"shaky"* . . . *"forthrightly for the full Civil Rights Program"*: WHD, February 27, 1964, Box 1.

244 *"What the hell is the presidency for?":* Michael Beschloss, speaking at John F. Kennedy Library at Presidential Historians Forum Series, January 30, 2002.

244 *"a marvelous televised statement": AWHD*, p. 174.

244 *"another step": AWHD*, p. 174.

244 *"with that sense of adventure": AWHD*, p. 175.

245 *"skeletons in the closet"* . . . *"depression and frustration": AWHD*, p. 139.

245 *"February or March 1968":* Ibid.

245 *"of course":* Lyndon Baines Johnson, *The Vantage Point: Perspectives of the Presidency, 1963–1969* (New York: Holt, Rinehart & Winston, 1971), p. 93.

248 *"to put their own 'squalid' tenant houses in order":* Marjorie Hunter, *New York Times*, May 15, 1964.

248 *"shocked"* . . . *"on the Johnson land were the worst":* Ibid.

248 *"explain Slum Lord Johnson":* Presidential Papers of LBJ, Box 62, Folder on Lady Bird, "June 1, 1964–June 19, 1964," LBJ Library,

249 *"batten down the hatches"* . . . *"jackass in a hailstorm":* WHD, May 13, 1964, Box 1.

249 *"trusted person":* Telephone conversation between Lyndon Johnson and Henry Luce, July 27, 1964, Citation #4350, WH6407.15, RTCM, LBJ Library.

250 *"Midas touch":* Keith Wheeler and William Lambert, *Life*, August 21, 1964, "The Man Who Is the President—How LBJ's Family Amassed Its Fortune," p. 62. This is part 2 of an article that began in August 14, 1964, issue with subtitle, "The Complex and Extraordinary Man Who Is the President." One full page of Part 2 lists the various holdings of the Johnson family—in ranch lands, banks, and businesses, with an estimated total value of $14 million.

251 *"legal delegation":* Memo from Lady Bird Johnson to the President, July 16, 1964, WHCF, Folder on Lady Bird, "July 16, 1964–October 1, 1964," LBJ Library.

252 *"I'll throw away the bottle":* Transcript, Claudia "Lady Bird" Johnson, Oral History Interview XXXVIII, August 1994, by Harry Middleton, Internet Copy, LBJ Library, p. 19.

252 *"snide jokes"* . . . *"this President and his wife are concerned":* Liz Carpenter, *Ruffles and Flourishes: The Warm and Tender Story of a Simple Girl Who Found Adventure in the White House* (Garden City, NY: Doubleday, book club edition, 1970), pp. 147–48.

252 *"I know the Civil Rights Act was right"* . . . *"I'm tired of people":* Ibid.

253 *"journey of the heart":* Ibid., p. 148.

253 *"because I feel at home":* Norma Ruth Holly Foreman, "The First Lady as a Leader of Public Opinion: A Study of the Role and Press Relations of Lady Bird Johnson" (Ph.D., University of Texas, 1971), p. 159.

253 *"Anyone can get into Atlanta":* Carpenter, *Ruffles and Flourishes*, p. 143.

254 *"half laughing at the whole idea"* . . . *"licking stamps and sealing envelopes":* Ibid.

254 *"a phony bone":* Transcript, Elizabeth Carpenter, Oral History Interview III, May 15, 1969, by Joe B. Frantz, LBJ Library, p. 35.

255 *"Blackbird, go home":* Bill Moyers's eulogy at funeral service of Mrs. Johnson, July 14, 2007. Access at www.c-span.org/video/?199909-1/lady-bird-johnson-funeral-service.

255 *"This is a country of many viewpoints"*: WHD, April 19, 1965, Box 2, discussing this speech at the time she returned to Columbia, South Carolina, for the funeral of a senator's wife. She also talks about how she handled hecklers in PBS documentary, *Lady Bird Johnson*, produced by MacNeil/Lehrer Productions and KLRU, Austin, 2001, Transcript, Part 3.

256 *"I've grown accustomed to your smell"*: Libby Cater Halaby to author, December 14, 2010.

257 *"Well, why the hell don't you find out?"*: Telephone conversation between LBJ and Lady Bird Johnson, October 7, 1964, Citation #5842, WH6410.04, RTCM, LBJ Library. The accusation takes place after minute 7 in what is a conversation of more than 13 minutes. Also in Michael Beschloss, *Reaching for Glory: Lyndon Johnson's Secret White House Tapes, 1964–1965* (New York: Simon & Schuster, 2001), p. 47. A subsequent phone call the same day between the president and first lady has him sounding more solicitous of her safety, and he talks with daughter Luci about the size of the crowds they are attracting and the number of hecklers.

257 *"working for Goldwater"*: Robert Dallek, *Flawed Giant: Lyndon Johnson and His Times, 1961–1973* (New York: Oxford University Press, 1998), p. 172.

258 *"two things"* . . . *"stay out of this"*: Telephone conversation between Lady Bird Johnson and LBJ, October 15, 1964, 9:12 a.m. Citation #5895, WH6410.11, RTCM, LBJ Library. Also in Beschloss, *Reaching for Glory*, pp. 84–87.

258 *"would have followed"* . . . *"My God, she was like a vessel"*: Merle Miller, *Lyndon: An Oral Biography* (New York: G. P. Putnam's Sons, 1980), p. 400.

259 *"great . . . and we did print it, of course"* . . . *"My heart is aching today"*: Miller, *Lyndon*, p. 604.

259 *"strange hour"*: WHD, November 17, 1964, Box 2.

260 *"I've had a headache"*: Telephone conversation between Lyndon Johnson and Dean Rusk, November 3, 1964, Citation #6110, WH6411.01, RTCM, LBJ Library. Also quoted in Beschloss, *Reaching for Glory*, p. 103.

260 *"my favorite first lady"*: Rosalynn Carter to author, May 27, 2011.

261 *"quiet"*: President's Daily Diary, November 4, 1964, LBJ Library.

261 *"a curious pall of sadness and inertia"*: WHD, November 17, 1964, Box 2.

262 *"tell-it-to-the-president"* . . . *"has been and continues to be deeply involved"*: Nan Robertson, *New York Times*, March 1, 1964.

14: Linchpin in the Launch of the Great Society

263 *"mean a lot"*: Nan Robertson, "Mrs. Johnson Holds the Bible for the Oath-Taking," *New York Times,* January 21, 1965.

263 *"sweet"*: WHD, January 20, 1965, Box 2.

264 *"relished [her] pillow talk"*: Joseph A. Califano, *The Triumph and Tragedy of Lyndon Johnson: The White House Years* (New York: Simon & Schuster, 1991), p. 27.

264 *"wonderful"* . . . *"went straight to my heart"*: Nan Robertson, "Mrs. Johnson Holds the Bible for the Oath-Taking," *New York Times,* January 21, 1965.

265 *"startled"* . . . *"fatigue"*: WHD, January 9, 1965, Box 2.

266 *"washed out"* . . . *"depressed":* WHD, January 29, 1965, Box 2.

266 *"How to fight it?":* Ibid.

267 *"Vietnam thing":* President's Daily Diary, March 4, 1965, LBJ Library.

267 *"Daddy duty":* Luci Baines Johnson, speaking on PBS documentary, *Lady Bird Johnson*, transcript, Part 4. She used same phrase speaking to Professor Harry Middleton's class, University of Texas, March 29, 2011.

267 *"routine physical checkup"* . . . *"sound"* . . . *"heavy load of tension"* . . . *"fog of depression":* Lady Bird Johnson, WHD, March 13, 1965, LBJ Library, Box 2. Also partially quoted in Beschloss, *Reaching for Glory,* p. 227.

267 *"great form"* . . . *"quite what sprung him":* WHD, March 14, 1965, Box 2.

268 *"given himself":* WHD, March 20, 1965, Box 2.

269 *"heaven": AWHD,* p. 260.

269 *"lashed to the mast"* . . . *"joyously":* Ibid.

269 *"earthy and colorful and true and fresh": AWHD,* p. 261.

269 *"deeply depressed":* Bill Moyers, quoted in Dallek, *Flawed Giant,* p. 282. Also see Robert Dallek, "Three New Revelations About LBJ," *Atlantic,* April 1, 1998. CTJ wrote in *AWHD,* p. 261, re April 19, 1965: "The mood is broken; the vacation ended," and she described the problems her husband faced.

269 *"creative people":* Transcript, J. Willis Hurst, Oral History Interview I, May 16, 1969, by T. H. Baker, Internet Copy, LBJ Library, p. 32.

270 *"lying in bed with the covers almost above his head":* Bill Moyers, in interview with Robert A. Dallek, which Dallek quoted in *Flawed Giant,* p. 282.

270 *"I worked in the residence":* Bess Abell to Will Swift, October 10, 2008.

271 *"superb salesman": AWHD,* p. 219.

271 *"spirit is lighter and his face less weary": AWHD,* p. 276.

271 *"Black Tuesday": AWHD,* p. 286.

271 *"culture"* . . . *"talks":* Eric F. Goldman, *The Tragedy of Lyndon Johnson* (New York: Alfred A. Knopf, 1969), p. 369.

271 *"what people create":* Ibid.

271 *"wince":* Ibid., p. 418.

272 *"our present foreign policy":* Richard F. Shepard, "Robert Lowell Rebuffs Johnson as Protest over Foreign Policy," *The New York Times,* June 3, 1965, p. 1.

273 *"greatest artists":* Eric F. Goldman, *The Tragedy of Lyndon Johnson,* p. 473.

273 *"She didn't even blink":* Jeanne Murray Vanderbilt to author, November 29, 2010.

273 *"public mask":* Richard Goodwin, *Remembering America* (Boston: Little, Brown, 1988), p. 399.

274 *"paranoid"* . . . *"a Senate or even an entire country":* Ibid., p. 398.

275 *"moving tribute"* . . . *"It's an honor that I haven't had done to me": New York Times,* July 31, 1965, p. 1.

276 *"probably the Kennedys":* Goodwin, *Remembering America,* p. 402.

277 *"backwoods of East Texas or Alabama"* . . . *"impact of Head Start": AWHD,* p. 310.

277 *"not-so-restful news": AWHD,* p. 311.

278 *"When he pulls his ear lobe":* Dallek, *Flawed Giant,* pp. 280–81.

279 *"I wouldn't appoint him to dog catcher now":* Goodwin, *Remembering America,* p. 401.

279 *"to crawl the walls of the White House"*: Jack Valenti, *A Very Human President* (New York: W. W. Norton, 1975), p. 312. Valenti made the comment in describing how irate President Johnson became when word got out that he was about to appoint Walter Washington mayor of Washington, D.C.

279 *"Her nose is a bit too long"*: "The White House: The First Lady Bird," *Time,* August 28, 1964.

280 *"to the best of his ability"*: *AWHD,* p. 198.

280 *"ice cream salesman"* . . . *"limp prick"*: Califano, *The Triumph and Tragedy of Lyndon Johnson,* p. 27.

280 *"You know Lyndon sometimes can confuse the messenger with the message"*: Ibid., pp. 280–81. Califano confirmed in interview with author, November 20, 2013, that details in his books were accurate.

281 *"corny"* . . . *"make the most of it!"*: *AWHD,* pp. 321–22.

282 *"from Lyndon's face to the flag"*: *AWHD,* p. 322.

282 *"We went in [to the church] as four"*: *AWHD,* p. 294

283 *"wisdom for the leaders of the nation"* . . . *"passages of the Episcopal prayer book"*: *AWHD,* p. 324.

284 *"let the whole world inspect"*: "Hurting Good," *Time,* October 29, 1965.

284 *"a man on whom an avalanche had suddenly fallen"*: WHD, October 12, 1965, Box 3.

284 *"I love ya"*: Telephone conversation between LBJ and Lady Bird Johnson, November 17, 1965, Citation #9180, WH6511.07, RTCM, LBJ Library.

285 *"Who knows how many disasters were averted"*: Bill Moyers's eulogy at funeral service of Mrs. Johnson, July 14, 2007. Access at www.c-span.org/video/?199909-1/lady-bird-johnson-funeral-service. A version of this was quoted to author in many interviews, including that of Ramsey Clark, September 27, 2013.

285 *"Walter Lippmann is a communist"* . . . *"Now, Lyndon"*: Goodwin, *Remembering America,* p. 404.

285 *"more than FDR ever did or ever thought of doing"*: Dallek, *Flawed Giant,* p. 231.

15: Beautification: A Legacy of Bird's Own

287 *"They're singing, 'We Shall Overcome'"*: Transcript, Sharon Francis, Oral History Interview I, May 20, 1969, by Dorothy Pierce McSweeney, Internet Copy, LBJ Library, p. 4.

288 *"I haven't been in a library since I left college"*: Eric F. Goldman, *The Tragedy of Lyndon Johnson* (New York: Alfred A. Knopf, 1969), p. 367.

289 *"to demand—and support"*: Lewis L. Gould, *Lady Bird Johnson: Our Environmental First Lady* (Lawrence: University Press of Kansas, 1999), p. 36.

289 *"natural parks and society"*: Transcript, Charles M. Haar, Oral History Interview I, June 14, 1971, by Joe B. Frantz, Internet Copy, LBJ Library, p. 11. Professor Haar confirmed sections of his oral history in interview with author, May 9, 2011.

290 *"Isn't that too much?"*: Transcript, Mary Lasker, Oral History Interview I, November 10, 1969, by Joe B. Frantz, Internet Copy, LBJ Library, p. 8.

290 *"anti-Negro and . . . anti-civil rights"*: Ibid., p. 12.

290 *"dent"* . . . *"crazy"*: Ibid., p. 13.

291 *"absolutely charming"*: Ibid.

291 *"very dear to me"*: Transcript, Claudia "Lady Bird" Johnson, Oral History Interview XL, August no date specified, 1994, by Harry Middleton, Internet Copy, LBJ Library, p. 24.

291 *"just marked time"*: Transcript, Mary Lasker, Oral History Interview I, November 10, 1969, by Joe B. Frantz, Internet Copy, LBJ Library, p. 19.

291 *"the appearance of the vast federal highway system"*: Ibid., p. 22.

291 *"victim . . . [of] totally treeless and hideous"*: Transcript, Mary Lasker, Oral History Interview II [mislabeled as Interview I], July 19, 1978, by Michael L. Gillette, Internet Copy, LBJ Library, p. 16.

294 *"jumped on a moving train"*: Cynthia Wilson to author, March 25, 2013.

294 *"really tore"*: Thomas Donahue to author, April 10, 2012.

295 *"just plain good business"*: Laurance Rockefeller, "Business and Beauty," *Vital Speeches of the Day* 15 (January 1966), p. 220.

295 *"any First Lady we've seen in this century"*: Norma Ruth Holly Foreman, "The First Lady as a Leader of Public Opinion: A Study of the Role and Press Relations of Lady Bird Johnson," (Ph.D., University of Texas, 1971), p. 139 lists these and other rave reviews for Mrs. Johnson.

295 *"two Washingtons"*: Lewis L. Gould, "Beautifying the Two Washingtons," in Gould, *Lady Bird Johnson*, p. 67.

296 *"cosmetic and trivial"*: Barbara Klaw, "Lady Bird Remembers," *American Heritage*, December 1980, p. 6. This is a verbatim record of Klaw's interview with CTJ.

297 *"the latest hair styles"*: . . *"Do you just do Mrs. Johnson's hair"*: Liz Carpenter, *Ruffles and Flourishes: The Warm and Tender Story of a Simple Girl Who Found Adventure in the White House* (Garden City, NY: Doubleday, book club edition, 1970), p. 237.

297 *"people in these neighborhoods can see the challenge"*: *AWHD*, p. 249.

297 *"a smooth briefcase operator"*: Milton Viorst, ed., *Hustlers and Heroes: An American Political Panorama* (New York: Simon & Schuster, 1971), pp. 250–51. This book of essays that Viorst wrote for various publications includes one entitled, "Walter Washington: Black Mayor, White Mind," pp. 240–65.

298 *"The word went out"*: Gould, *Lady Bird Johnson*, p. 65.

299 *"commanding . . . [with] something of the quality"*: *AWHD*, p. 308.

300 *"prepared to learn"* . . . *"That was honest"* . . . *"decisive factor"* . . . *"Hirshhorn is crazy about her"*: Barry Hyams, *Hirshhorn: Medici from Brooklyn* (New York: Dutton, 1979), pp. 149–52.

300 *"Lady Bird Johnson did that"*: Margaret McDermott to author, April 9, 2012, was among many who passed along to author this quote from taxi drivers. McDermott, a Texan, heard it when she visited the capital long after the Johnsons left the White House. She had passed it on to Mrs. Johnson, adding, "It's the people, you know, that count."

301 *"areas of commercial and industrial use"*: Gould, *Lady Bird Johnson*, p. 95.

302 *"You know I love that woman"*: Joseph A. Califano, *The Triumph and Tragedy of Lyndon Johnson: The White House Years* (New York: Simon & Schuster, 1991), p. 84. Califano confirmed in interview with author.

303 *"Imagine me keeping company with Chief Justice Warren!"*: *AWHD*, p. 325.

16: War Clouds

306 *"imaginative propaganda"*: David G. Nes, Interviewed by Ted Gittinger, November 10, 1982, Association for Diplomatic Studies and Training Foreign Affairs Oral History Project, Internet Copy, Courtesy of the National Archives and Records Service, LBJ Library, Interview I, no page.

306 August 4, 1964: Composed by Steven Stucky, with libretto by Gene Scheer.

306 *"rather trivial things"*: WHD, August 4, 1964, Box 2.

306 *"extraordinarily grave"*: Ibid.

306 *"relax at the most amazing times"*: Ibid.

308 *"open aggression on the high seas"*: Robert Dallek, *Flawed Giant: Lyndon Johnson and His Times, 1961–1973* (New York: Oxford University Press, 1998), p. 153. Full text is in *The New York Times*, August 4, 1964, p. 1.

308 *"frozen with dismay"*: Katharine Graham, *Personal History* (New York, Alfred A. Knopf, 1997), pp. 482–83.

308 *"his substantial organ"*: Dallek, *Flawed Giant*, p. 491.

309 *manic depressive:* D. Jablow Hershman, *Power Beyond Reason: The Mental Collapse of Lyndon Johnson* (Fort Lee, NJ: Barricade, 2002), p. 15: "The mental illness that afflicted Lyndon Johnson was . . . manic depression."

309 *"dismaying"*: Transcript, Harry McPherson, Oral History Interview III, January 16, 1969, by T. H. Baker, Internet Copy, LBJ Library, p. 1. In interview with author June 29, 2010, Mr. McPherson said LBJ could "hit dumps harder than anybody I've ever seen . . . angry . . . impatient." But McPherson noted that these depressed phases did not extend over long periods.

309 *"very up and monopolized"*: Transcript, Victoria Murphy, and Simon McHugh, Oral History Interview V, June 9, 1975, by Michael L. Gillette, LBJ Library, p. 5. Quoted by permission of Victoria Murphy.

309 *"on air"* . . . *"manic depressive"*: Transcript, George Reedy, Oral History Interview VIII, August 16, 1983, by Michael L. Gillette, Internet Copy, LBJ Library, p. 66.

309 *"Lyndon Johnson exhibited behavior patterns"*: Robert E. Gilbert, "Psychological Dysfunction and Great Achievement: The Presidency of Lyndon B. Johnson," *Politics, Culture and Socialization*, Spring 2011, pp. 7–8.

309 *"perhaps as extraordinary"*: Ibid., p. 1.

310 *"a very great asset"*: Transcript, J. Willis Hurst, Oral History Interview I, May 16, 1969, by T. H. Baker, Internet Copy, LBJ Library, p. 22.

310 *"key helper"*: Robert E. Gilbert to author, email, May 24, 2013.

310 *"one foot in front of the other"*: WHD, June 9, 1964, Box 2.

311 *"I would walk over hot coals for her"*: Bill Fisher to author, April 6, 2011.

311 *"against the backdrop of air strikes"*: AWHD, pp. 247–48.

312 *"It's like shooting the rapids"*: AWHD, pp. 246–47.

312 *"I can't get out"*: AWHD, p. 248.

312 *"It was just a hell of a thorn"*: Dallek, *Flawed Giant*, p. 283, quoting Mrs. Johnson to Dallek.

312 *"Win or lose, it's the right thing to do"*: Dallek, *Flawed Giant*, p. 283, quoting Mrs. Johnson to Dallek.

312 *"for the light at the end of the tunnel":* Dallek, *Flawed Giant*, p. 255.
313 *"amazingly calm":* Cynthia Wilson to author, March 27, 2013.
313 *Bird, slim in a two-piece:* LBJ Library Video, Lady Bird Johnson's Home Movies, HM34, Mrs. Johnson at the Virgin Islands, June 1965.
314 *"drove myself"* . . . *"read":* Lady Bird Johnson, Official White House Diary, entry for June 18, 1966, in Mrs. Johnson's handwriting and shorthand, Copy supplied to author by LBJ Library.
314 *"supper alone"* . . . *"early":* Ibid.
314 *"what to do tonight":* President's Daily Diary, entry for June 18, 1966, Copy supplied to author by LBJ Library.
315 *"It takes $8 to make me presentable":* WHD, February 16, 1967, Box 4.
316 *"You know, Mother":* WHD, July 7, 1965, Box 3.
316 *"I felt selfish":* Ibid.
317 *"in the palm of her small cherub hand":* WHD, September 19, 1965, Box 3.
317 *"almost sad":* WHD, April 11, 1964, Box 1.
317 *"was cut out for destiny":* WHD, May 12, 1964, Box 1.
318 *"reliable, planning-ahead"* . . . *"lark":* WHD, August 26, 1965, Box 3.
318 *"You might as well try to bottle sunshine":* WHD, January 27, 1965, Box 2.
318 *"impossible":* WHD, March 3, 1964, Box 1.
318 *"the world"* . . . *"to taste it all":* WHD, January 27, 1965, Box 2.
318 *"mutual appreciation":* WHD, February 13, 1965, Box 2.
318 *"looks down":* WHD, March 18, 1965, Box 2.
319 *"reach out to other people":* WHD, November 14, 1965, Box 3.
319 *"bobby socks and loafers":* WHD, February 22, 1965, Box 2.
319 *"I had just gotten my driver's license":* Luci Johnson, speaking at conference, "Modern First Ladies: Private Lives and Public Duties," Gerald R. Ford Museum, April 19, 1984.
319 *"rushed . . . helpless and disturbed":* Katie Louchheim Papers, Library of Congress Manuscripts, Washington, D.C., Box 79, Folder 6, "December 1965 to March 1966," p. 39.
320 *"wicked and delightful city"* . . . *"leading the sort of life":* WHD, March 3, 1964, Box 1.
320 *"taste the cream of life":* WHD, July 28, 1964, Box 2.
321 *"awkward age"* . . . *"I'm afraid I'm the one":* Transcript, Claudia "Lady Bird" Johnson, Oral History Interview XXVII, January 30, 1982, by Michael L. Gillette, Internet Copy, LBJ Library, p. 30.
321 *Bird's home movies:* LBJ Library Video, Lady Bird Johnson's Home Movies, HM33, LBJ Ranch, 1965
321 *"a few too many women crazy about him":* WHD, February 6, 1966, Box 3.
321 *"Excitement is a new mood for Lynda":* AWHD, p. 346.
322 *"jolted herself back into this world":* Transcript, J. Willis Hurst, Oral History Interview II, June 16, 1970, by T. H. Baker, Internet Copy, LBJ Library, p. 13.
322 *"Washington was burning":* Cynthia Wilson to author, March 26, 2013.
323 *"looking for communists under every bed":* WHD, March 10, 1967, Box 4.
323 "like Pearl Harbor or the Alamo": Transcript, Claudia "Lady Bird" Johnson, Oral History Interview XV, January 4–5, 1980, by Michael L. Gillette, Internet Copy, LBJ Library, p. 8.

323 *"Of course not"*: *American Heritage* 57, no. 6 (November–December 2006), p. 50. Access at www.americanheritage.com on May 28, 2014.

324 *"big enough"*: Jan Jarboe Russell, *Lady Bird: A Biography of Mrs. Johnson* (New York: Scribner, 1999), p. 281.

17: Outlandish LBJ

325 *"You can play with Lyndon"*: Traphes Bryant with Frances Spatz Leighton, *Dog Days at the White House: The Outrageous Memoirs of the Presidential Kennel Keeper* (New York: Macmillan, 1975), p. 110.

326 *"When people ask me these sort of things"*: Jan Jarboe Russell, *Lady Bird: A Biography of Mrs. Johnson* (New York: Scribner, 1999), p. 12.

326 *"enjoyed his physical power"*: White House staff member, email to author, April 1, 2013.

326 *"me coming in and out of a few women's bedrooms"*: Hal C. Wingo, who was *Life* magazine's reporter on the White House in 1963, describing a conversation in December 1963, in a letter to *The New Yorker*, April 23, 2012, p. 3.

327 *"if he did not"*: Robert Dallek, *An Unfinished Life: John F. Kennedy* (New York: Little, Brown, 2003), p. 476.

327 *"all the wifely chores"* . . . *"vicious"*: Joe Phipps, *Summer Stock: Behind the Scenes with LBJ in '48* (Fort Worth: Texas Christian University Press, 1992), p. 328.

327 *"Well, believe me, we celebrated my father's death with more hilarity than was exhibited on that trip"*: Transcript, George E. Reedy Oral History Interview XXI, January 7, 1987, by Michael L. Gillette, Internet Copy, LBJ Library, p. 9.

328 *"antique silver tray"*: Mary Margaret Valenti to author, May 20, 2011.

330 *"went out of her way to be nice"*: Randall B. Woods, *LBJ: Architect of American Ambition* (New York: Free Press, 2006), p. 406, quotes what Marie Fehmer Chiarodo told Woods on December 12, 2000. On January 12, 2015, Professor Woods confirmed in email to author that he had encountered nothing after his interview with Marie Fehmer Chiarodo that "would discredit or challenge her version."

330 *"Mr. President, You're Fun"* . . . *"baby-blue eyes"* . . . *"sex life of a bull"*: *Time*, April 10, 1964, p. 23

330 *"a younger crowd"*: WHD, March 4, 1964, Box 2.

331 *"put his shoes under my bed any night"*: Transcript, Elizabeth Carpenter, Oral History Interview II, April 4, 1969, by Joe B. Frantz, LBJ Library, p. 12.

331 *"skimmed over"*: Edna O'Brien, *Country Girl: A Memoir* (New York: Little, Brown, 2012), p. 277.

331 *"to confront, humiliate"*: Ted Sorensen, *Counselor: A Life at the Edge of History* (New York: HarperCollins, 2008), p. 122.

331 *"Nor do I know"*: Ibid.

332 *"loves the chase and is bored with the conquest"*: Letter is quoted in Katharine Q. Seelye, "Jackie Kennedy's Letters Taken Off the Auction Block," *New York Times*, May 23, 2014.

332 *"blonde bimbo"* . . . *"This is the girl"*: Dallek, *An Unfinished Life*, p. 477.

332   *"nothing less than making love":* Quoted in Sally Bedell Smith, *Grace and Power: The Private World of the Kennedy White House* (New York: Random House, 2004), p. 275.

333   *"from time to time for intimate evenings":* Ibid., p. 71.

334   *"a fly on the wedding cake":* Nancy Dickerson, *Among Those Present* (New York: Ballantine, 1977), p. 139.

334   *"I know Ike":* Ruth Montgomery, "An Intimate Portrait of Our Vivacious First Lady," *Look*, February 23, 1954, p. 31.

335   *"under the . . . skirt":* Jan Jarboe Russell, "Alone Together," *Texas Monthly*, August 1999, quotes Horace Busby describing what happened during the Senate years.

335   *"liked women":* Transcript, Helen Thomas, Oral History Interview I, April 19, 1977, by Joe B. Frantz, Internet Copy, LBJ Library, p. 2.

336   *"vigorous activity":* Dickerson, *Among Those Present*, p. 37.

336   *"actress":* Telephone conversation between Lyndon Johnson and Mary Lasker, January 20, 1964, Citation #1442, WH6401.17, RTCM, LBJ Library.

337   *"These women":* Telephone conversation between Lyndon Johnson and Dean Rusk, April 26, 1965, Citation #7365, WH6504.05, RTCM, LBJ Library.

337   *"best [boss] I ever had":* Grace Halsell, *In Their Shoes* (Fort Worth: Texas Christian University Press, 1996), p. 112.

337   *"Come over here!":* Ibid., p. 114.

338   *"on his feet":* Ibid., p. 115.

338   *"did not want to engage my mind" . . . "bigger man" . . . "small creature":* Ibid., p. 114.

338   *"Gary Cooper without a script":* Ibid., p. 115.

338   *"never had children":* Ibid., p. 116.

338   *"more for display than passion":* Ibid.

339   *"Aphrodite or Galatea":* Ibid., p. 117.

339   *"good behinds":* Ibid., p. 119.

339   *"If you wear a tight dress like that":* Ibid.

339   *"a matinee":* Ibid., p. 120.

339   *"rested up":* Ibid.

339   *"The more he belittled":* Ibid., p. 119.

340   *"fierce, dynamic energy":* Madeleine Duncan Brown, *Texas in the Morning: The Love Story of Madeleine Brown and President Lyndon Baines Johnson* (Baltimore: Harrison Edward Livingstone book, Conservatory Press, 1997), p. 60.

341   *"goddamn dumb Dora" . . . "your ass will be in a hell of a lot of trouble":* Ibid., pp. 60–61.

341   *"crumpled, overweight, haggard-looking":* Ibid., pp. 211–13.

341   *"continue with the financial arrangements":* Those who discredit Brown's account point to many errors in her claim that LBJ was implicated in the assassination of JFK. She admitted to an acquaintance with Jack Ruby, and she claimed to have heard Lyndon promise shortly before November 22 that "those goddamn Kennedys will never embarrass me again." After her death in 2002, David B. Perry, who identified himself as her friend, published a highly critical assessment of Brown's book in an online article, "Texas in the Imagination." For Randall Woods's account, see *Architect of Ambition*, p. 247.

342 *"tacky"* . . .*"Can't somebody teach that girl how to dress?":* Lou Hill Davidson to author, May 20, 2011.

343 *"the fact that [Mathilde's] so pretty":* WHD, August 6, 1965, Box 3.

343 *" likes to have the prettiest woman beside him":* WHD, April 10, 1966, Box 4.

344 *"gone to bed and Dickerson is covering him"* . . . *"sex had nothing to do with it":* Dickerson, *Among Those Present*, p. 139.

344 *"had no peer":* Ibid., p. 138.

344 *"I had a great love affair":* Russell, *Lady Bird*, p. 22.

344 *"like a magic wand passed over her":* Transcript, Elizabeth Carpenter, Oral History Interview I, August 27, 1968, by Joe B. Frantz, LBJ Library, p. 18.

18: Wrapping Up "Our" Presidency

346 *"our presidency":* AWHD, p. 553, talking about the time "when our tenure of the presidency ends."

346 *"open-ended stay in a concentration camp":* AWHD, p. 518.

346 *"simply did not want to face another campaign":* AWHD, p. 566.

346 *"roaring energy"* . . . *"unbearably painful":* AWHD, p. 567.

346 *"If we ever get sick":* Ibid.

346 *"picking out friend and foe and question mark"* . . . *"stoney":* WHD, January 10, 1967, Box 4.

346 *"Now is indeed the 'Valley of the Black Pig' ":* AWHD, p. 469, entry for January 5, 1967.

347 *"castor oil":* WHD, July 23, 1965, Box 2.

347 *"the ugliest thing I ever saw"* . . . *"damn rude"* . . . *"could not have been kinder"* . . . *"lived to be 1000."* Nan Robertson, "Johnson Dislikes His Likeness, Terms Portrait 'Ugliest Thing I Ever Saw,' " *New York Times,* January 6, 1967.

348 *"End of the Trail"* . . . *"Ladybird's Johnson":* "Chicago's Art World Takes Aim at Johnson": *New York Times*, February 4, 1967.

348 *"brilliantly illuminated":* AWHD, p. 470.

349 *"sloppy fat and drank too much"* . . . *"splendid mind and wrote well":* Transcript, Claudia "Lady Bird" Johnson, Oral History Interview XLI, August, no date specified, 1994, by Harry Middleton, Internet Copy, LBJ Library, p. 9.

349 *"I'm all right":* Bill Moyers's eulogy at funeral service of Mrs. Johnson, July 14, 2007. Access at www.c-span.org/video/?199909-1/lady-bird-johnson -funeral-service.

349 *"like a stone on my heart":* WHD, August 27, 1965, Box 3.

350 *"I love you":* Transcript, Claudia "Lady Bird" Johnson, Oral History Interview XLIV, November 26, 1996, by Harry Middleton, Internet Copy, LBJ Library, p. 14.

351 *"nervous exhaustion":* William Manchester, *Controversy* (Boston: Little, Brown, 1976), p. 14.

351 *"shortest distance between two points was a tunnel"* . . . *"practitioner of political tergiver-sation":* Ibid., pp. 21–22.

351 *"a planned wave of attacks":* WHD, August 29, 1966, Box 4.

352 *"I believed, as did many other soldiers":* Member of 1st Military Police, living in Florida, email to author, January 29, 2013.

352 *"itching": AWHD*, p. 620.

353 *"knew a little bit [about anger] too": AWHD*, p. 623.

354 *"I'll take care of it"* . . . *"This chili's too hot"*: Bill Fisher to author, April 6, 2011.

354 *"I'm more bewildered by Lyndon"*: Bill Moyers's eulogy at funeral service of Mrs. Johnson, July 14, 2007. Access at www.c-span.org/video/?199909-1/lady-bird-johnson-funeral-service.

355 *"My daughter just made me a grandfather"*: Luci Baines Johnson, speaking at Harry Middleton's class, LBJ Library, March 22, 2011.

355 *"loneliness in his voice": AWHD*, p. 553.

357 *"tenderness and understanding": AWHD*, p. 598.

357 *"The White House": AWHD*, p. 600.

358 *"That dog is not going to be in this picture"*: Nash Castro to author, December 17, 2010.

358 *"disappointment"* . . . *"after Lynda and Chuck have gone"*: WHD, December 9, 1967, LBJ Library, Box 5.

359 *"hugging and kissing him": AWHD*, p 605.

359 *"his mind was lashed [to the job]": AWHD*, p. 615.

360 *"Why do we have to be in Vietnam?"* . . . *"If that happens to Chuck"* . . . *"since his mother died": AWHD*, p. 642.

361 *"emotional, crying and distraught"* . . . *"affect the morale"* . . . *"rather distantly": AWHD*, p. 644.

361 *"Remember—pacing and drama": AWHD*, p. 645.

361 *"Accordingly, I shall not seek . . . and I will not accept": AWHD*, pp. 645–46.

362 *"Dr. King's been shot"* . . . *"nightmare quality": AWHD*, p. 647.

363 *"historic towns and blooming fields of wildflowers"* . . . *"foreign writers that there are places": AWHD*, p. 649.

363 *"black people [who] were unreliable"* . . . *"no parks, no trees"*: Transcript, Sharon Francis, Oral History Interview I, September 5, 1980, by Dorothy Pierce McSweeney, Internet Copy, LBJ Library, pp. 49–50.

365 *"I seek, to celebrate": . . "Camp of Peace": AWHD*, p. 783. Mrs. Johnson attributed the lines to *India's Love Lyrics*, a volume of Laurence Hope poetry published posthumously in 1906. It may be that is where she read the poem "The End," because Hope's poetry appeared in several different collections after her death. But "The End" was originally published in the volume *Stars of the Desert*, now available free to ebook readers.

19: Calming Anchor for a "Holy Terror"

366 *"This is my ranch"*: Jan Jarboe Russell, *Lady Bird: A Biography of Mrs. Johnson* (New York: Scribner, 1999), p. 306. The sofa pillow is also shown in Mrs. Johnson's interview with Brian Lamb, November 11, 1999, on C-Span.

369 *"private and confidential"*: Memo, Ashton Gonella to Marvin Watson, July 3, 1965, WHCF, Ex WH11, "Supplies, Materials, Services," Box 21, LBJ Library. Supplied to author by archivist Barbara Cline, LBJ Library, May 2, 2014.

369   *"my time": AWHD*, pp. vii–viii.

369   *"I* like *writing": AWHD,* p. viii.

370   *"bowl of jelly":* Claudia Anderson to author, April 23, 2009.

370   *"You are killing my darlings": AWHD*, p. ix.

371   *"The velocity at which Mrs. Johnson flew":* Jean Stafford, "Birdbath," *New York Review of Books,* December 3, 1970.

371   *"presidential":* Robert Hardesty, "With Lyndon Johnson in Texas," in Richard Norton Smith and Timothy Walch, eds., *Farewell to the Chief: Former Presidents in American Public Life* (Worland, WY: High Plains Publishing, 1990), p. 104.

372   *"For Christ's sake get that vulgar language of mine out of there":* Doris Kearns Goodwin, *Lyndon Johnson and the American Dream* (New York: St. Martin's, 1991), p. 355.

372   *"would have been more exciting":* Transcript, Jewell Malechek Scott, Oral History Interview II, May 30, 1990, by Michael L. Gillette, Internet Copy, LBJ Library, p. 12.

372   *"as a study in political psychopathology":* David Halberstam, *New York Times Book Review*, October 31, 1971, p. 1.

373   *"a kid kicking off his shoes":* Bill Porterfield, "Back Home Again in Johnson City," *New York Times Magazine*, March 2, 1969.

373   *"deep depression":* Robert Dallek, *Flawed Giant: Lyndon Johnson and His Times* (New York: Oxford University Press, 1998), p. 605. Dallek interviewed Elizabeth Wickenden December 20, 1986.

373   *"normal manic depressive self":* Dallek, *Flawed Giant*, p. 605.

374   *"one great adventure":* Robert Hardesty, "With Lyndon Johnson in Texas," in Smith and Walch, eds., *Farewell to the Chief*, p. 99.

374   *"quieted right down":* Russell, *Lady Bird,* p. 306.

374   *"Dr. Schles-ing-er"* . . . *"crazy":* Merle Miller, *Lyndon: An Oral Biography* (New York: G. P. Putnam's Sons, 1980), pp. 545–46.

375   *"psychopathic":* H. R. Haldeman, *The Haldeman Diaries: Inside the Nixon White House* (New York: G. P. Putnam's Sons, 1994), pp. 82–83, quoted in Dallek, *Flawed Giant*, p. 606.

375   *"The only thing more impotent than a former president":* Robert Hardesty, "With Lyndon Johnson in Texas," in Smith and Walch, eds., *Farewell to the Chief*, p. 106.

375   *"freeze out":* Tom Johnson to author, March 15, 2012.

375   *"The fact that Tom is loyal to Bill Moyers":* Ibid. Edwina Johnson participated in the interview and substantiated this account.

376   *"It must be for one of your lady friends":* Russell, *Lady Bird*, p. 307.

376   *"Too late now, Lyndon":* Libby Cater Halaby to author, December 14, 2010.

376   *"a holy terror":* Russell, *Lady Bird*, p. 307.

377   *"My mother never let me do anything like this before":* Charlotte Curtis, "Bustling Summer Capital of International Society," *New York Times*, August 24, 1969, p. 74.

378   *"I thought the President was really a virile man":* Transcript, Gordon Bunshaft, Oral History Interview I, June 25, 1969, by Paige E. Mulhollan, Internet Copy, LBJ Library, p. 27.

378 *"we felt like she could sell"*: Transcript, William W. Heath, Oral History Interview II, May 20, 1970, by Joe B. Frantz, Internet Copy, LBJ Library, p. 20. Two interviews were done same day but pagination is separate for each one.

379 *"sheer beauty"*: WHD, April 2, 1967, Box 5.

380 *"with the bark off"*: Frank Cormier, *LBJ: The Way He Was* (Garden City, NY: Doubleday, 1976), Preface quotes LBJ at library opening as saying: "It is all here; the story of our time—with the bark off." Luci Baines Johnson used a similar phrase in her introductory remarks at the conference, "Revisiting the Great Society," Hunter College, New York City, March 15, 2012.

382 *"just stare at the ceiling"*: Jan Jarboe Russell, interview with David Gergen, *PBS NewsHour*, November 17, 1999.

383 *"hard to imagine life without"*: Lady Bird Johnson said of A.W. Moursund, *"We'd be lonesome without him."* LBJ Library Video, Lady Bird Johnson's Home Movies, HM30, LBJ Ranch, 1965.

383 *"We decided to split the blanket"*: Leo Janos, "The Last Days of the President," *Atlantic Monthly*, July 1973, p. 40.

384 *"As the Days Dwindle Down"*: *New York Times,* September 21, 1972, p. 47.

385 *"where the best years of my life were spent"*: Lady Bird Johnson, interview with *Houston Post*, in undated clipping, Reference File on Lady Bird Johnson, Post Presidential folder, LBJ Library.

385 *"at utter peace"*: "Johnson Still a Man of Contrasts," *New York Times*, October 10, 1971, p. 51.

385 *"so clearly in charge of the day-to-day management of his life"* . . . *"impossible: depressed one minute, raging the next"*: Russell, *Lady Bird*, p. 306.

385 *"I don't know what he would have done without her"*: Russell, *Lady Bird*, quotes George Christian, p. 307.

386 *"I'm kind of ashamed of myself"*: John Herbers, "Johnson Mediates a Rights Dispute," *New York Times*, December 13, 1972, p. 1.

387 *"He very much loved her"*: Sharon Francis to author, March 20, 2013.

387 *"he loved her"*: Helen Thomas to author, November 1, 2011.

387 *"Don't think a day doesn't pass"*: Transcript, Russell M. Brown, Oral History Interview I, January 10, 1978, by Michael L. Gillette, Internet Copy, LBJ Library, p. 72.

387 *"very much"*: Mrs. Johnson's interview with Brian Lamb, November 11, 1999, on C-Span.

387 *"This time we didn't make it"*: Dallek, *Flawed Giant*, p. 623.

388 *"end the war and bring peace with honor in Vietnam"*: *New York Times*, transcript, January 24, 1973.

388 *"I know that somewhere, sometime"*: Dallek, *Flawed Giant*, p. 623.

389 *"Both the glory and the tragedy"*: *New York Times*, January 24, 1973.

389 *"human puzzle"*: Dallek, *Lone Star Rising*, p. 6.

389 *"thirteen of the most exasperating men I ever met"*: Bill Moyers, Conference on the Great Society, Hunter College, March 15, 2012.

389 *"Ah, but didn't he live well"*: Roy Reed, "Thousands at Johnson Bier," *New York Times*, January 24, 1973, p. 1

389 *"Lyndon pushed me"*: PBS documentary, *Lady Bird Johnson*, produced by MacNeil/Lehrer Productions and KLRU, Austin, 2001, Transcript, Part 1.

389 *"The Lord knew what he was doing"*: PBS documentary, *Lady Bird Johnson*, Transcript, Part 5. Access at www.pbs.org/ladybird/windingdown/windingdown_index.html.

390 *"She tempered his rashness"*: Robert Hardesty, "With Lyndon Johnson in Texas," in Smith and Walch, eds., *Farewell to the Chief*, p. 99.

20: Flying Solo

391 *"impertinent"* . . . *"hand and foot"*: Barbara Walters, *Audition: How to Talk with Practically Anybody About Practically Anything* (New York: Alfred A. Knopf, 2008), p. 402.

392 *"Politics was Lyndon's life"*: Barbara Klaw, "Lady Bird Remembers," *American Heritage*, December 1980, p. 17.

392 *"When it gets as close as your son-in-law"*: Ibid., p. 7.

393 *"What was the name of that film?"*: University of Texas professor to author, Austin, Texas, April 23, 2009.

393 *"Well, I wonder if we just made the cover"*: Harry Middleton's eulogy at funeral service of Mrs. Johnson, July 14, 2007. Access at www.c-span.org/video/?199909-1/lady-bird-johnson-funeral-service.

394 *"last hurrah"*: Lewis L. Gould, *Lady Bird Johnson and the Environment* (Lawrence: University Press of Kansas, 1988), p. 242.

394 *"rent for the space"*: Lewis L. Gould, *Lady Bird Johnson: Our Environmental First Lady* (Lawrence: University Press of Kansas, 1999), p. 124.

394 *"redbud, crepe myrtle"*: Gould, *Lady Bird and the Environment*, p. 241.

396 *"grandchildren proof"*: Lady Bird Johnson to Jacqueline Kennedy Onassis, June 11, 1982, in Reference File for Lady Bird Johnson, Folder on Jacqueline Kennedy Onassis, LBJ Library. Same folder has Jacqueline Onassis's reply.

396 *"delicious meal, your guests"*: Lady Bird Johnson to Jacqueline Kennedy Onassis, August 18, 1993, in Reference File for Lady Bird Johnson, Folder on Jacqueline Kennedy Onassis, LBJ Library.

397 *"But I thought we agreed"*: Clipping, *Austin American-Statesman*, August 2, 2009, in Reference File on Lady Bird Johnson, Post Presidential folder, LBJ Library.

398 *The Johnson daughters produced a total of seven children:* The Nugents had Patrick Lyndon, born June 21, 1967; Nicole Marie, born January 11, 1970; Rebekah Johnson, born July 10, 1974; and Claudia Taylor, born March 17, 1976. The Robbs had Lucinda Desha, born October 25, 1968; Catherine Lewis, born June 5, 1970; and Jennifer Wickliffe, born June 20, 1978.

399 *"mild stroke in a bad place"*: Shirley James to author, June 3, 2010.

400 *"the least needy, quietly confident person":* Lucinda Robb Florio, speaking at funeral service of Mrs. Johnson, July 14, 2007. Access at www.c-span.org /video/?199909-1/lady-bird-johnson-funeral-service.

400 *"whale of fun":* Harry Middleton's eulogy at funeral service of Mrs. Johnson, July 14, 2007. Access at www.c-span.org/video/?199909-1/lady-bird -johnson-funeral-service.

INDEX

ABOUT THE AUTHOR

Betty Boyd Caroli is the author of *First Ladies: From Martha Washington to Michelle Obama, Inside the White House*, and *The Roosevelt Women*. Caroli frequently appears on national television and the BBC to discuss the role of presidents' wives in American politics and has been a guest on *Today, The O'Reilly Factor, The NewsHour with Jim Lehrer*, Al Jazeera, *Booknotes* with Brian Lamb, and many others. A graduate of Oberlin College, Caroli holds a master's degree in Mass Communications from the Annenberg School of the University of Pennsylvania and a Ph.D. in American Civilization from New York University. A Fulbright scholar to Italy, she also held fellowships and grants from the National Endowment for the Humanities, the Franklin and Eleanor Roosevelt Institute, the Hoover Presidential Library, and others. After studying in Salzburg, Austria, and Perugia, Italy, she taught in Palermo and Rome, Italy, and later joined the faculty at the City University of New York. She currently resides in New York City and Venice, Italy.